The Prince of Tennis anime is also being shown in Korea. When I had the chance to see it, I thought the voices were perfect; they felt really natural. The voice actors over there are amazing!

And finally, starting in June, the manga will be sold in America. I hope many people around the world get to read it.

— Takeshi Konomi, 2004

About Takeshi Konomi

Takeshi Konomi exploded onto the manga scene with the incredible **THE PRINCE OF TENNIS**. His refined art style and sleek character designs proved popular with **Weekly Shonen Jump** readers, and **THE PRINCE OF TENNIS** became the number one sports manga in Japan almost overnight. Its cast of fascinating male tennis players attracted legions of female readers even though it was originally intended to be a boys' comic. The manga continues to be a success in Japan and has inspired a hit anime series, as well as several video games and mountains of merchandise.

THE PRINCE OF TENNIS
VOL. 22
The SHONEN JUMP Manga Edition

STORY AND ART BY
TAKESHI KONOMI

Translation/Joe Yamazaki
Consultant/Michelle Pangilinan
Touch-up Art & Lettering/Vanessa Satone
Design/Sam Elzway
Editor/Leyla Aker

Editor in Chief, Books/Alvin Lu
Editor in Chief, Magazines/Marc Weidenbaum
VP of Publishing Licensing/Rika Inouye
VP of Sales/Gonzalo Ferreyra
Sr. VP of Marketing/Liza Coppola
Publisher/Hyoe Narita

Published by VIZ Media, LLC
P.O. Box 77010
San Francisco, CA 94107

SHONEN JUMP Manga Edition
10 9 8 7 6 5 4 3 2 1
First printing, November 2007

PARENTAL ADVISORY
THE PRINCE OF TENNIS
is rated A and is suitable
for readers of all ages.
ratings.viz.com

www.viz.com

THE WORLD'S
MOST POPULAR MANGA

www.shonenjump.com

SHONEN JUMP Manga

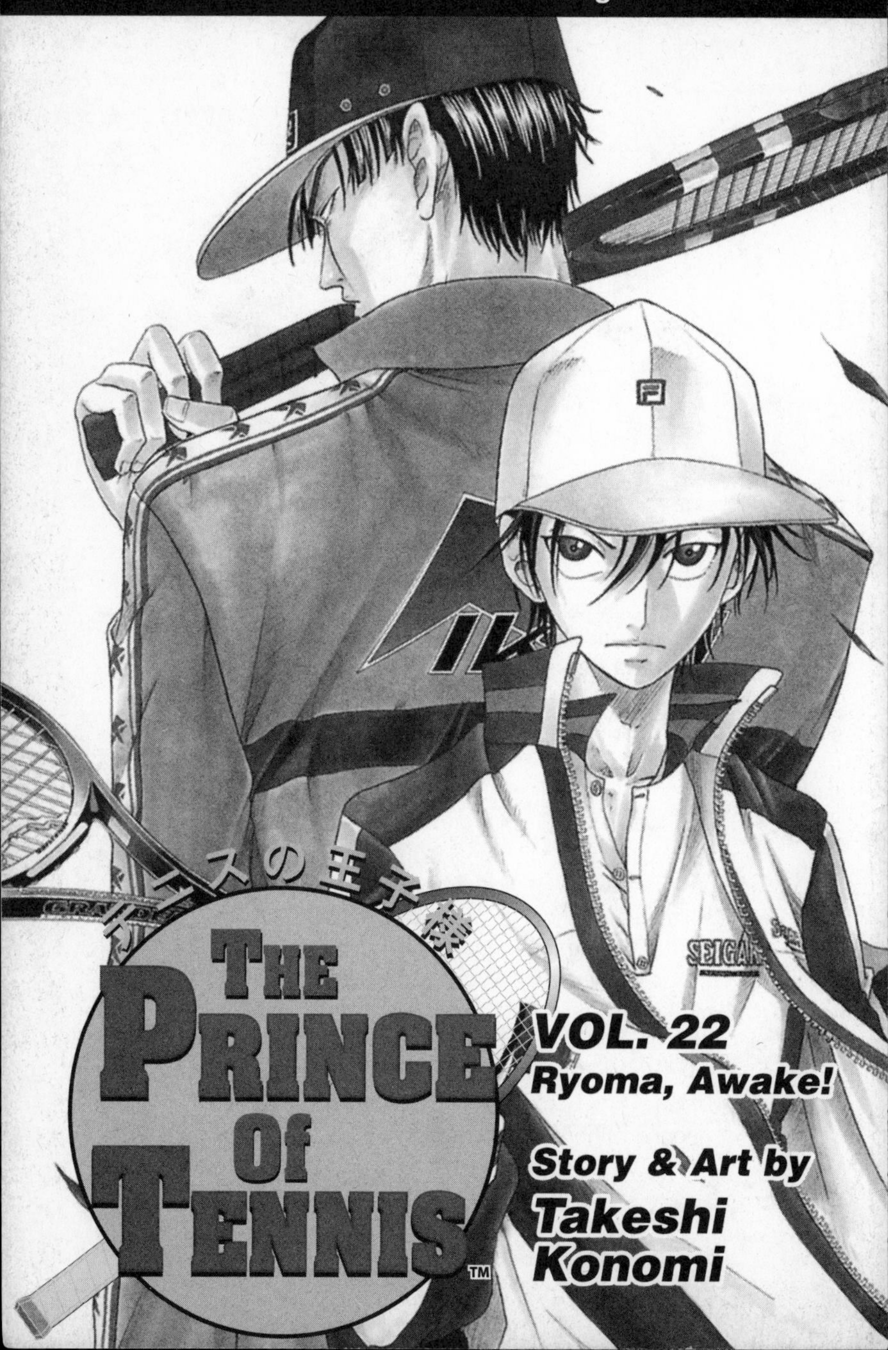

THE PRINCE OF TENNIS™

VOL. 22
Ryoma, Awake!

Story & Art by
Takeshi Konomi

ENNIS CLUB

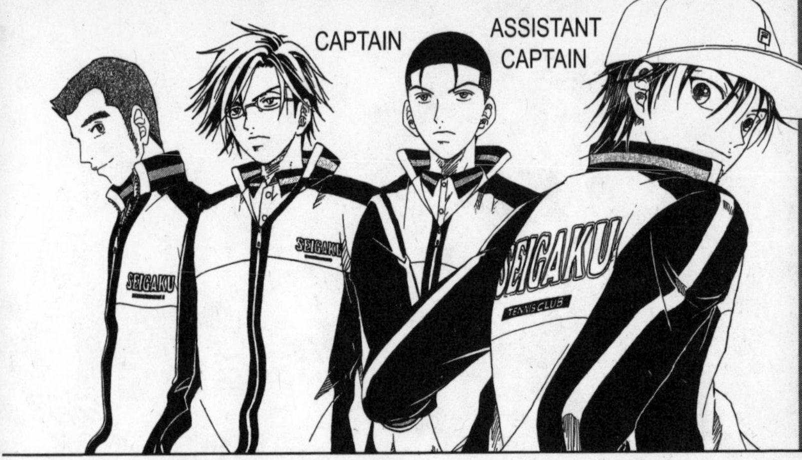
CAPTAIN
ASSISTANT CAPTAIN

• TAKASHI KAWAMURA • KUNIMITSU TEZUKA • SHUICHIRO OISHI • RYOMA ECHIZEN •

STORY & HARACTERS

Seishun Academy student Ryoma Echizen is a tennis prodigy with wins in four consecutive U.S. Junior tournaments under his belt. Then he became a starter as a 7th grader and led his team to the District Preliminaries! Despite a few mishaps, Seishun won the District Prelims and City Tournament, and even earned a ticket to the Kanto Tournament.

The Kanto Tournament begins and Seishun's first-round opponent is last year's Nationals runner-up, Hyotei. Seishun come away victorious from a close match, but Kunimitsu injures his shoulder and leaves the team to seek treatment in Kyushu. Although missing Kunimitsu and Shuichiro, Seishun nevertheless strengthen their team unity and defeat Midoriyama and Rokkaku to reach the finals. But their finals match is against Rikkai, who are going for their third straight national title! After watching Rikkai's humiliation of Fudomine in the semifinals, the Seishun players are shocked at their opponent's power...

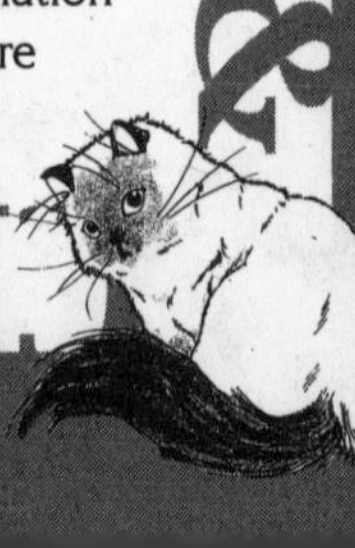

SEIGAKU T

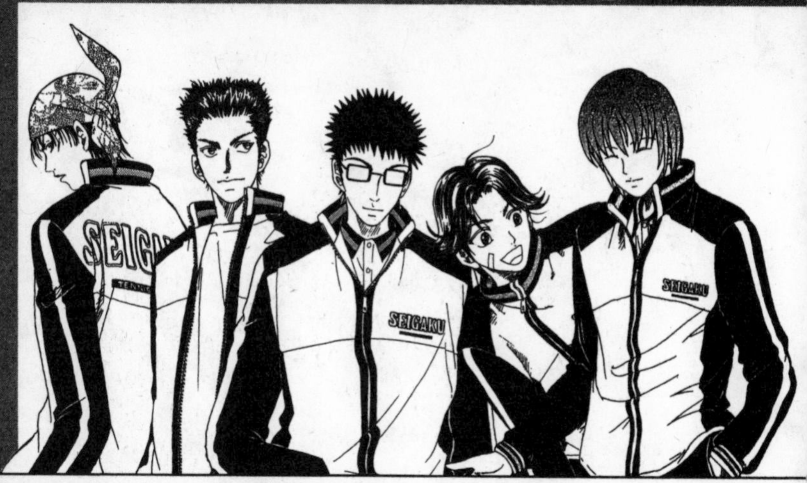

SEIGAKU
SEIGAKU

● KAORU KAIDO ● TAKESHI MOMOSHIRO ● SADAHARU INUI ● EIJI KIKUMARU ● SHUSUKE FUJI ●

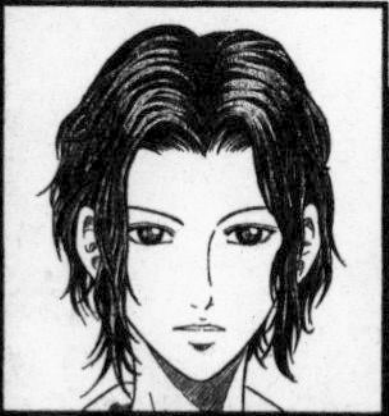

RIKKAI

SEIICHI YUKIMURA

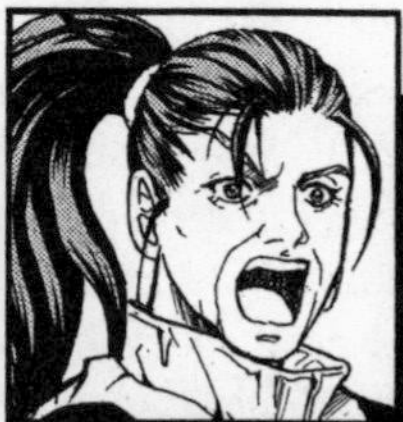

SEISHUN ACADEMY TENNIS COACH

SUMIRE RYUZAKI

THE PRINCE OF TENNIS

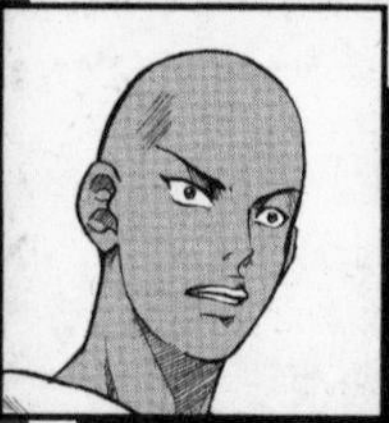

RIKKAI

JACKAL KUWAHARA

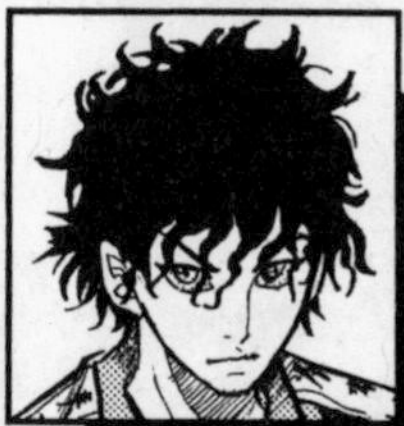

RIKKAI

AKAYA KIRIHARA

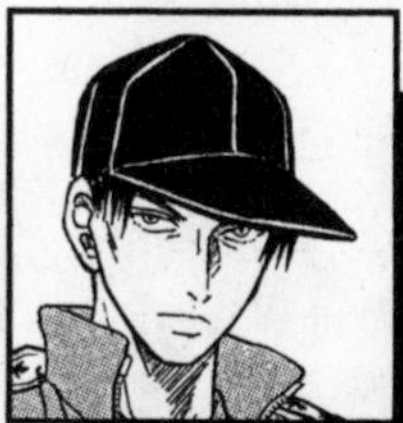

RIKKAI

GENICHIRO SANADA

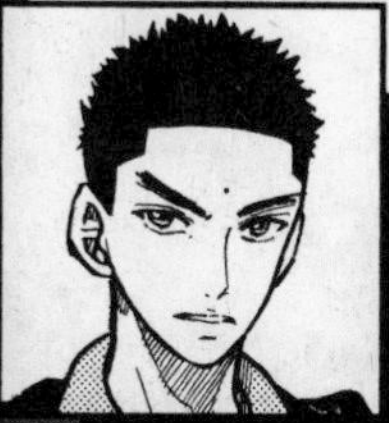

FUDOMINE

KIPPEI TACHIBANA

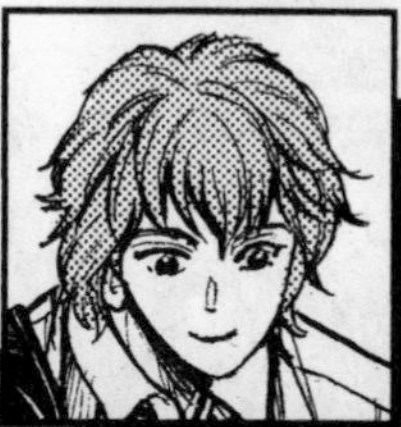

RIKKAI

BUNTA MARUI

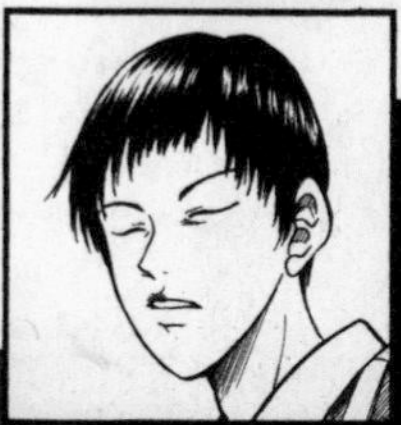

RIKKAI

RENJI YANAGI

CONTENTS

Vol. 22
Ryoma, Awake!

Genius 186: Surprise Attack   7

Genius 187: 2 minutes 11 seconds   27

Genius 188: Signs of Danger   47

Genius 189: The Terrifying Knuckle Serve   67

Genius 190: Relentless Attack   87

Genius 191: Ryoma, Awake!   104

Genius 192: Signs of Awakening   125

Genius   0: The Samurai's Story   145

GENIUS 186: SURPRISE ATTACK

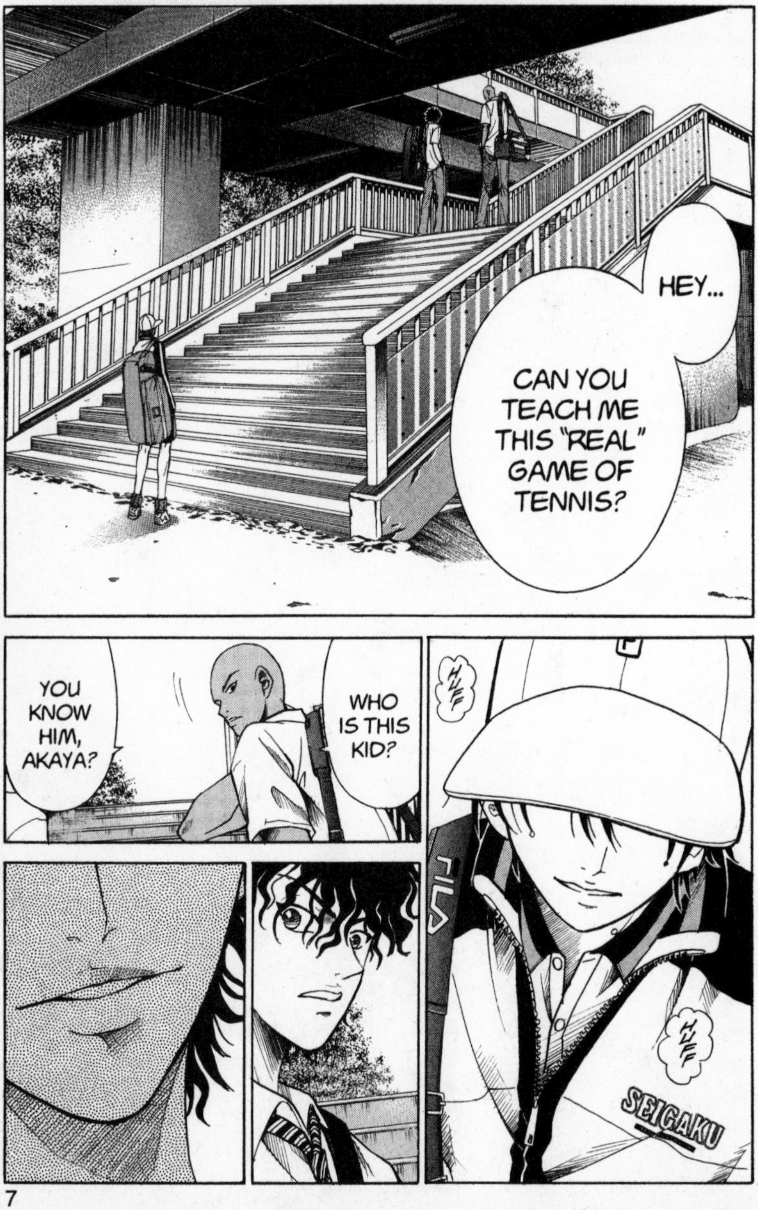
HEY...
CAN YOU TEACH ME THIS "REAL" GAME OF TENNIS?
HUFF
HUFF
SEIGAKU
WHO IS THIS KID?
YOU KNOW HIM, AKAYA?

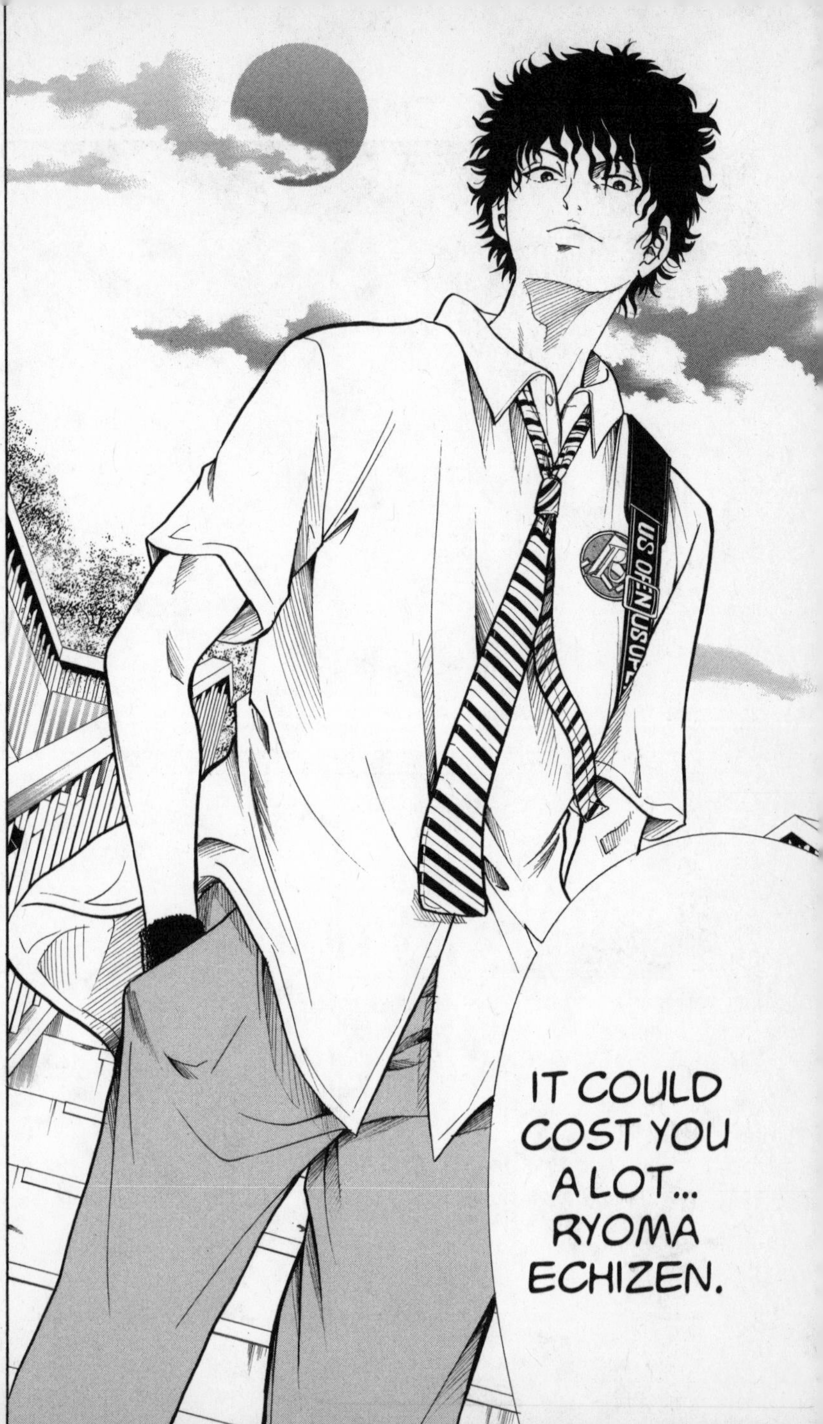
US OPEN
US OPEN
IT COULD COST YOU A LOT... RYOMA ECHIZEN.

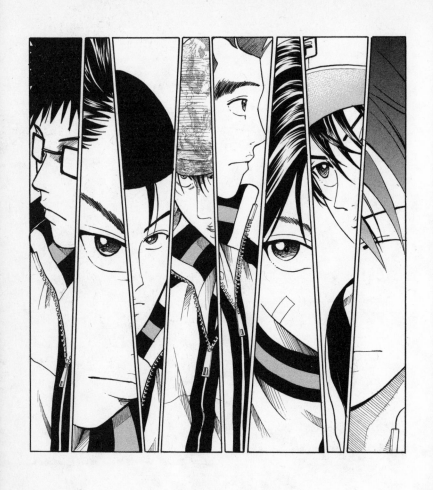

GENIUS 186: SURPRISE ATTACK

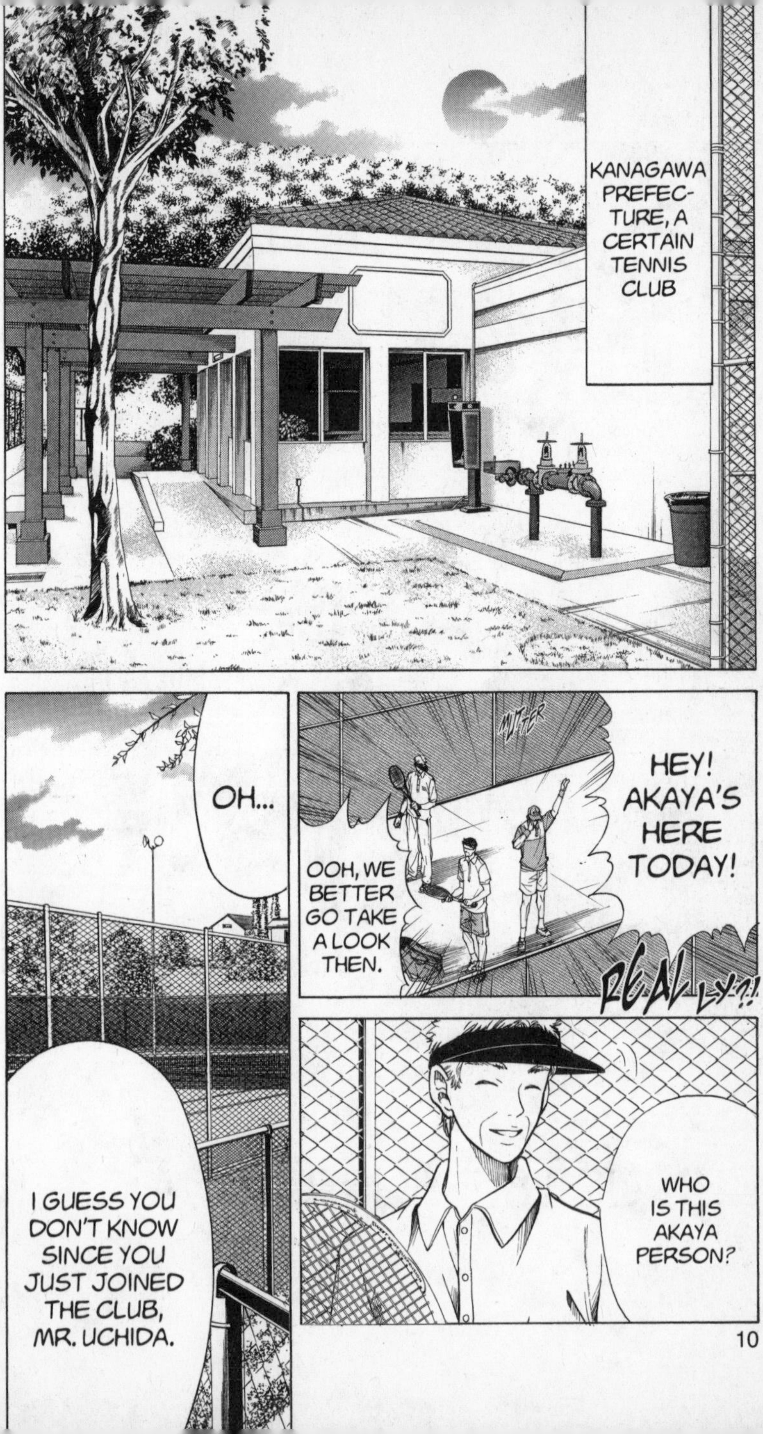
KANAGAWA PREFECTURE, A CERTAIN TENNIS CLUB
HEY! AKAYA'S HERE TODAY!
MUTTER
OOH, WE BETTER GO TAKE A LOOK THEN.
REALLY?!
WHO IS THIS AKAYA PERSON?
OH...
I GUESS YOU DON'T KNOW SINCE YOU JUST JOINED THE CLUB, MR. UCHIDA.

READ THIS WAY

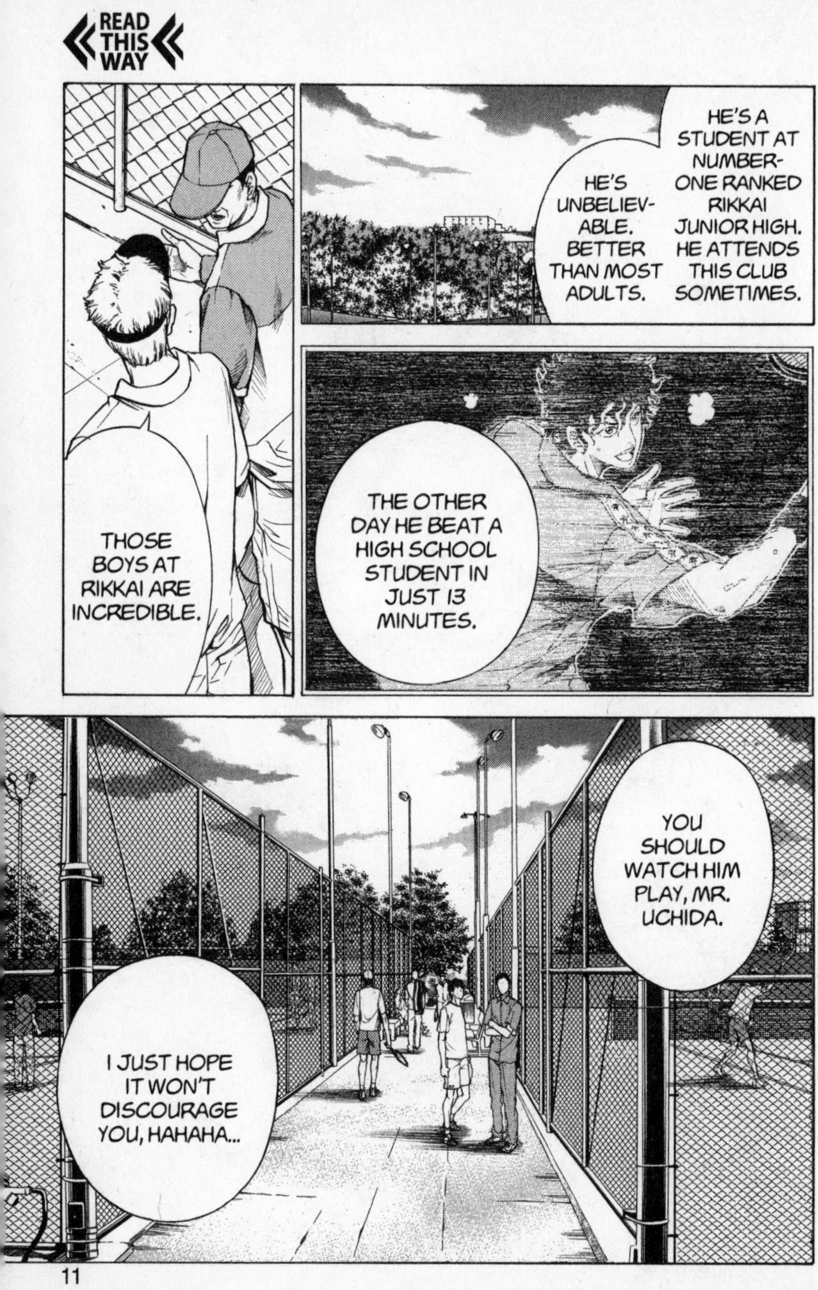
HE'S A STUDENT AT NUMBER-ONE RANKED RIKKAI JUNIOR HIGH. HE ATTENDS THIS CLUB SOMETIMES.
HE'S UNBELIEV-ABLE. BETTER THAN MOST ADULTS.
THE OTHER DAY HE BEAT A HIGH SCHOOL STUDENT IN JUST 13 MINUTES.
THOSE BOYS AT RIKKAI ARE INCREDIBLE.
YOU SHOULD WATCH HIM PLAY, MR. UCHIDA.
I JUST HOPE IT WON'T DISCOURAGE YOU, HAHAHA...

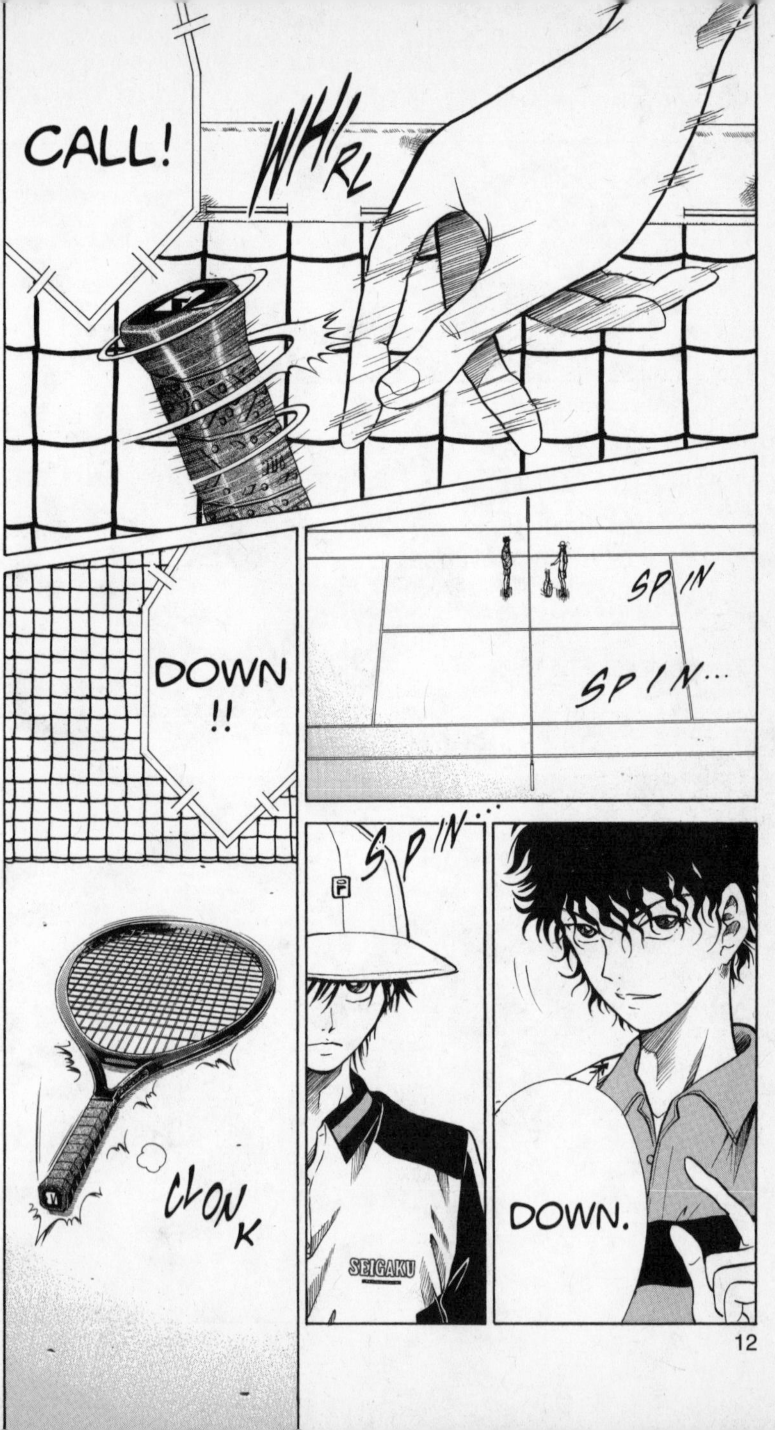
CALL!
WHIRL
SPIN
SPIN...
DOWN.
SPIN...
DOWN !!
CLONK
SEIGAKU

READ THIS WAY

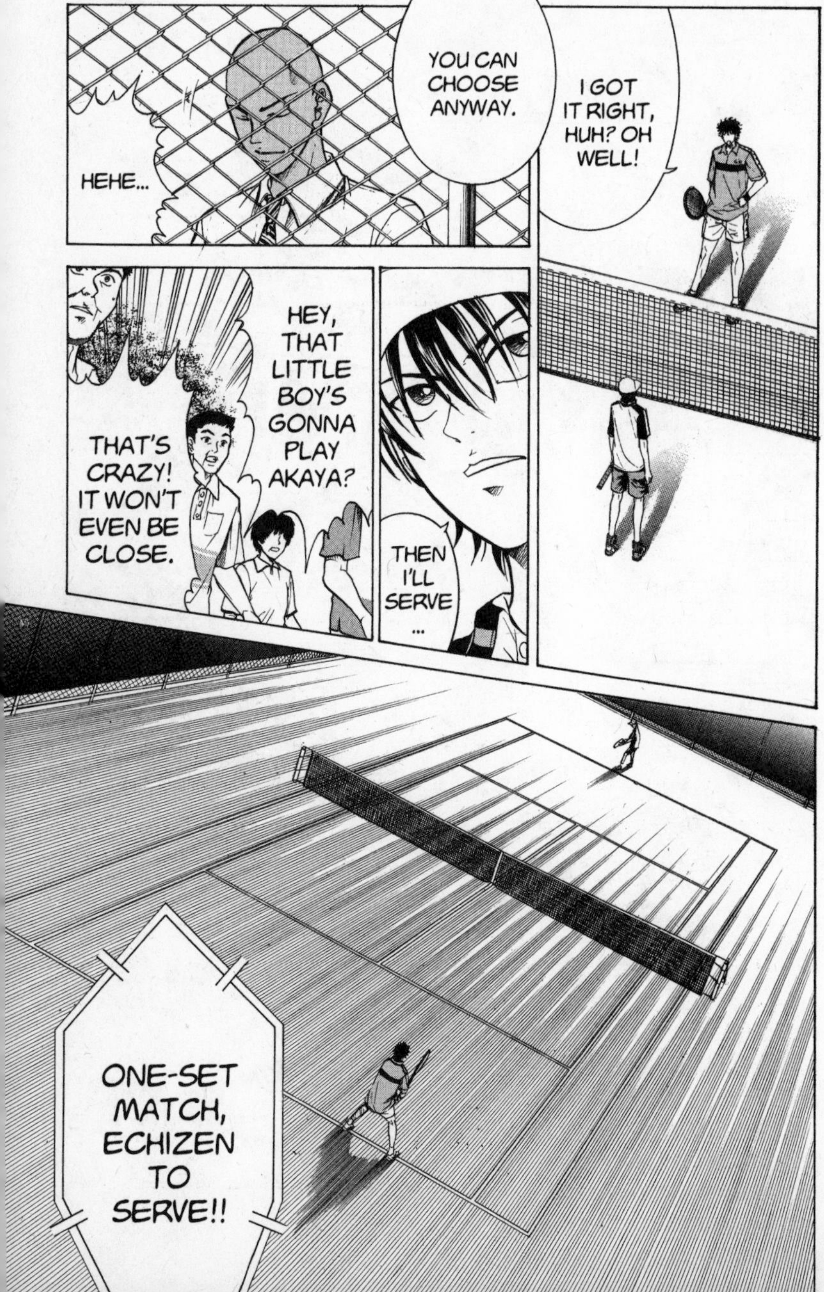
I GOT IT RIGHT, HUH? OH WELL!
YOU CAN CHOOSE ANYWAY.
HEHE...
THEN I'LL SERVE ...
HEY, THAT LITTLE BOY'S GONNA PLAY AKAYA?
THAT'S CRAZY! IT WON'T EVEN BE CLOSE.
ONE-SET MATCH, ECHIZEN TO SERVE!!

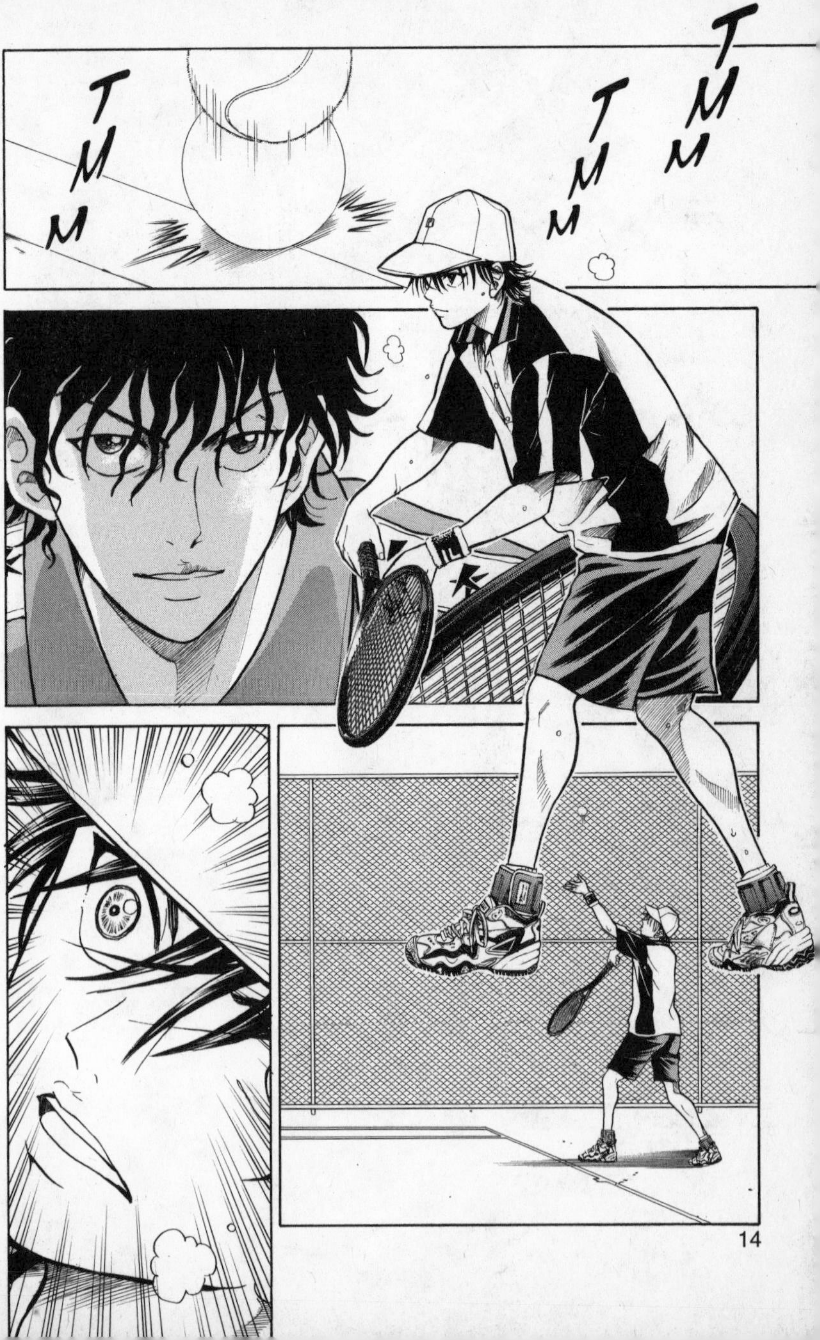
TMM
TMM
TMM

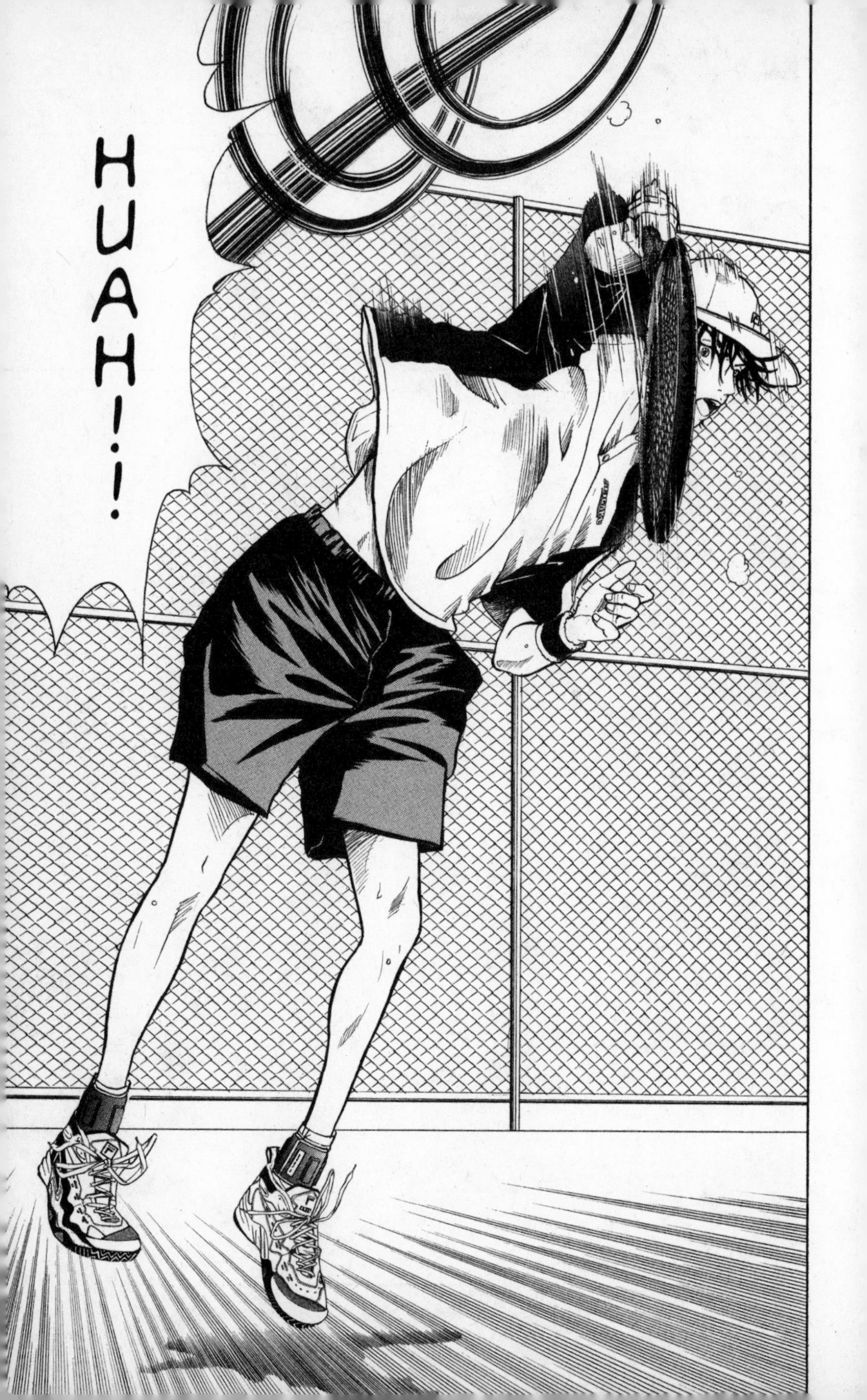
HUAH!!

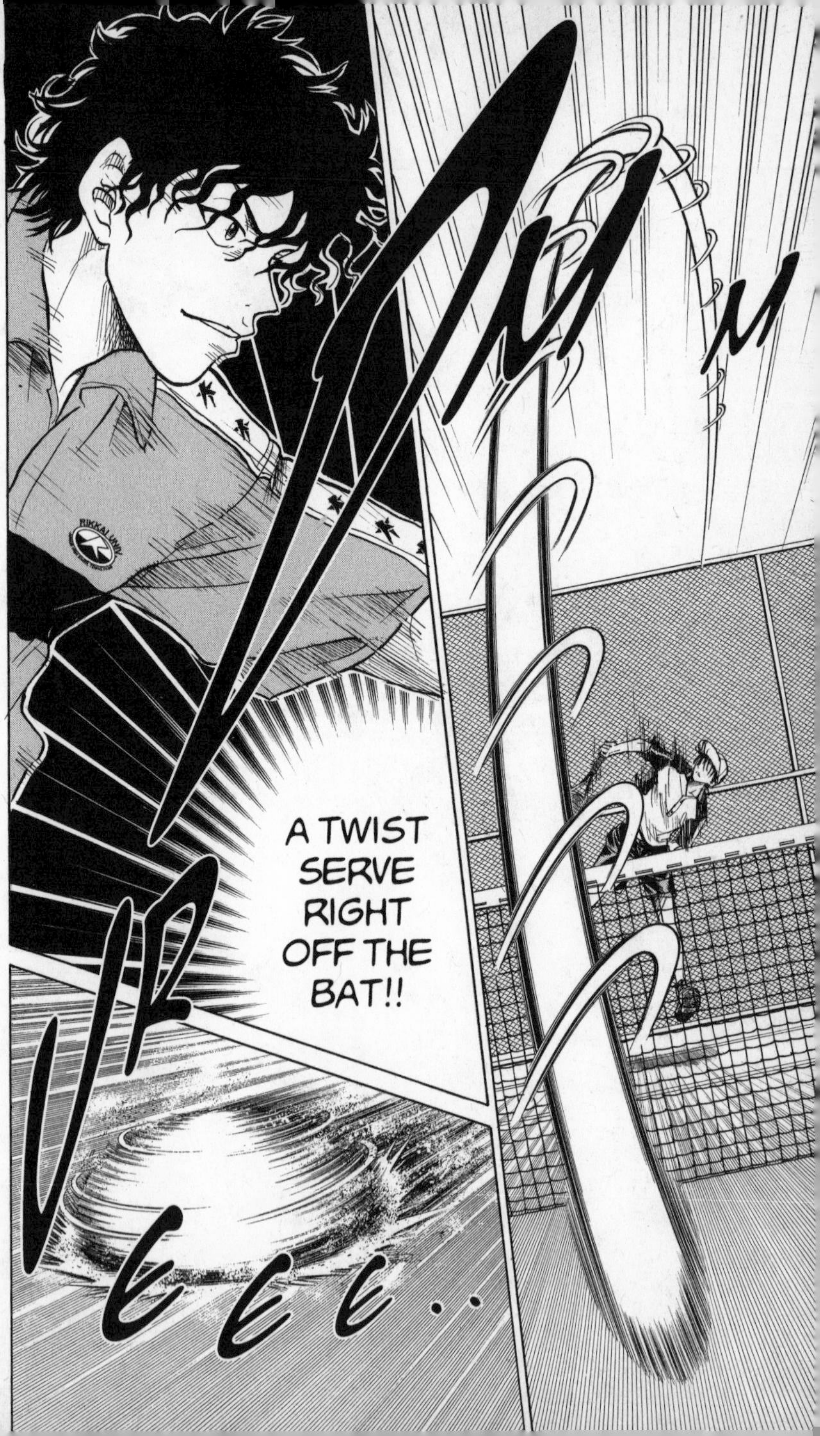
A TWIST SERVE RIGHT OFF THE BAT!!

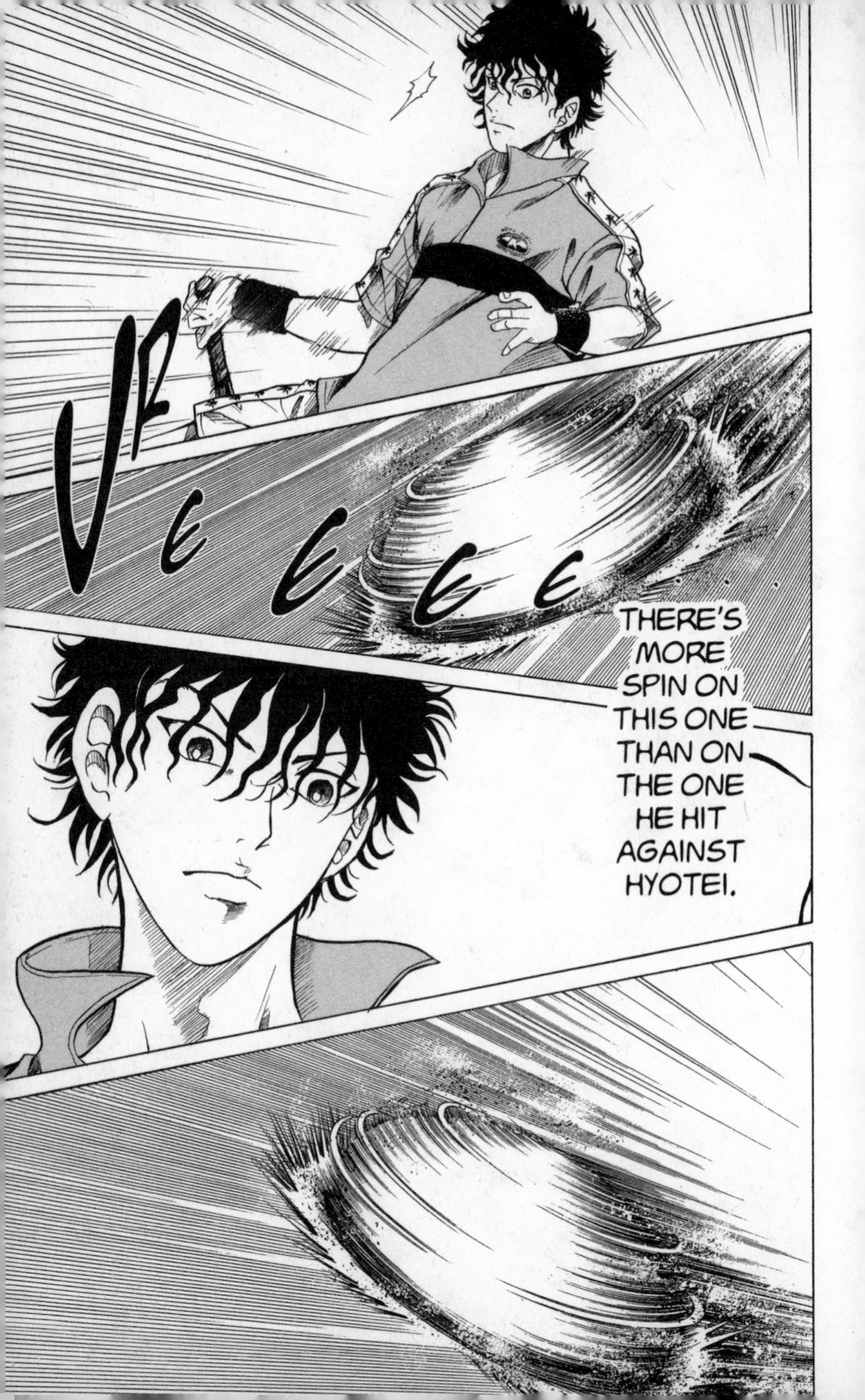
VREEEE
THERE'S MORE SPIN ON THIS ONE THAN ON THE ONE HE HIT AGAINST HYOTEI.

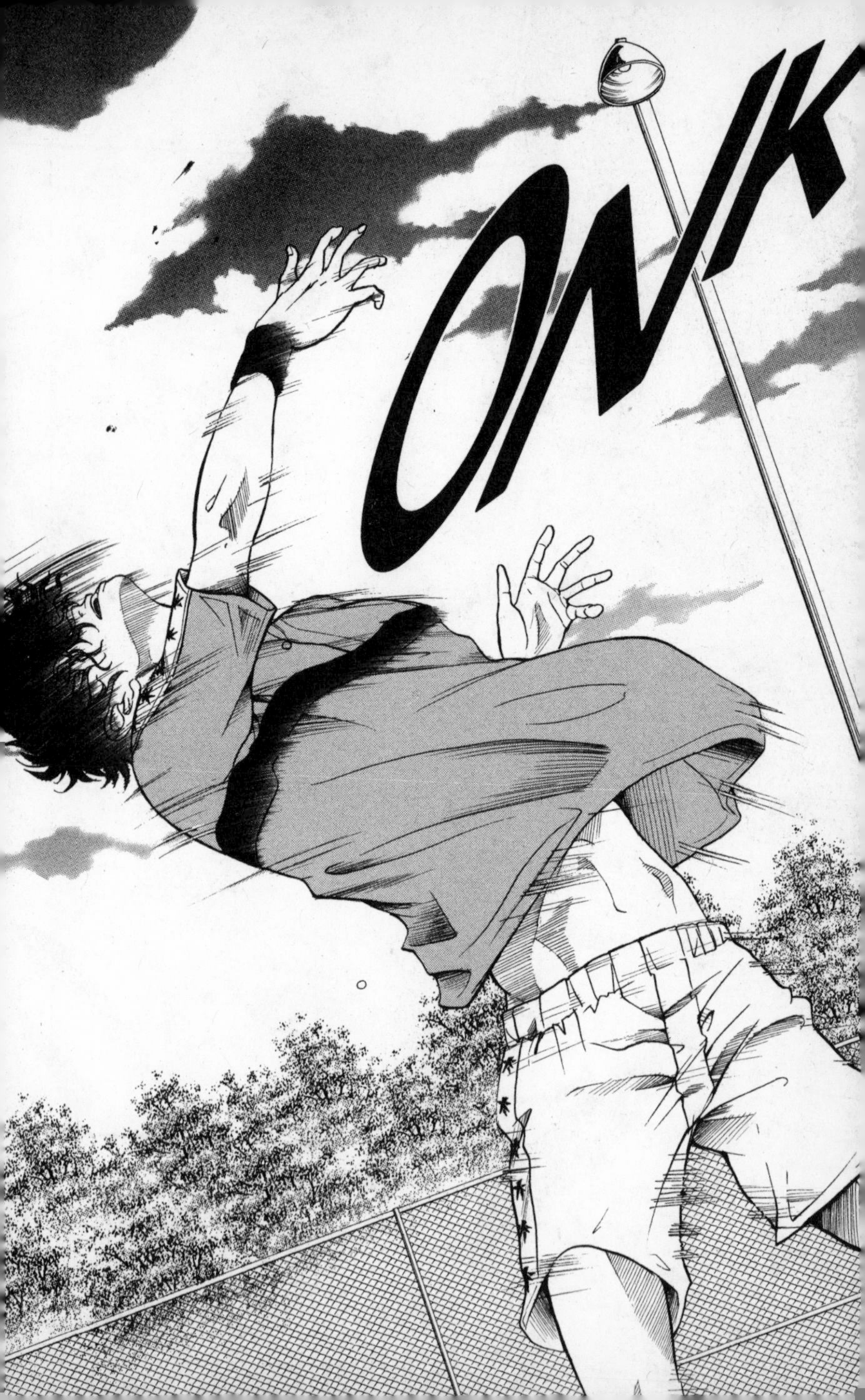
ONK

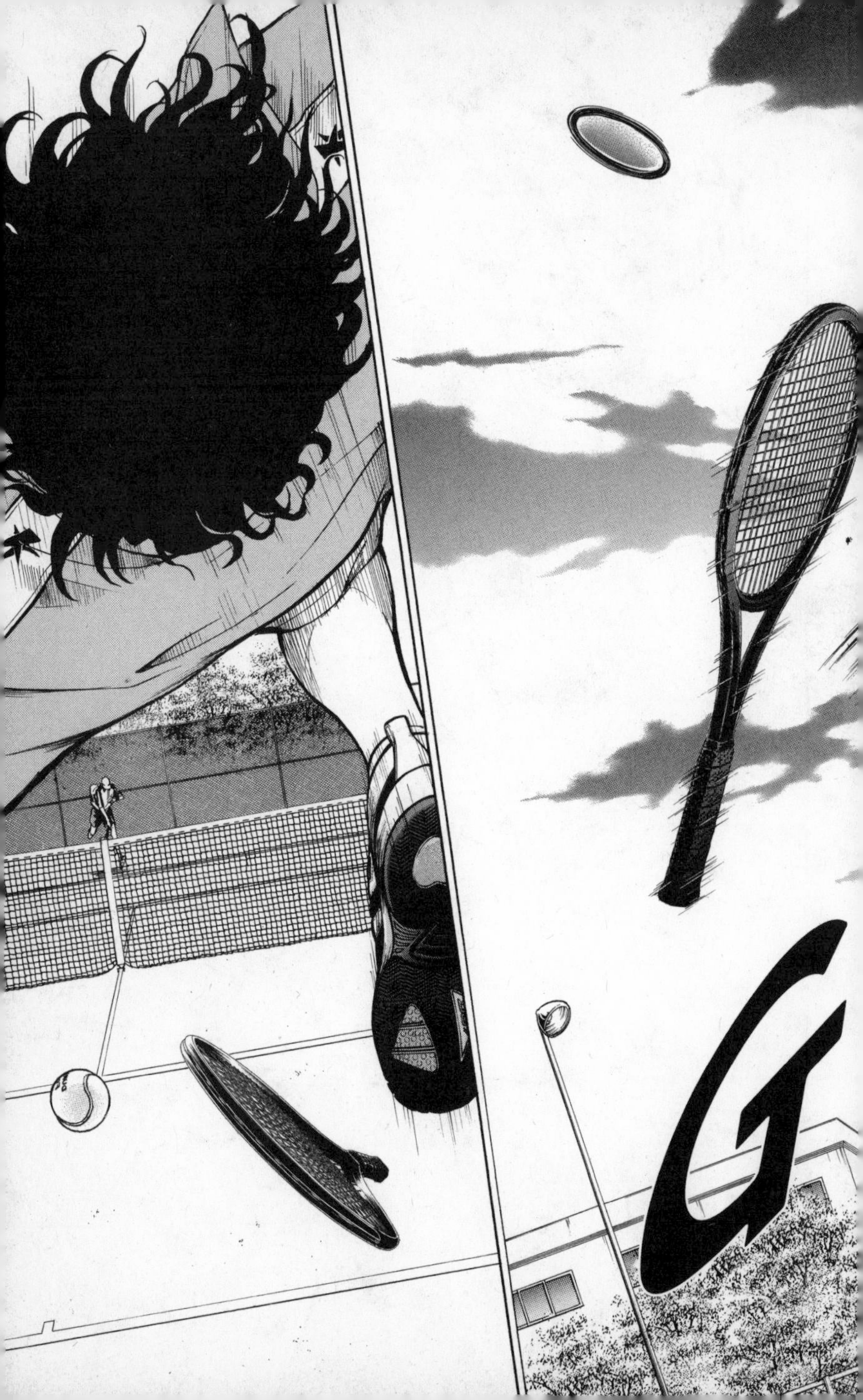
G

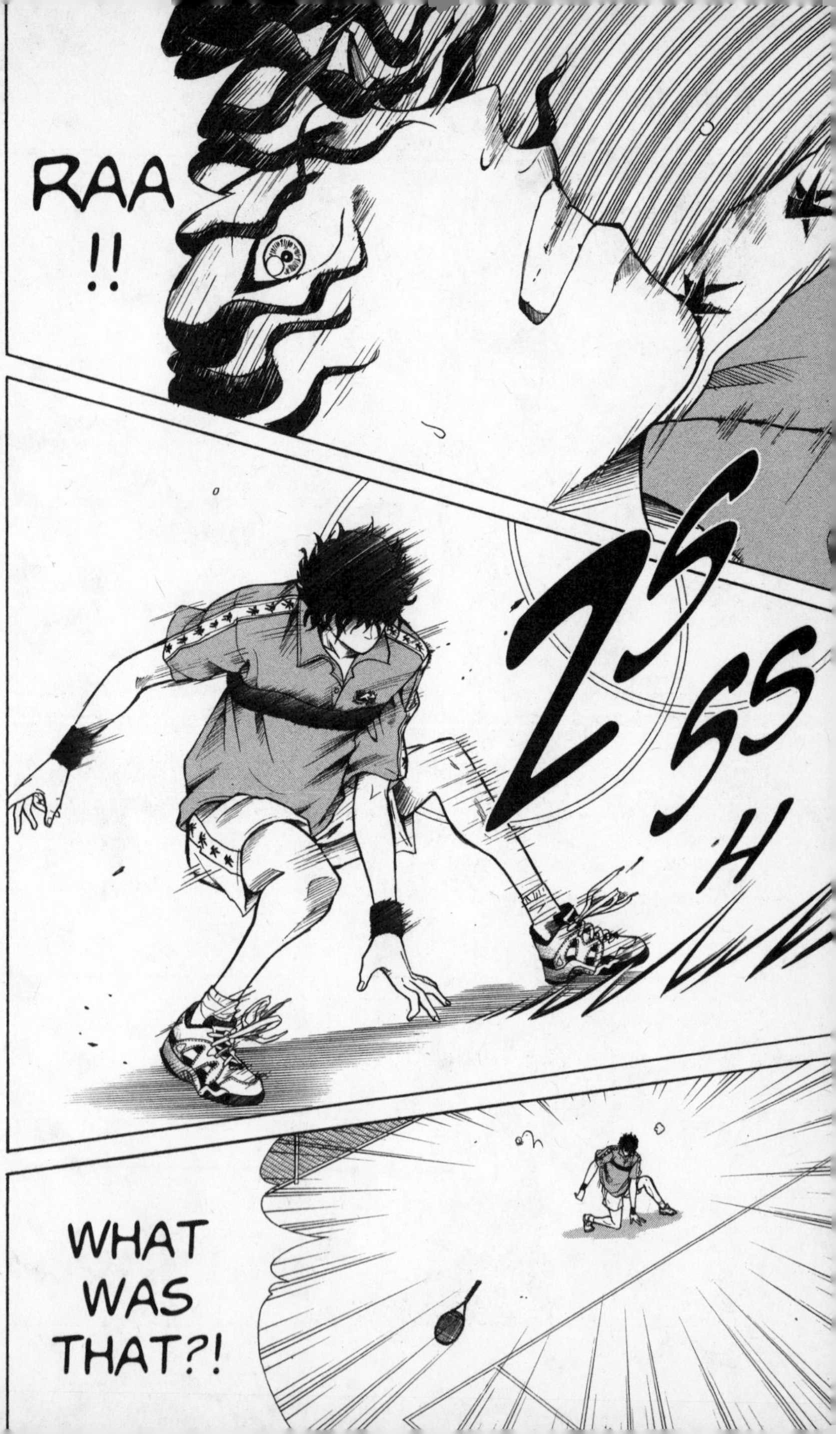
RAA !!
ZSSSH
WHAT WAS THAT?!

READ THIS WAY

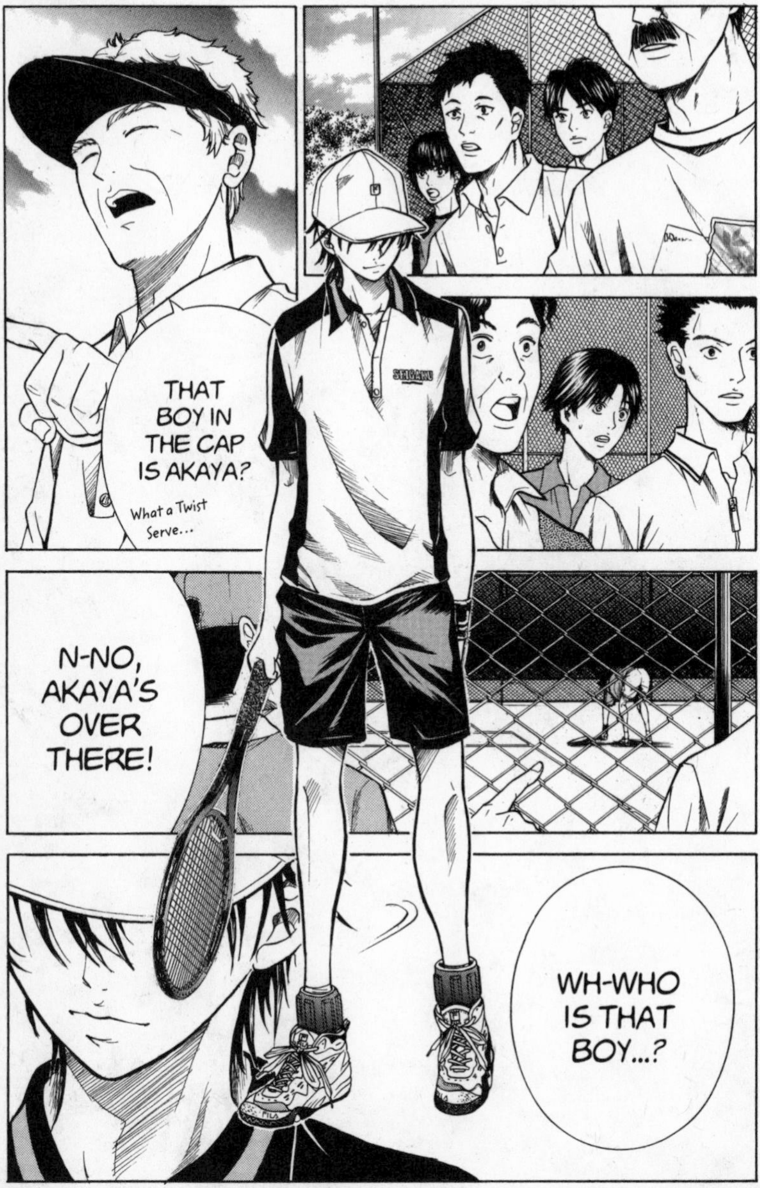
THAT BOY IN THE CAP IS AKAYA?
What a Twist Serve...
N-NO, AKAYA'S OVER THERE!
WH-WHO IS THAT BOY...?

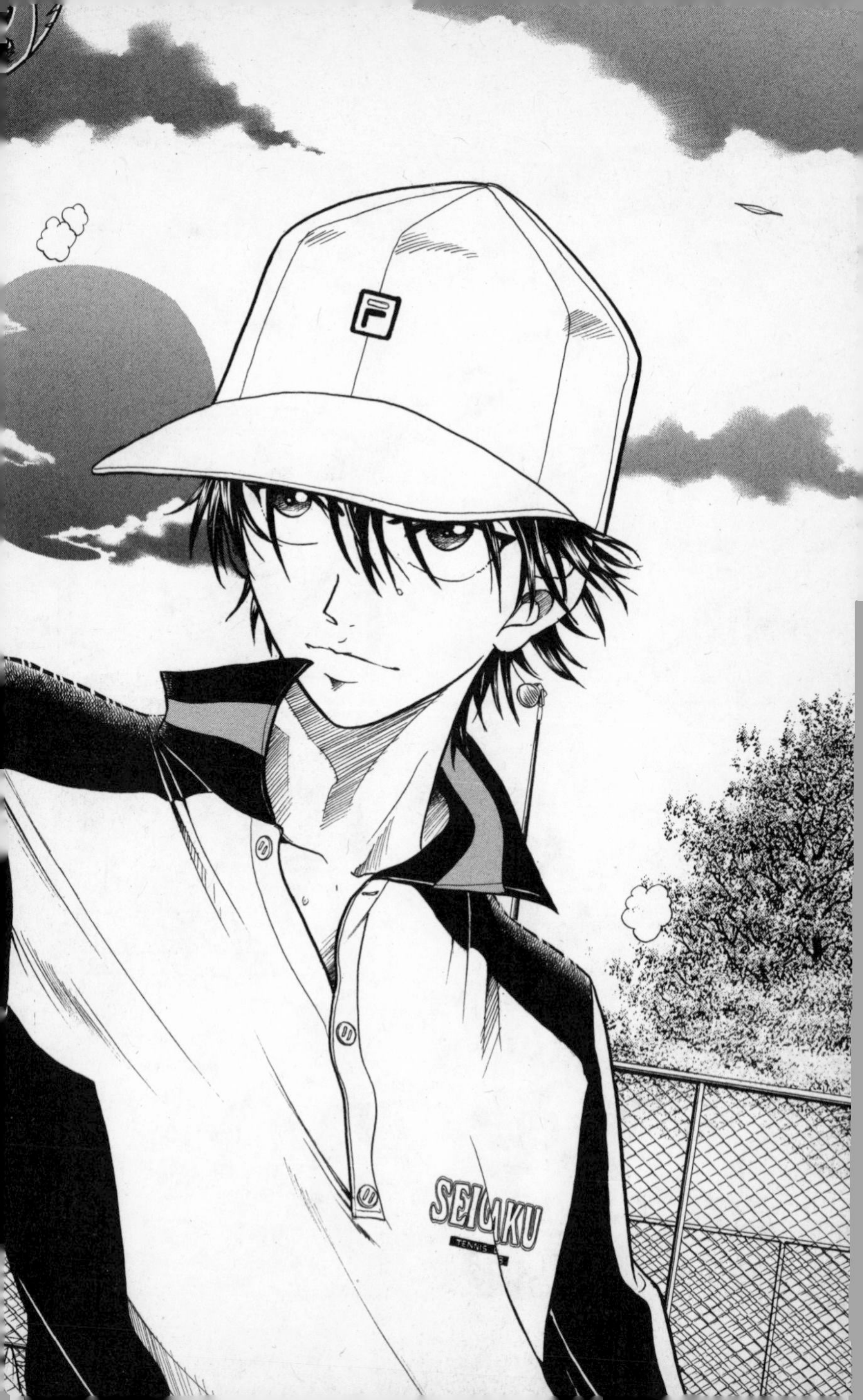

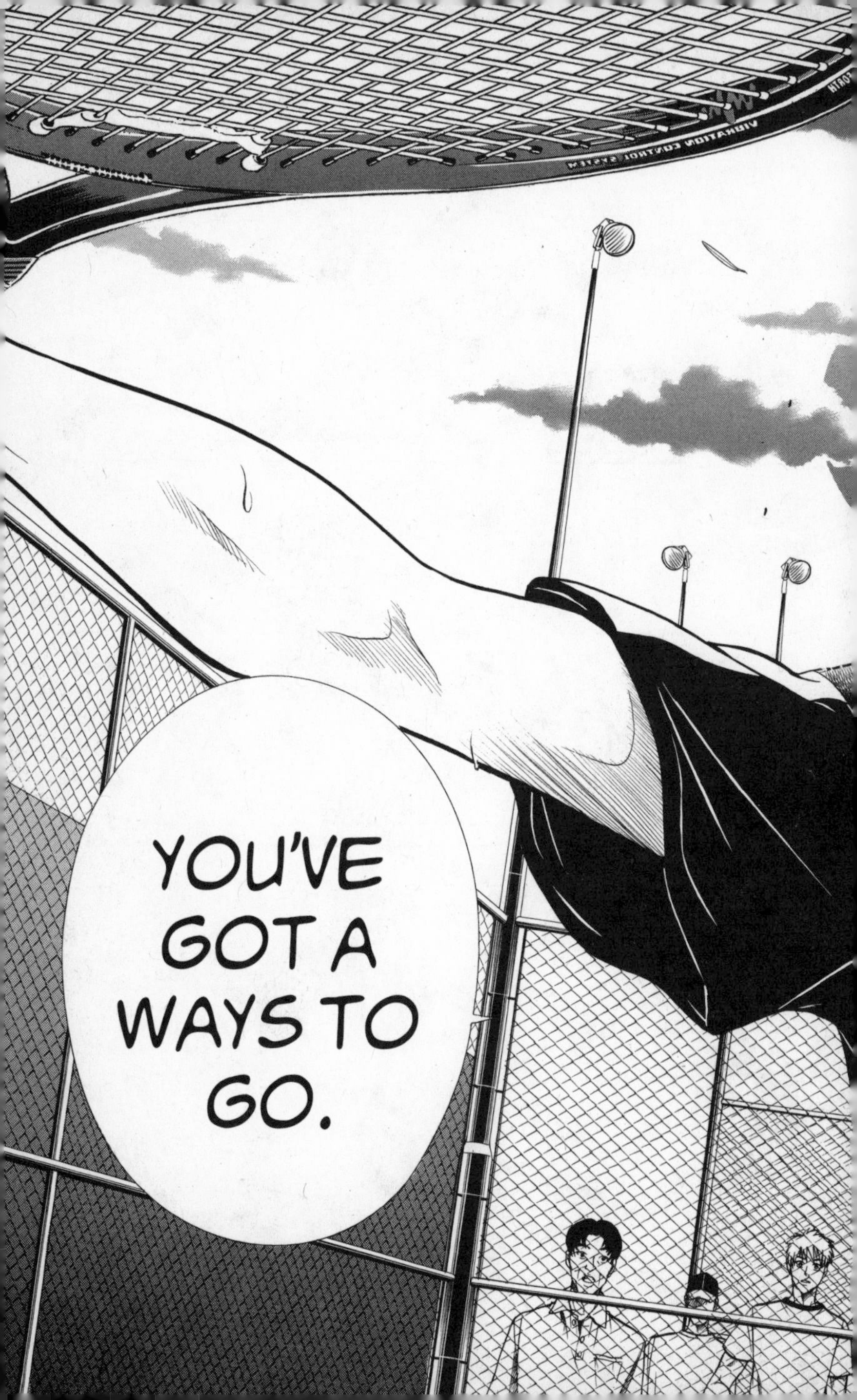
YOU'VE GOT A WAYS TO GO.

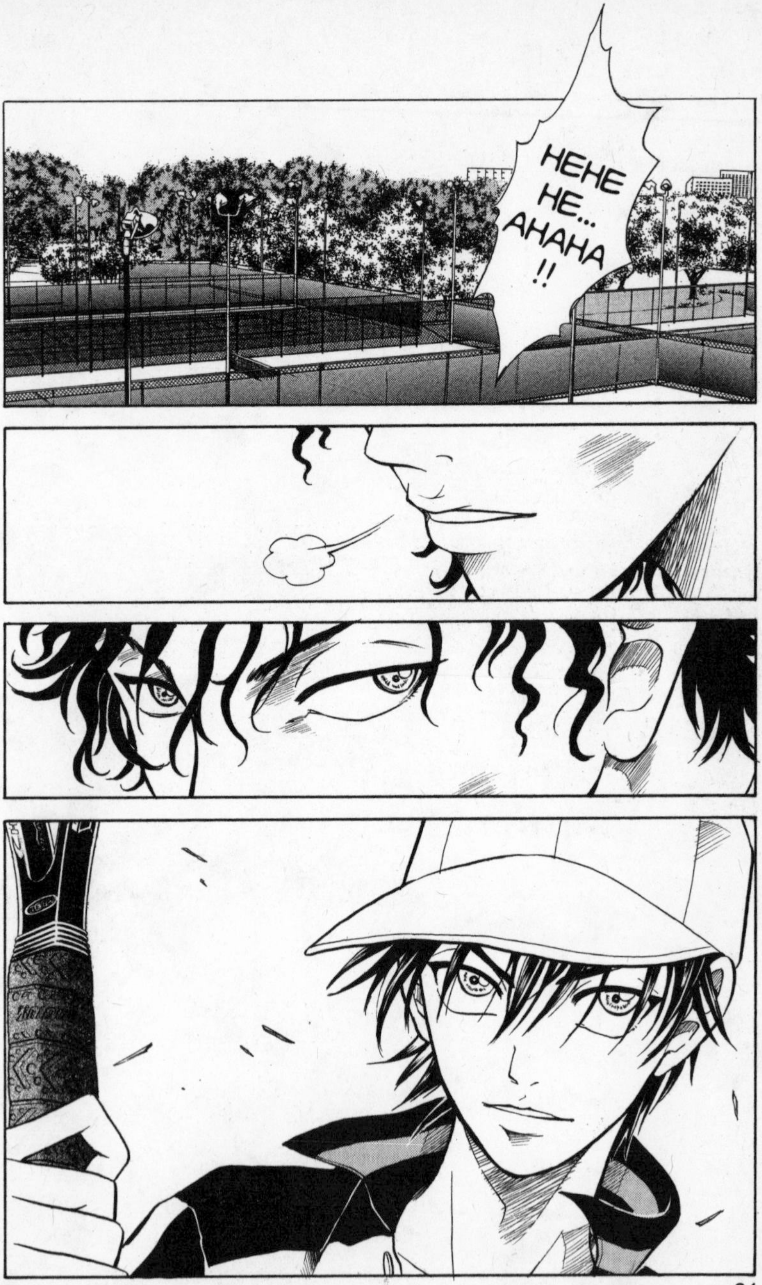
HEHE HE... AHAHA !!

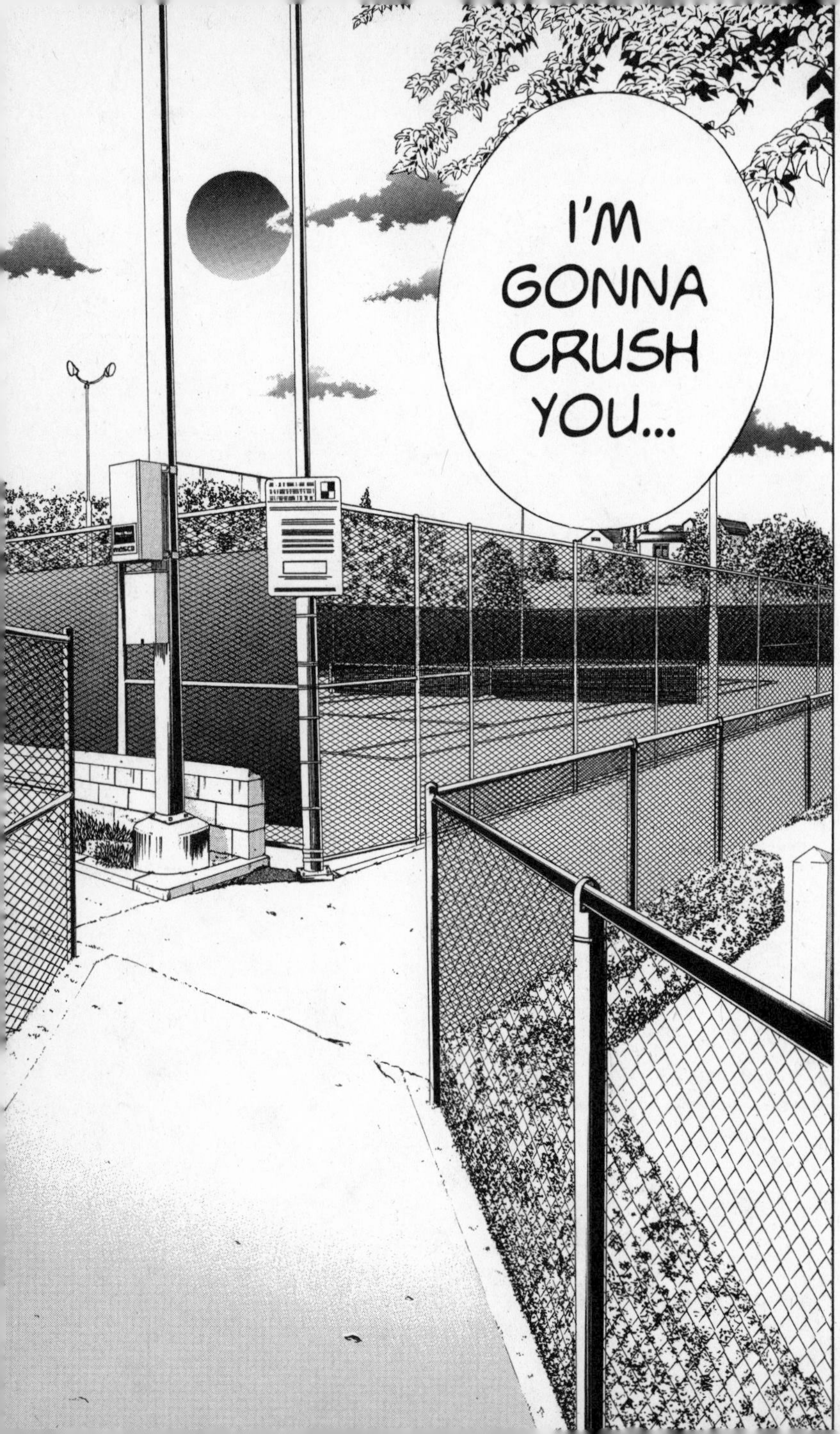
I'M GONNA CRUSH YOU...

テニスの王子様

THE PRINCE OF TENNIS™

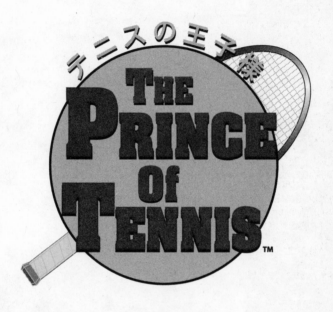

GENIUS 187: 2 MINUTES 11 SECONDS

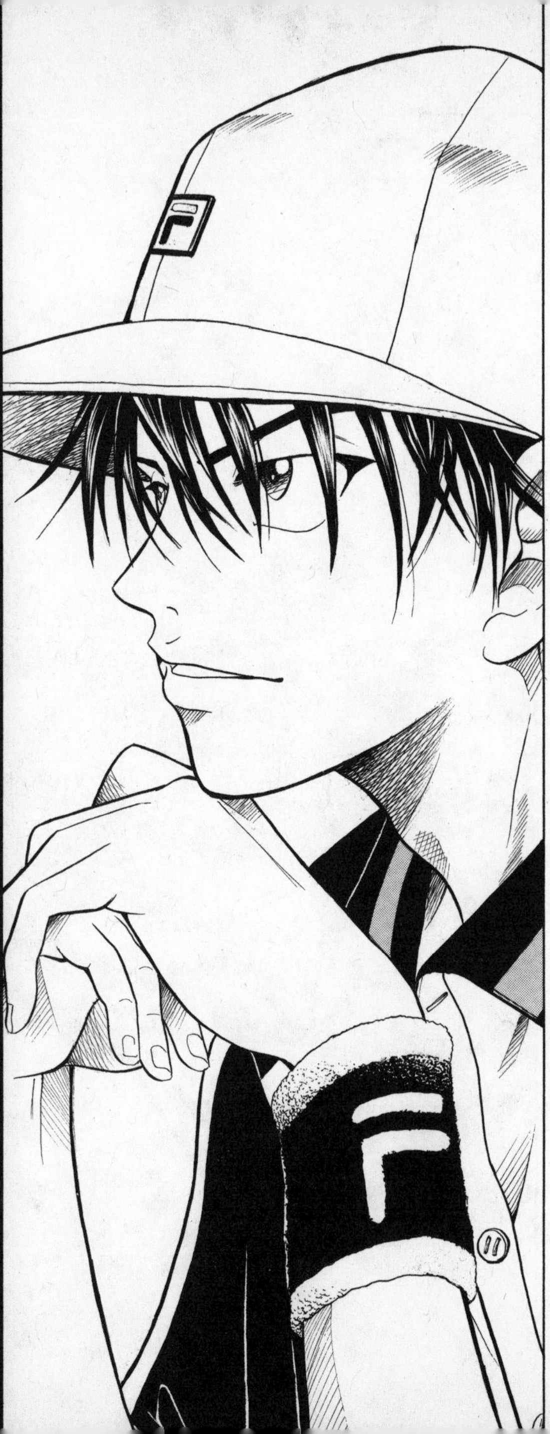

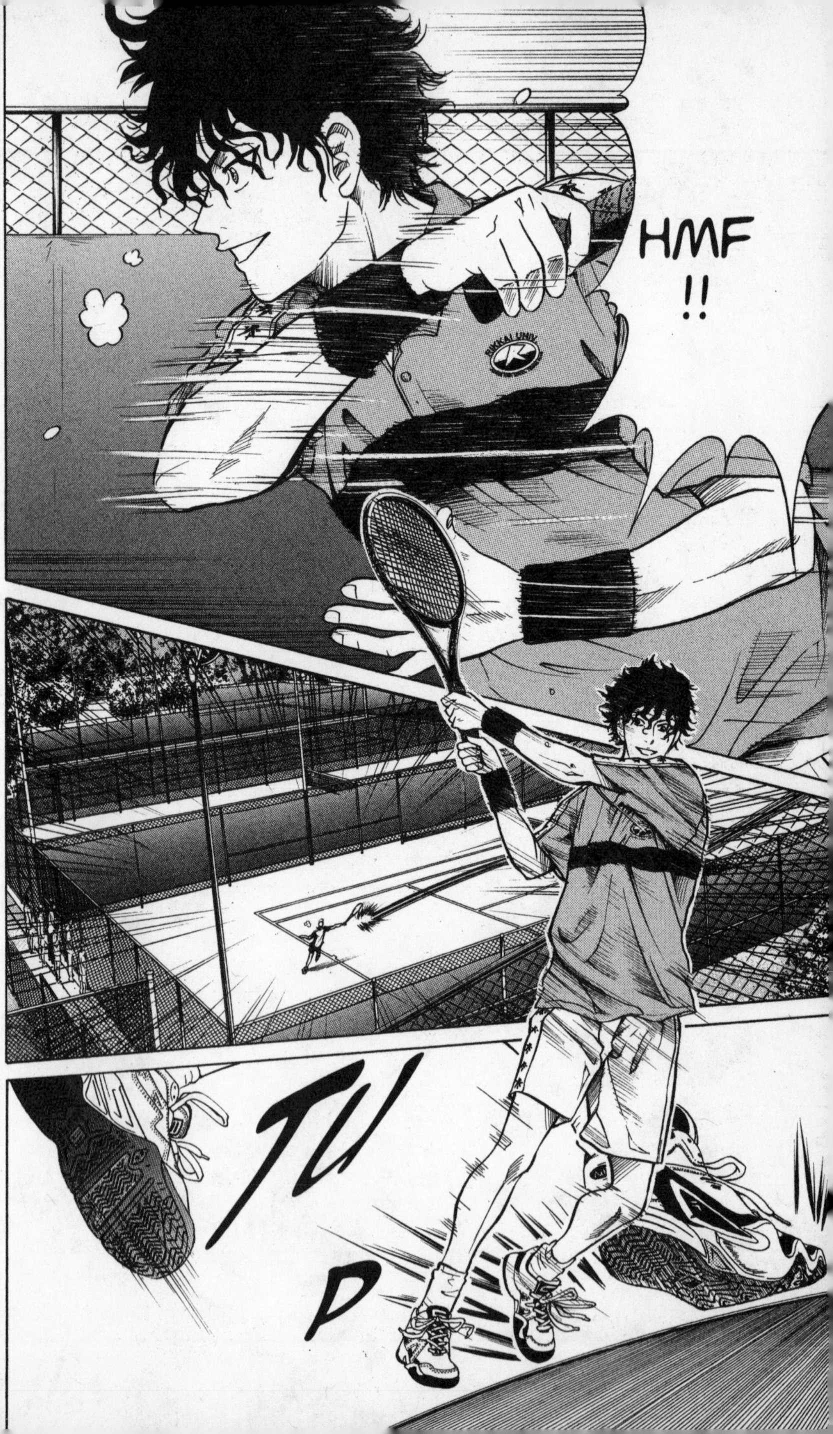
HMF
!!
TU
D

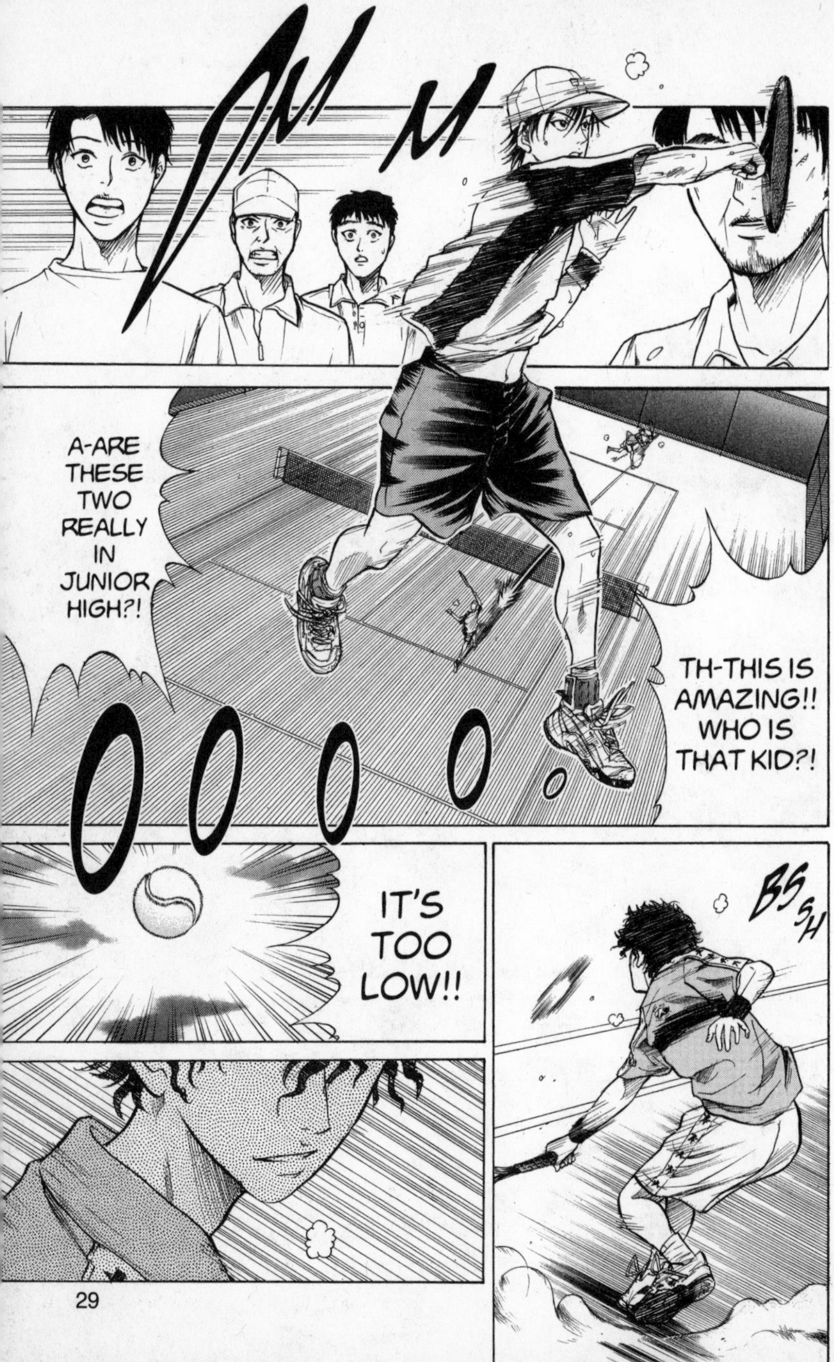
TH-THIS IS AMAZING!! WHO IS THAT KID?!
A-ARE THESE TWO REALLY IN JUNIOR HIGH?!
BSSH
IT'S TOO LOW!!

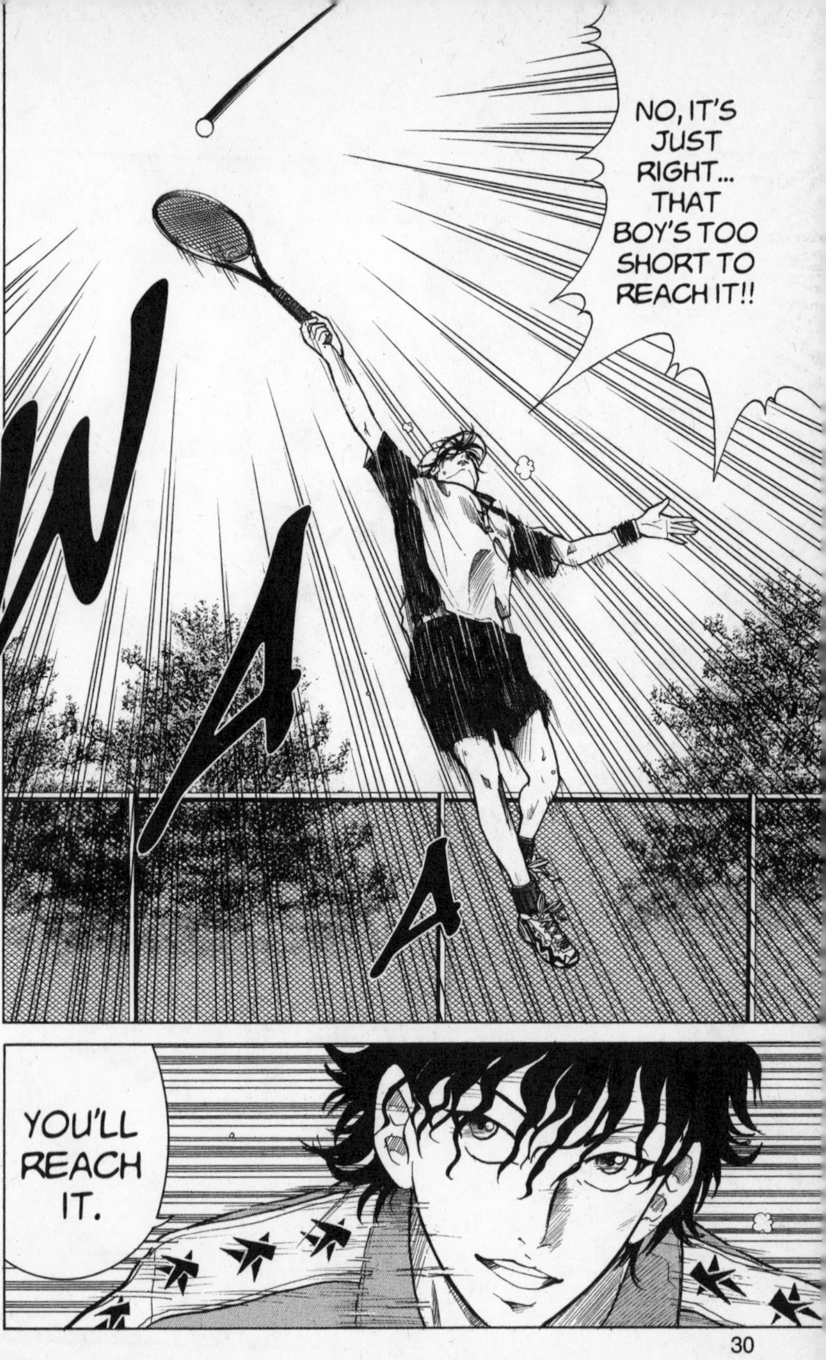
NO, IT'S JUST RIGHT... THAT BOY'S TOO SHORT TO REACH IT!!
WAA
YOU'LL REACH IT.

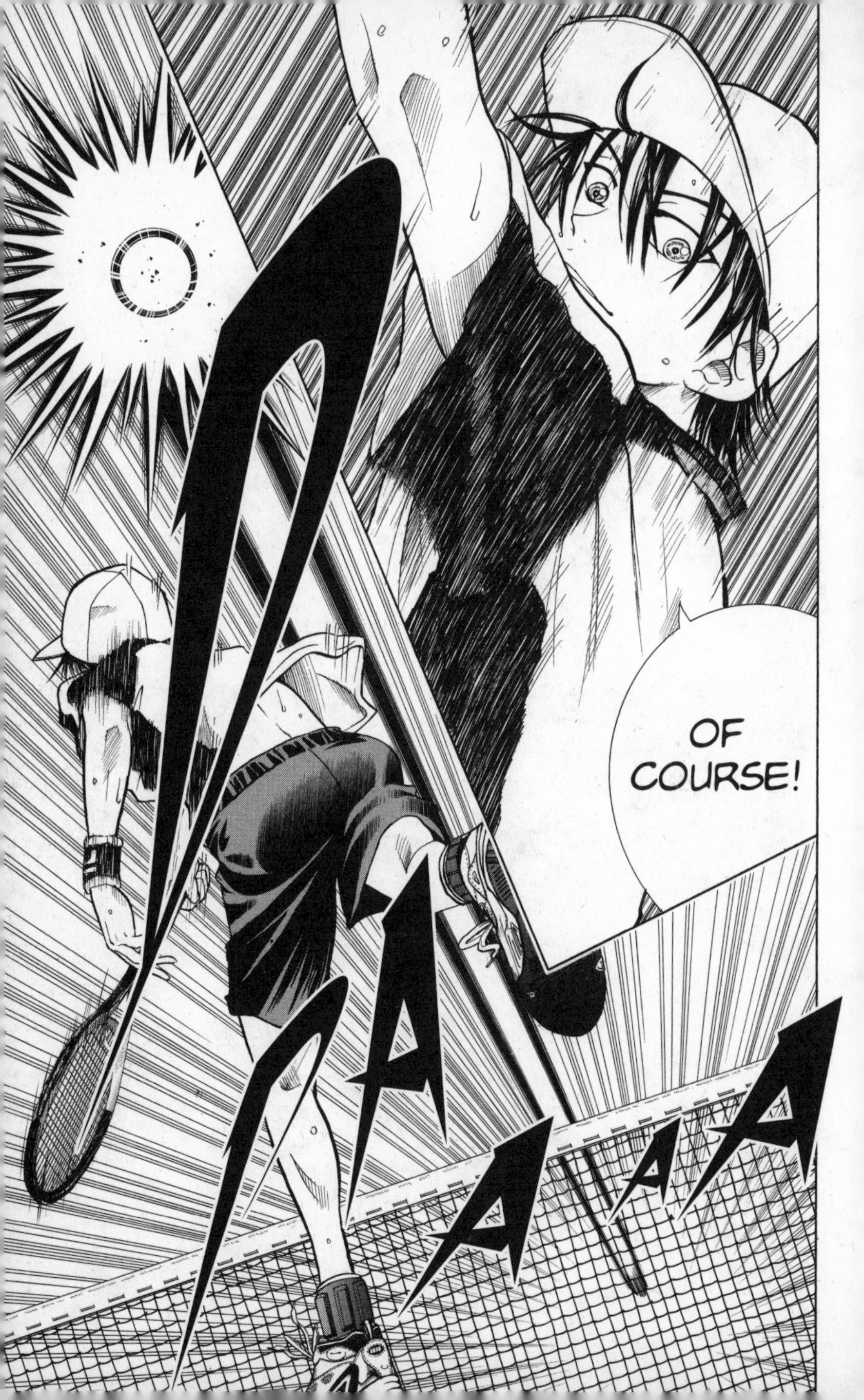
OF COURSE!

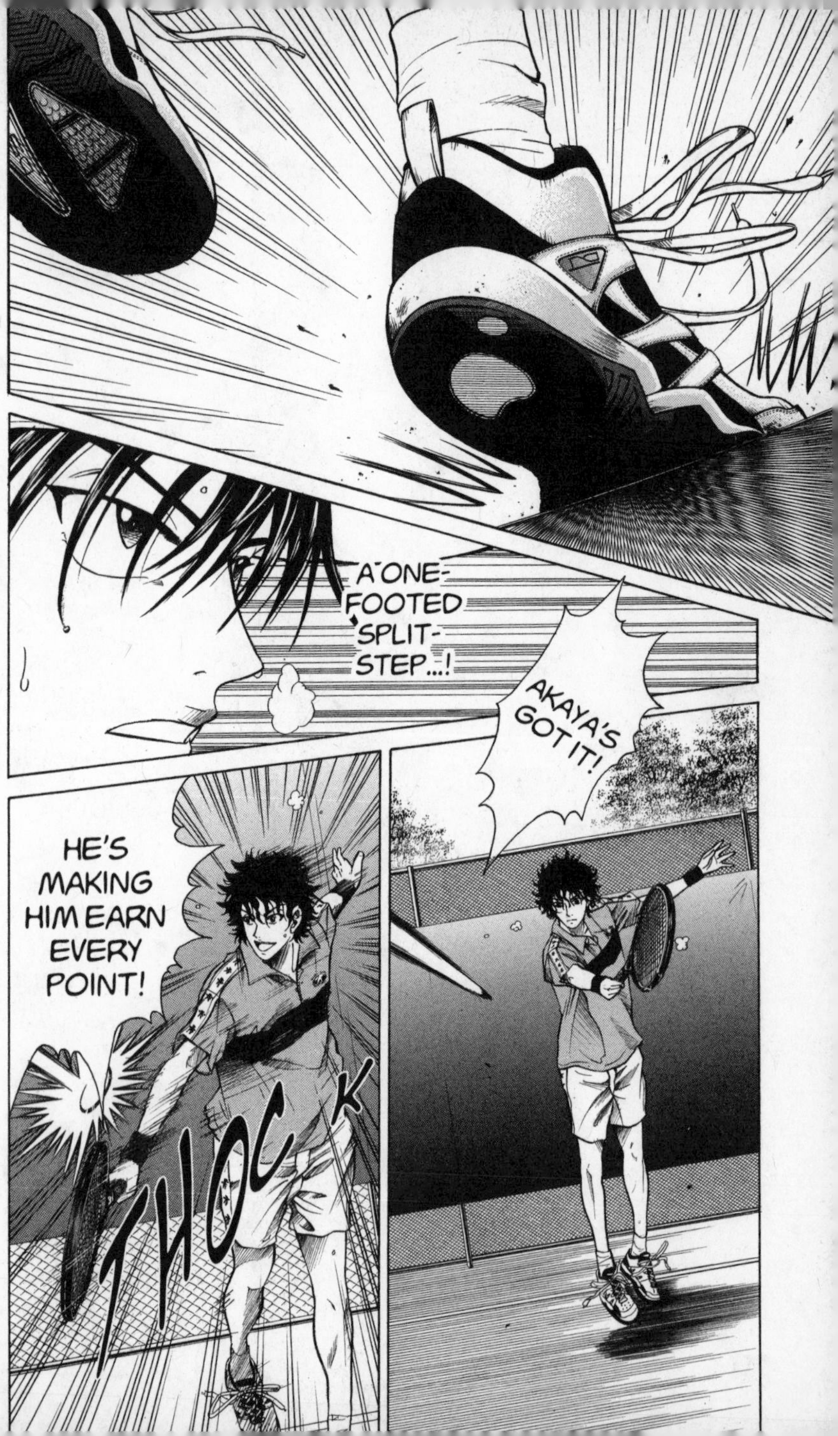
A ONE-FOOTED SPLIT-STEP...!
AKAYA'S GOT IT!
HE'S MAKING HIM EARN EVERY POINT!
THOCK

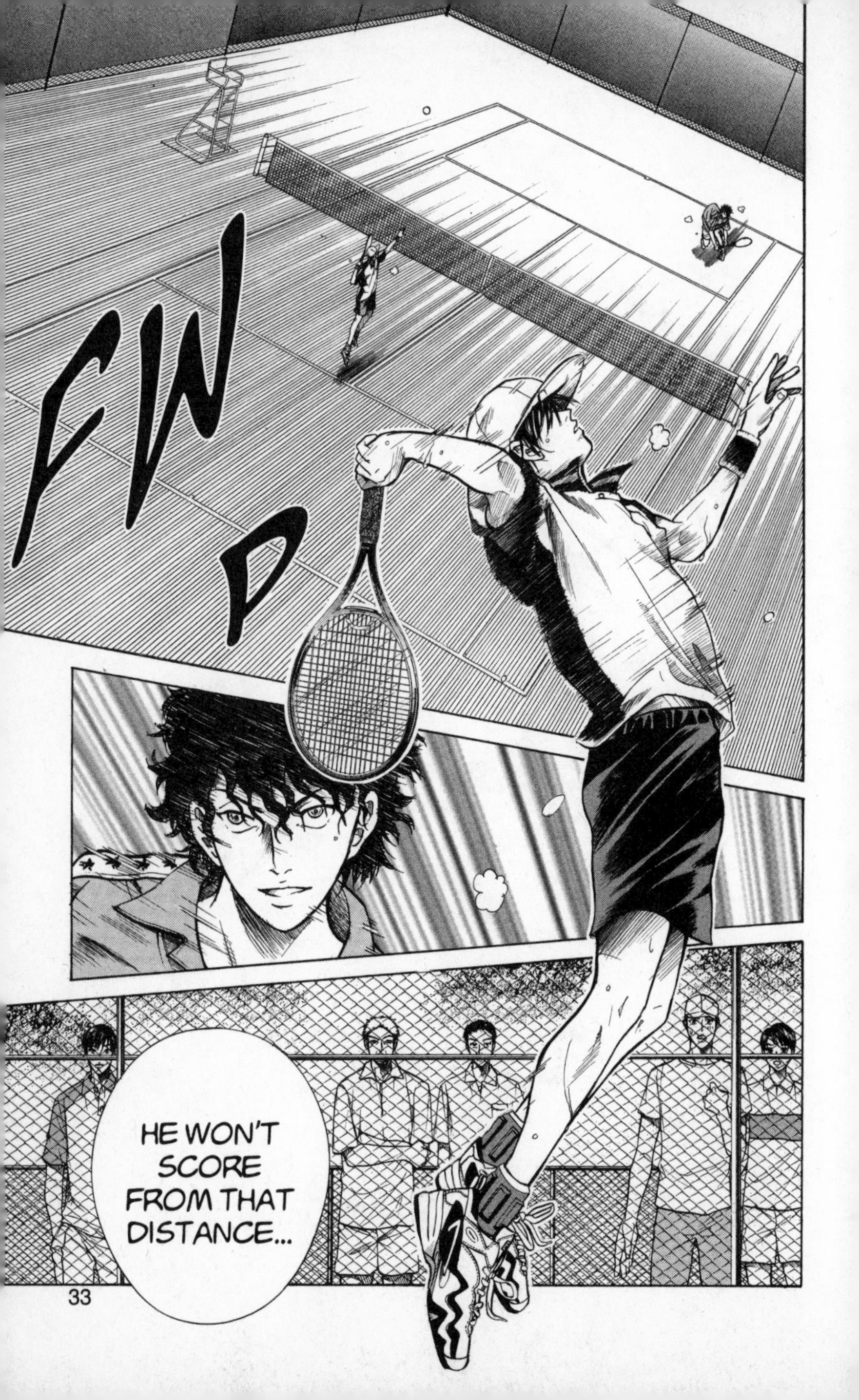
FWP
HE WON'T SCORE FROM THAT DISTANCE...

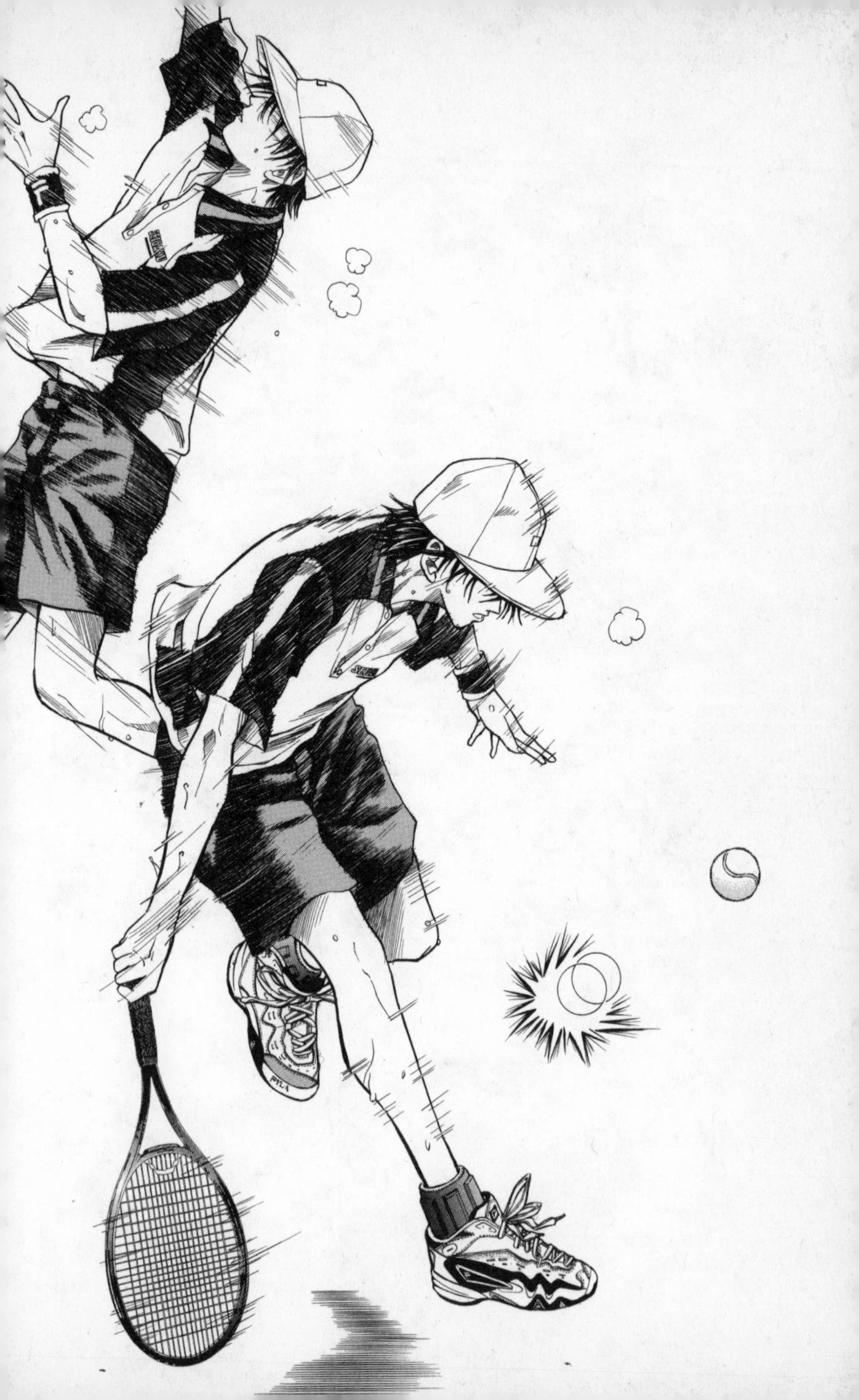

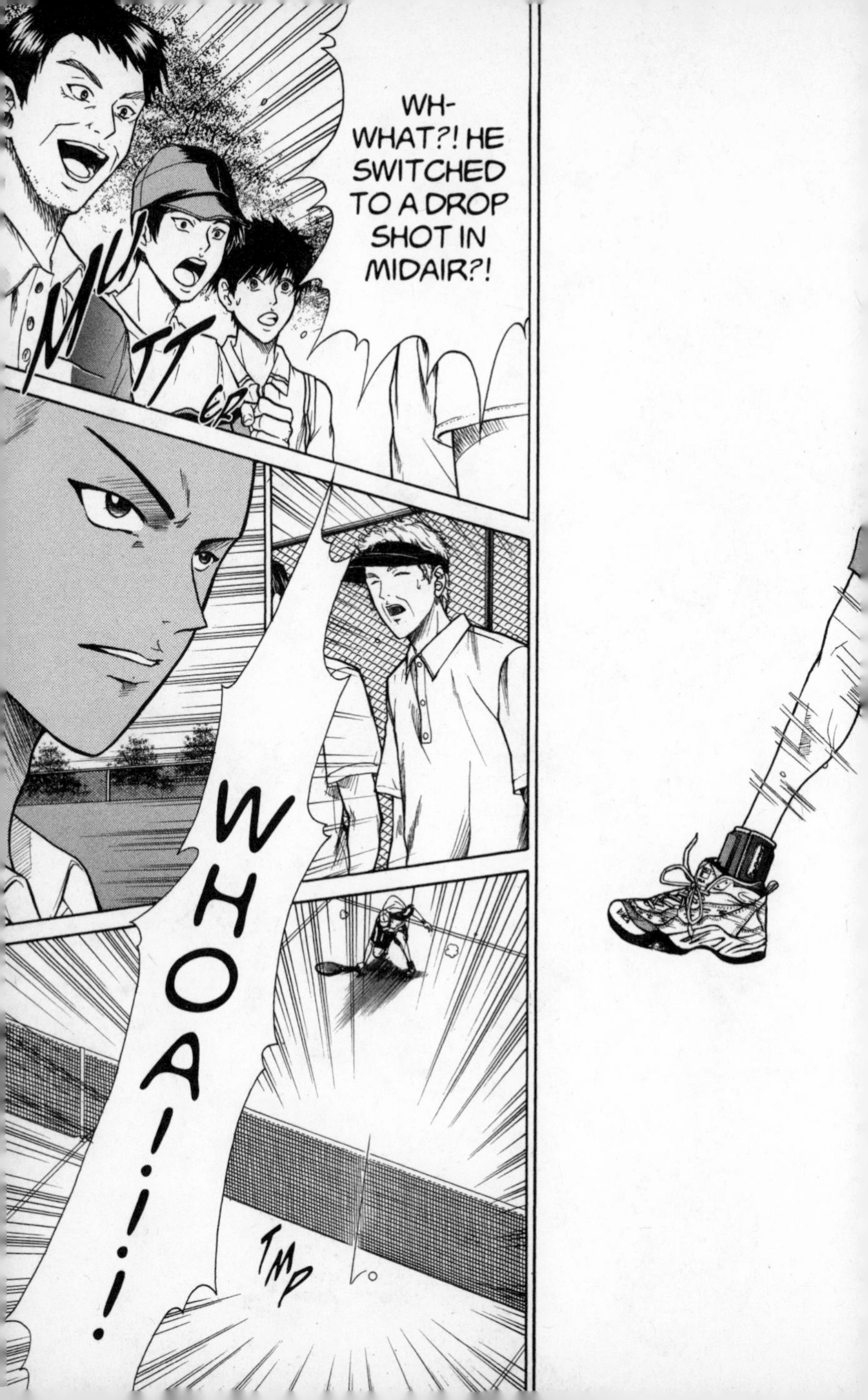
WH- WHAT?! HE SWITCHED TO A DROP SHOT IN MIDAIR?!
MUTTER
WHOA!!!!
TMP

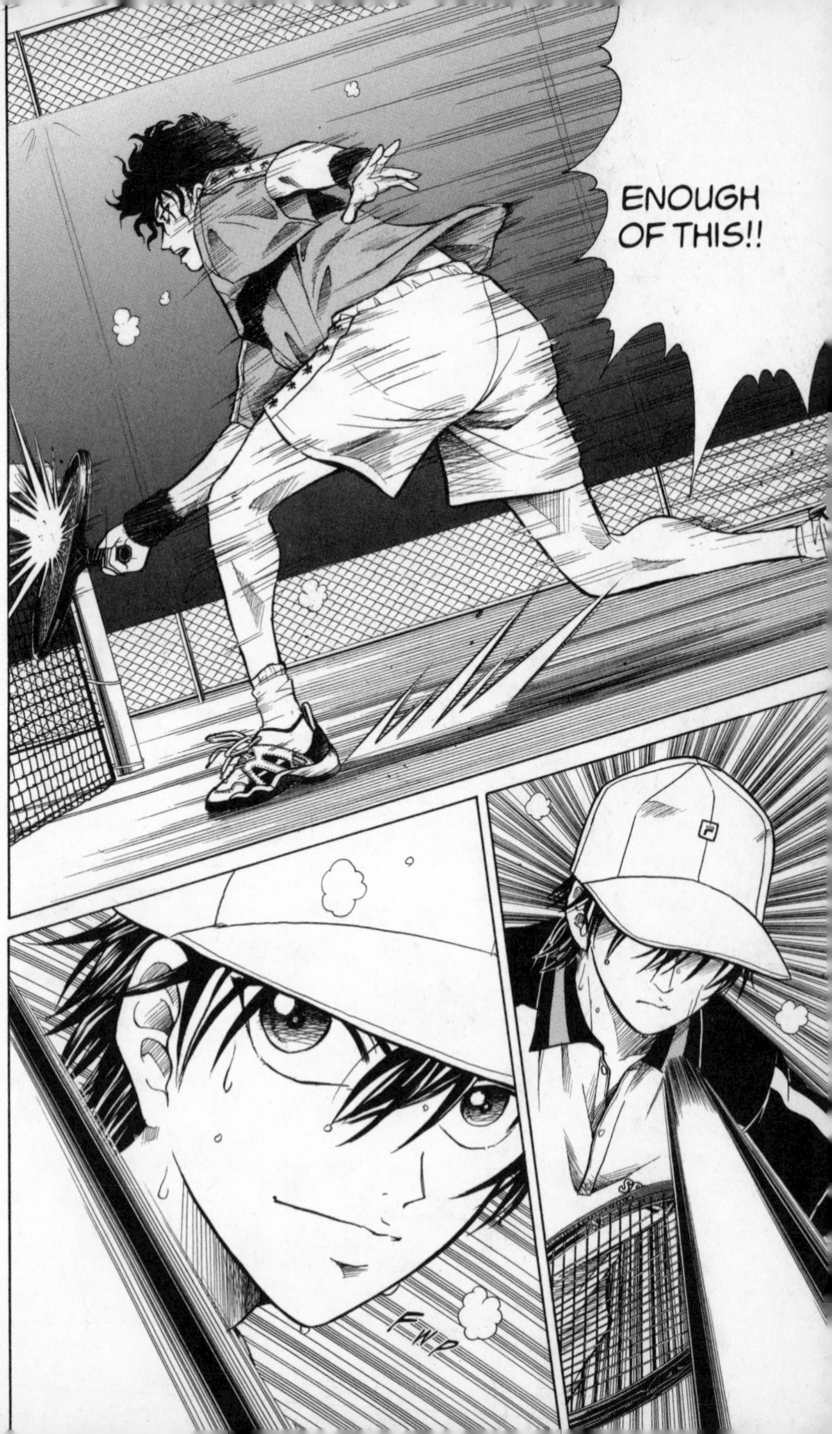
ENOUGH OF THIS!!
F-W-P

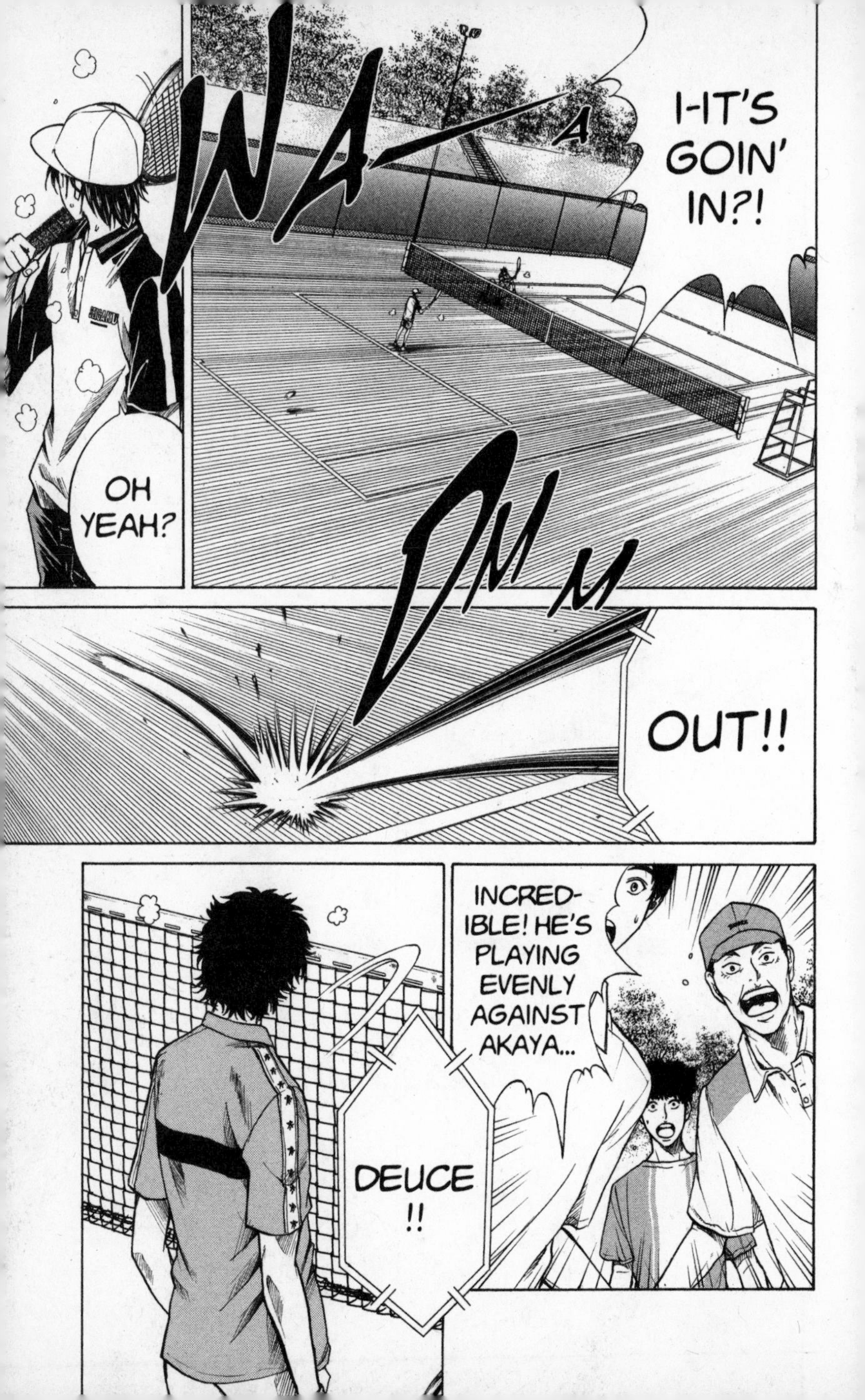
WA—A
I-IT'S GOIN' IN?!
DMM
OH YEAH?
OUT!!
INCRED-IBLE! HE'S PLAYING EVENLY AGAINST AKAYA...
DEUCE!!

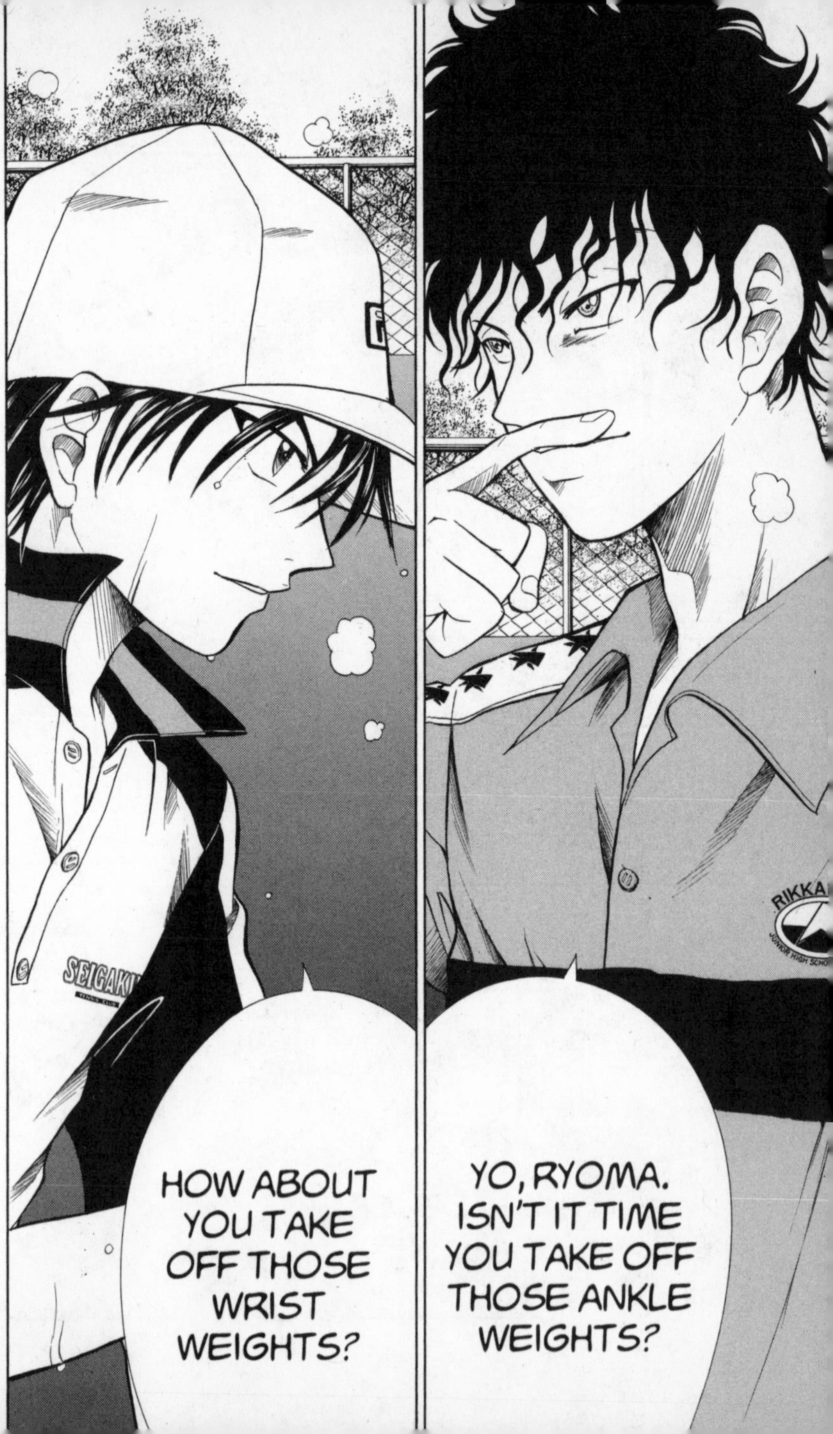
YO, RYOMA. ISN'T IT TIME YOU TAKE OFF THOSE ANKLE WEIGHTS?
HOW ABOUT YOU TAKE OFF THOSE WRIST WEIGHTS?

READ THIS WAY

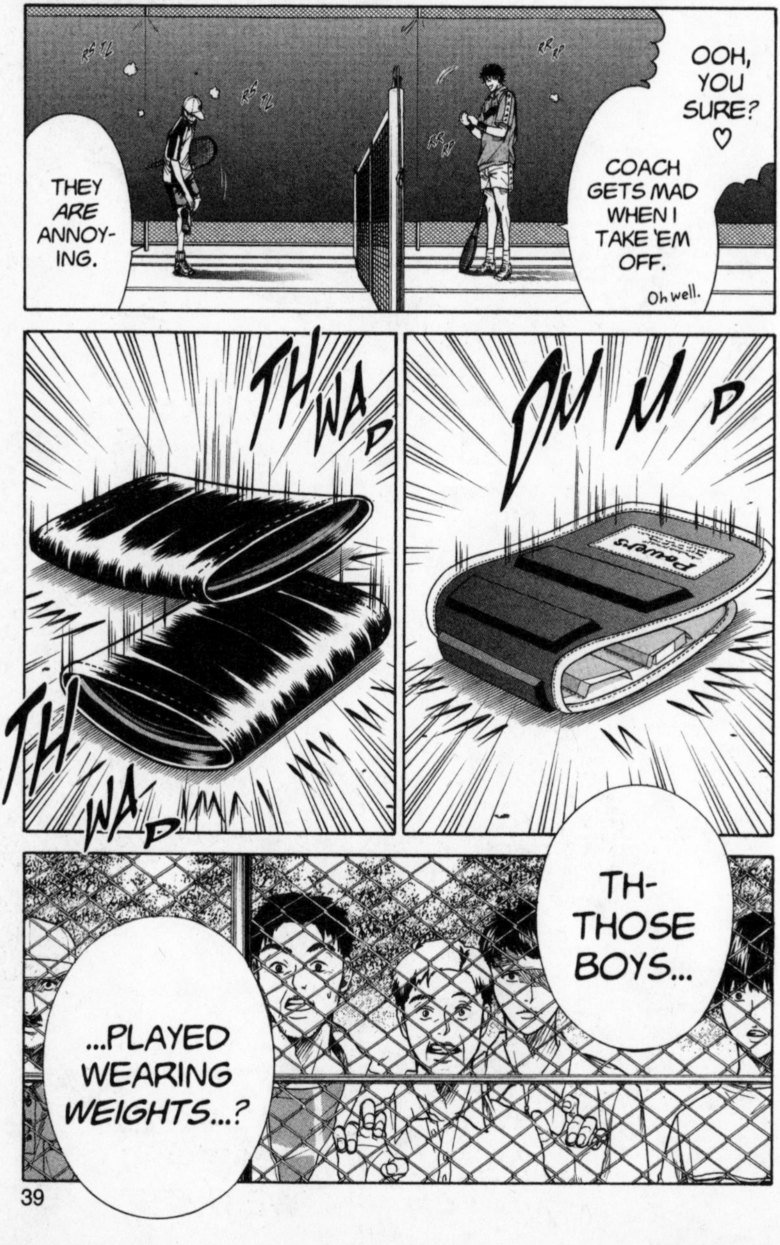
OOH, YOU SURE? ♡
COACH GETS MAD WHEN I TAKE 'EM OFF.
Oh well.
THEY ARE ANNOYING.
DUMP
THWAP
THWAP
TH-THOSE BOYS...
...PLAYED WEARING WEIGHTS...?

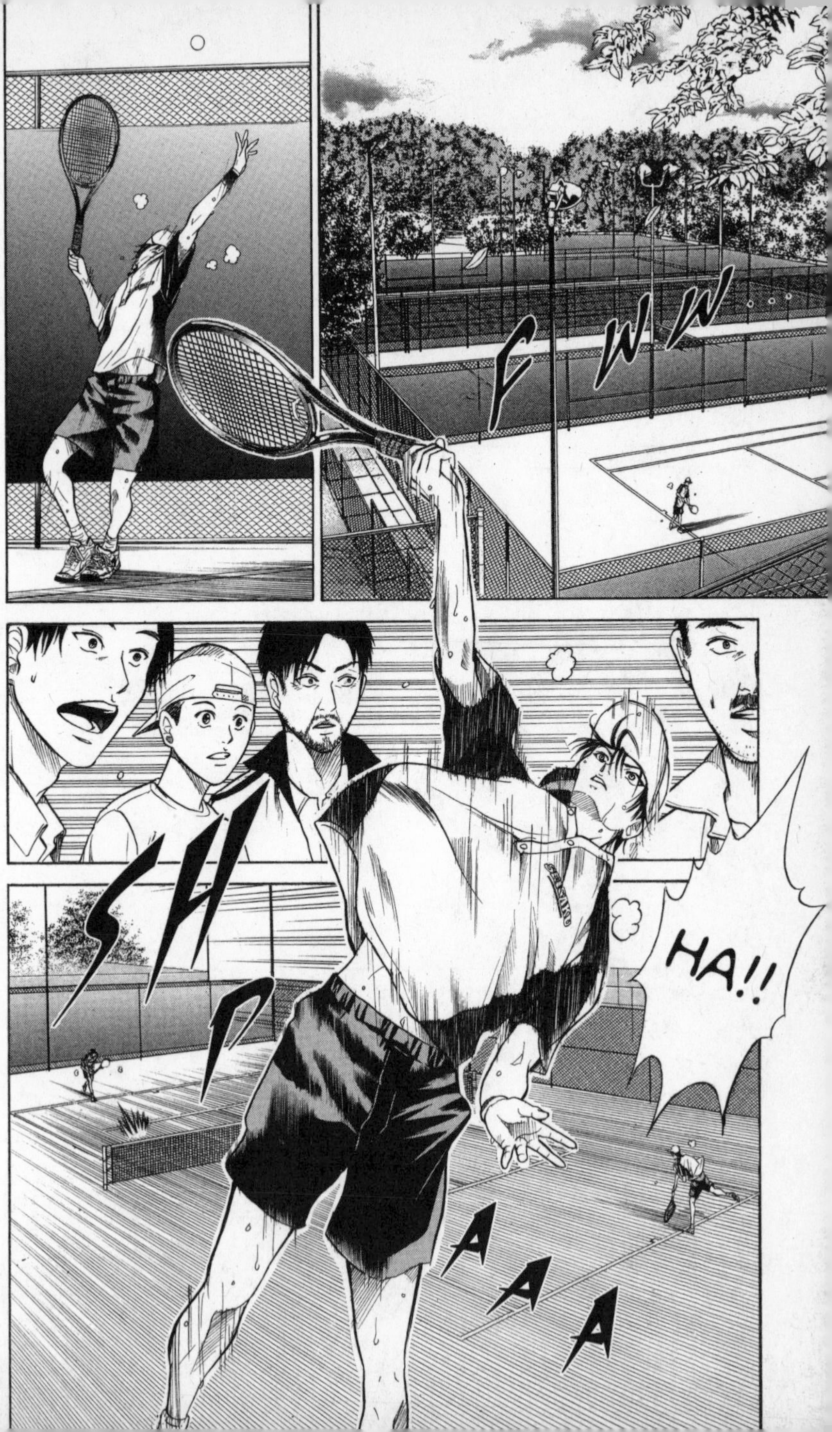
FWW
HA!!
SHN
AAA

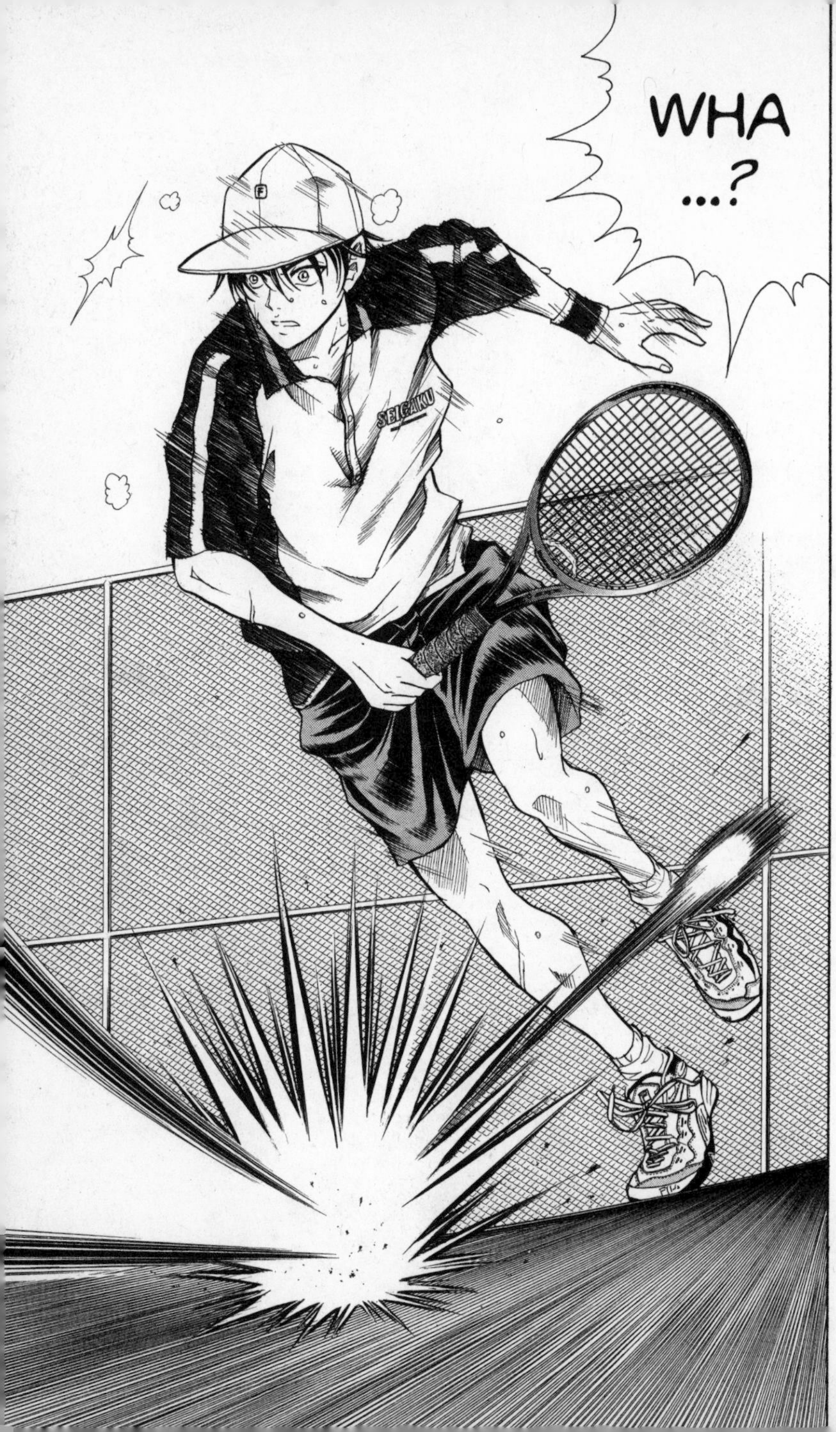
WHA
...?
SEIGAKU

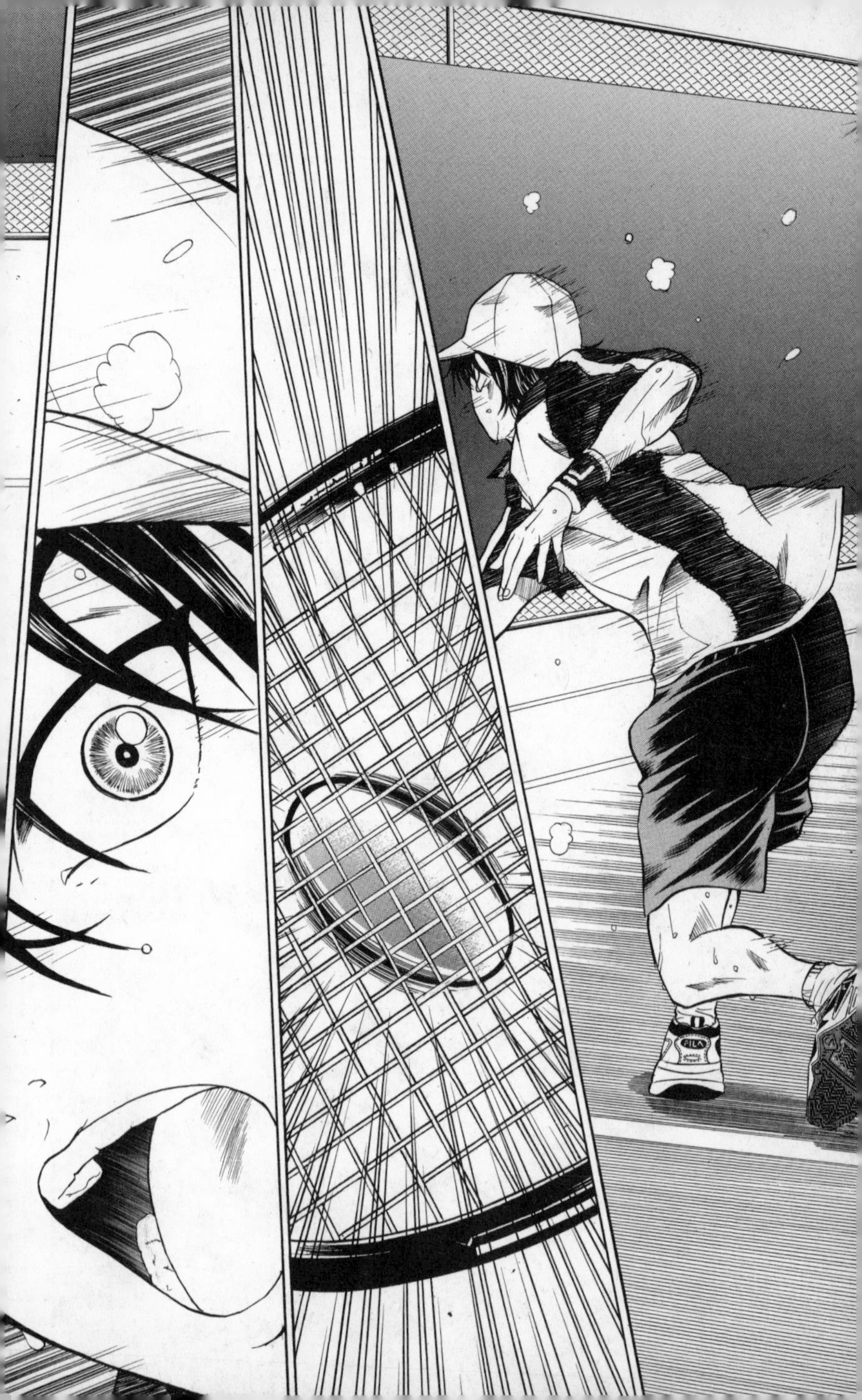

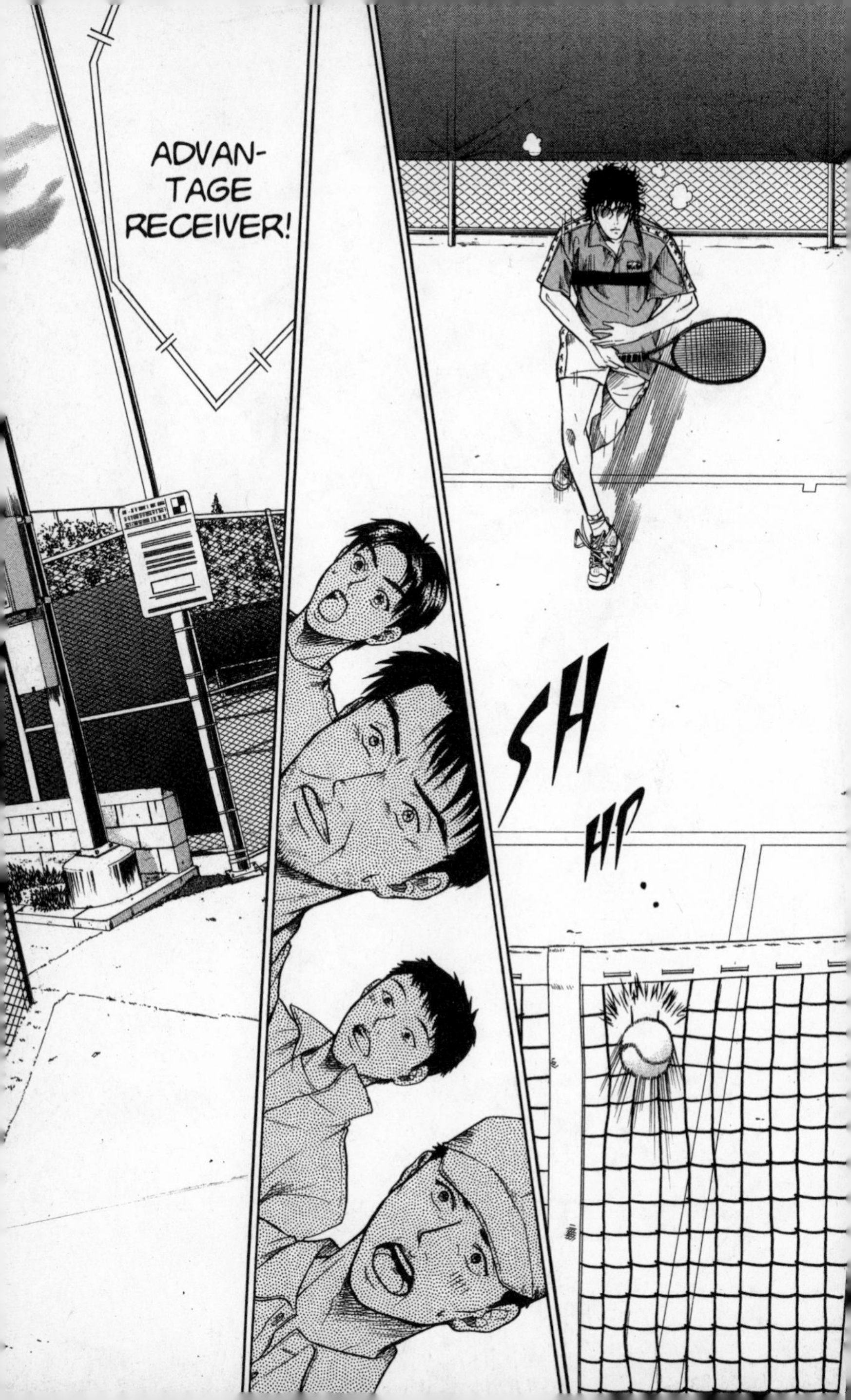
SH
HP
ADVAN-
TAGE
RECEIVER!

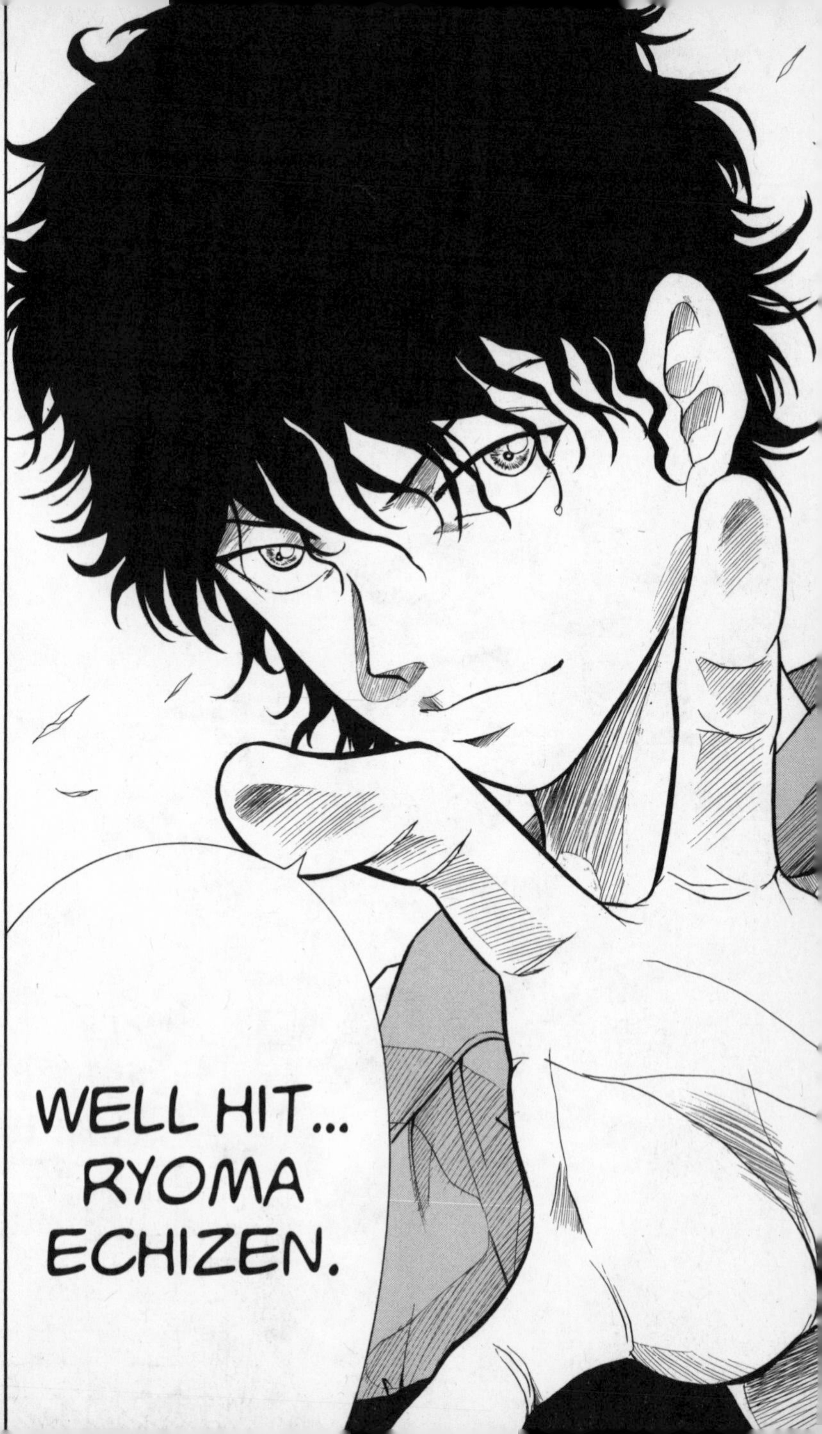
WELL HIT... RYOMA ECHIZEN.

READ THIS WAY

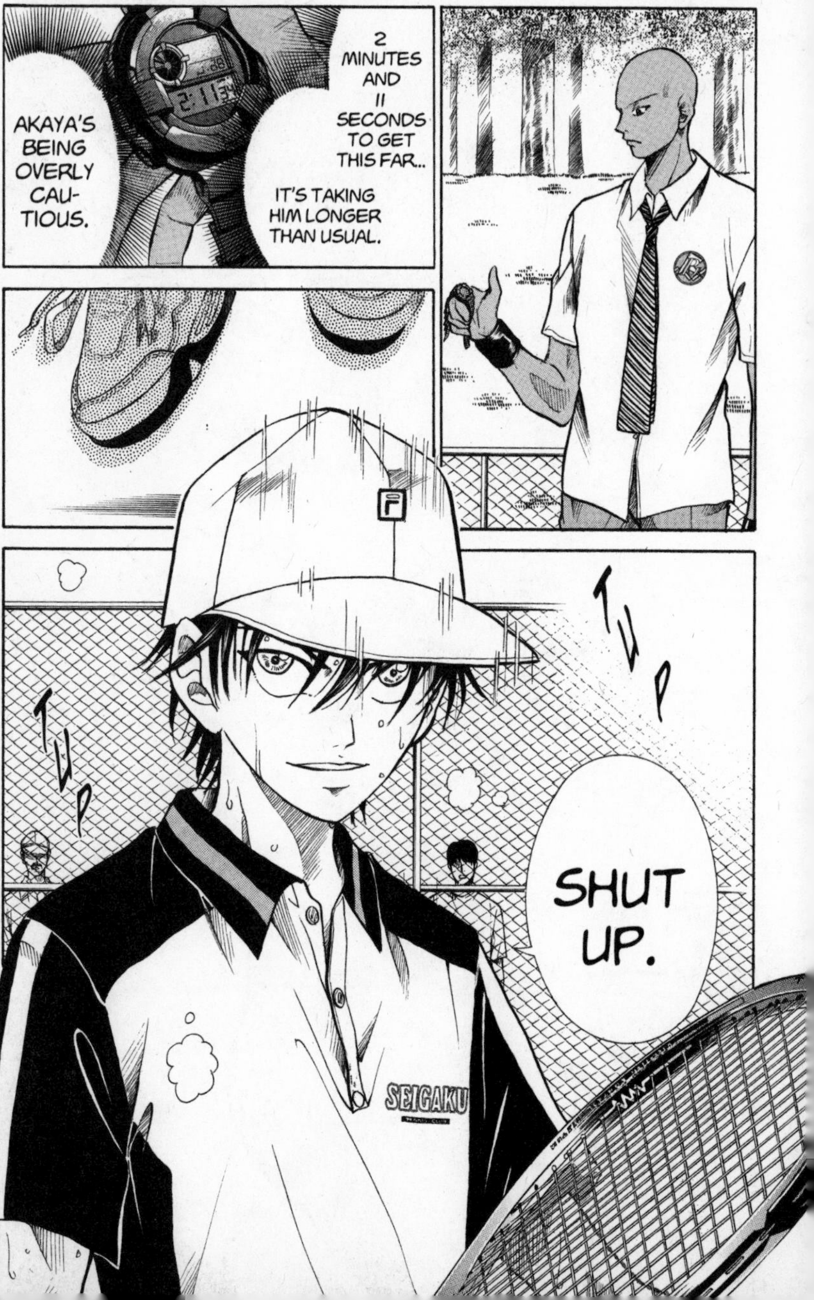
2 MINUTES AND 11 SECONDS TO GET THIS FAR..
IT'S TAKING HIM LONGER THAN USUAL.
AKAYA'S BEING OVERLY CAU-TIOUS.
TUP
SHUT UP.
TUP
SEIGAKU

テニスの王子様

THE PRINCE OF TENNIS™

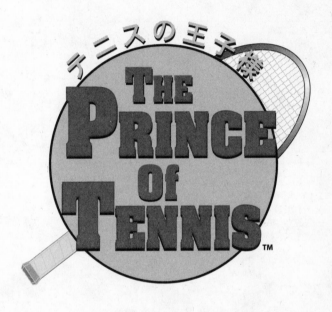

GENIUS 188: SIGNS OF DANGER

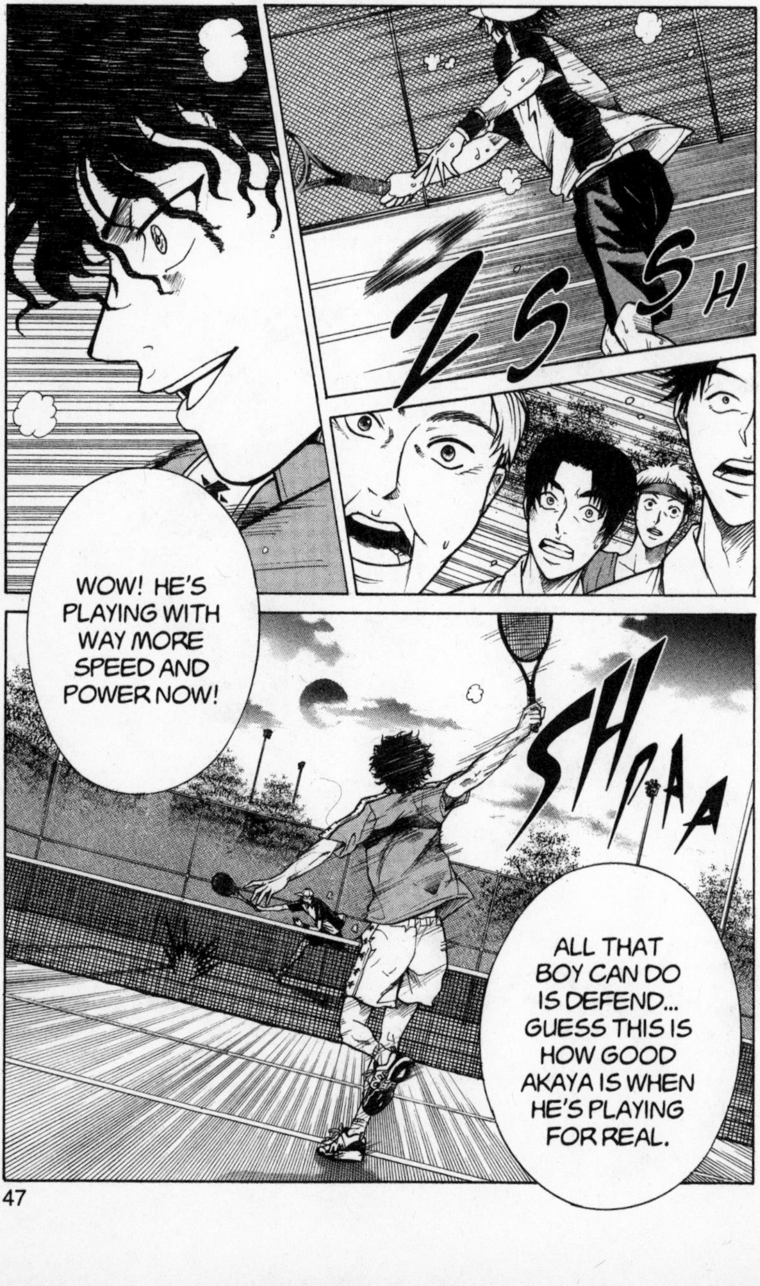
ZSSH
WOW! HE'S PLAYING WITH WAY MORE SPEED AND POWER NOW!
SHAA
ALL THAT BOY CAN DO IS DEFEND... GUESS THIS IS HOW GOOD AKAYA IS WHEN HE'S PLAYING FOR REAL.

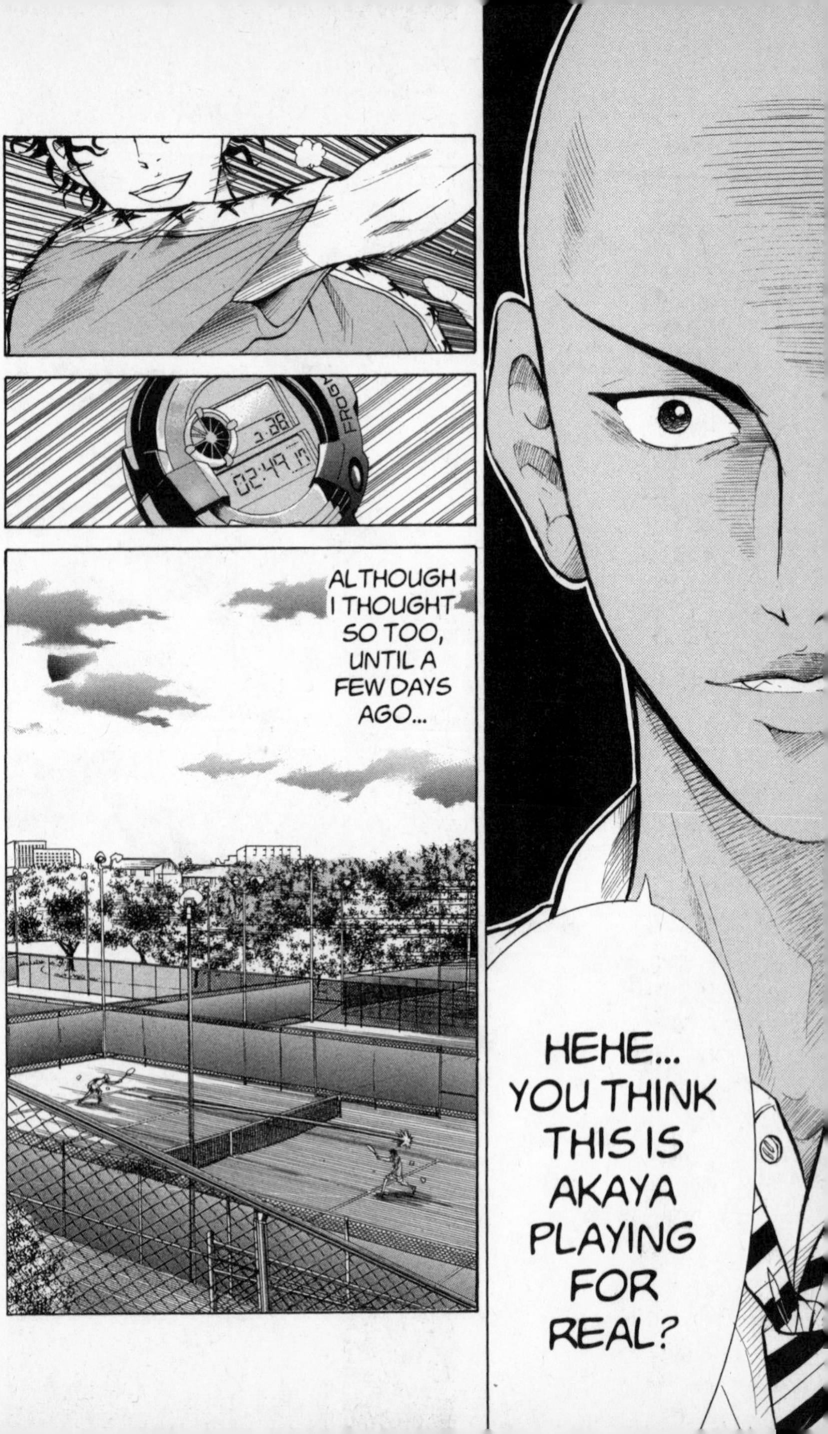
HEHE... YOU THINK THIS IS AKAYA PLAYING FOR REAL?
ALTHOUGH I THOUGHT SO TOO, UNTIL A FEW DAYS AGO...

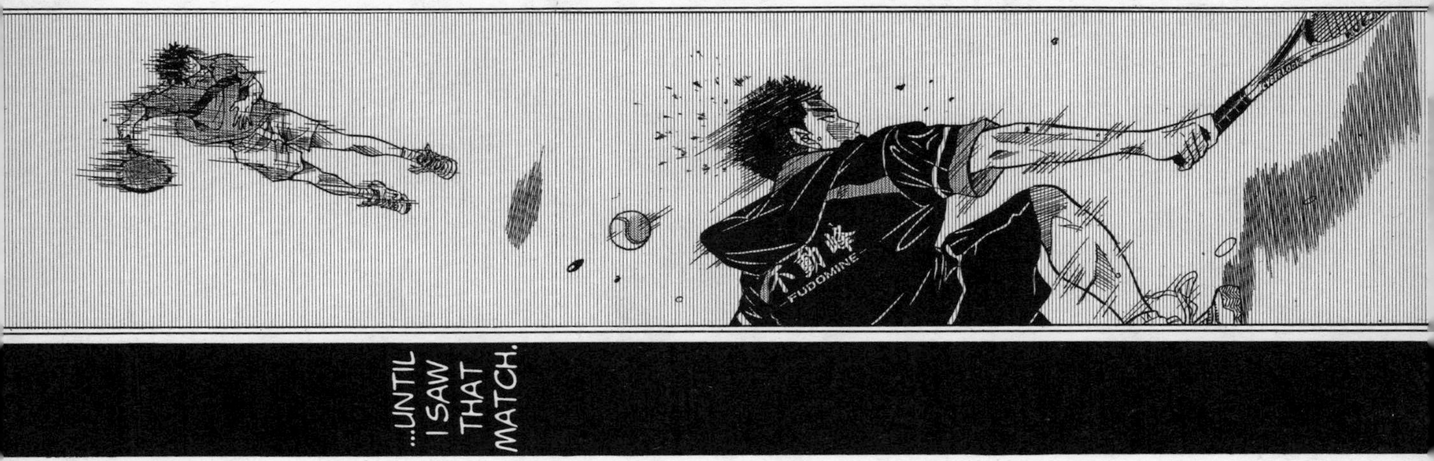
...UNTIL I SAW THAT MATCH.

GENIUS 188: SIGNS OF DANGER

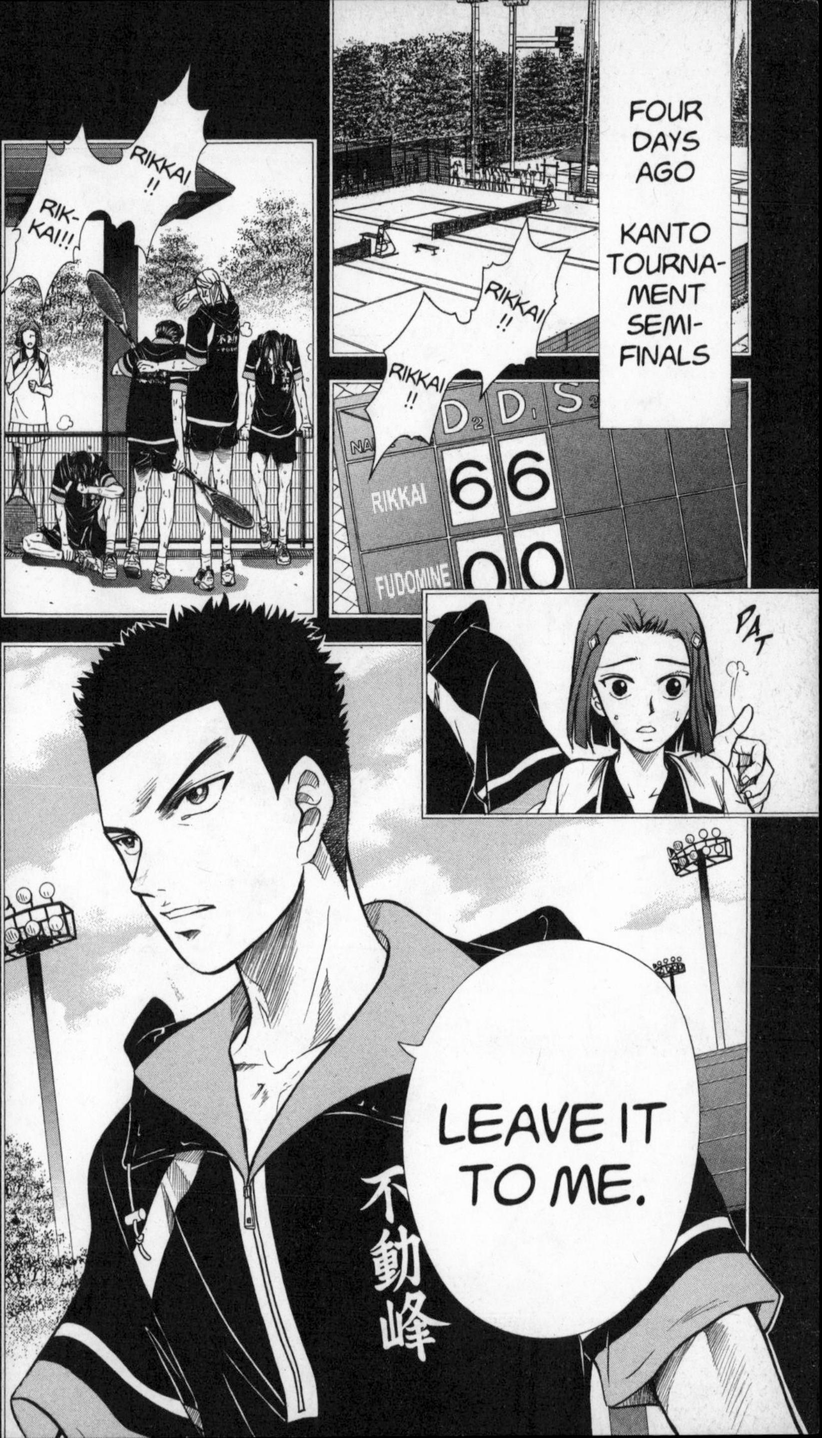
FOUR DAYS AGO
KANTO TOURNAMENT SEMI-FINALS
RIKKAI!!
RIKKAI!!
D2 D1 S3
RIKKAI 6 6
FUDOMINE 0 0
RIKKAI!!
RIK-KAI!!!
DAT
LEAVE IT TO ME.
不動峰

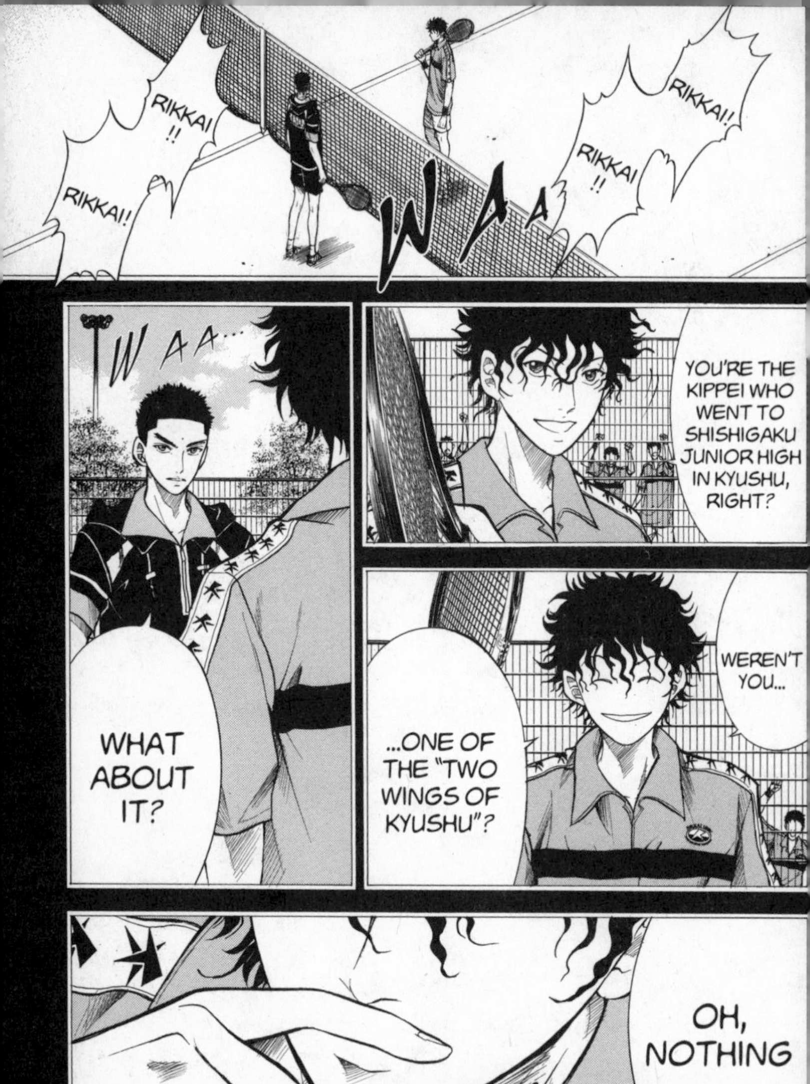
RIKKAI!!
RIKKAI !!
WAA
RIKKAI !!
RIKKAI!!
YOU'RE THE KIPPEI WHO WENT TO SHISHIGAKU JUNIOR HIGH IN KYUSHU, RIGHT?
WEREN'T YOU...
...ONE OF THE "TWO WINGS OF KYUSHU"?
WAA...
WHAT ABOUT IT?
OH, NOTHING ...
SCRUB

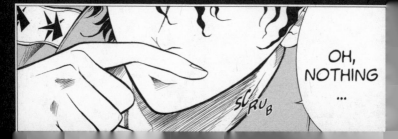

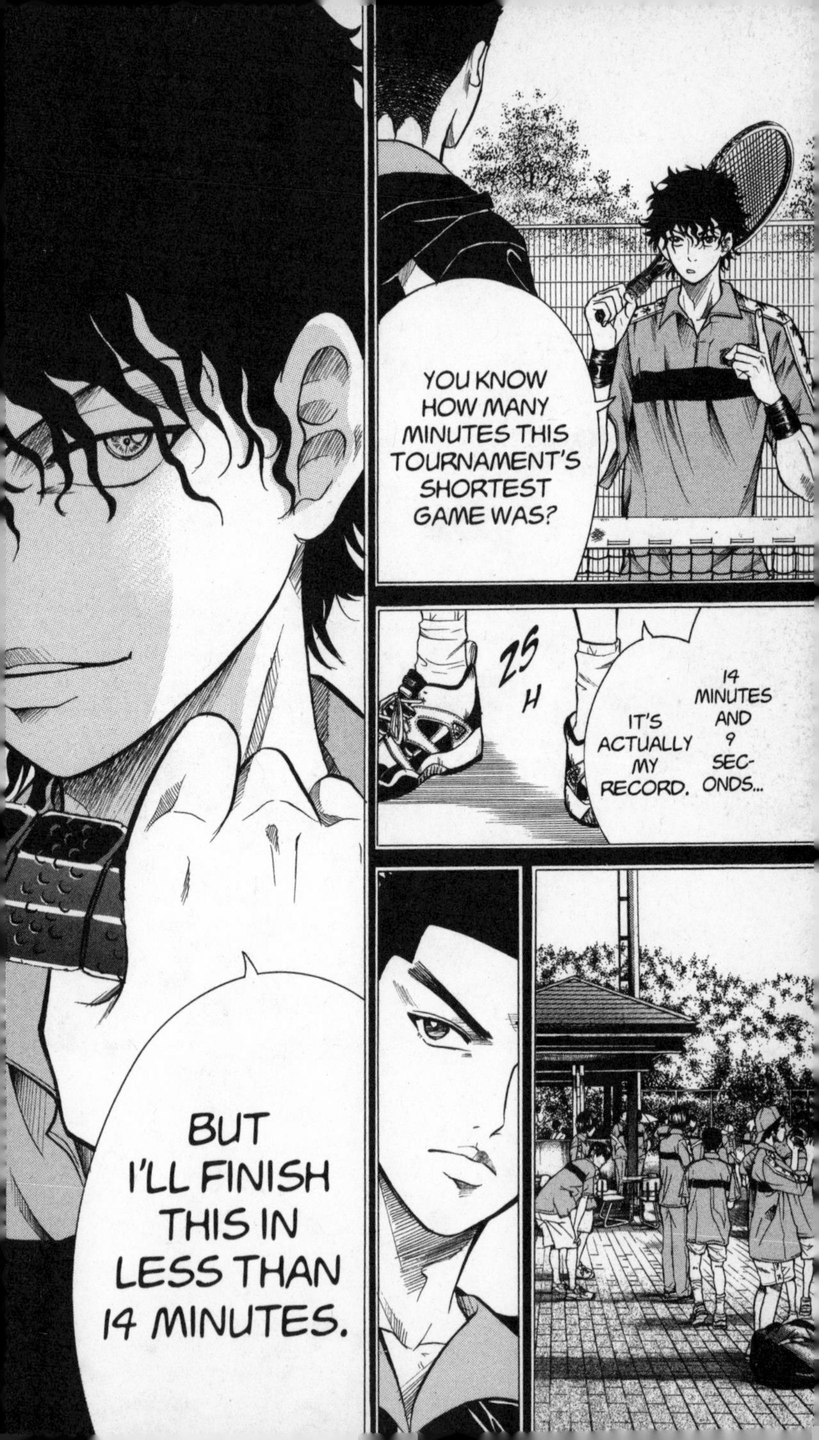
YOU KNOW HOW MANY MINUTES THIS TOURNAMENT'S SHORTEST GAME WAS?
14 MINUTES AND 9 SEC-ONDS...
IT'S ACTUALLY MY RECORD.
ZSH
BUT I'LL FINISH THIS IN LESS THAN 14 MINUTES.

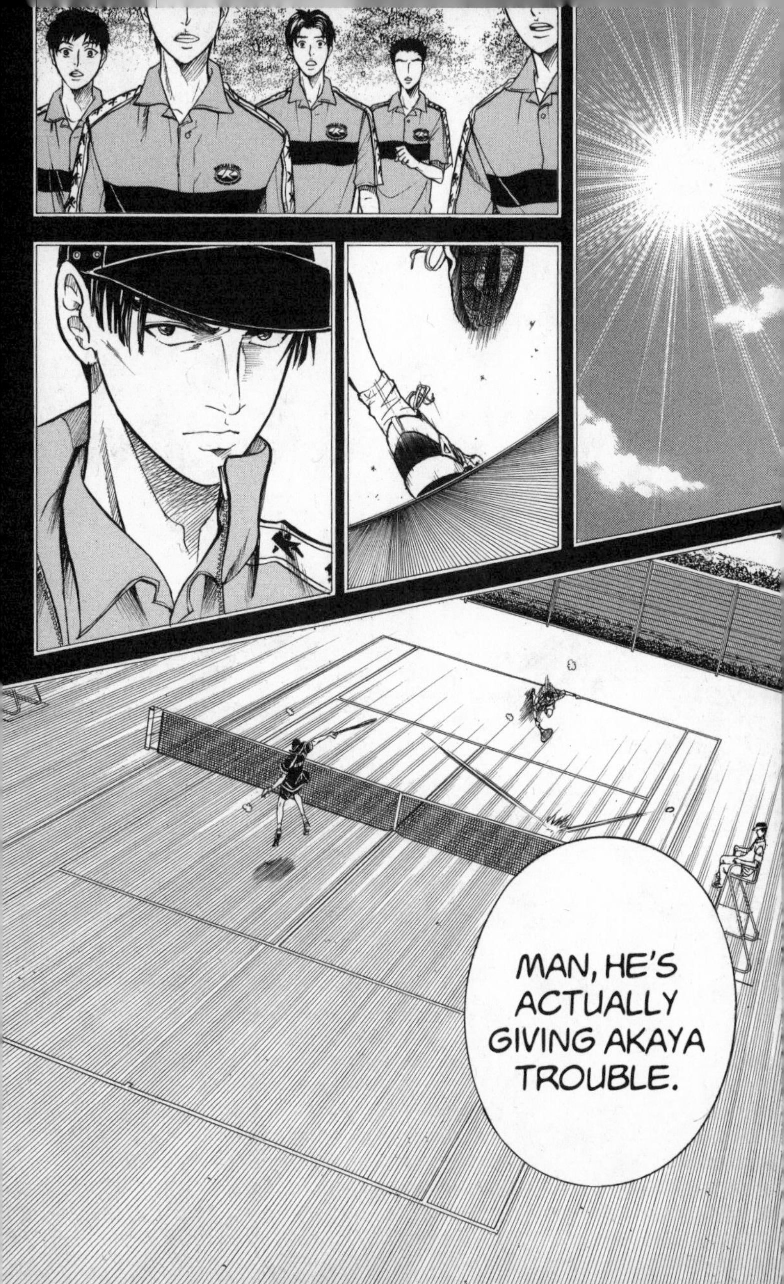
MAN, HE'S ACTUALLY GIVING AKAYA TROUBLE.

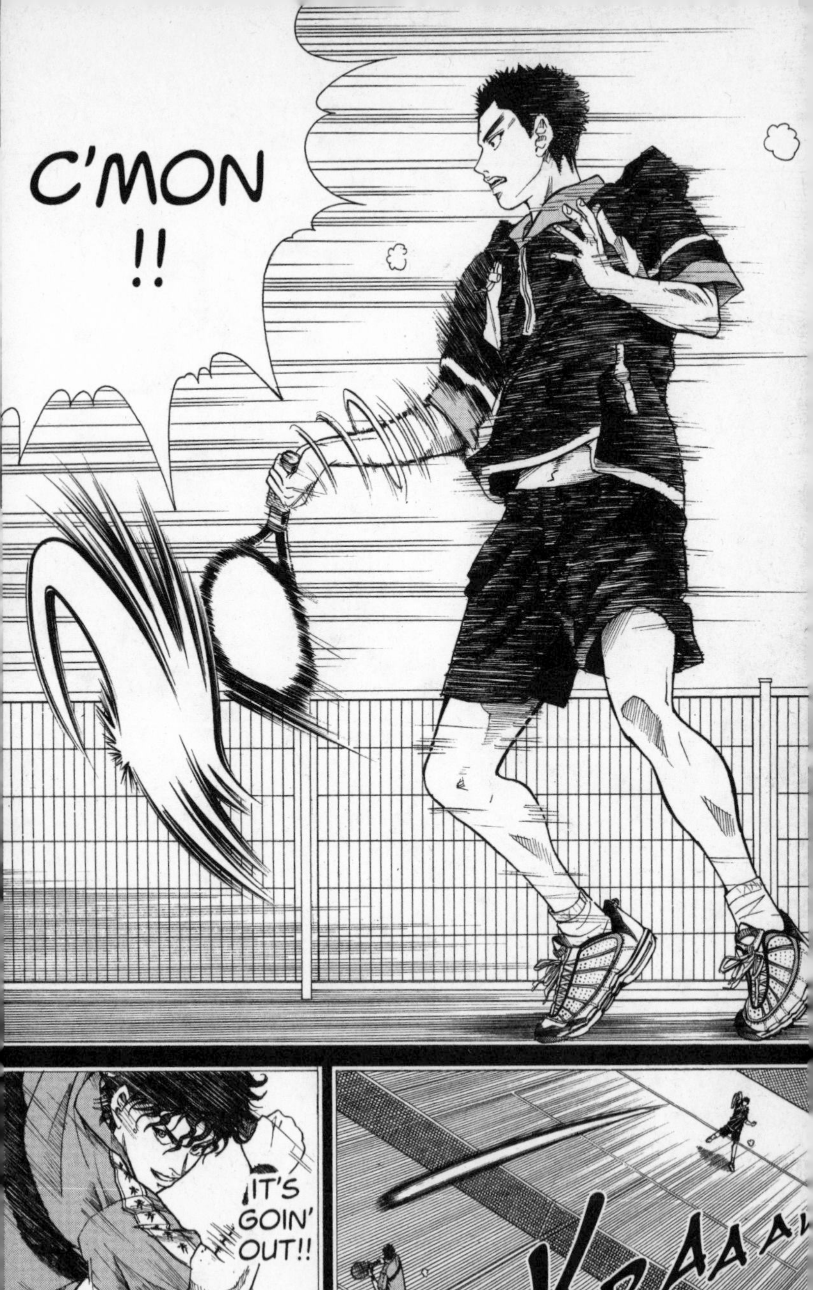
C'MON !!
KDAAA
IT'S GOIN' OUT!!

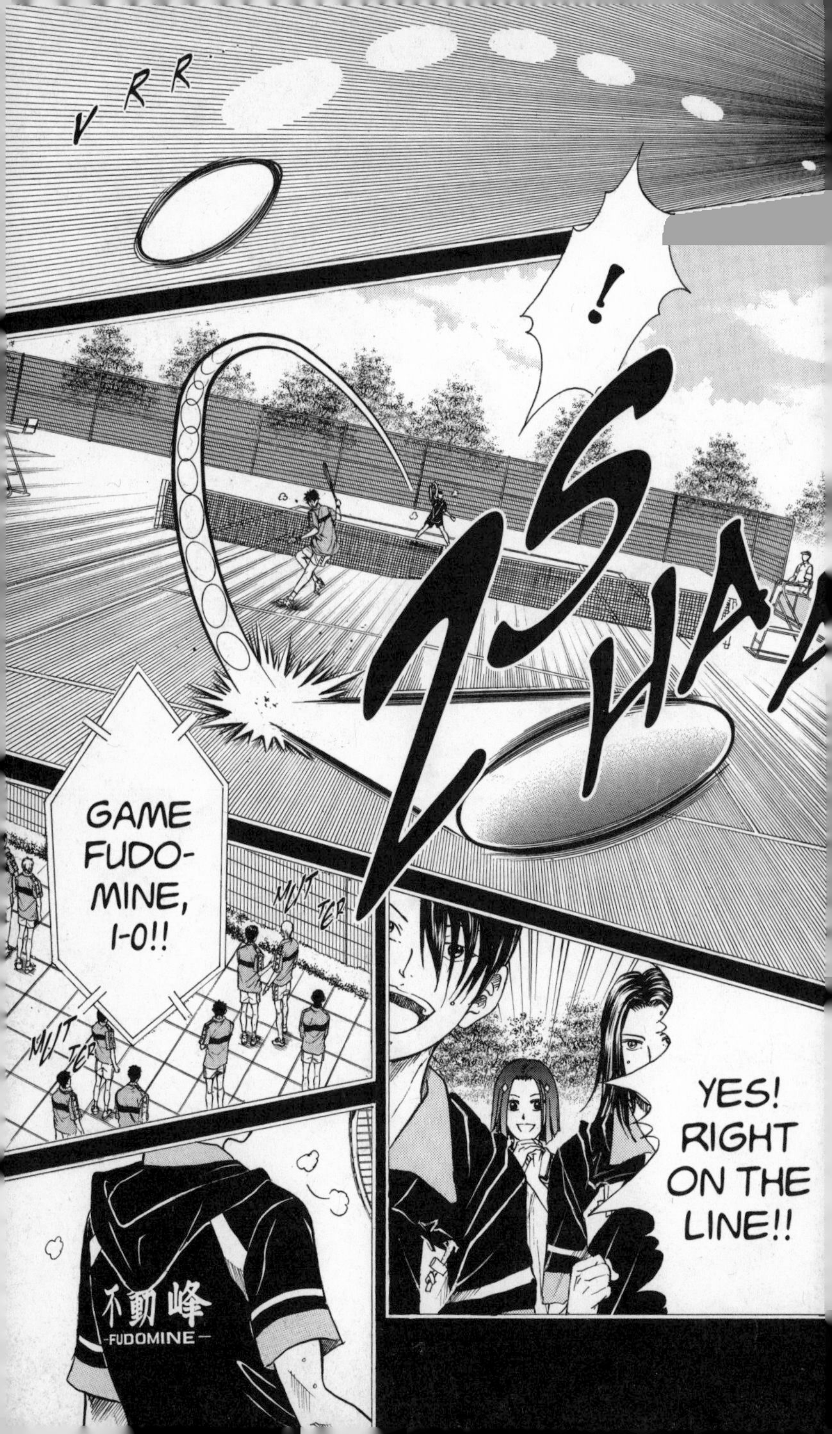
VRR
!
GAME FUDO-MINE, 1-0!!
YES! RIGHT ON THE LINE!!
MUTTER
MUTTER
不動峰
-FUDOMINE-

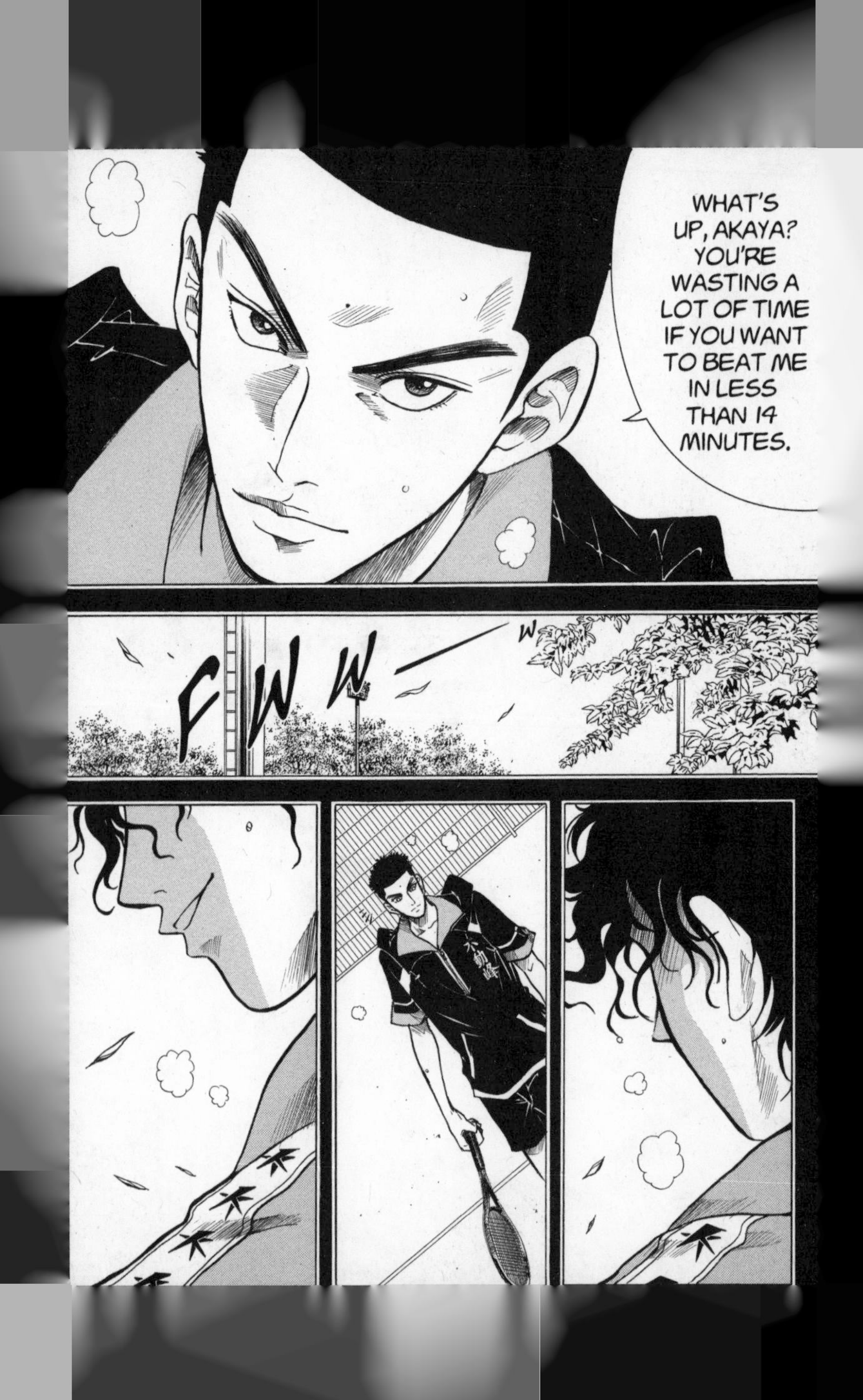
WHAT'S UP, AKAYA? YOU'RE WASTING A LOT OF TIME IF YOU WANT TO BEAT ME IN LESS THAN 14 MINUTES.
FWW—W

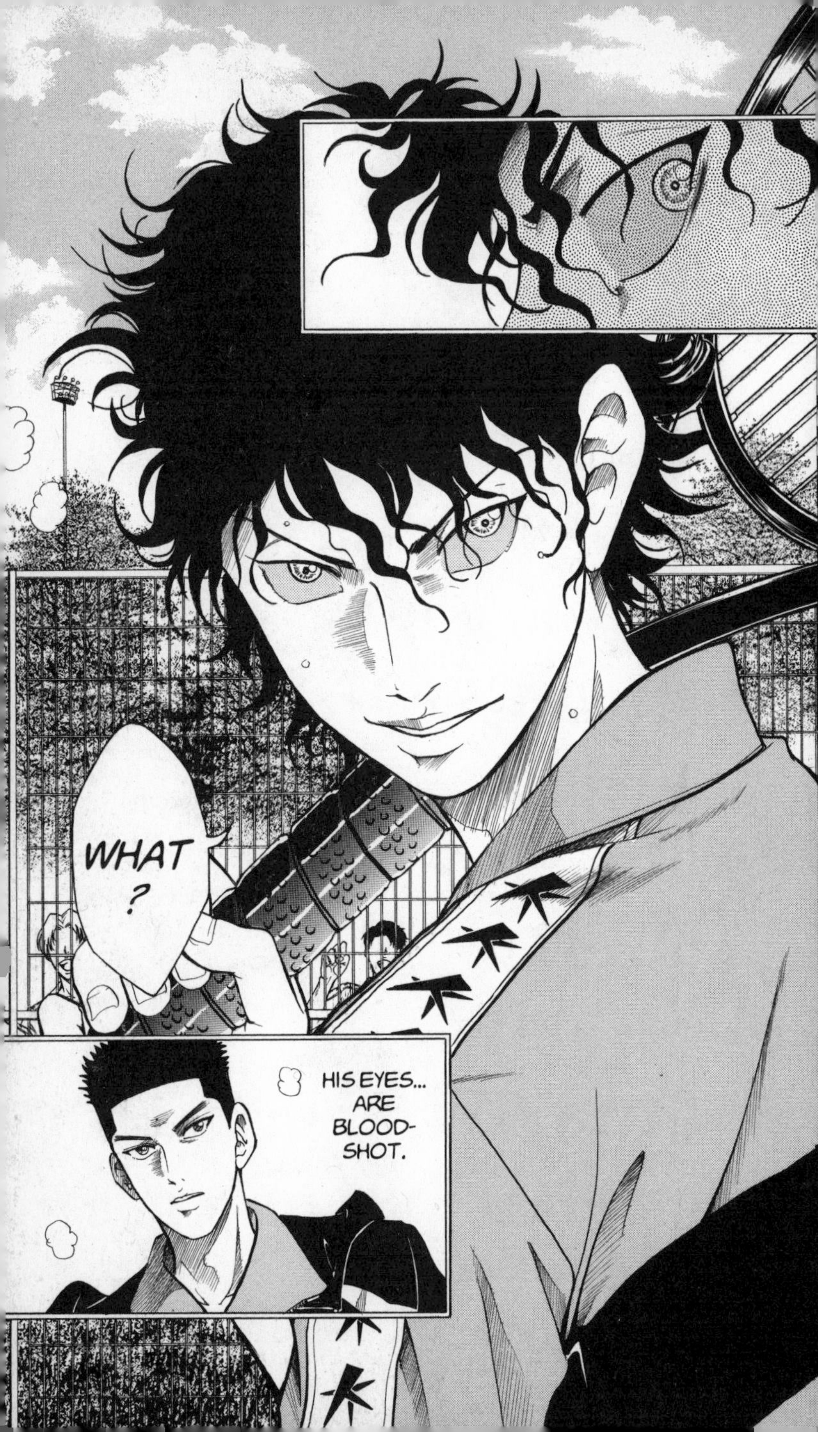
WHAT?
HIS EYES... ARE BLOOD-SHOT.

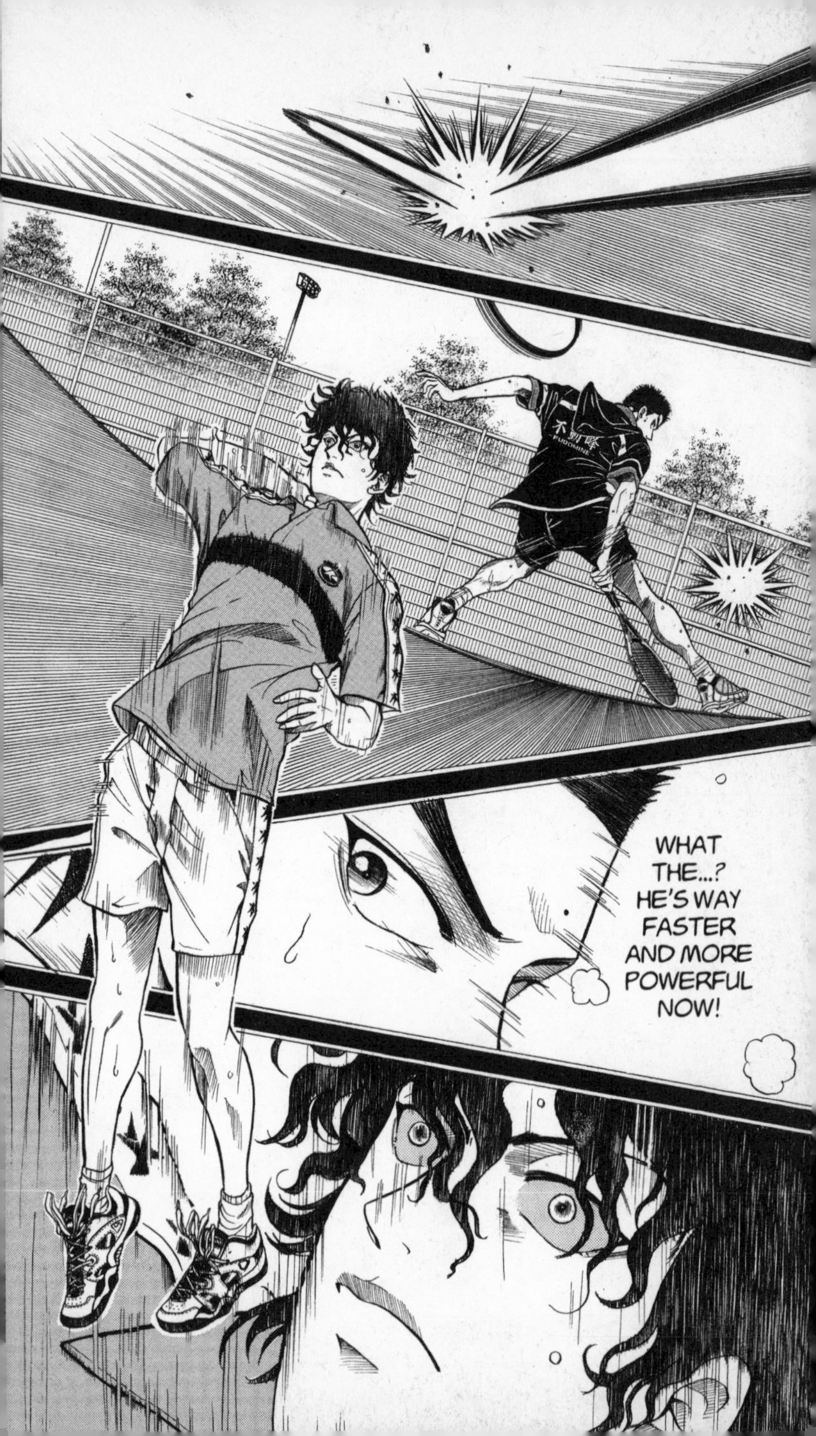
WHAT THE...? HE'S WAY FASTER AND MORE POWERFUL NOW!

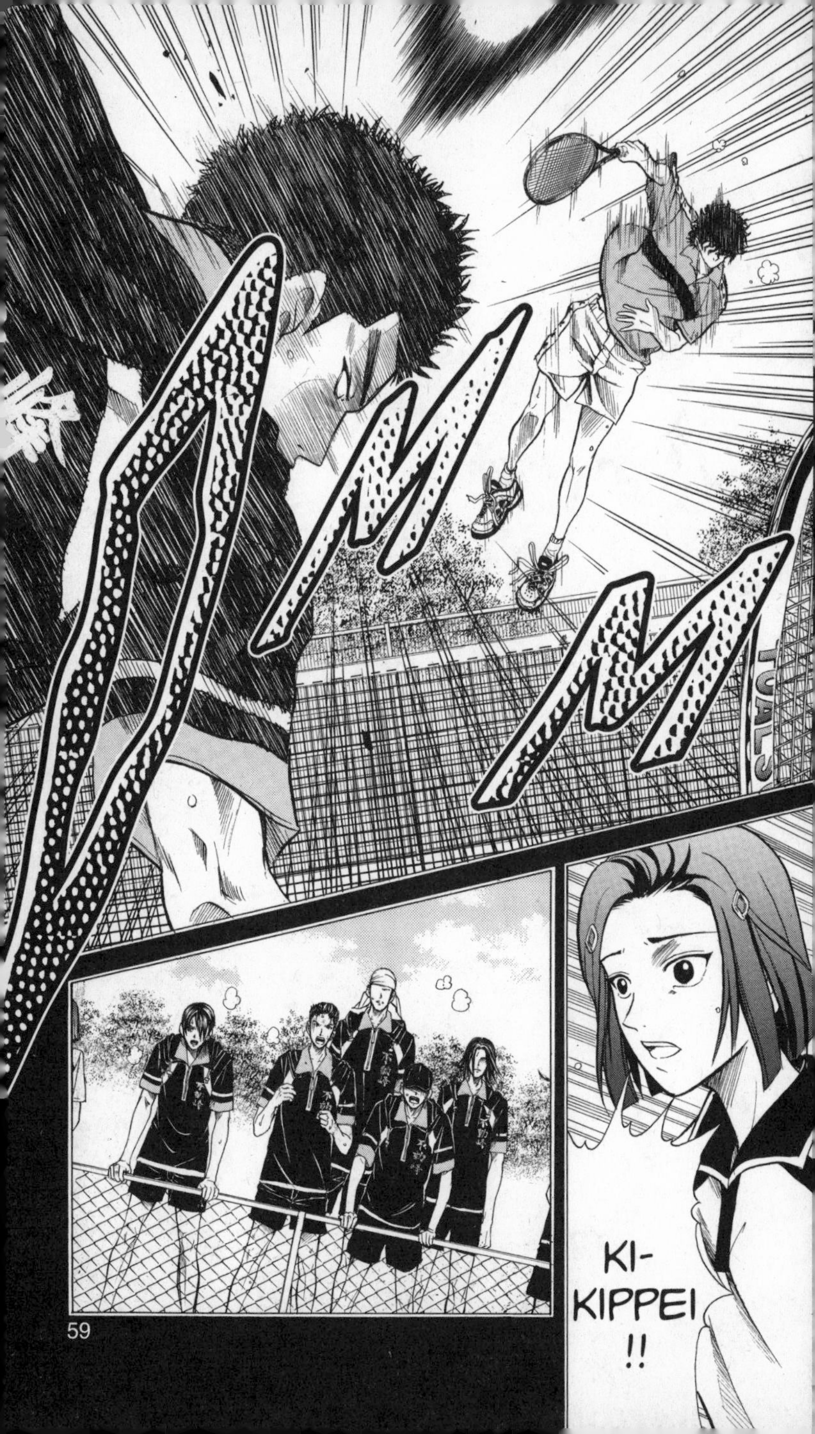
KI-
KIPPEI
!!

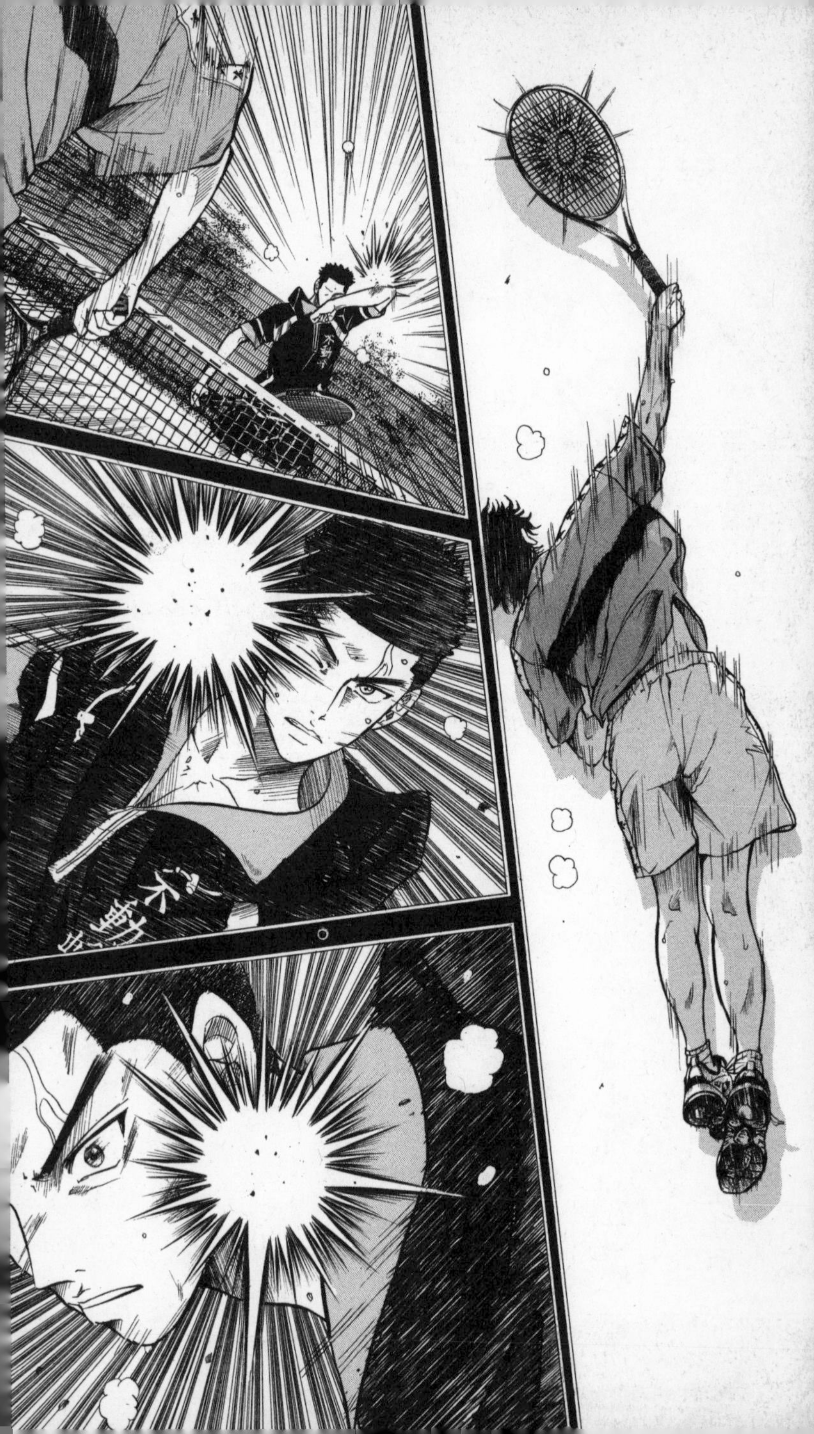
不動

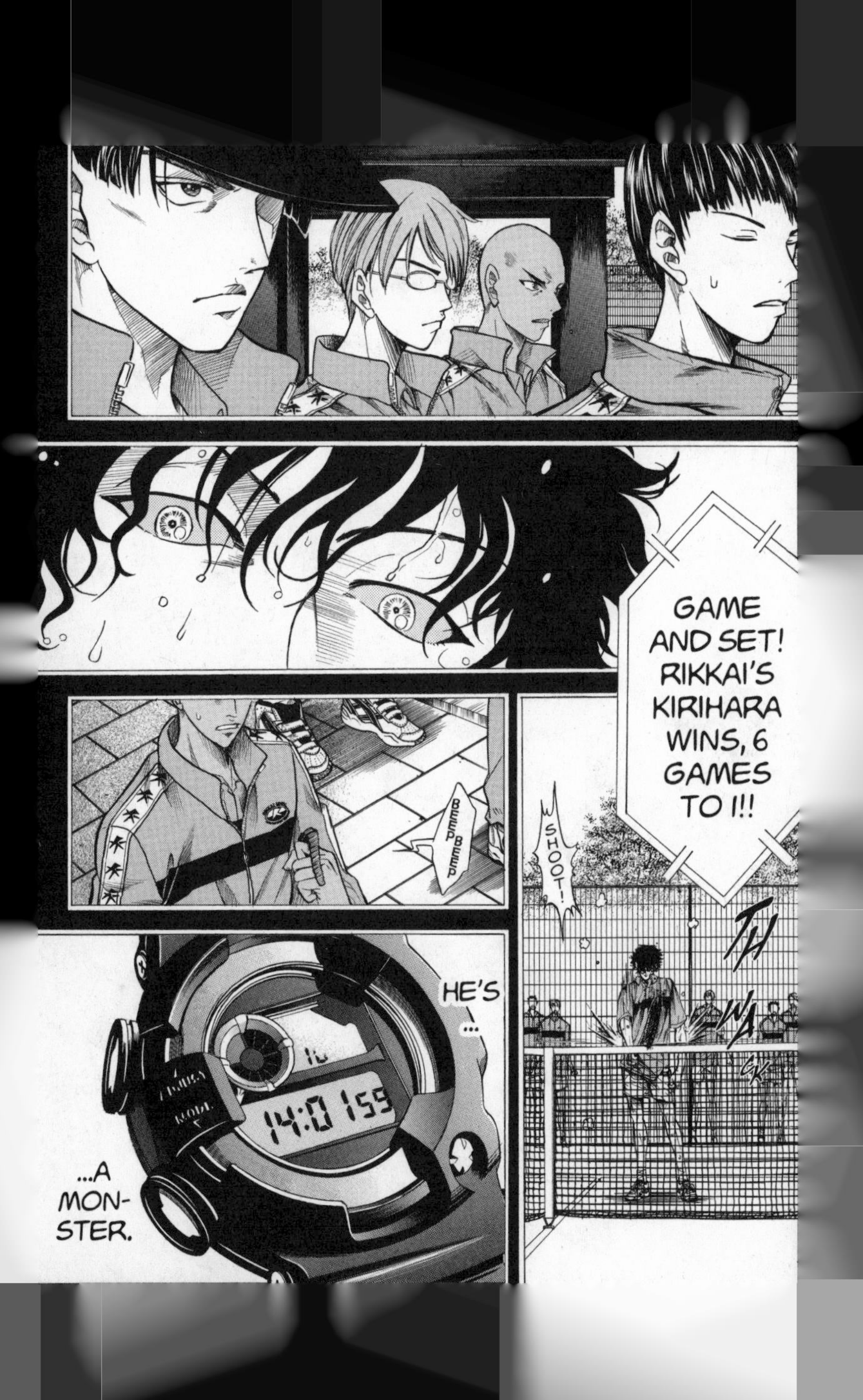
GAME AND SET! RIKKAI'S KIRIHARA WINS, 6 GAMES TO 1!!
SHOOT!
THWACK
BEEP BEEP BEEP
HE'S...
...A MONSTER.

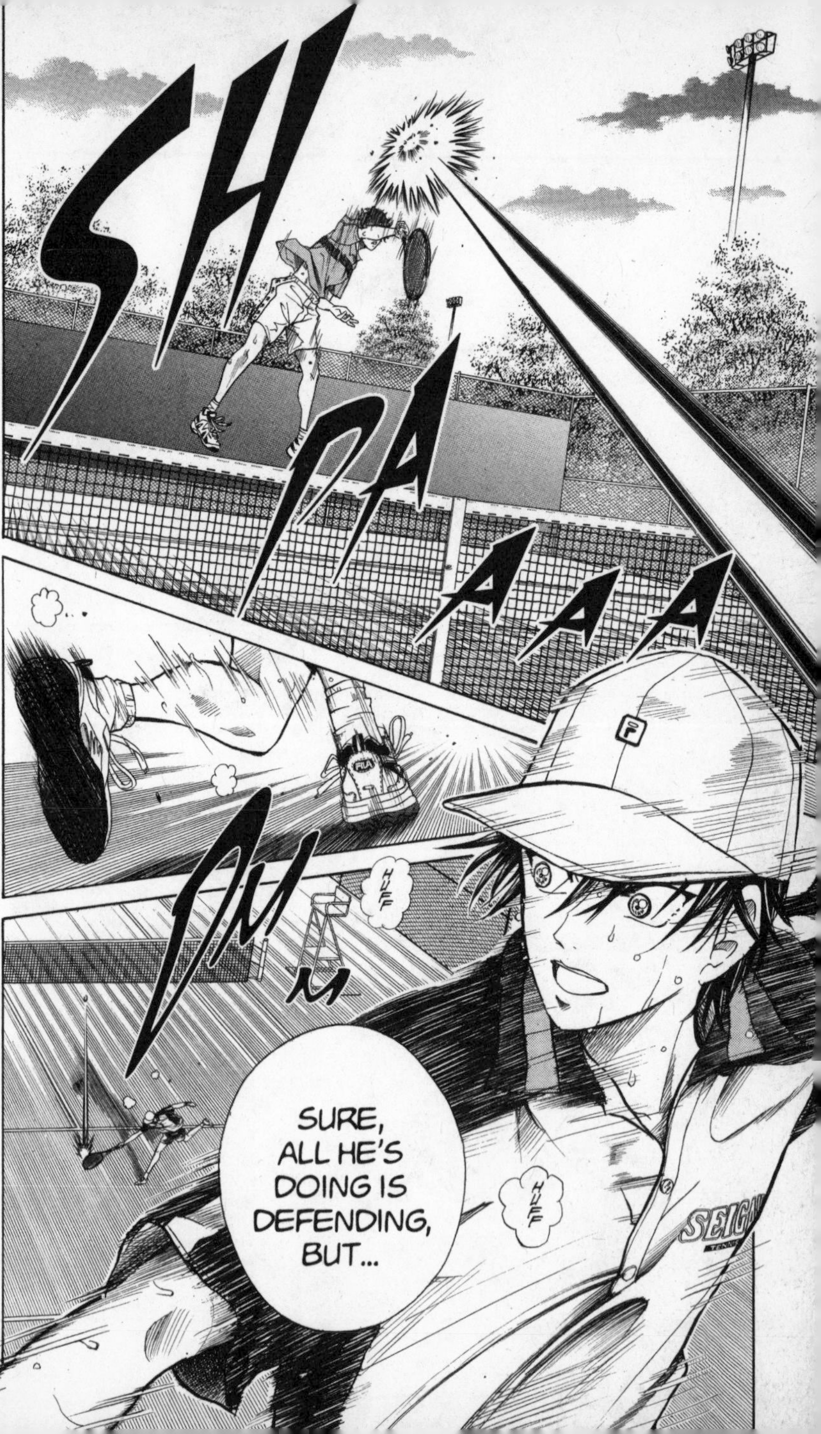
SHPAAAAA
...
HUFF
SHUMM
SURE, ALL HE'S DOING IS DEFENDING, BUT...
HUFF

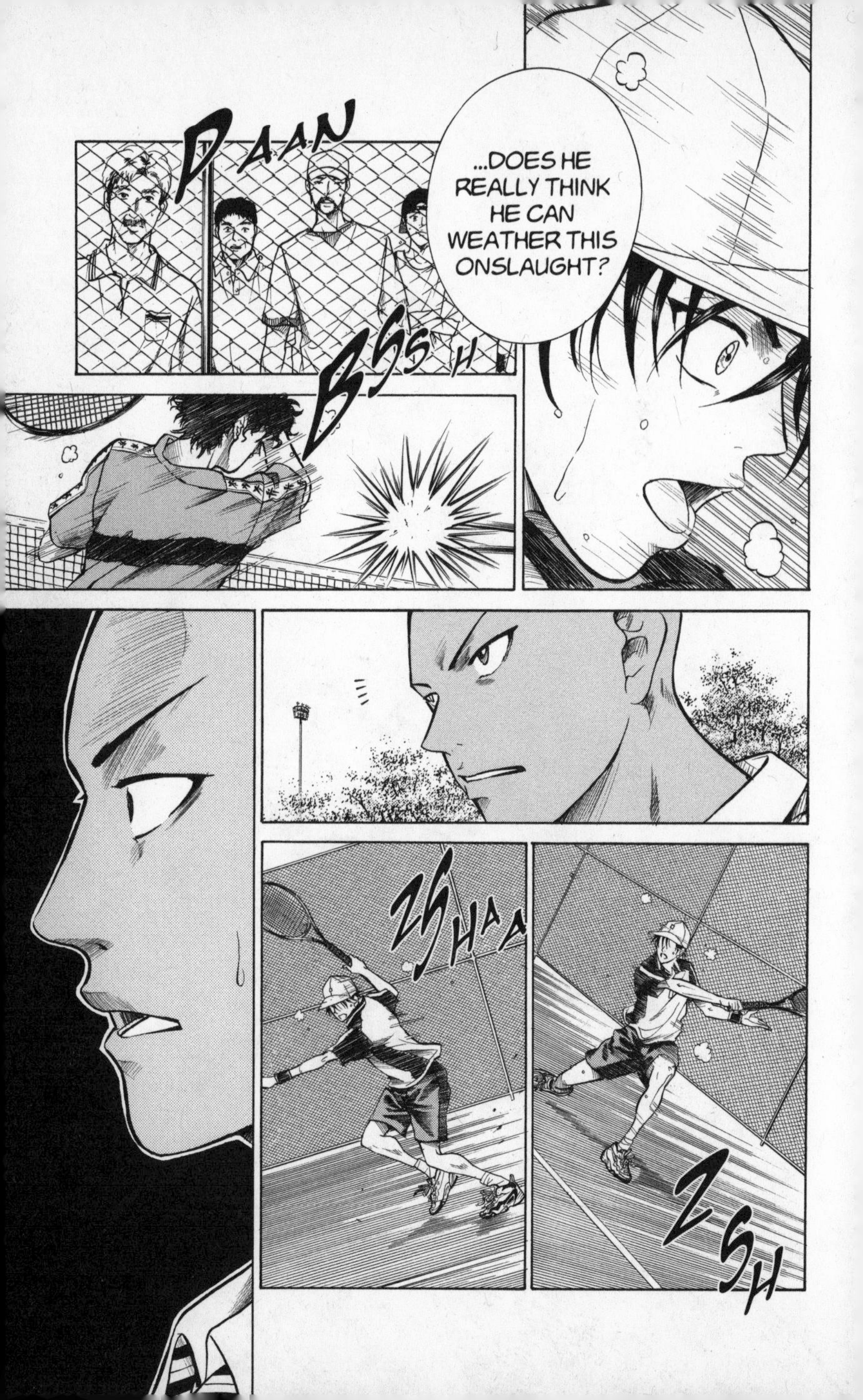
...DOES HE REALLY THINK HE CAN WEATHER THIS ONSLAUGHT?
DAAN
BSSH
ZSH
ZSHAA

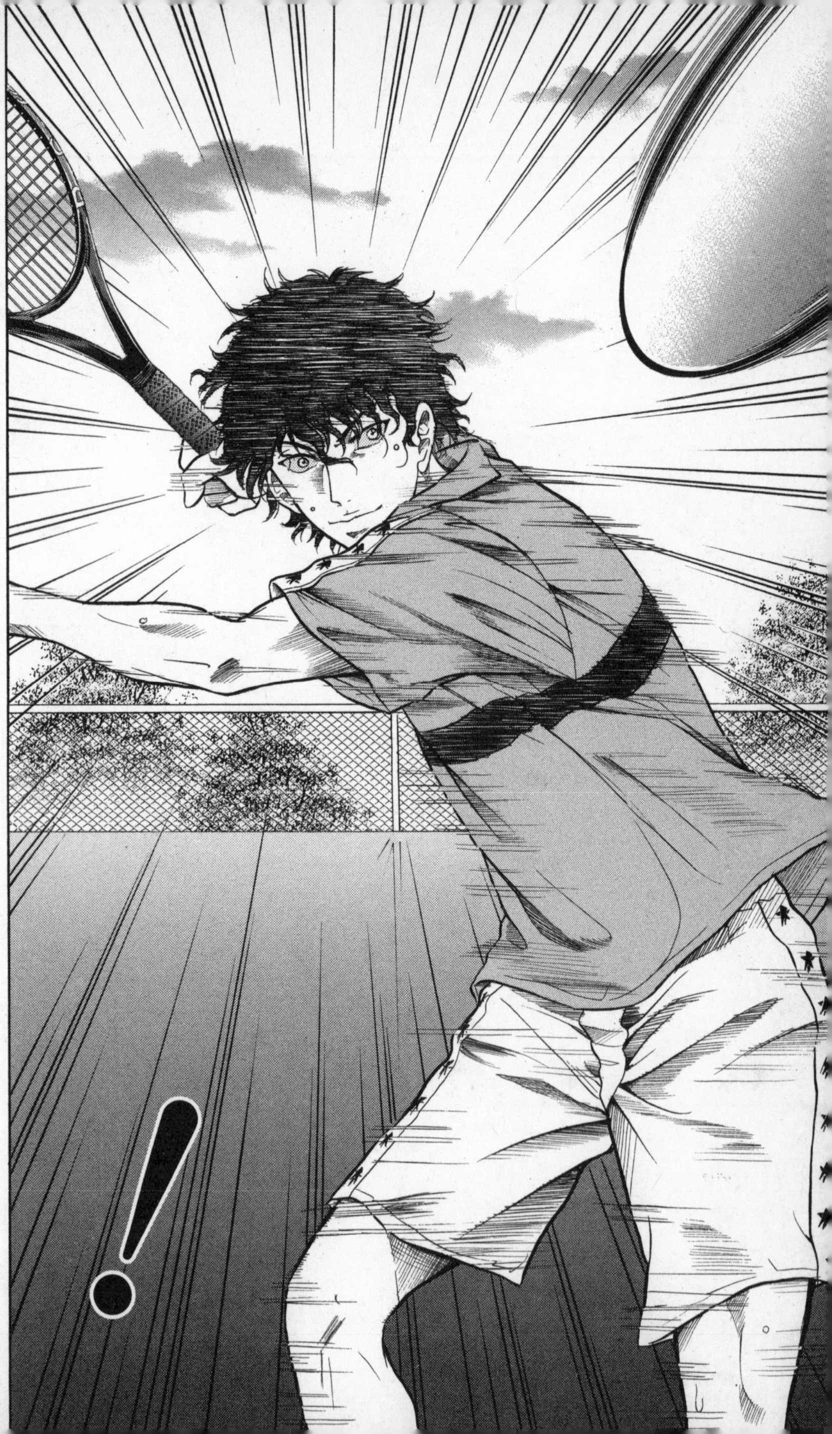
!

READ THIS WAY

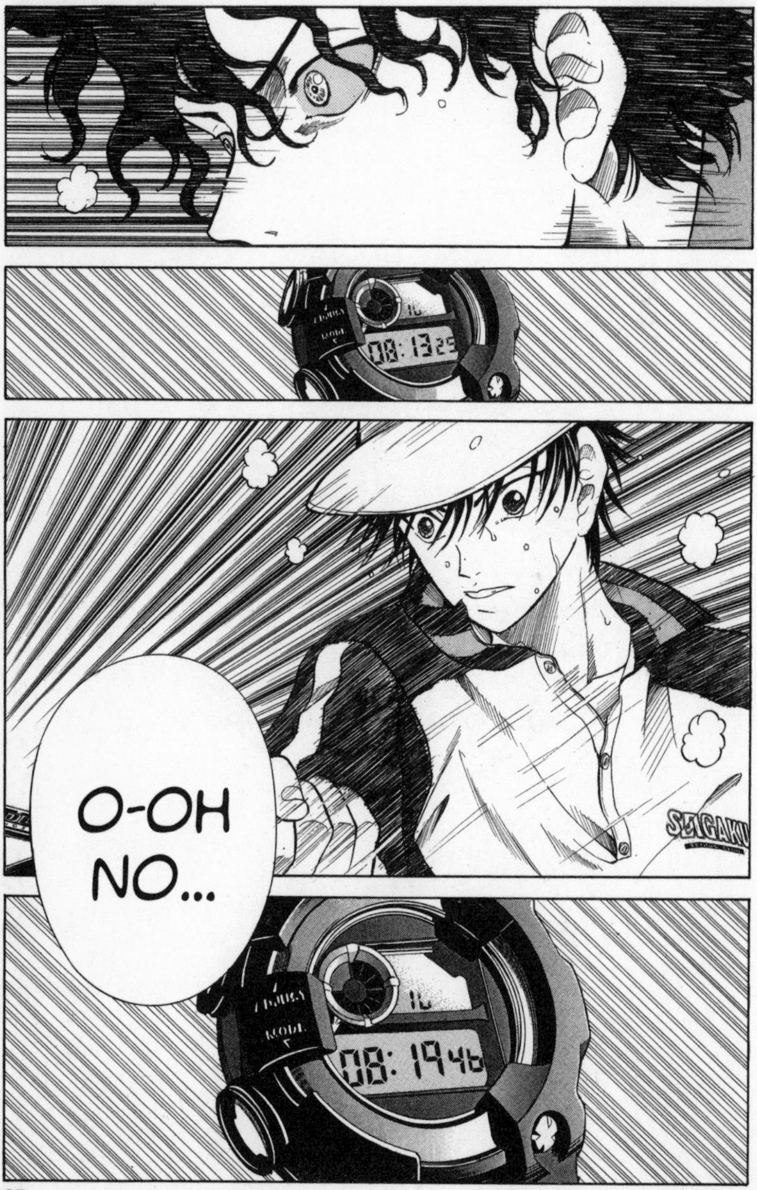
O-OH NO...

テニスの王子様

THE PRINCE OF TENNIS™

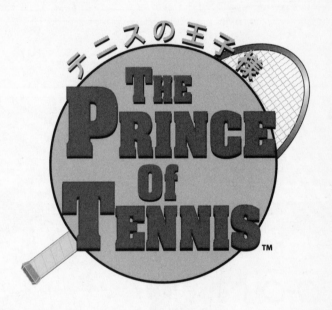

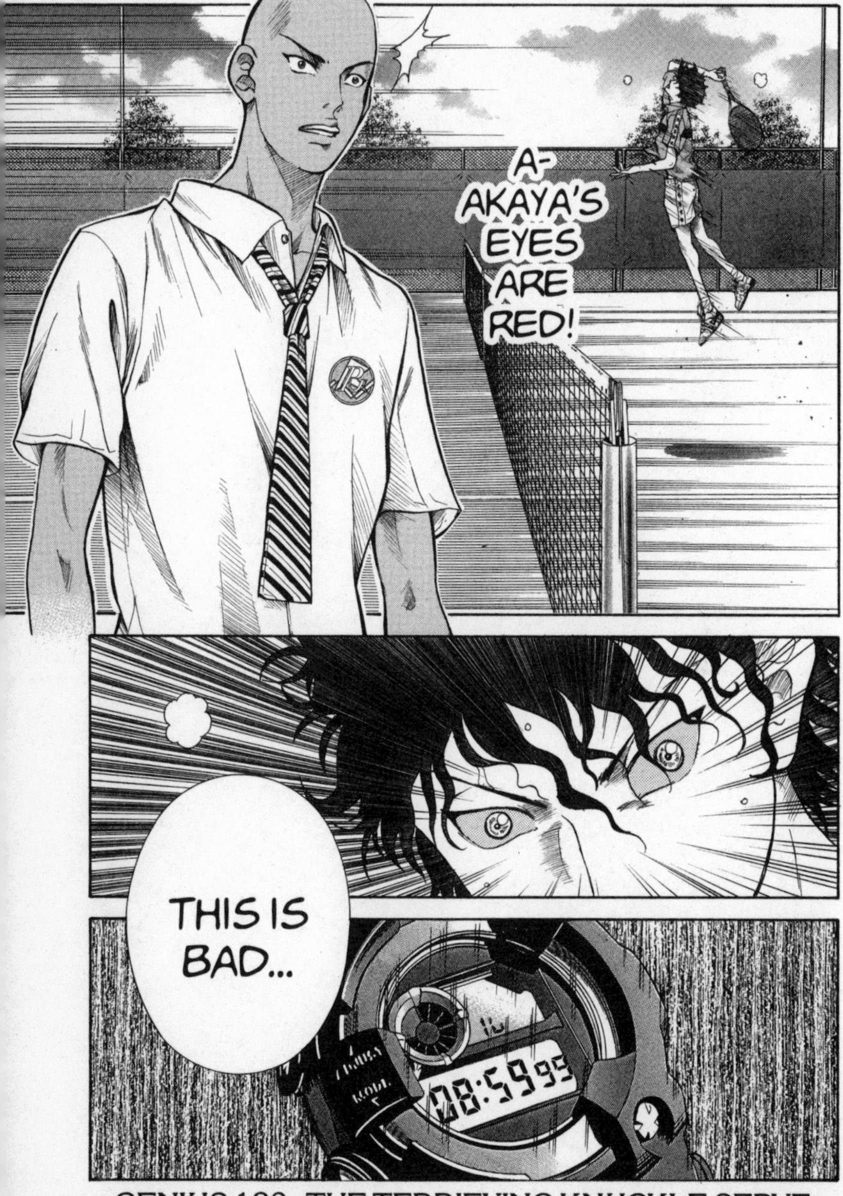
A-AKAYA'S EYES ARE RED!
THIS IS BAD...
08:59 99

GENIUS 189: THE TERRIFYING KNUCKLE SERVE

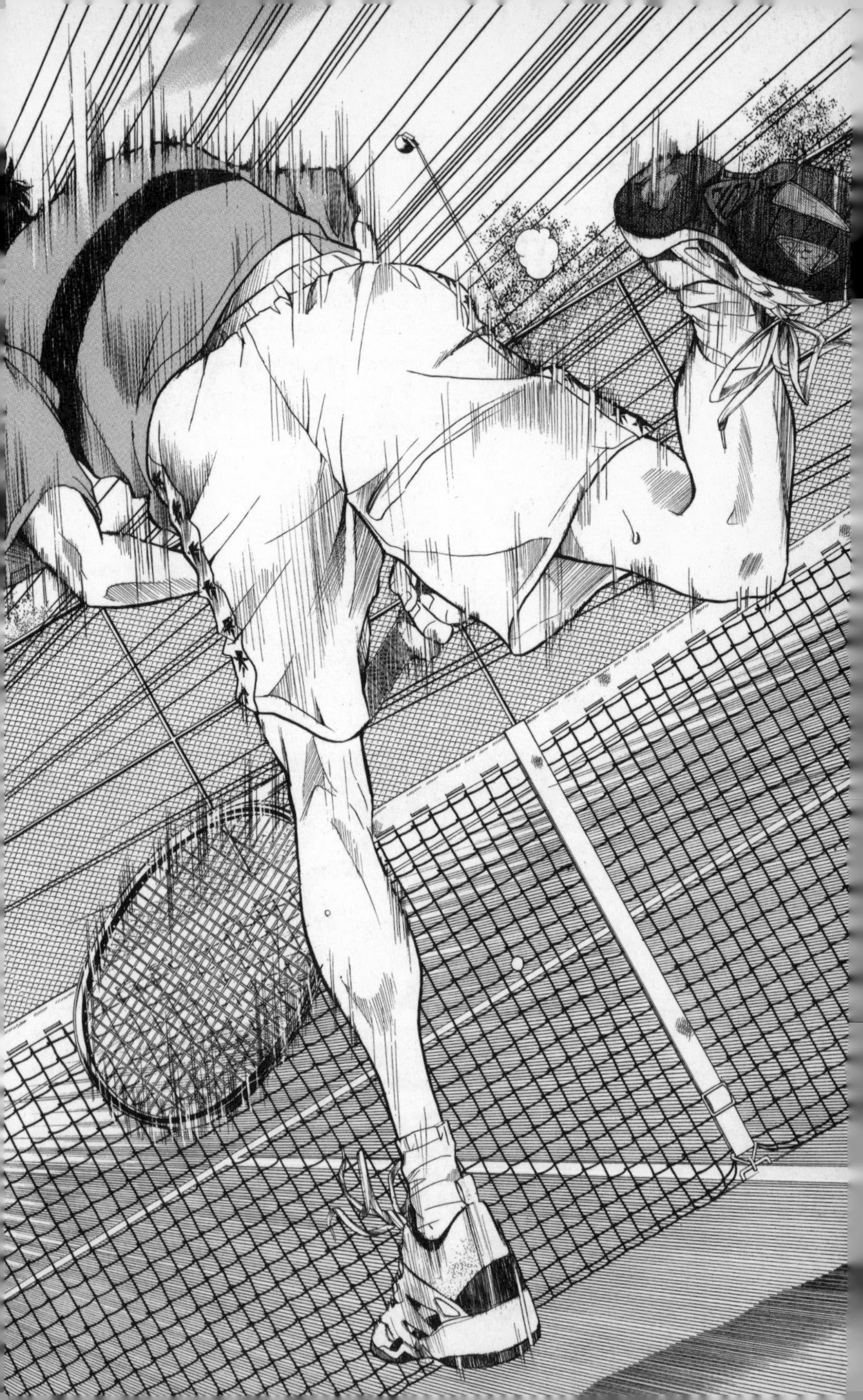

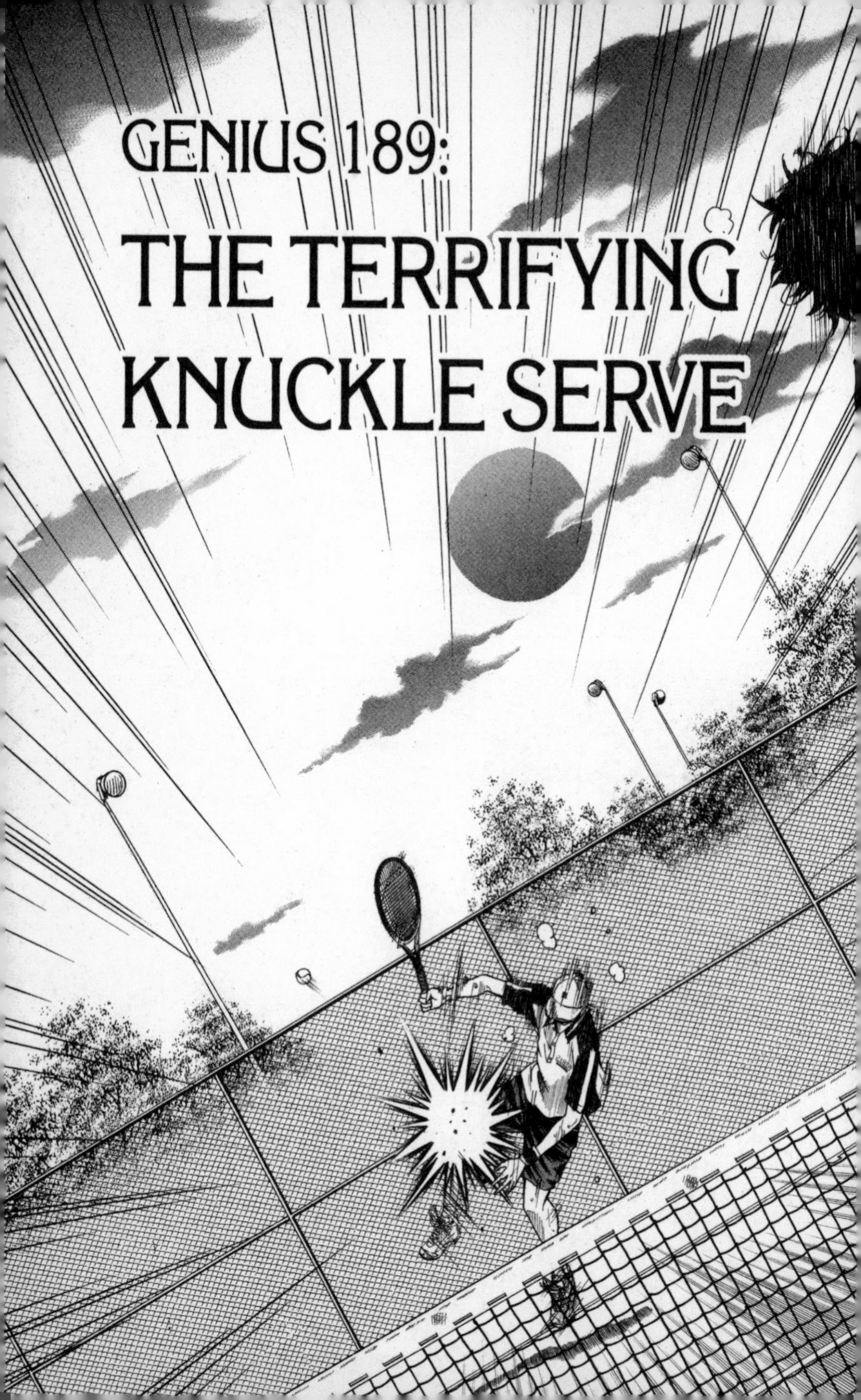
GENIUS 189:
THE TERRIFYING KNUCKLE SERVE

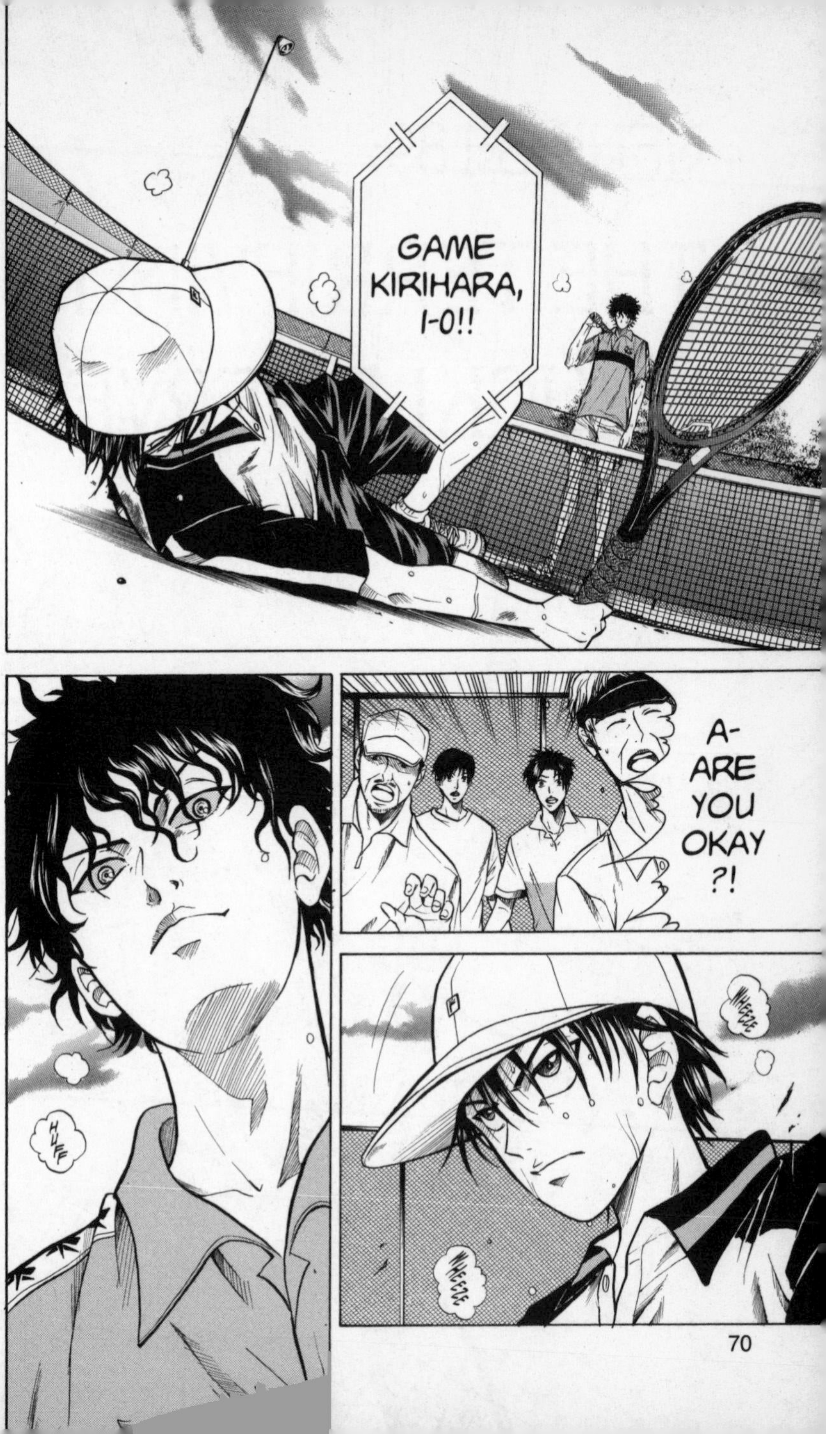
GAME KIRIHARA, 1-0!!
A- ARE YOU OKAY ?!
WHEEZE
WHEEZE
HUFF

READ THIS WAY

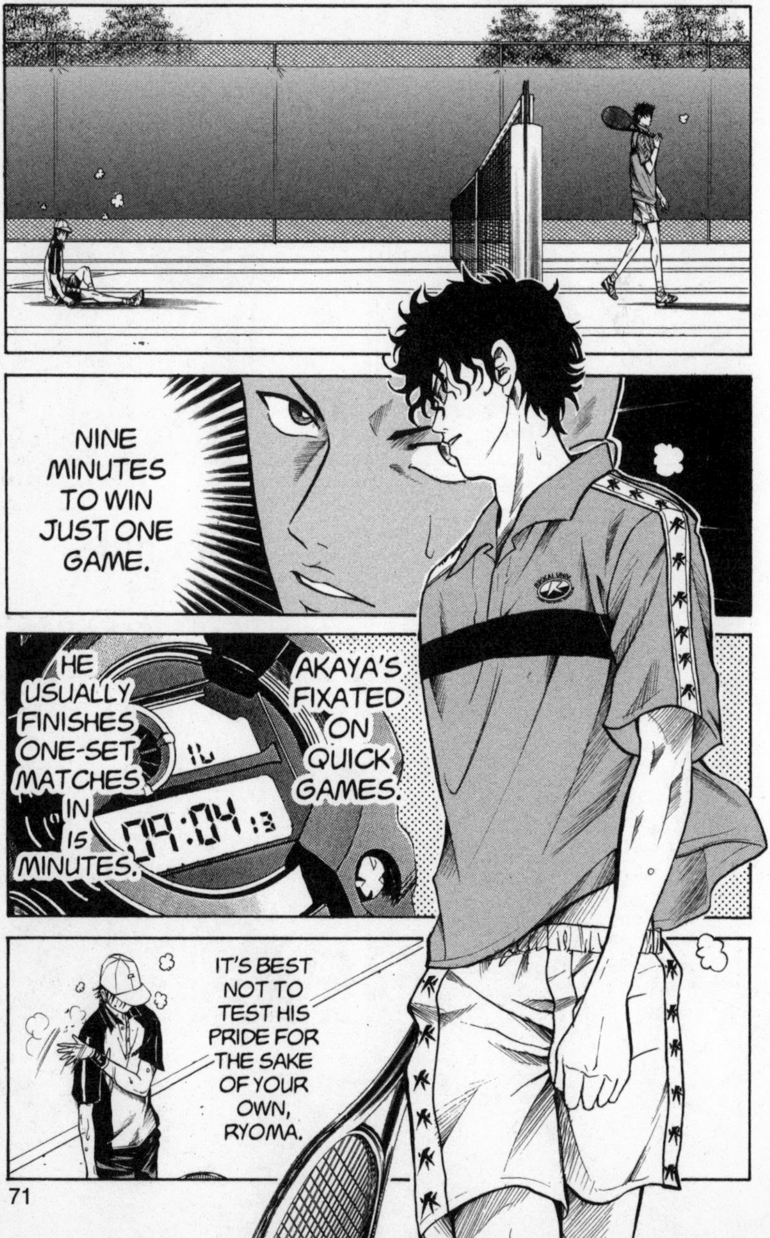
NINE MINUTES TO WIN JUST ONE GAME.
AKAYA'S FIXATED ON QUICK GAMES.
HE USUALLY FINISHES ONE-SET MATCHES IN 15 MINUTES.
09:04
IT'S BEST NOT TO TEST HIS PRIDE FOR THE SAKE OF YOUR OWN, RYOMA.

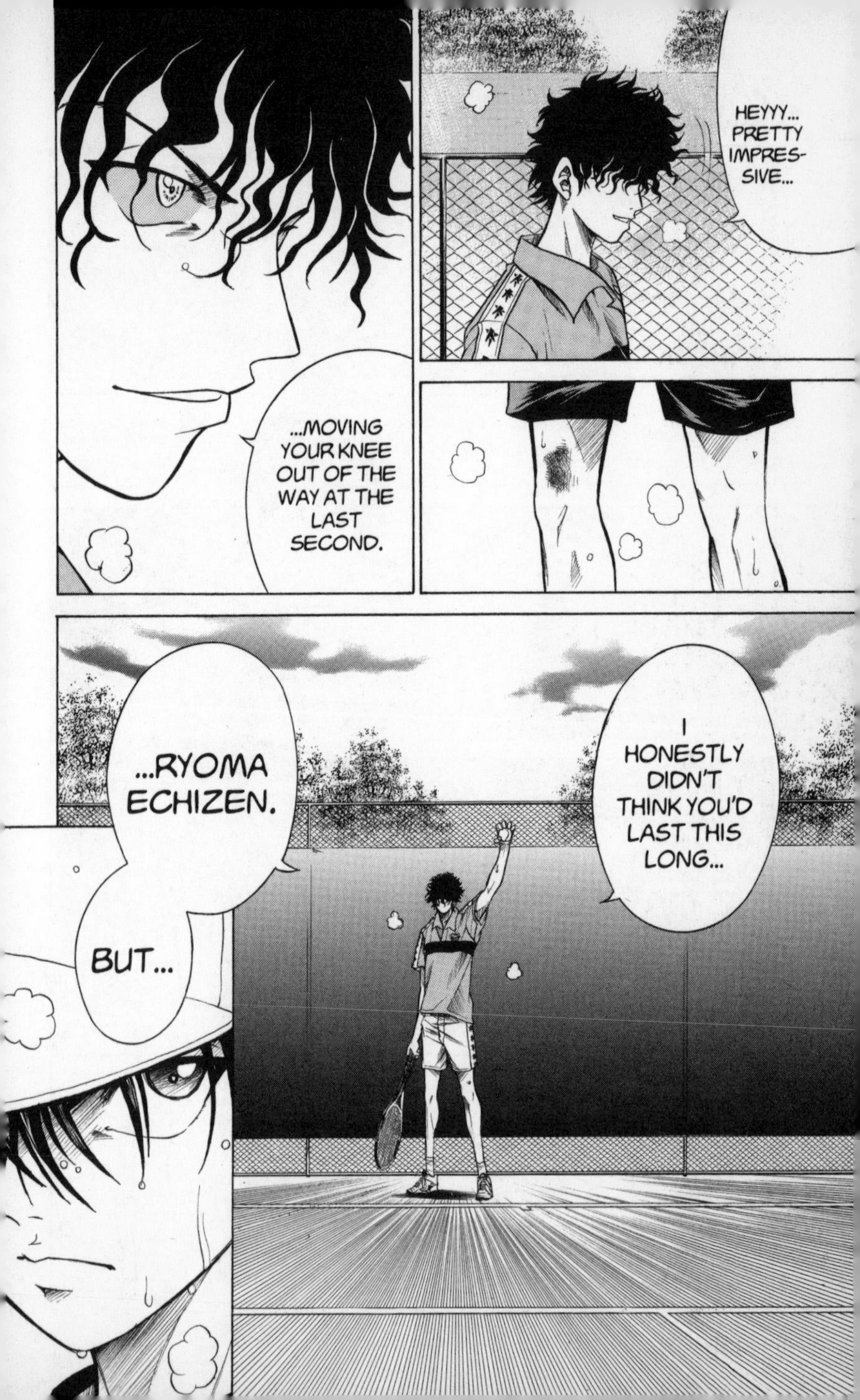
HEYYY... PRETTY IMPRES-SIVE...
...MOVING YOUR KNEE OUT OF THE WAY AT THE LAST SECOND.
I HONESTLY DIDN'T THINK YOU'D LAST THIS LONG...
...RYOMA ECHIZEN.
BUT...

READ THIS WAY

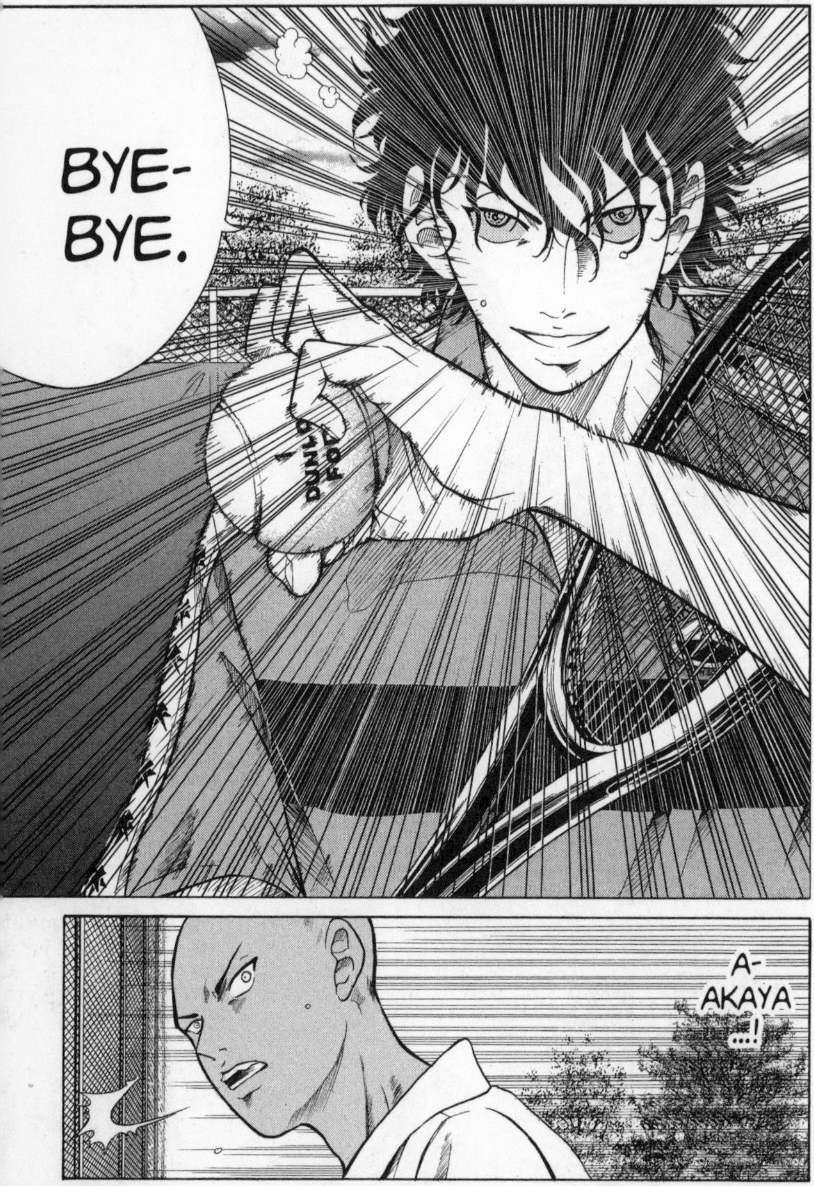
BYE-BYE.
A-AKAYA...!

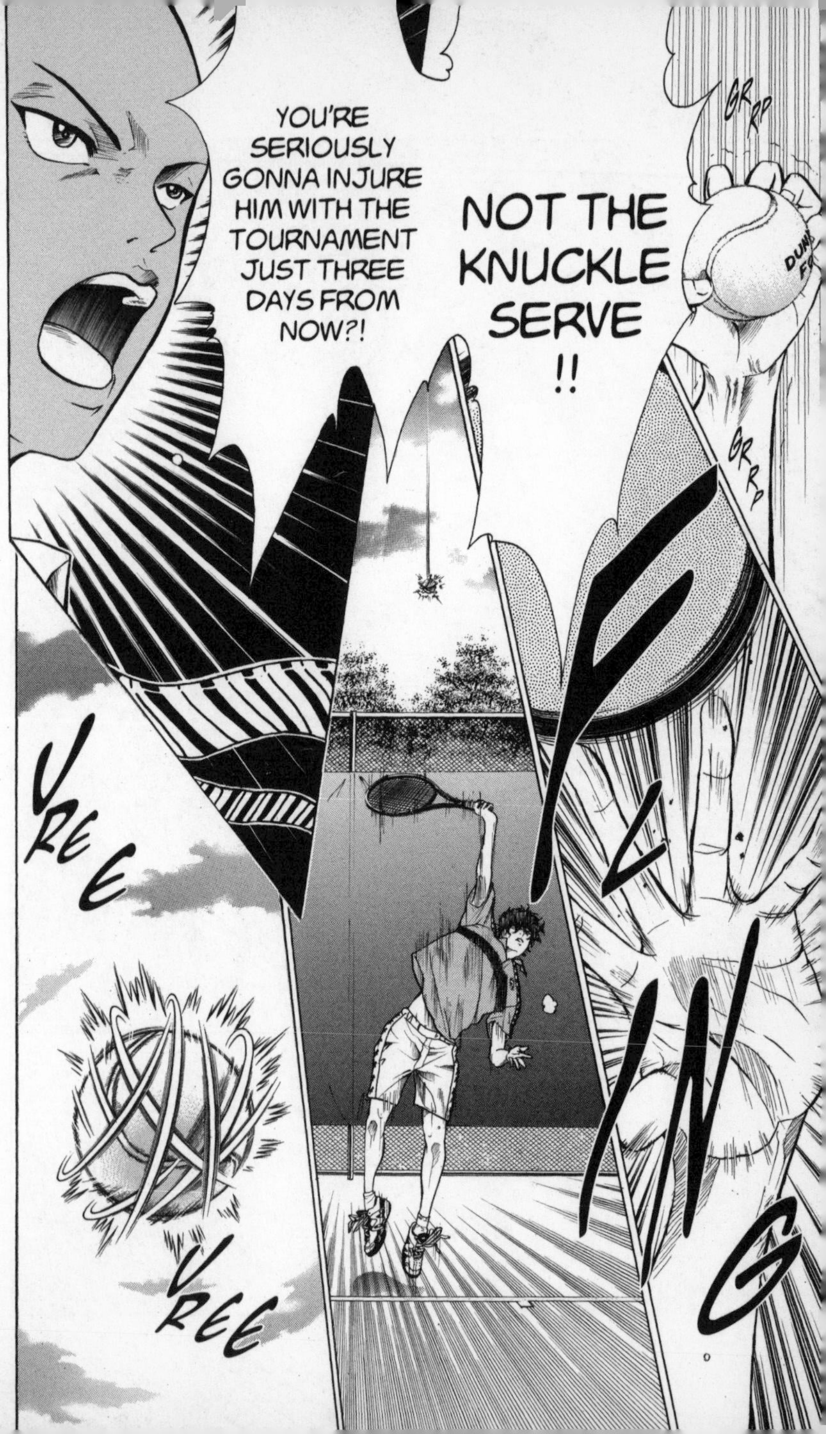
GRRP
NOT THE KNUCKLE SERVE!!
YOU'RE SERIOUSLY GONNA INJURE HIM WITH THE TOURNAMENT JUST THREE DAYS FROM NOW?!
GRRP
FWING
VREEE
VREE

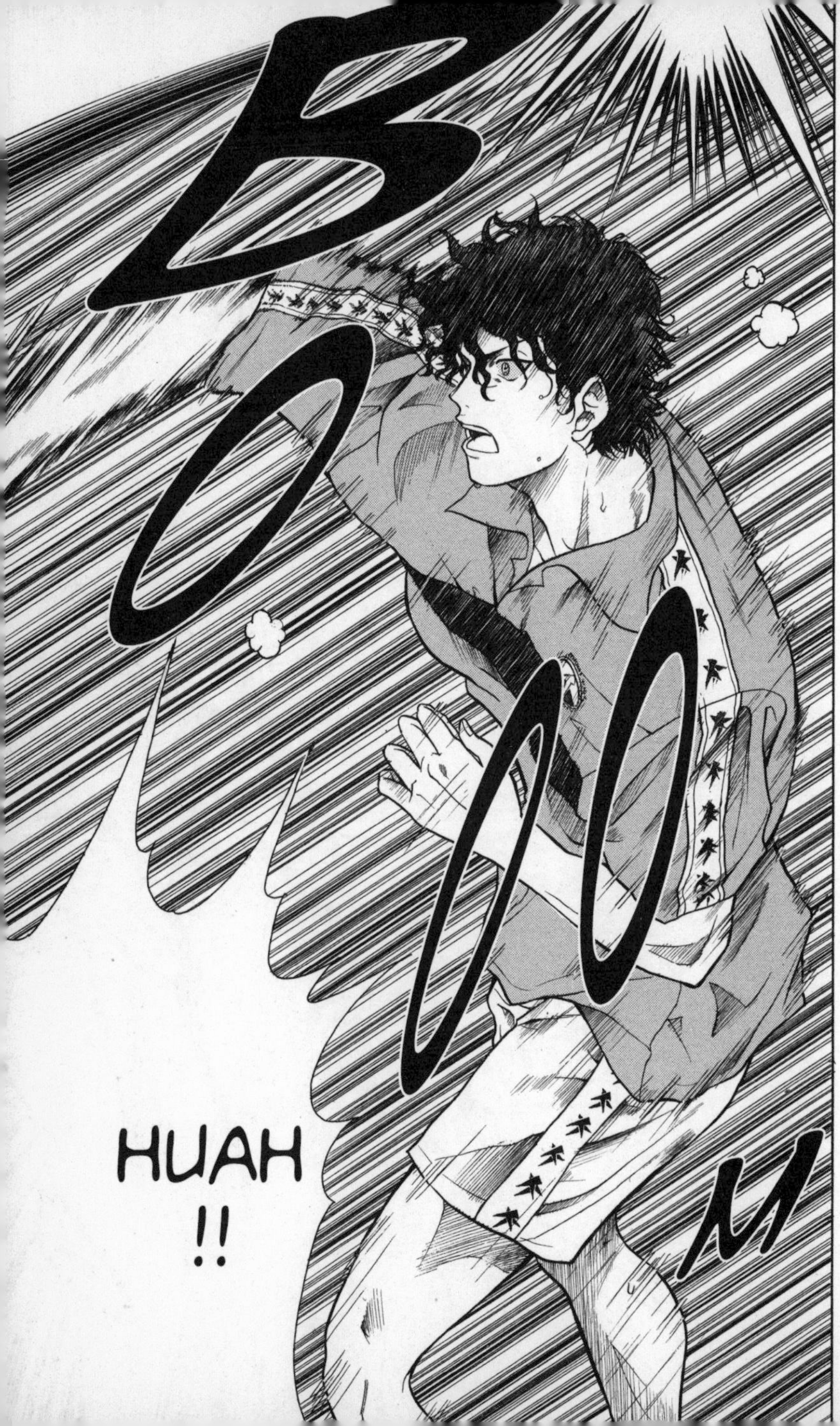
BOOOOM
HUAH !!

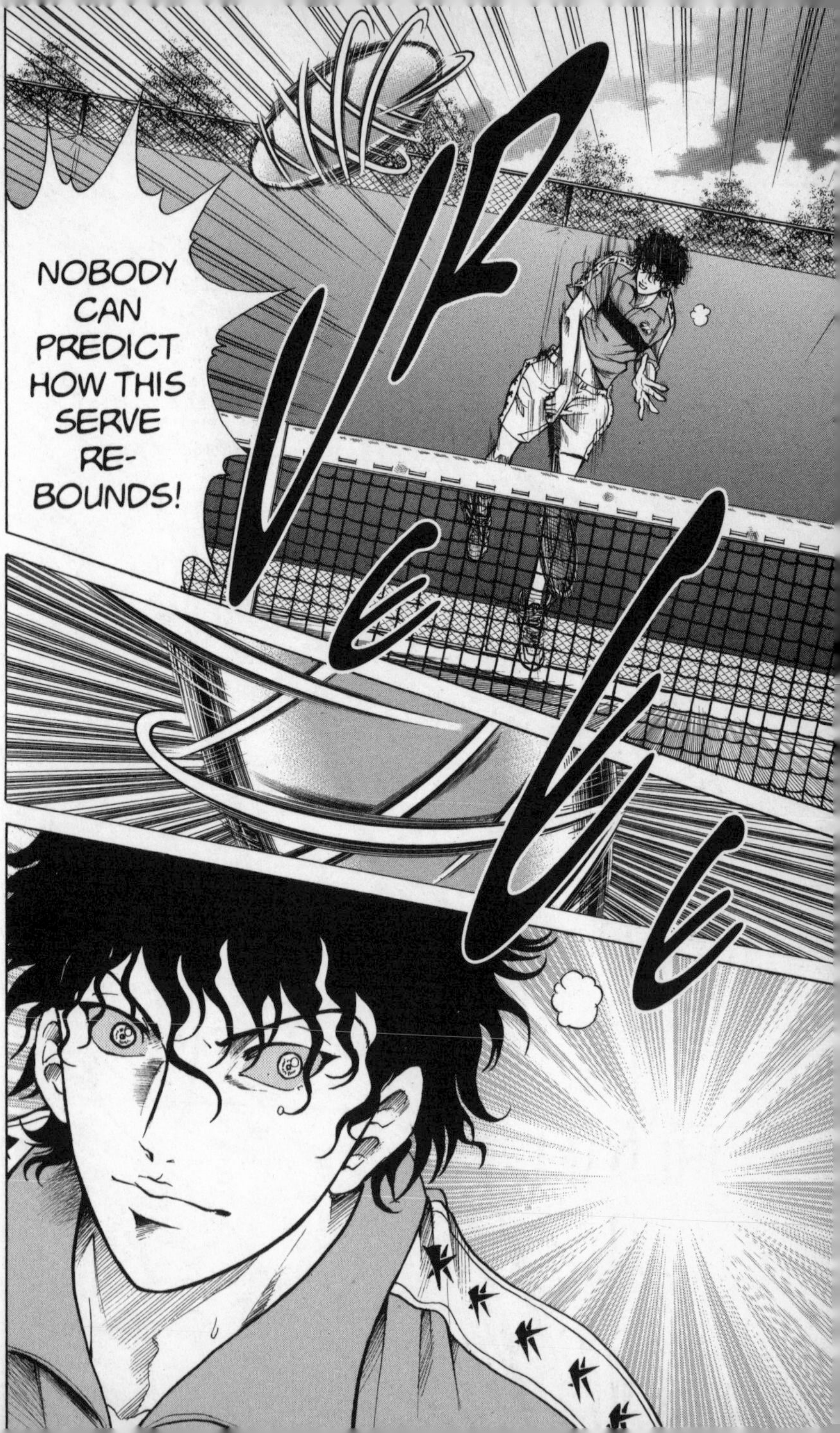
NOBODY CAN PREDICT HOW THIS SERVE RE-BOUNDS!

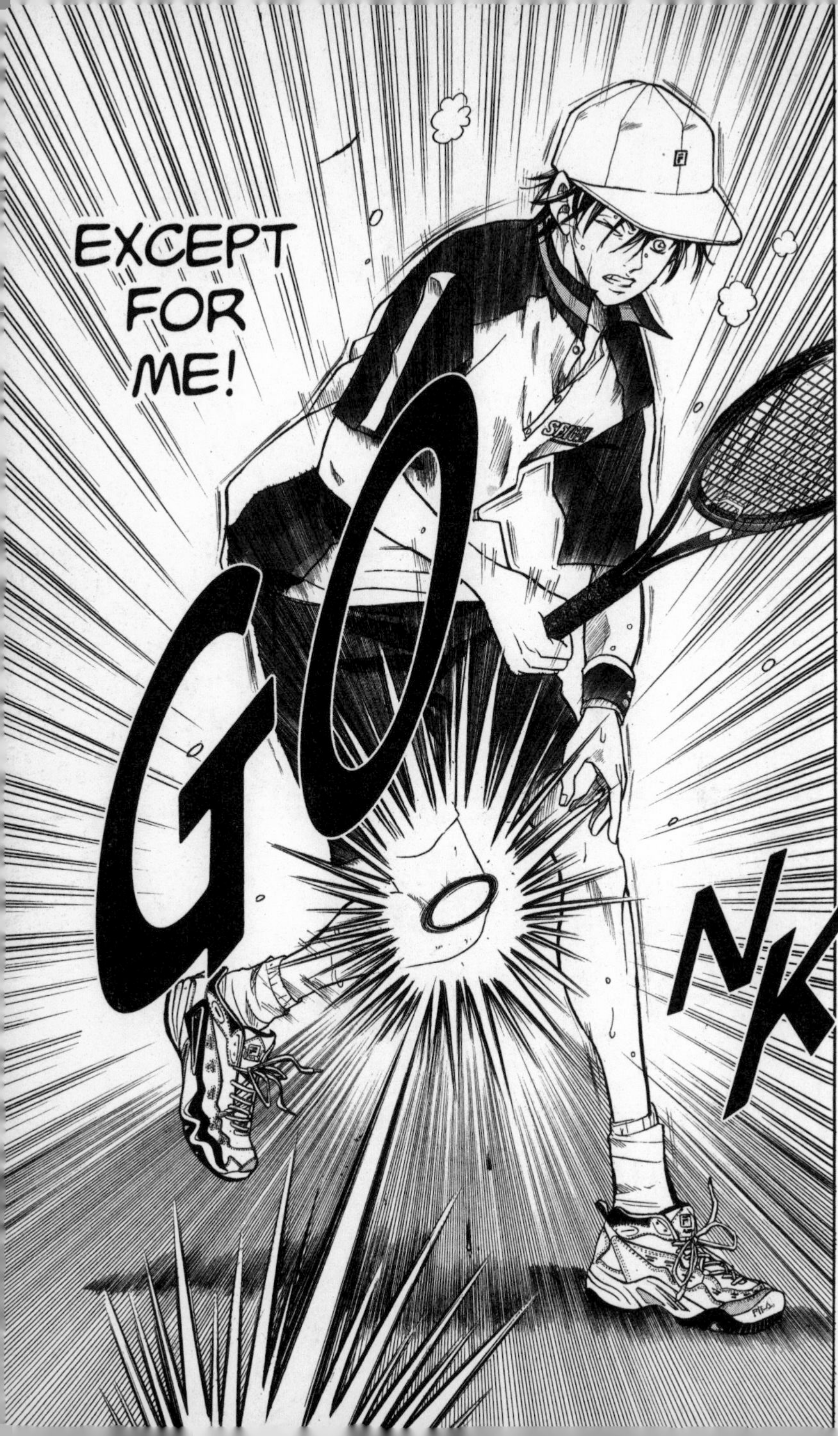
EXCEPT FOR ME!
GONK

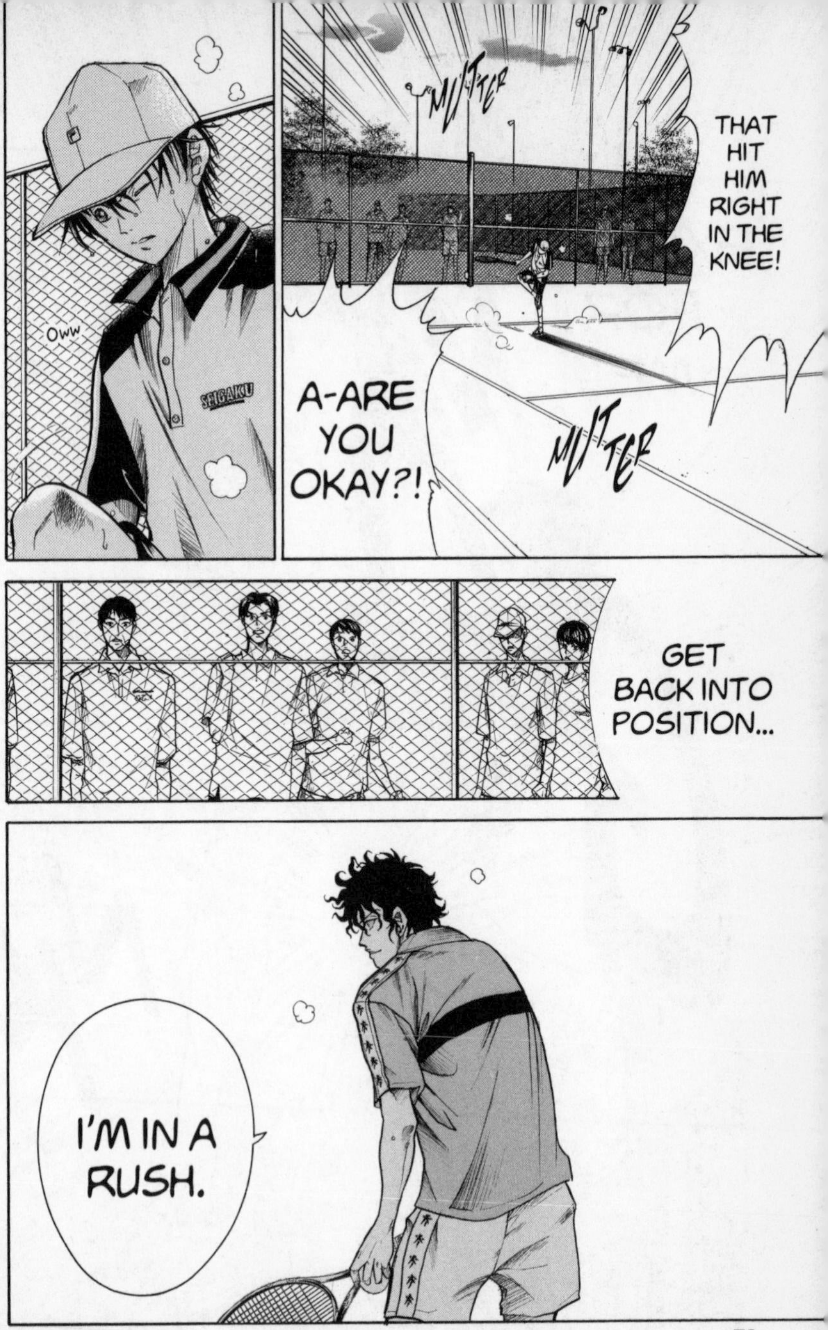
THAT HIT HIM RIGHT IN THE KNEE!
MUTTER
A-ARE YOU OKAY?!
MUTTER
OWW
GET BACK INTO POSITION...
I'M IN A RUSH.

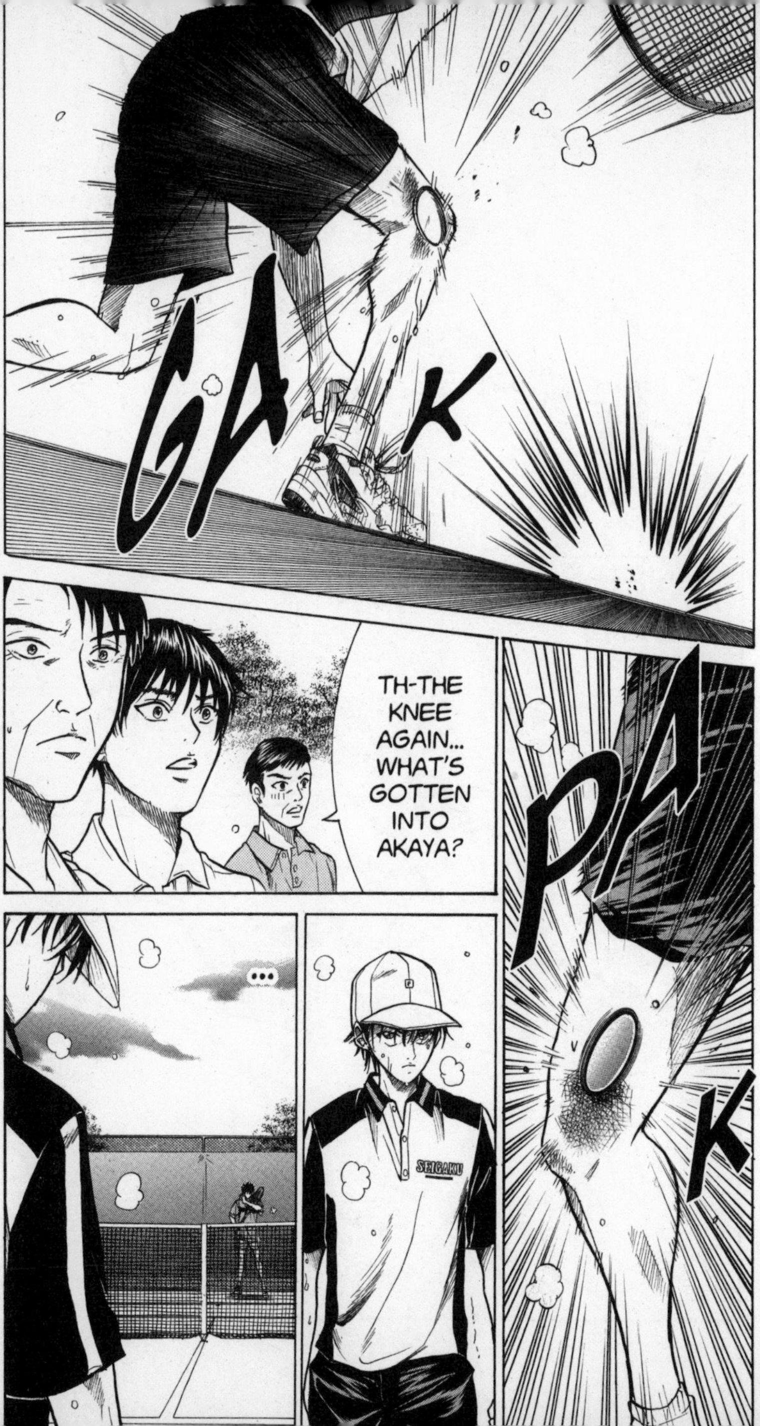
GAK
PAK
TH-THE KNEE AGAIN... WHAT'S GOTTEN INTO AKAYA?
SEIGAKU
...

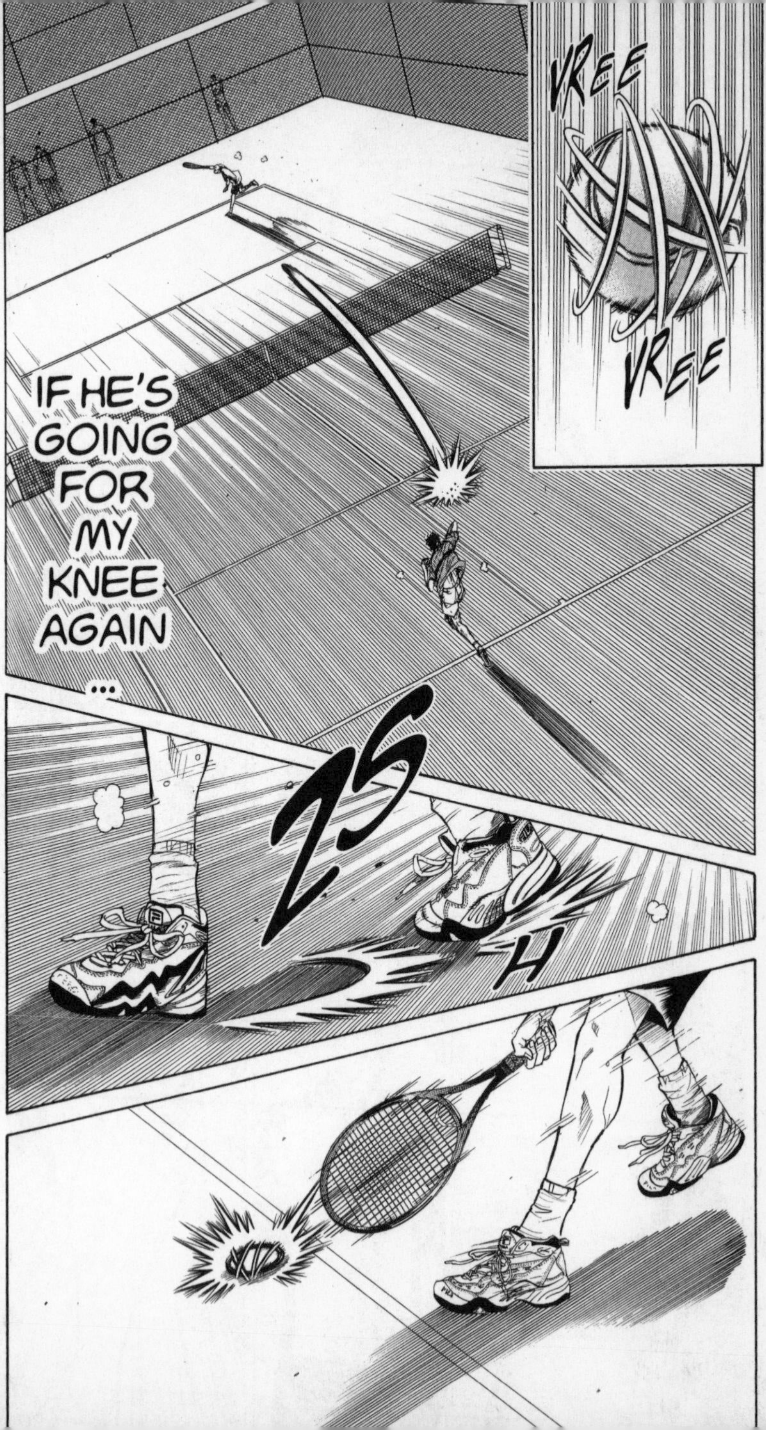
VREE
VREE
IF HE'S GOING FOR MY KNEE AGAIN ...
ZSH

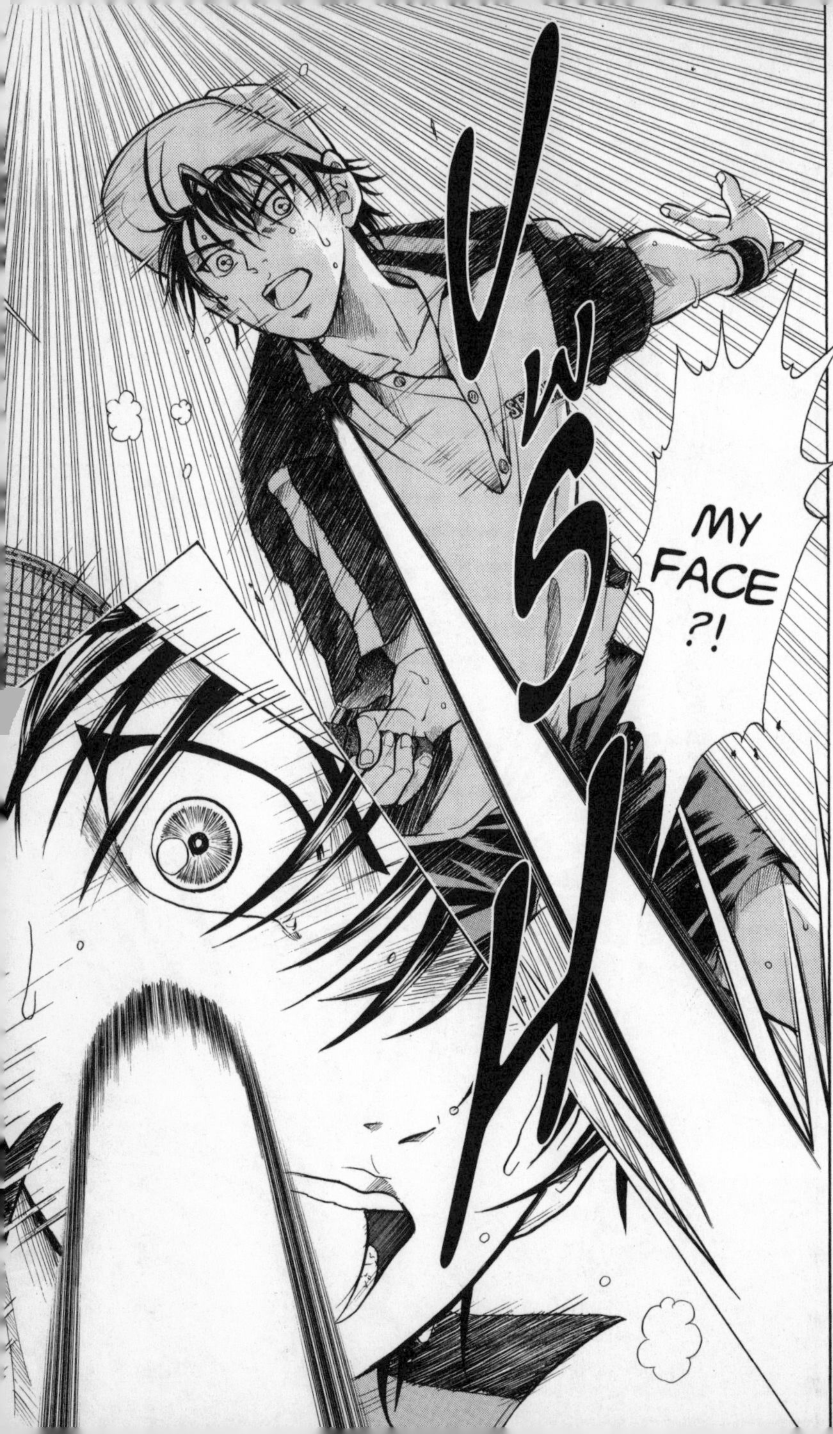
MY FACE ?!

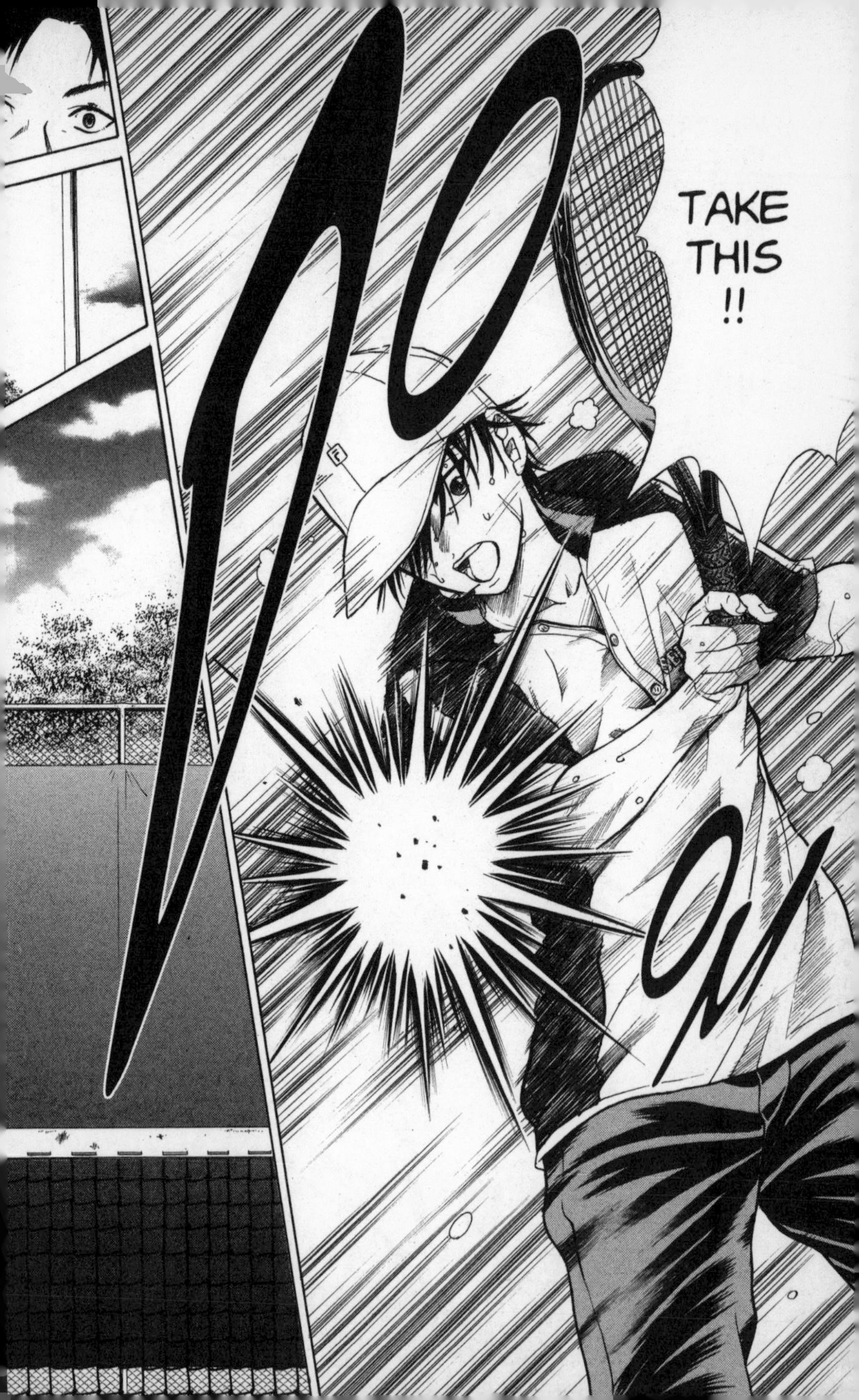
TAKE THIS !!

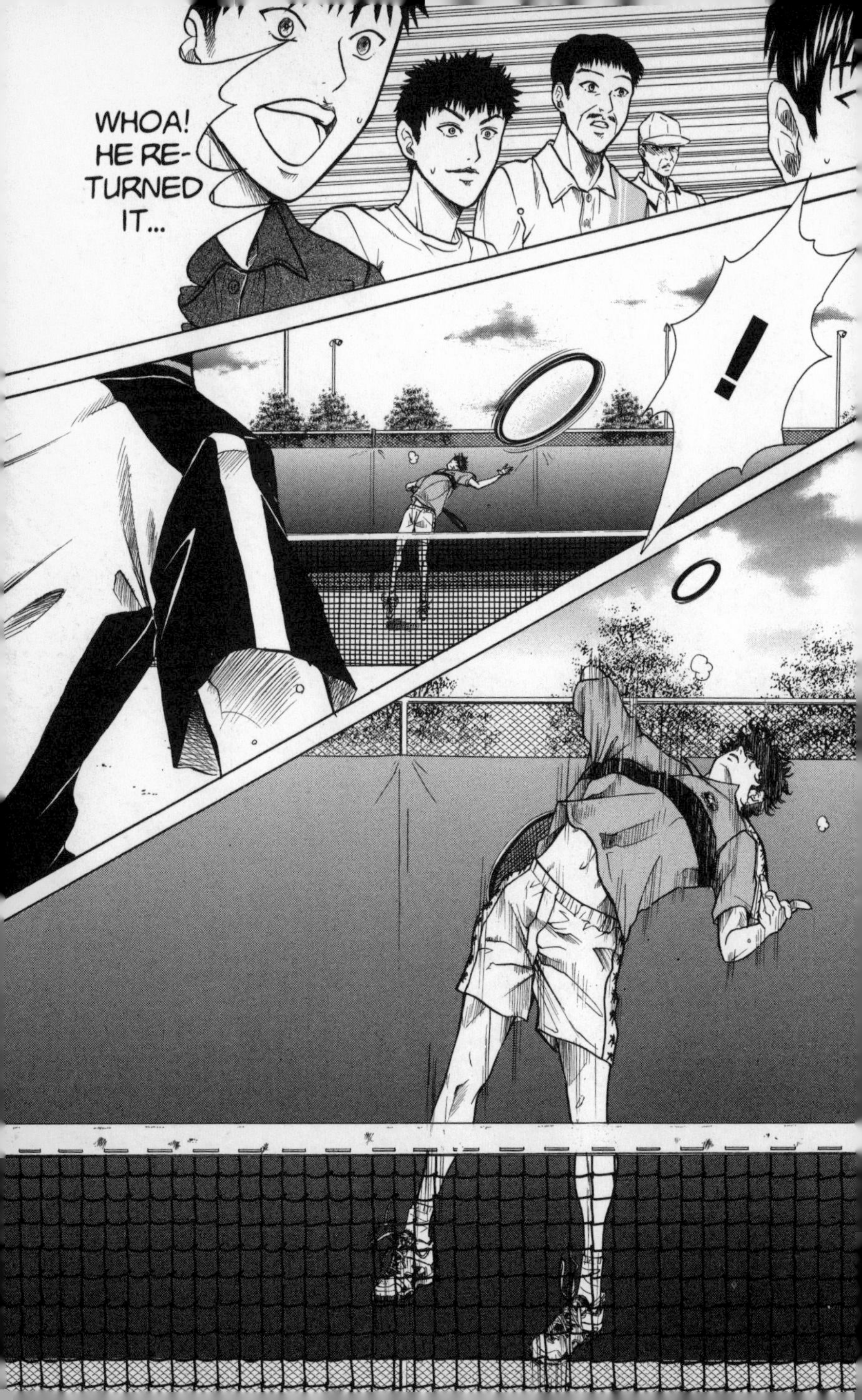
WHOA! HE RE-TURNED IT...
!

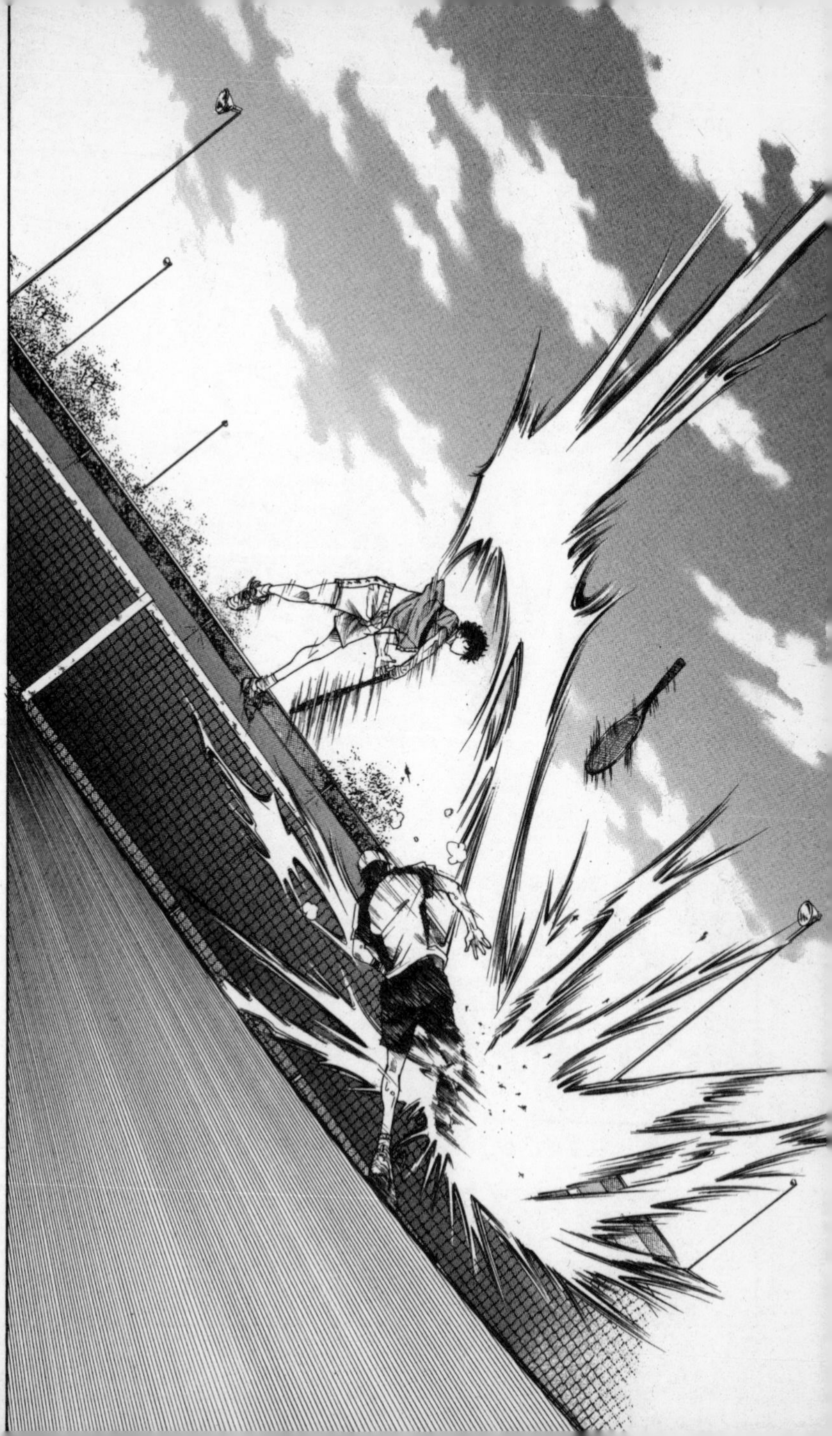

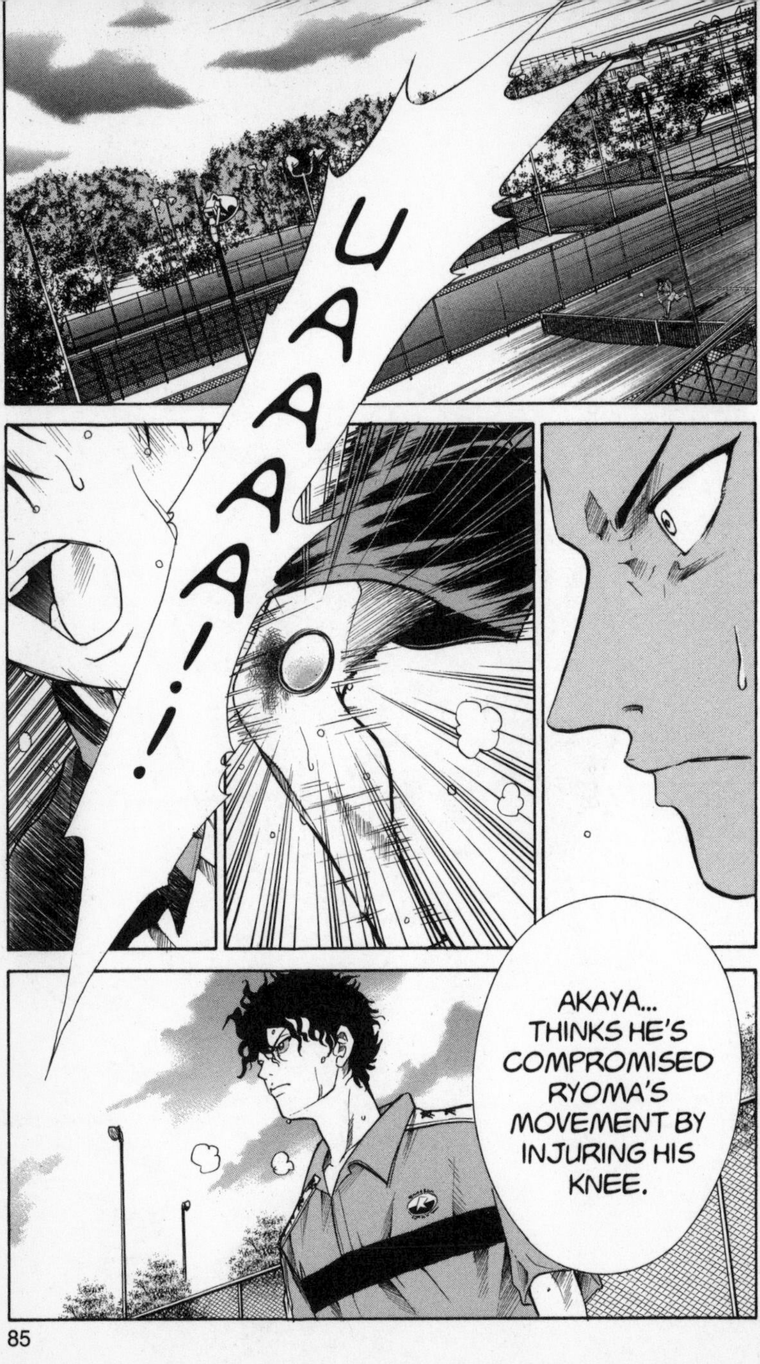
UAAAAA!!
AKAYA... THINKS HE'S COMPROMISED RYOMA'S MOVEMENT BY INJURING HIS KNEE.

テニスの王子様

THE PRINCE OF TENNIS™

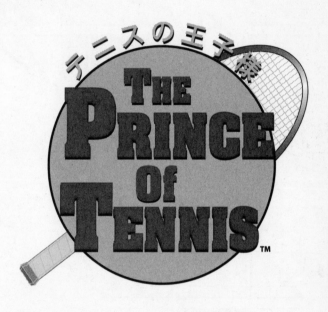

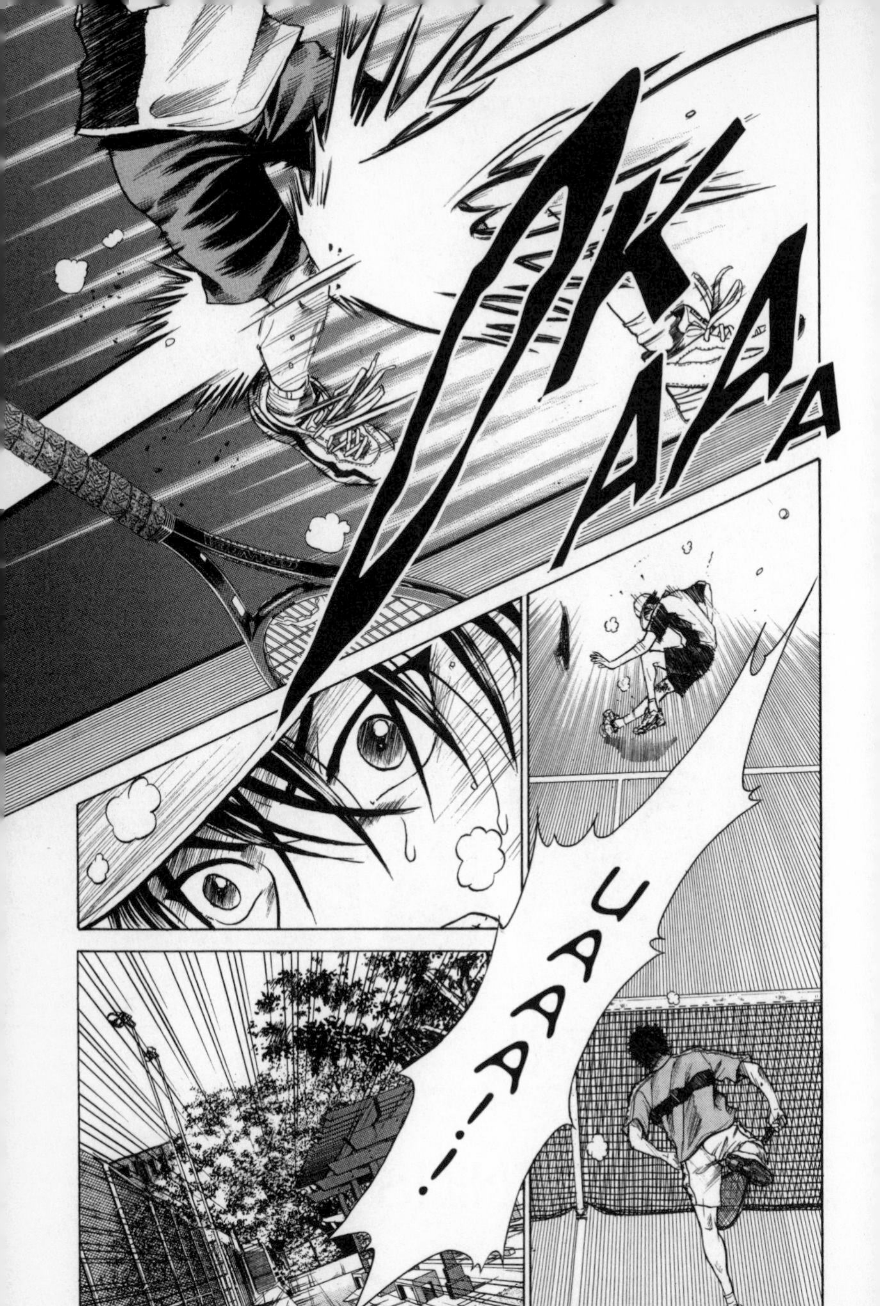
UAAA–!!

GENIUS 190: RELENTLESS ATTACK

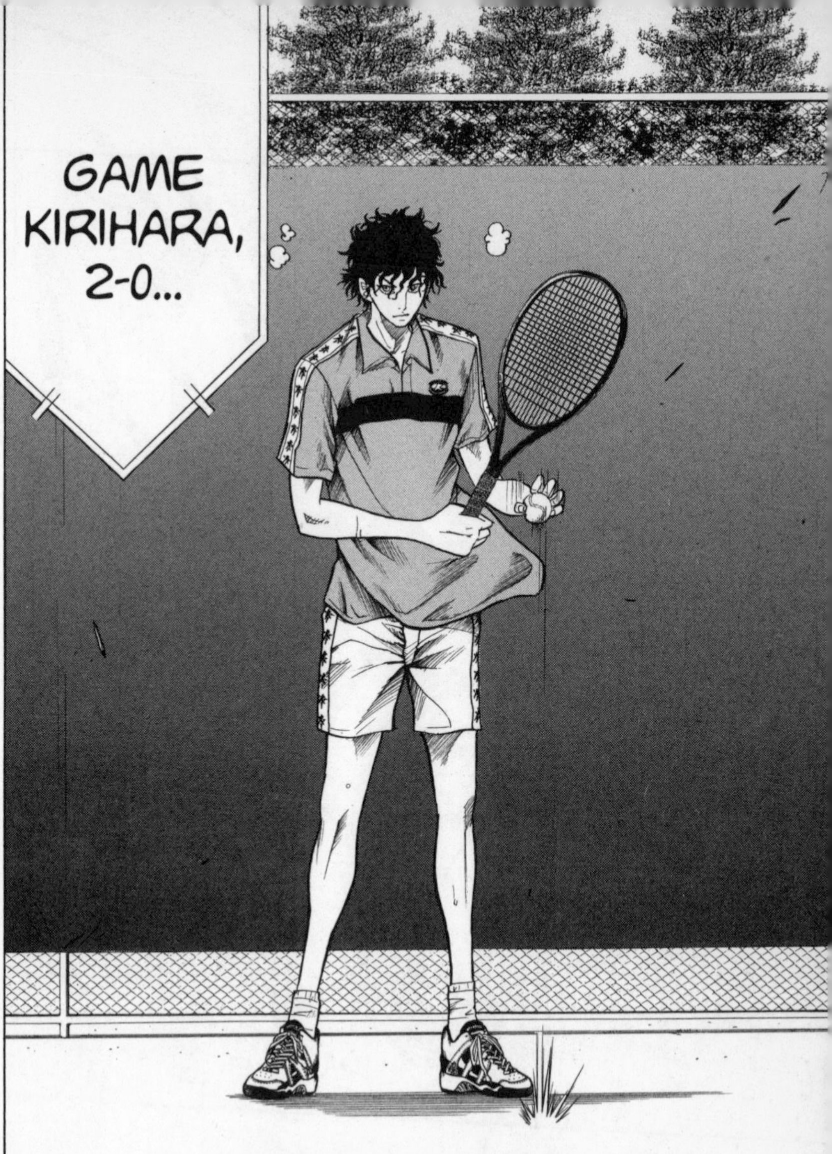
GAME KIRIHARA, 2-0...

GENIUS 190: RELENTLESS ATTACK

READ THIS WAY

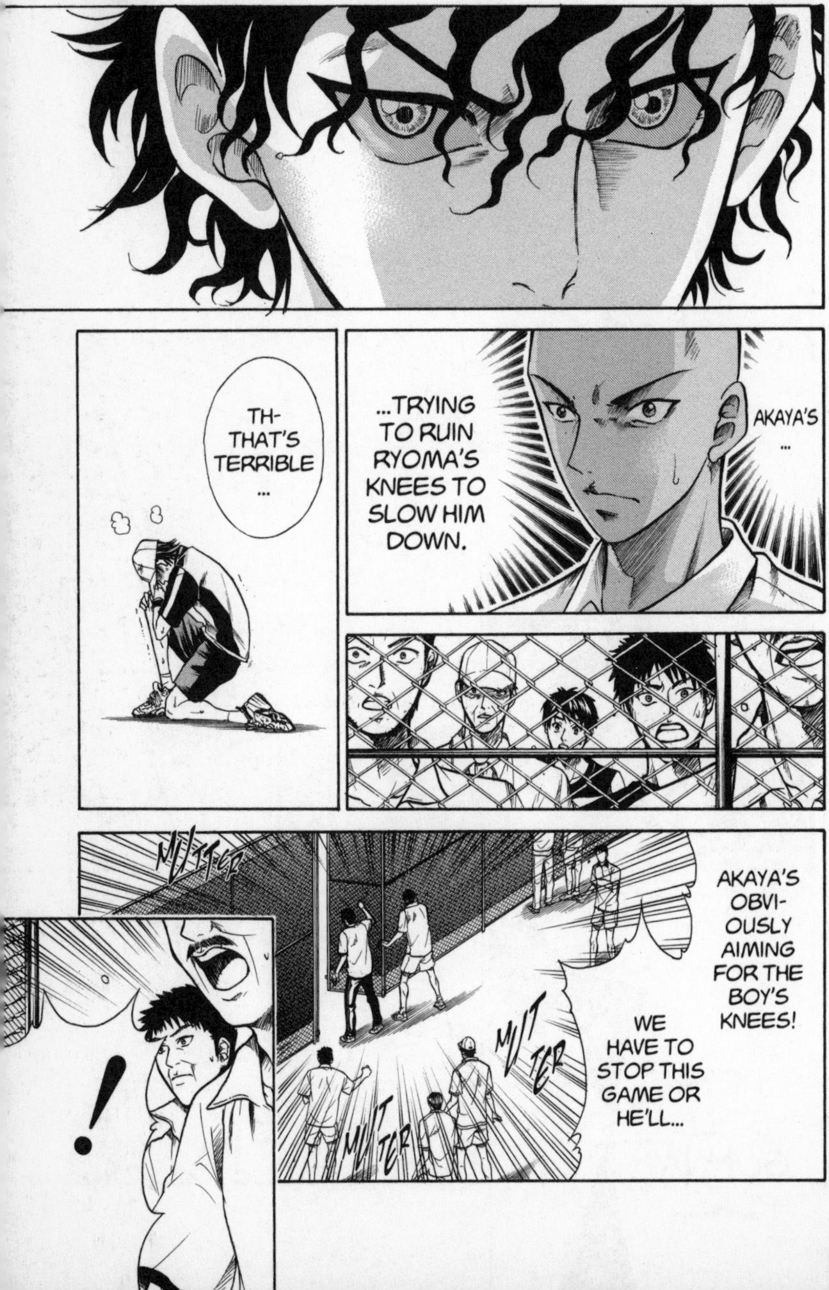
AKAYA'S ...
...TRYING TO RUIN RYOMA'S KNEES TO SLOW HIM DOWN.
TH-THAT'S TERRIBLE ...
MUTTER
AKAYA'S OBVIOUSLY AIMING FOR THE BOY'S KNEES!
WE HAVE TO STOP THIS GAME OR HE'LL...
MUTTER
MUTTER
!

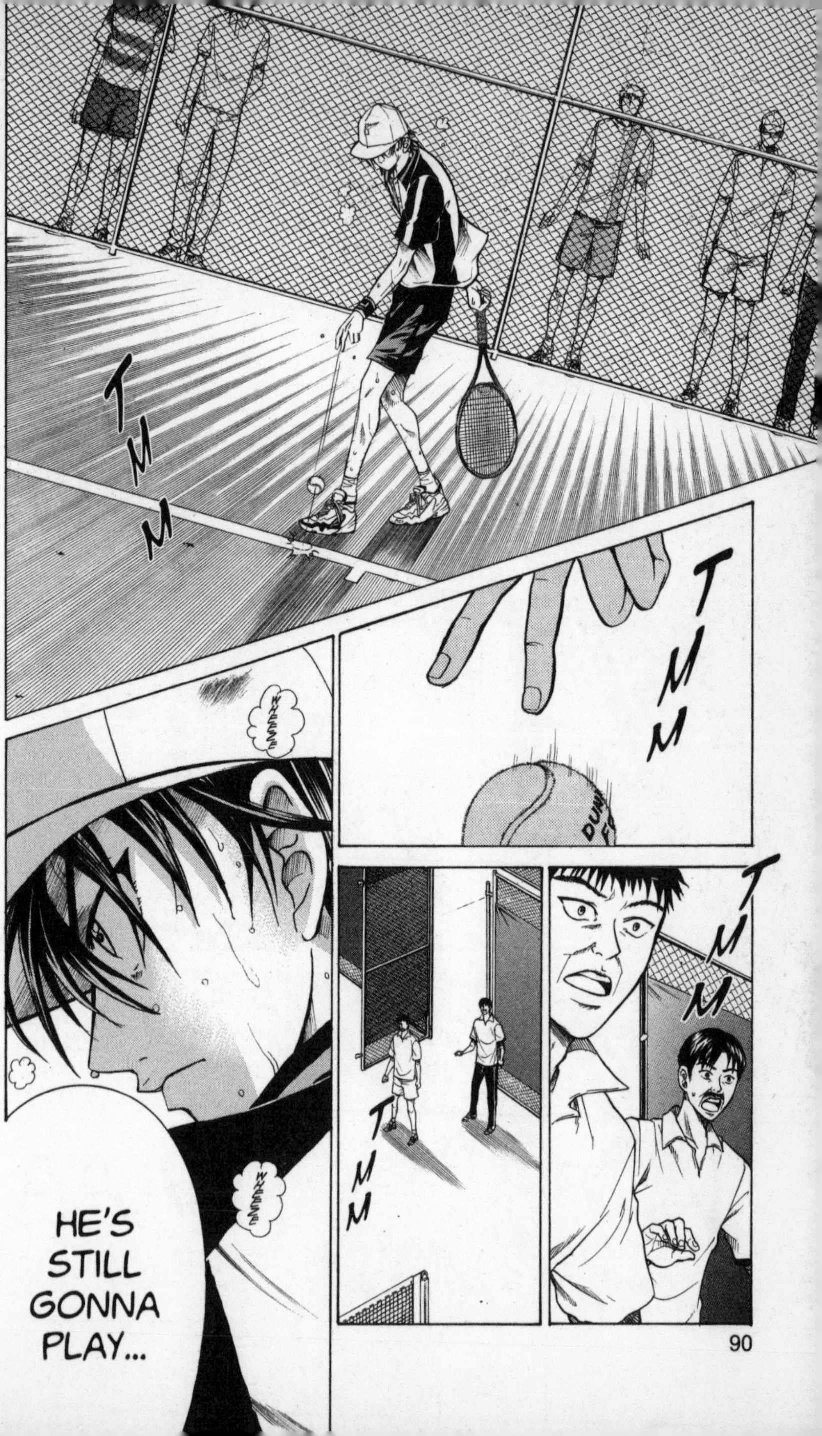
TMM
TMM
TMM
TMM
WHEEZE
WHEEZE
HE'S STILL GONNA PLAY...

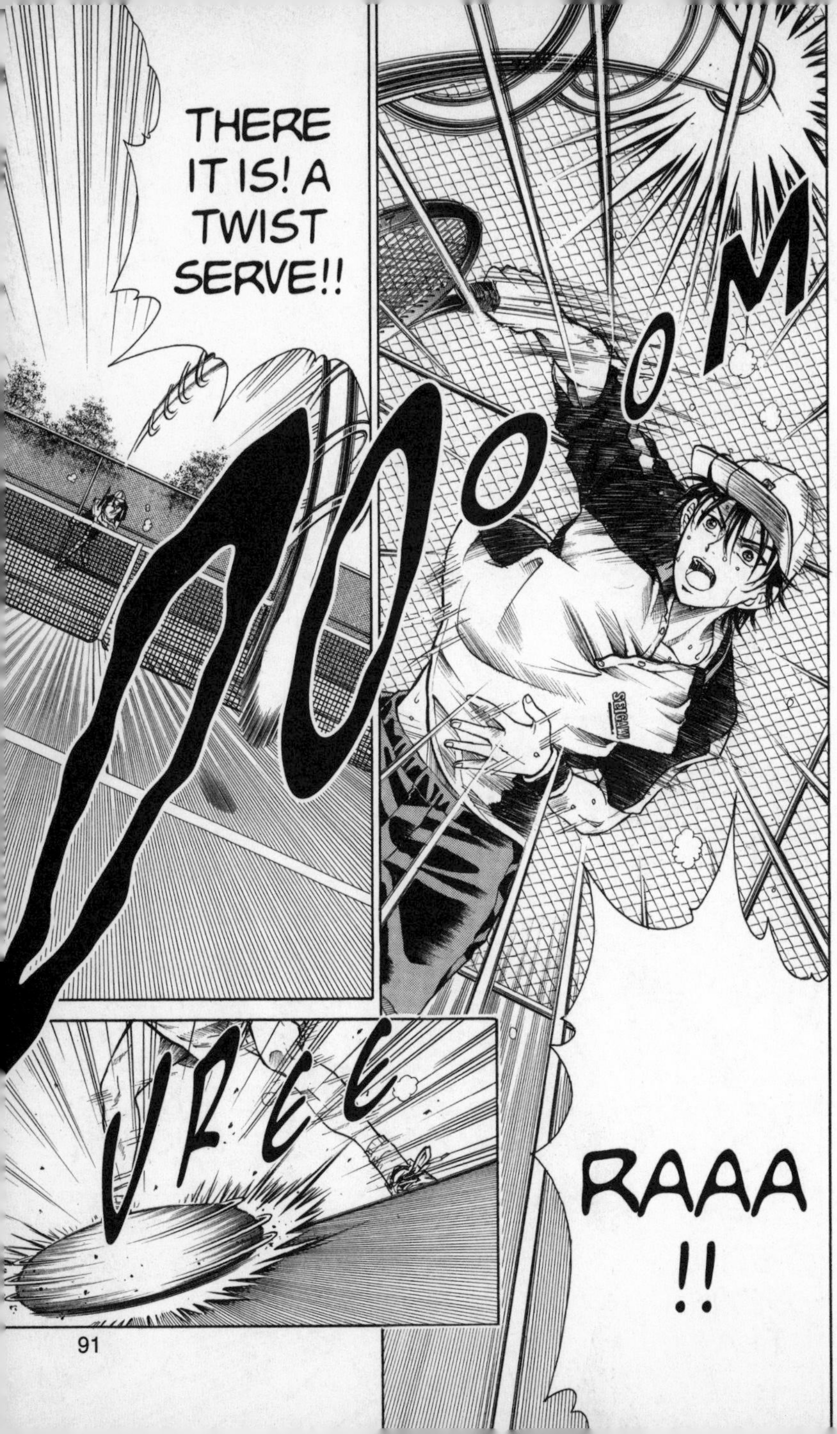
THERE IT IS! A TWIST SERVE!!
RAAA !!

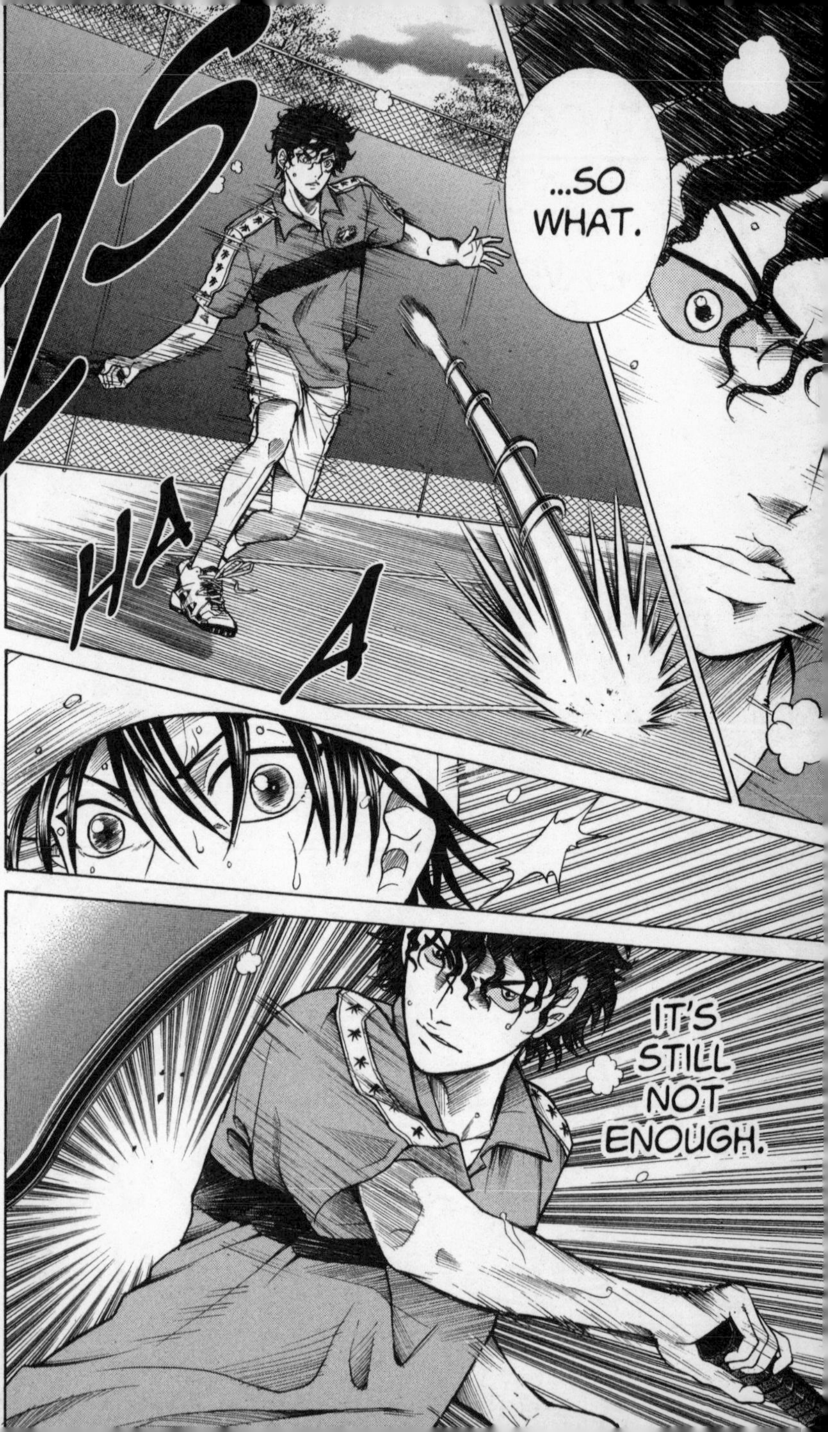
...SO WHAT.
ZS
HA A
IT'S STILL NOT ENOUGH.

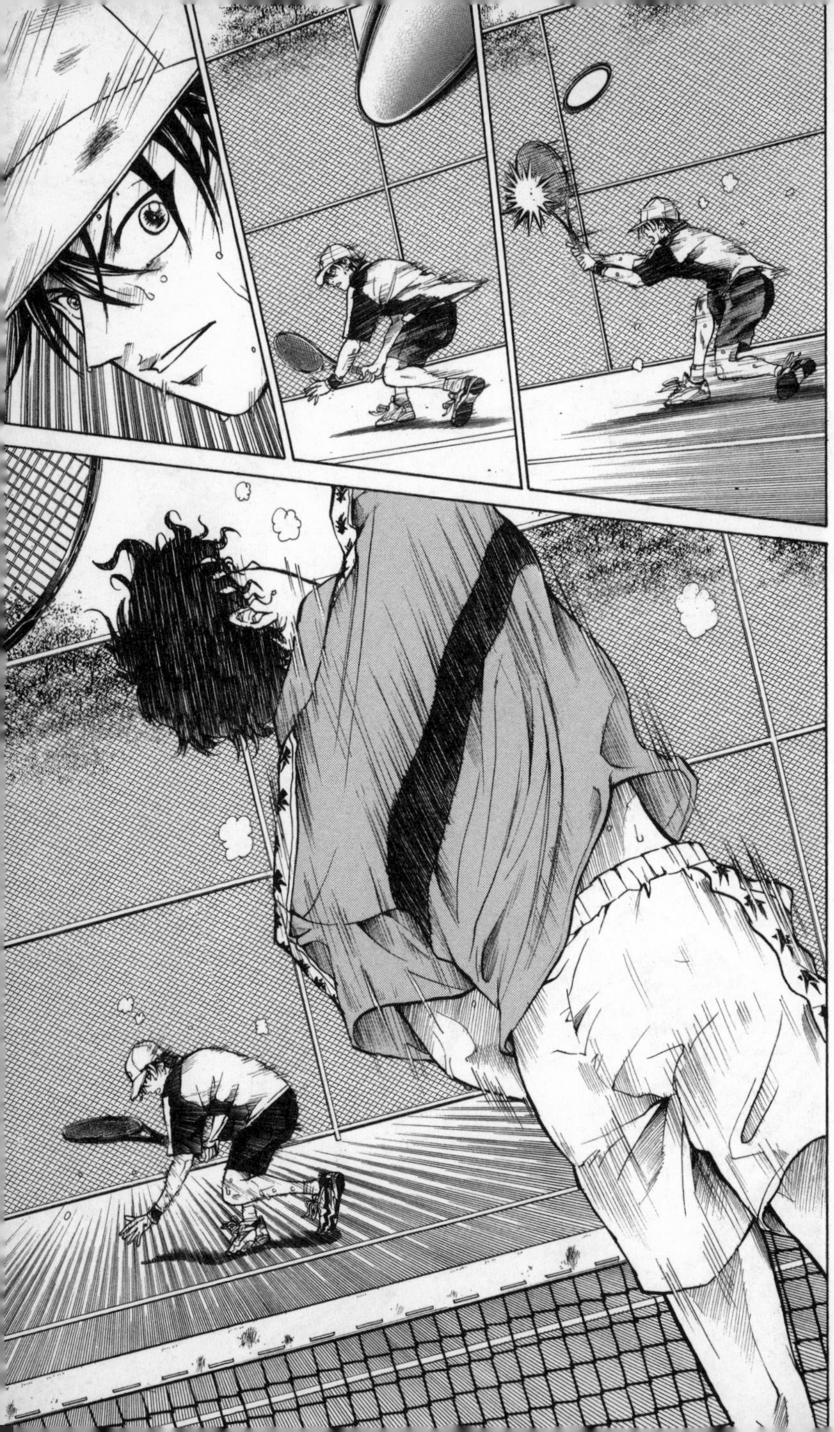

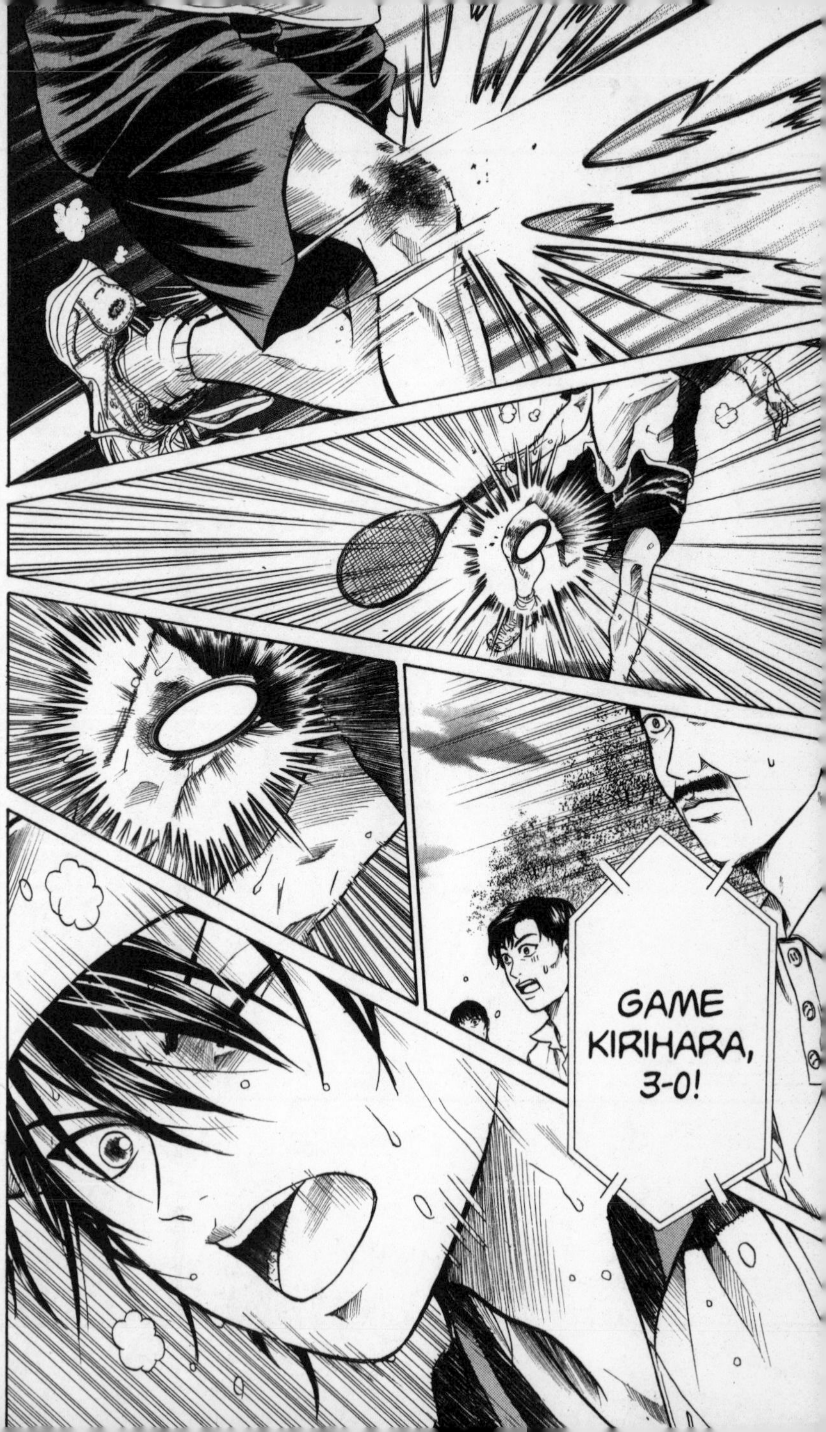
GAME KIRIHARA, 3-0!

READ THIS WAY

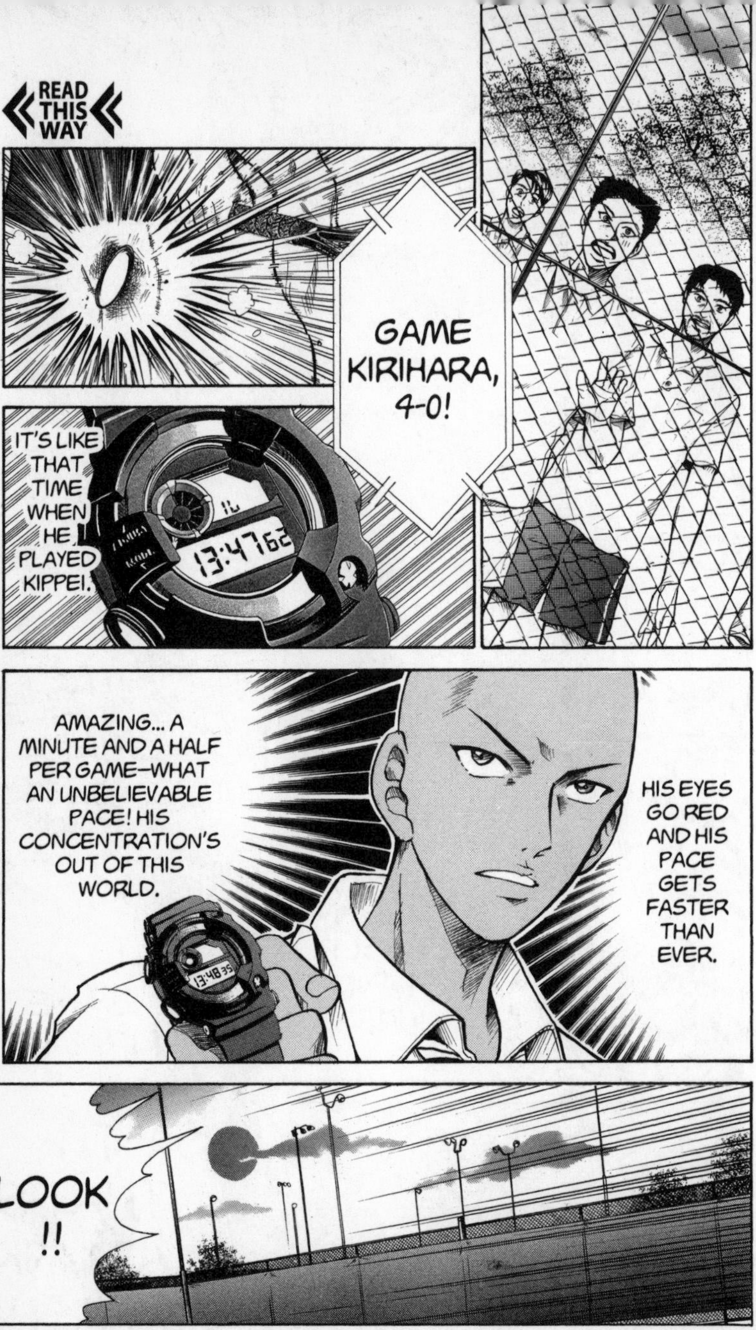
GAME KIRIHARA, 4-0!
IT'S LIKE THAT TIME WHEN HE PLAYED KIPPEI.
HIS EYES GO RED AND HIS PACE GETS FASTER THAN EVER.
AMAZING... A MINUTE AND A HALF PER GAME–WHAT AN UNBELIEVABLE PACE! HIS CONCENTRATION'S OUT OF THIS WORLD.
LOOK !!

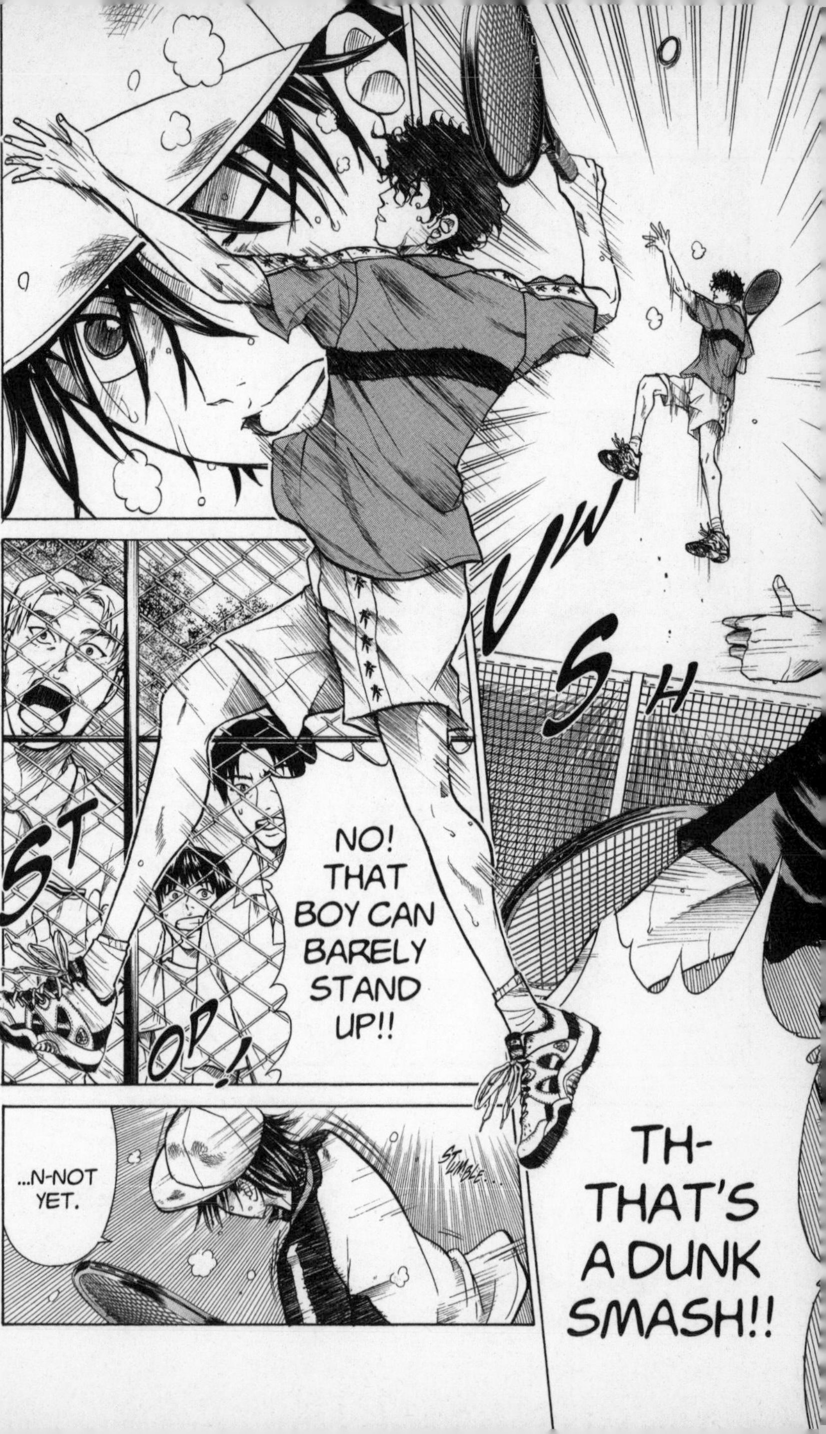
TH- THAT'S A DUNK SMASH!!
NO! THAT BOY CAN BARELY STAND UP!!
STOP!!
STUMBLE...
...N-NOT YET.

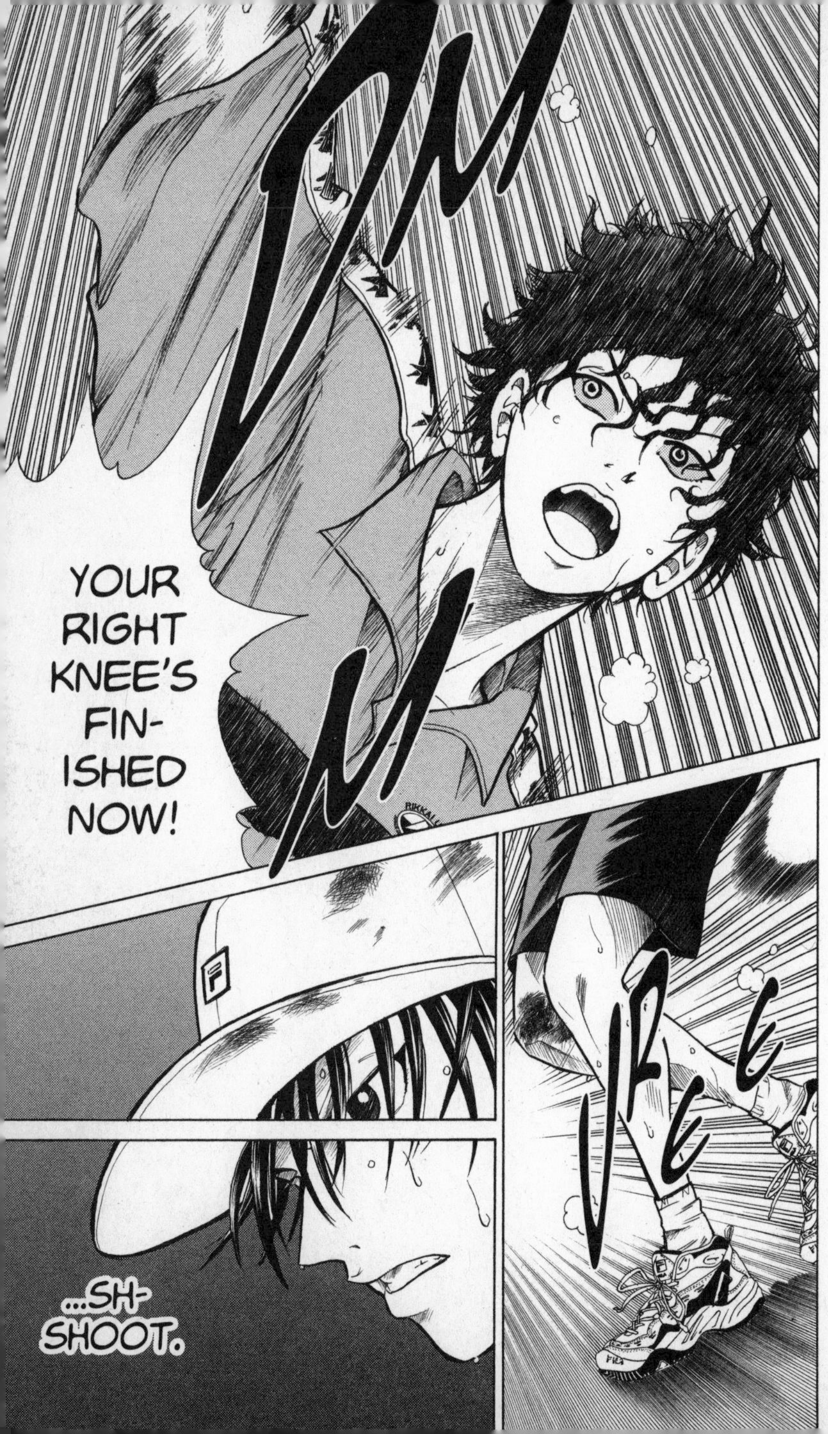
YOUR RIGHT KNEE'S FIN-ISHED NOW!
...SH-SHOOT.

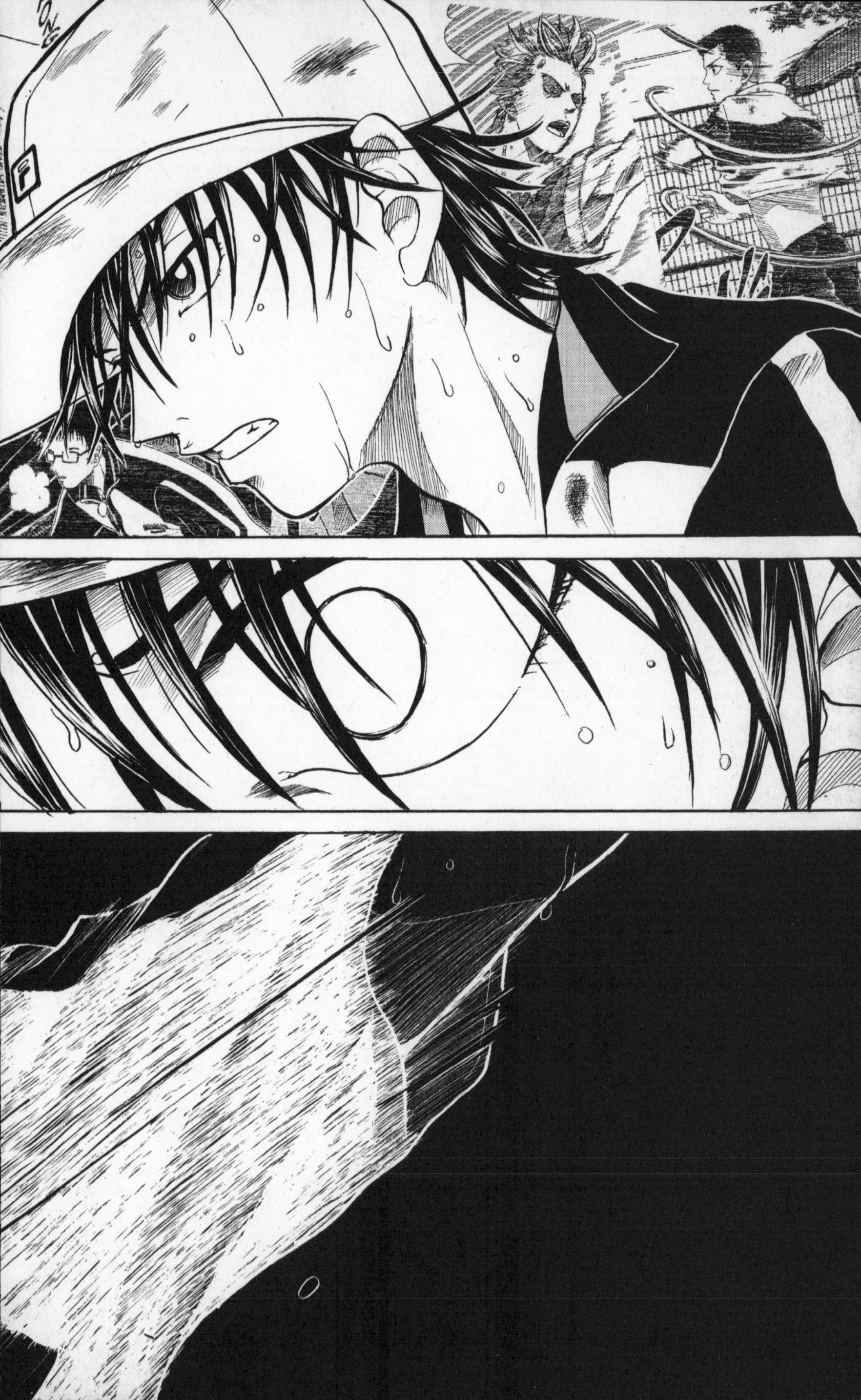

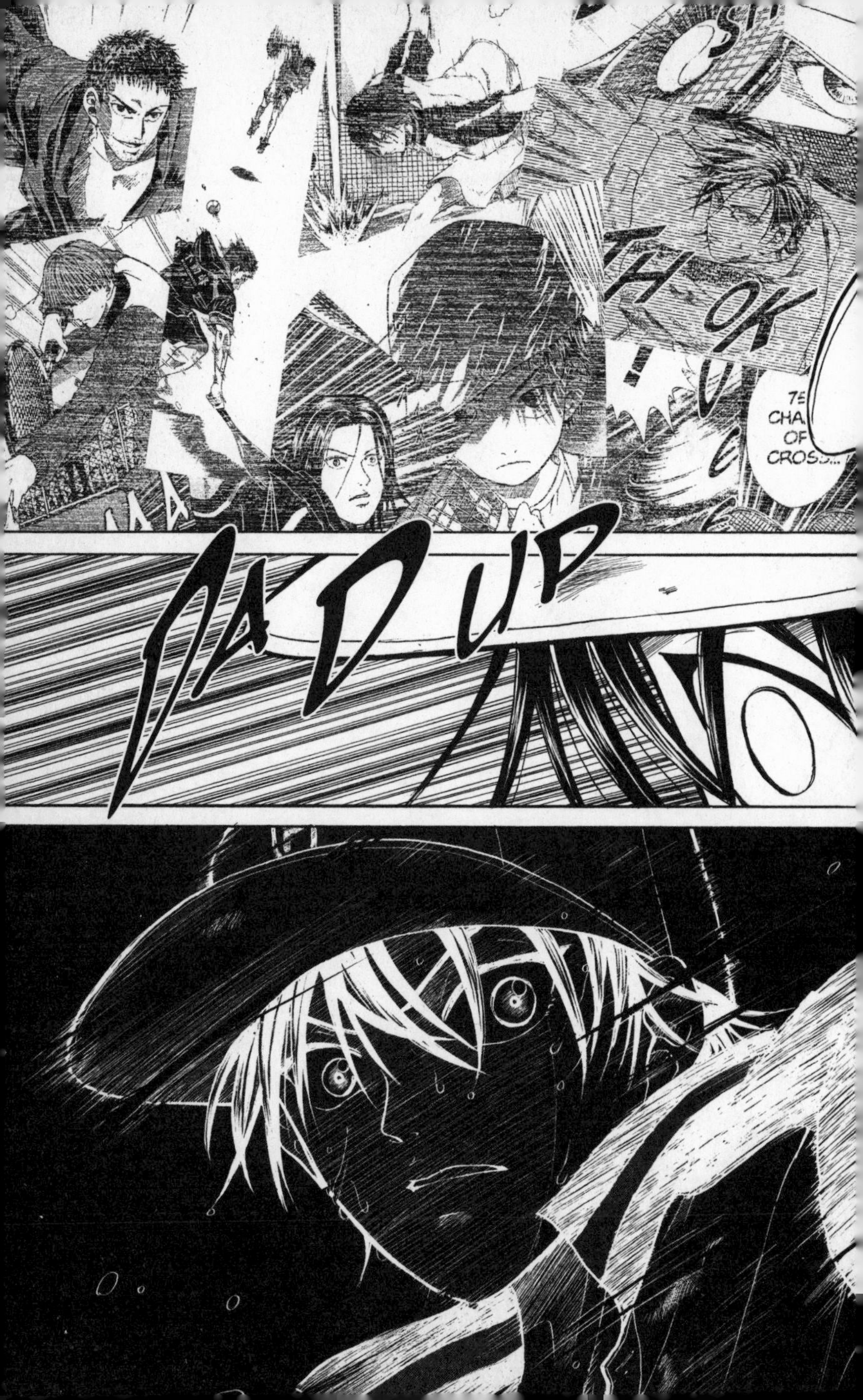
THOK!
75
CHA
OF
CROSS...
DA DUP

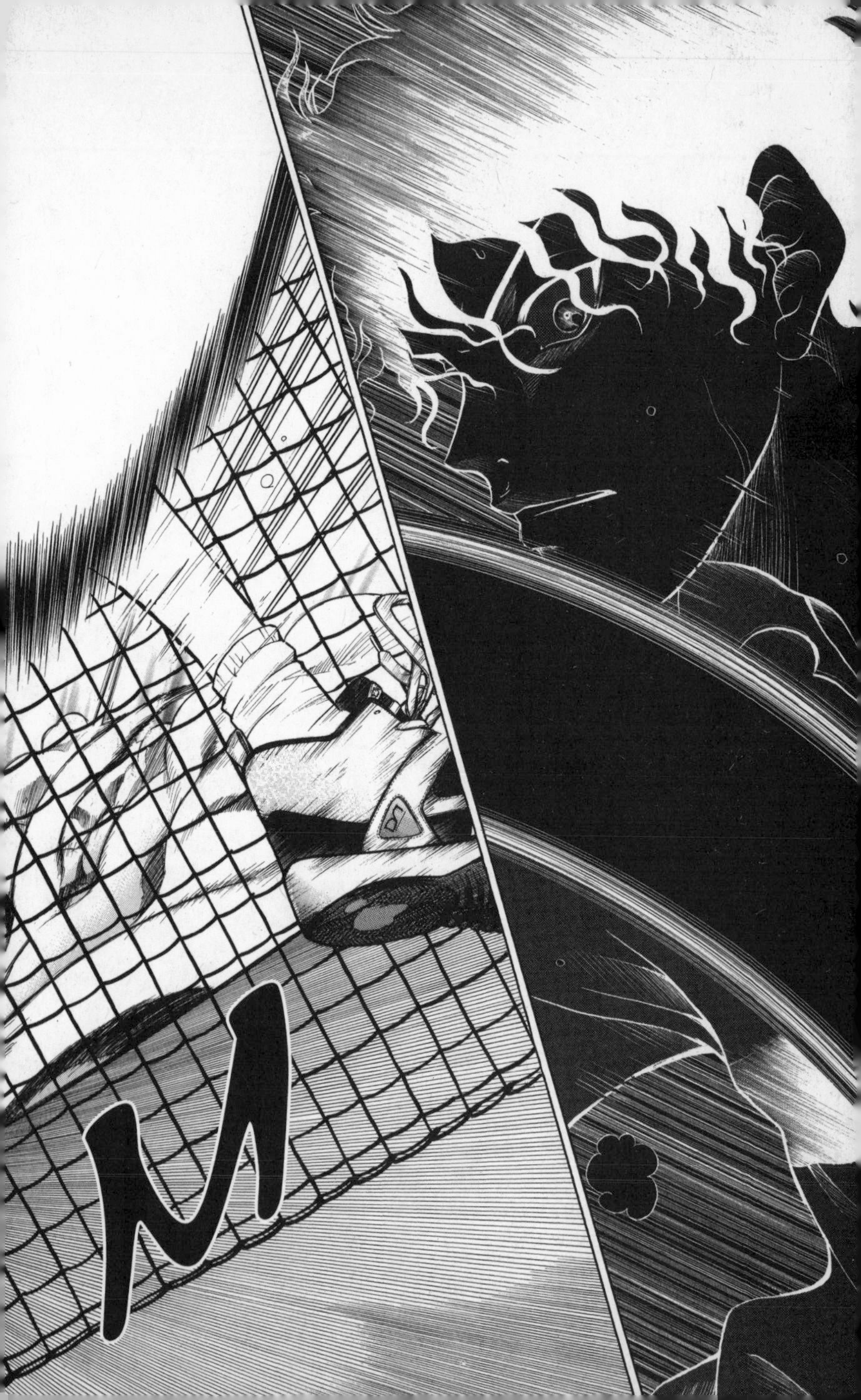
M

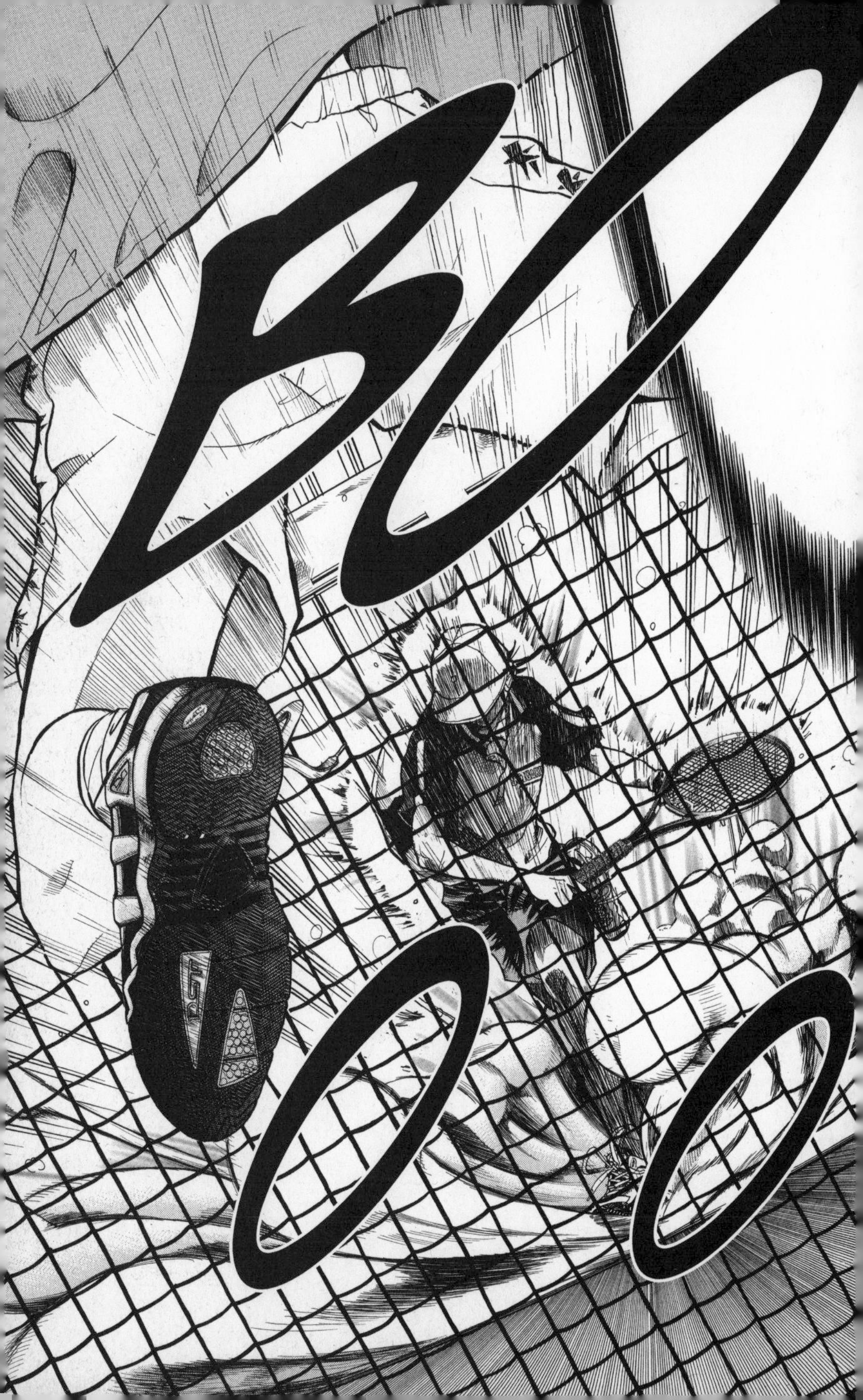
BOOO

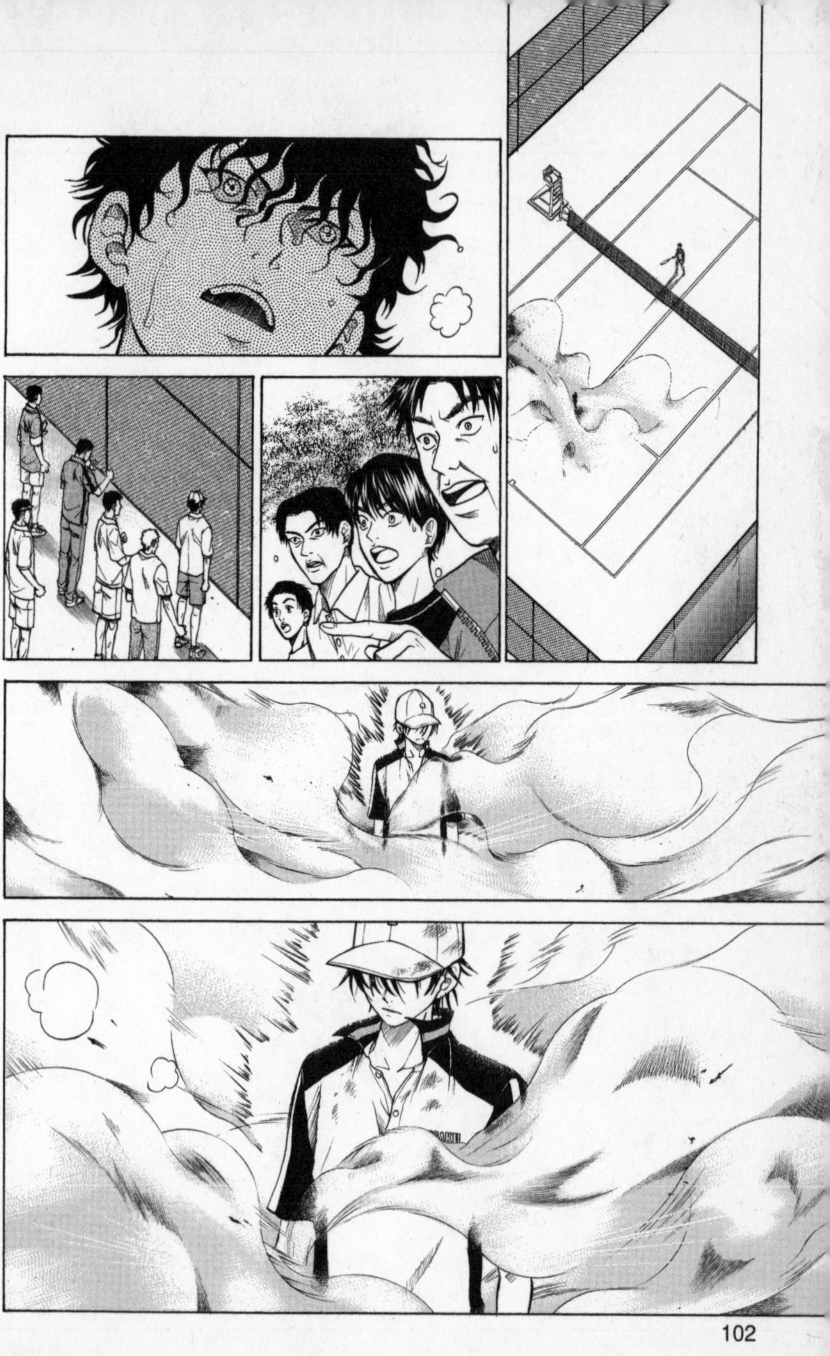

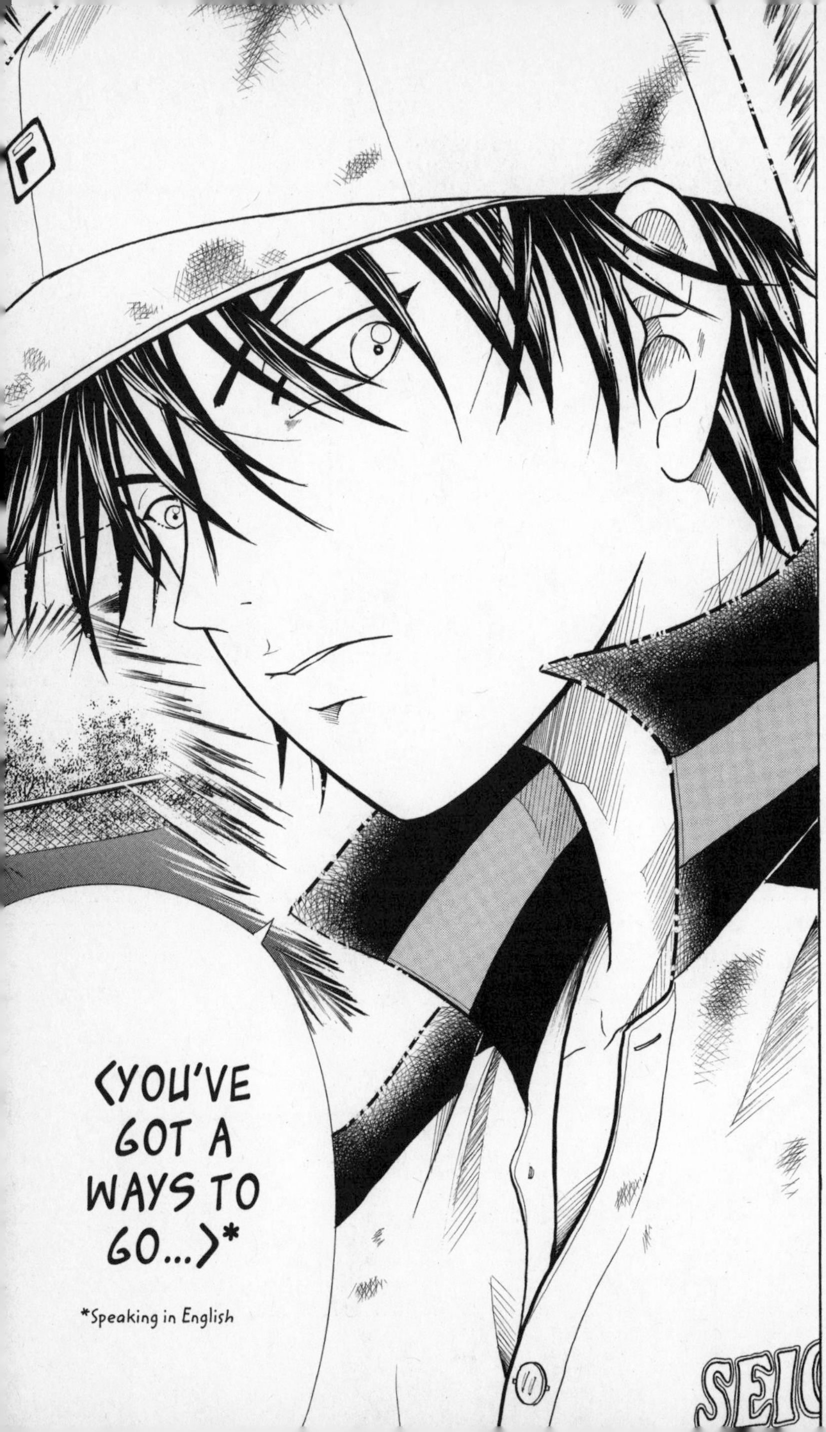
<YOU'VE GOT A WAYS TO GO...>*
*Speaking in English

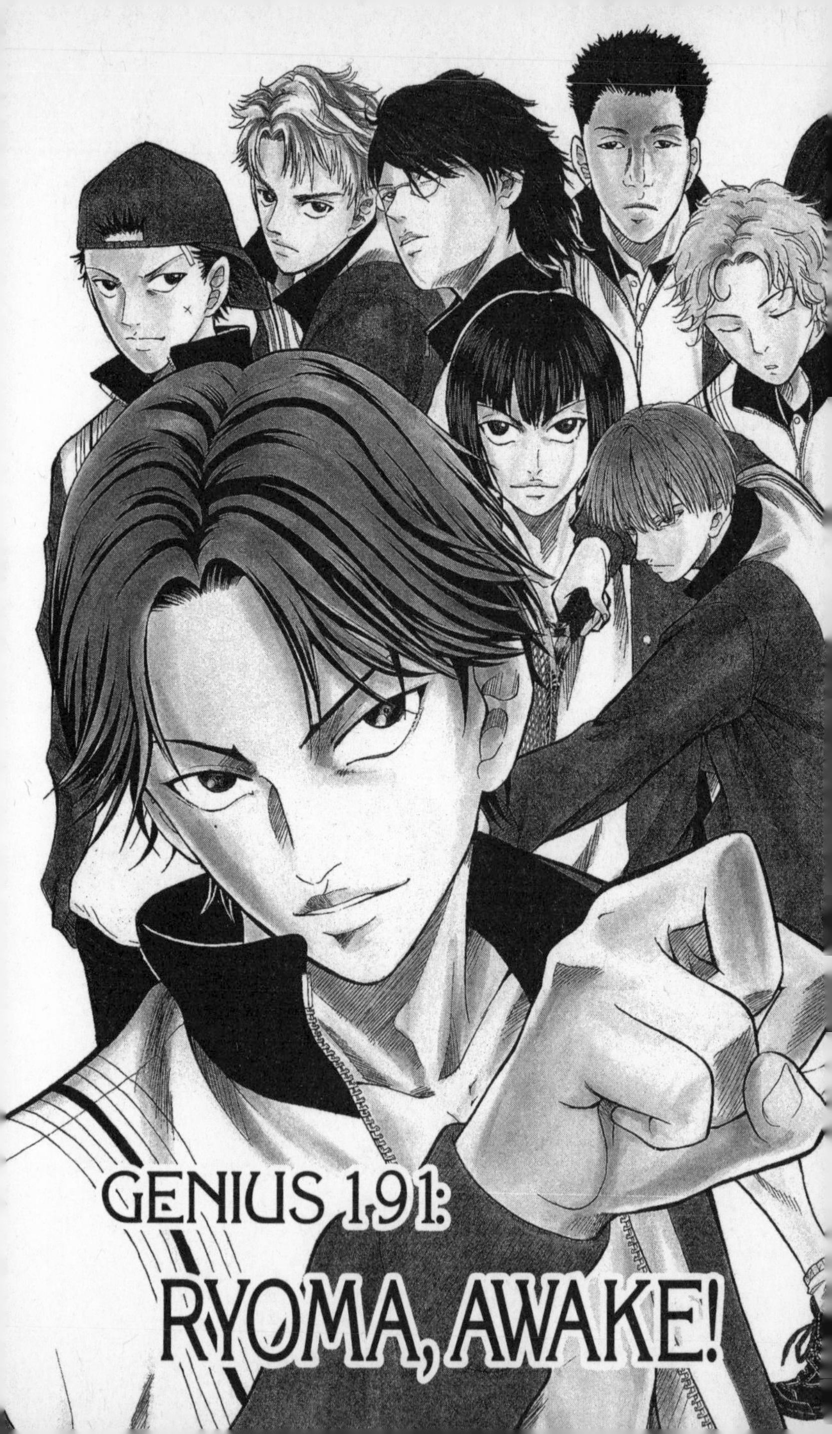
GENIUS 191:
RYOMA, AWAKE!

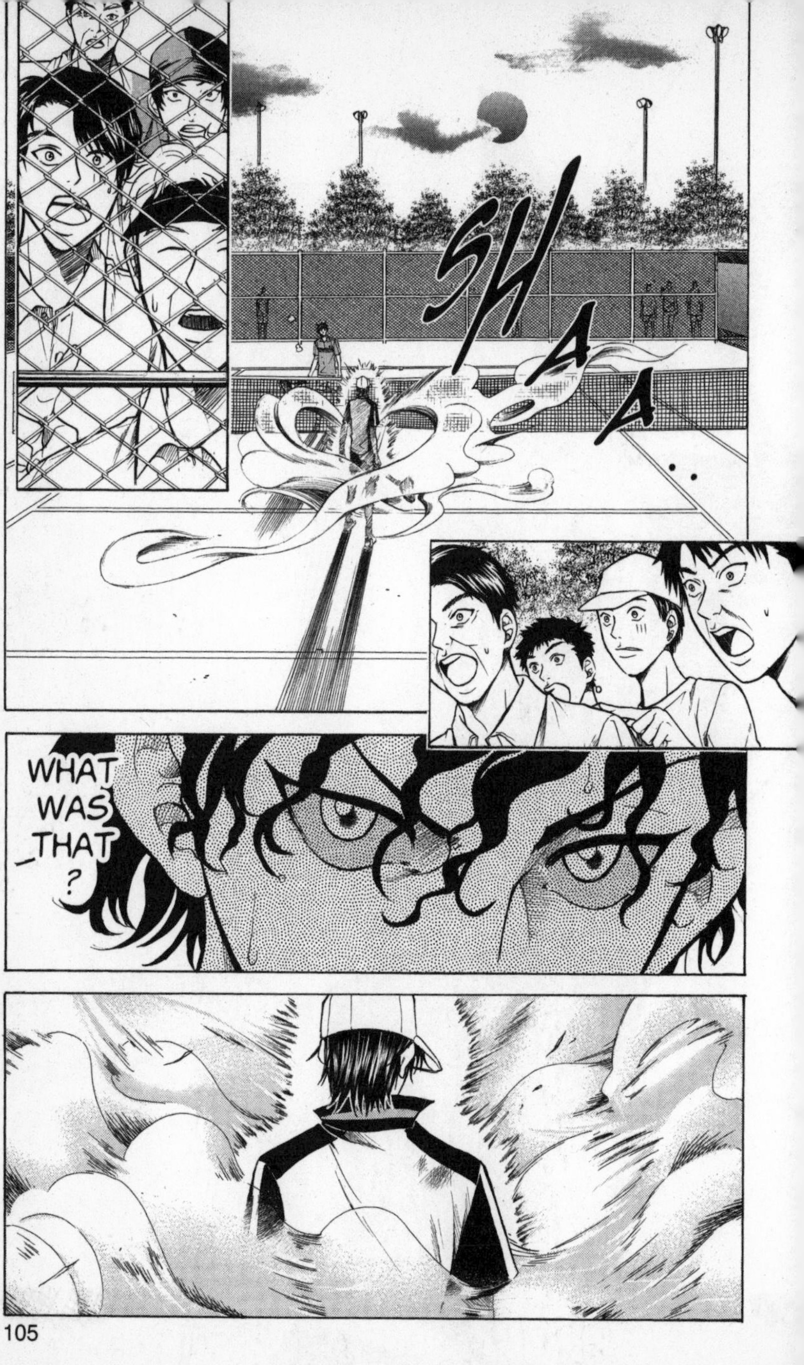
SHAA..
WHAT WAS THAT?

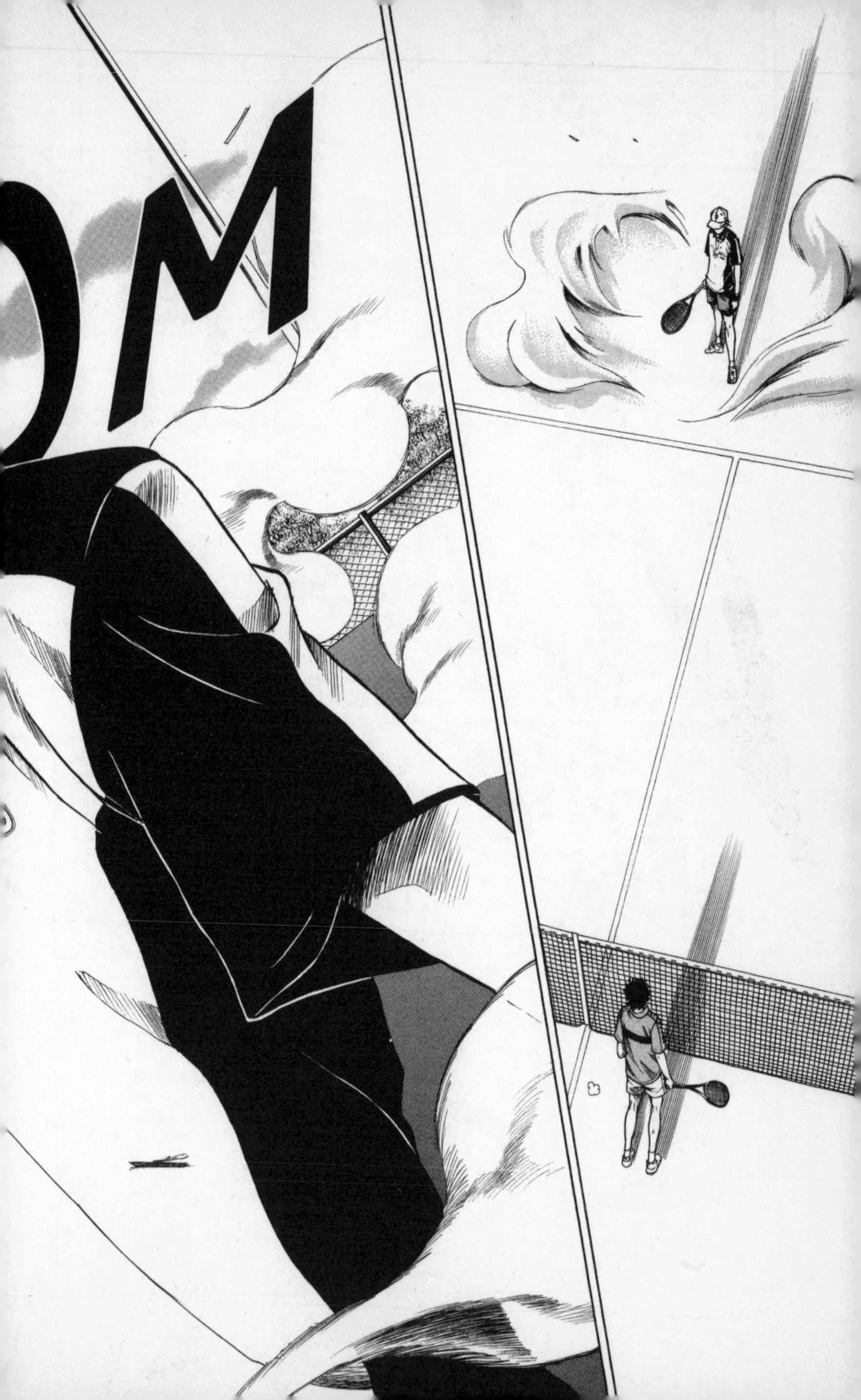
OM

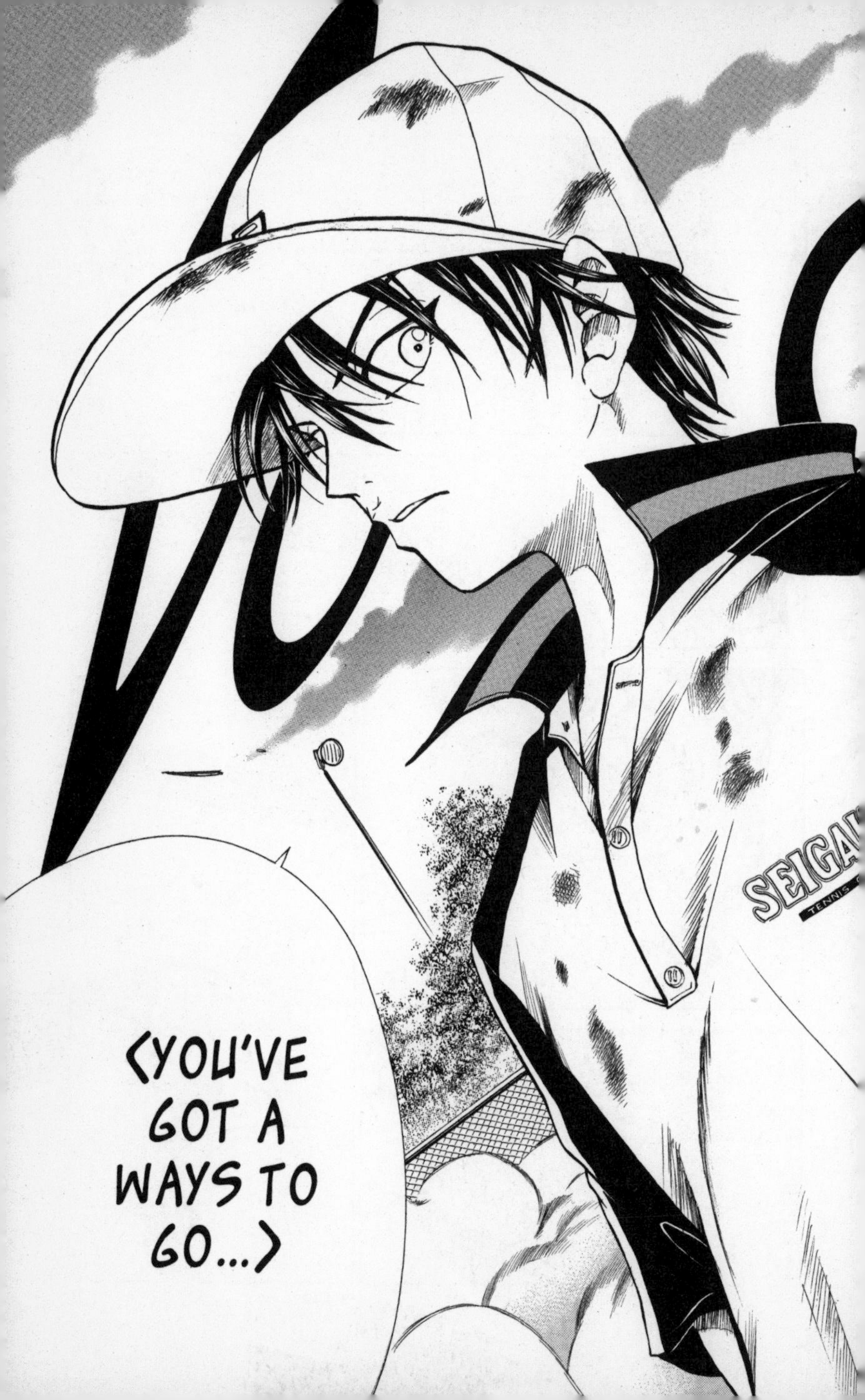
<YOU'VE GOT A WAYS TO GO...>

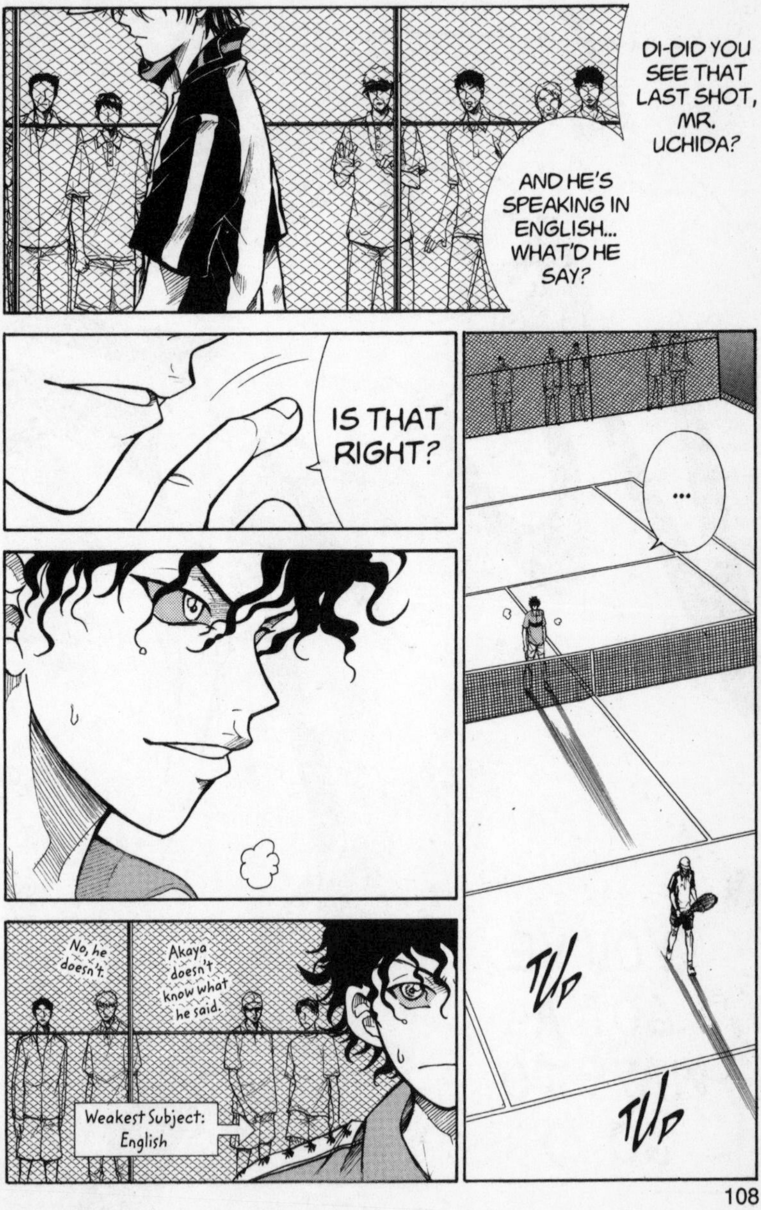
DI-DID YOU SEE THAT LAST SHOT, MR. UCHIDA?
AND HE'S SPEAKING IN ENGLISH... WHAT'D HE SAY?
...
TUD
TUD
IS THAT RIGHT?
Akaya doesn't know what he said.
No, he doesn't.
Weakest Subject: English

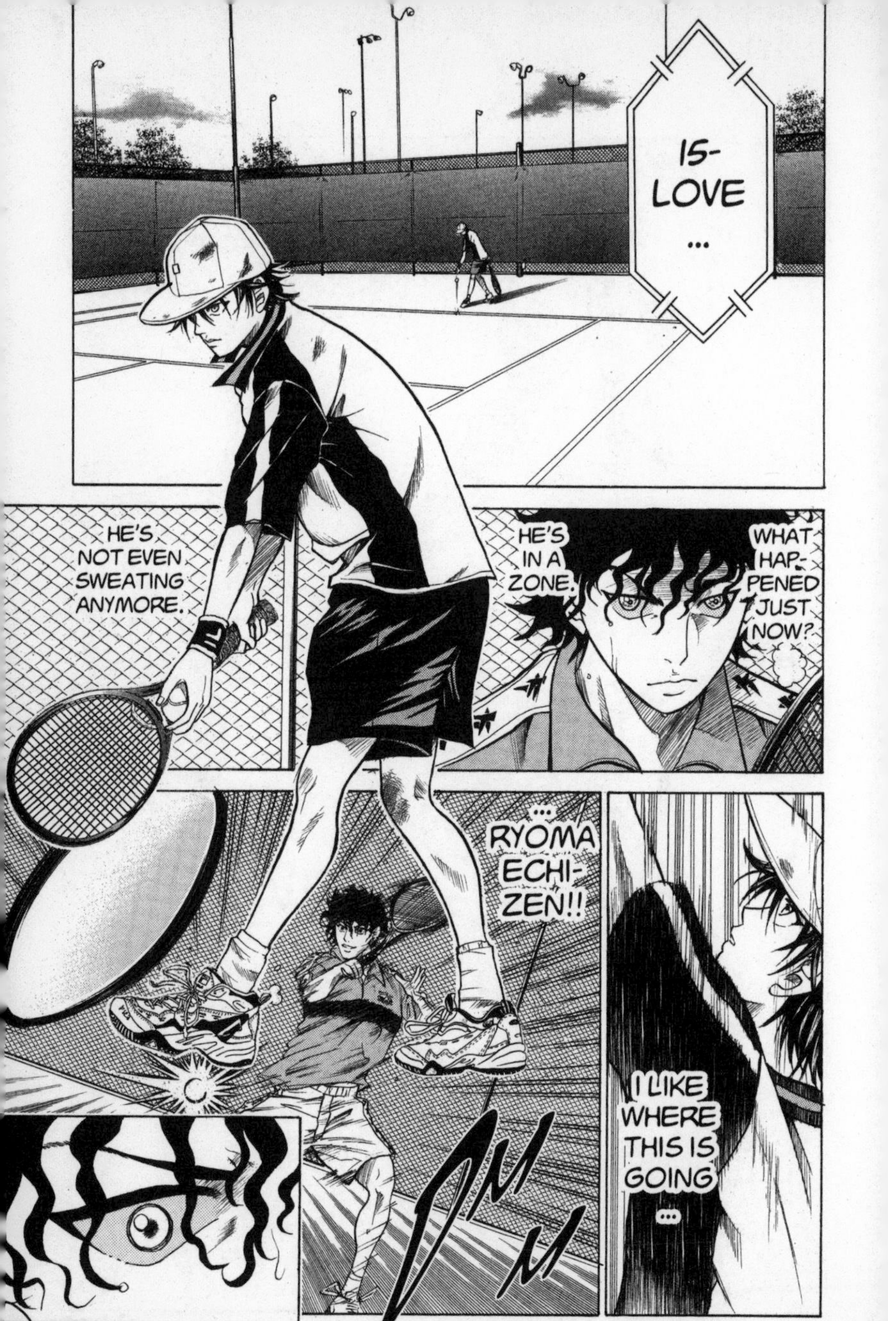
15-LOVE ...
WHAT HAPPENED JUST NOW?
HE'S IN A ZONE.
HE'S NOT EVEN SWEATING ANYMORE.
I LIKE WHERE THIS IS GOING ...
... RYOMA ECHIZEN!!

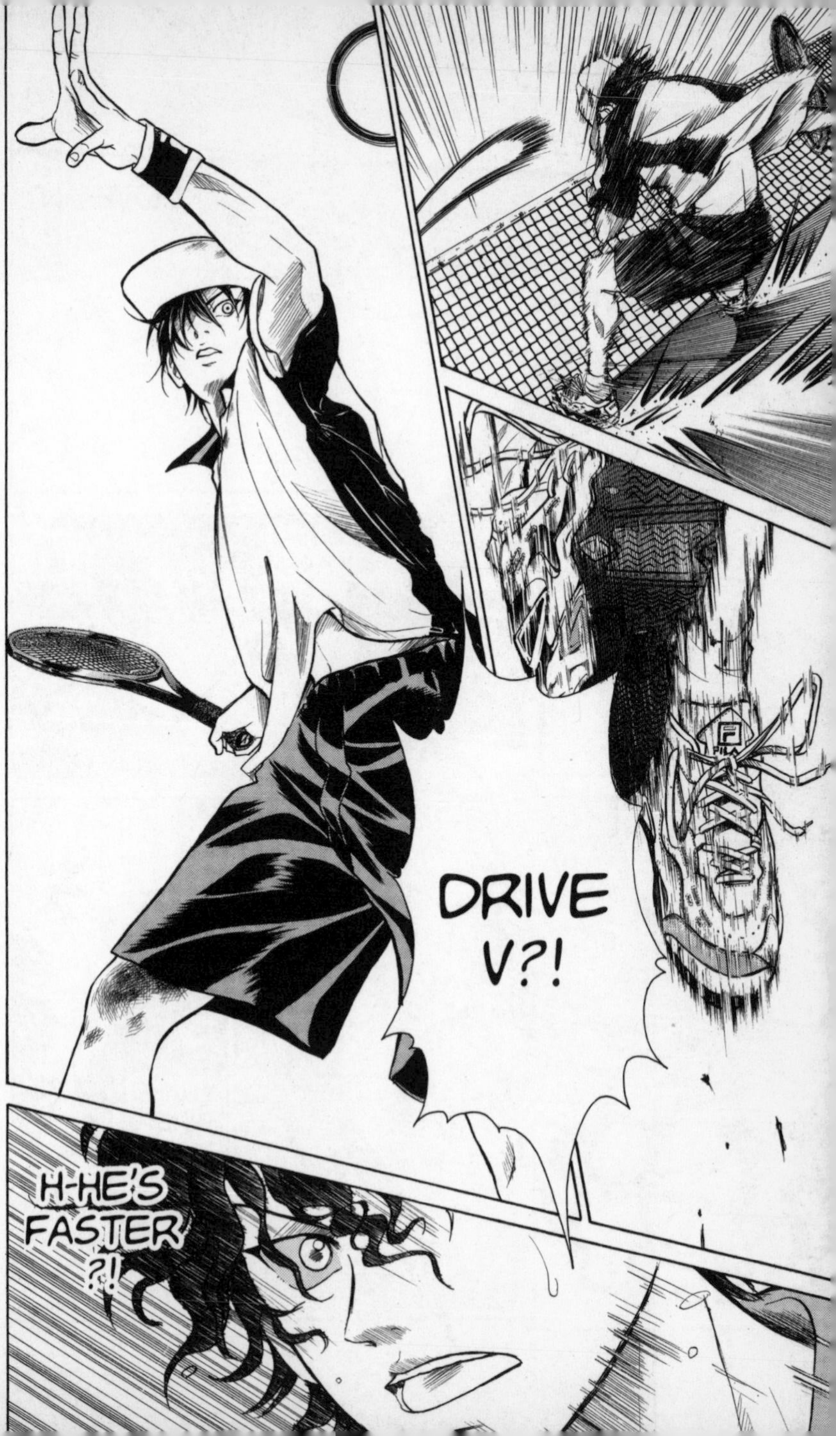
DRIVE V?!
H-HE'S FASTER ?!

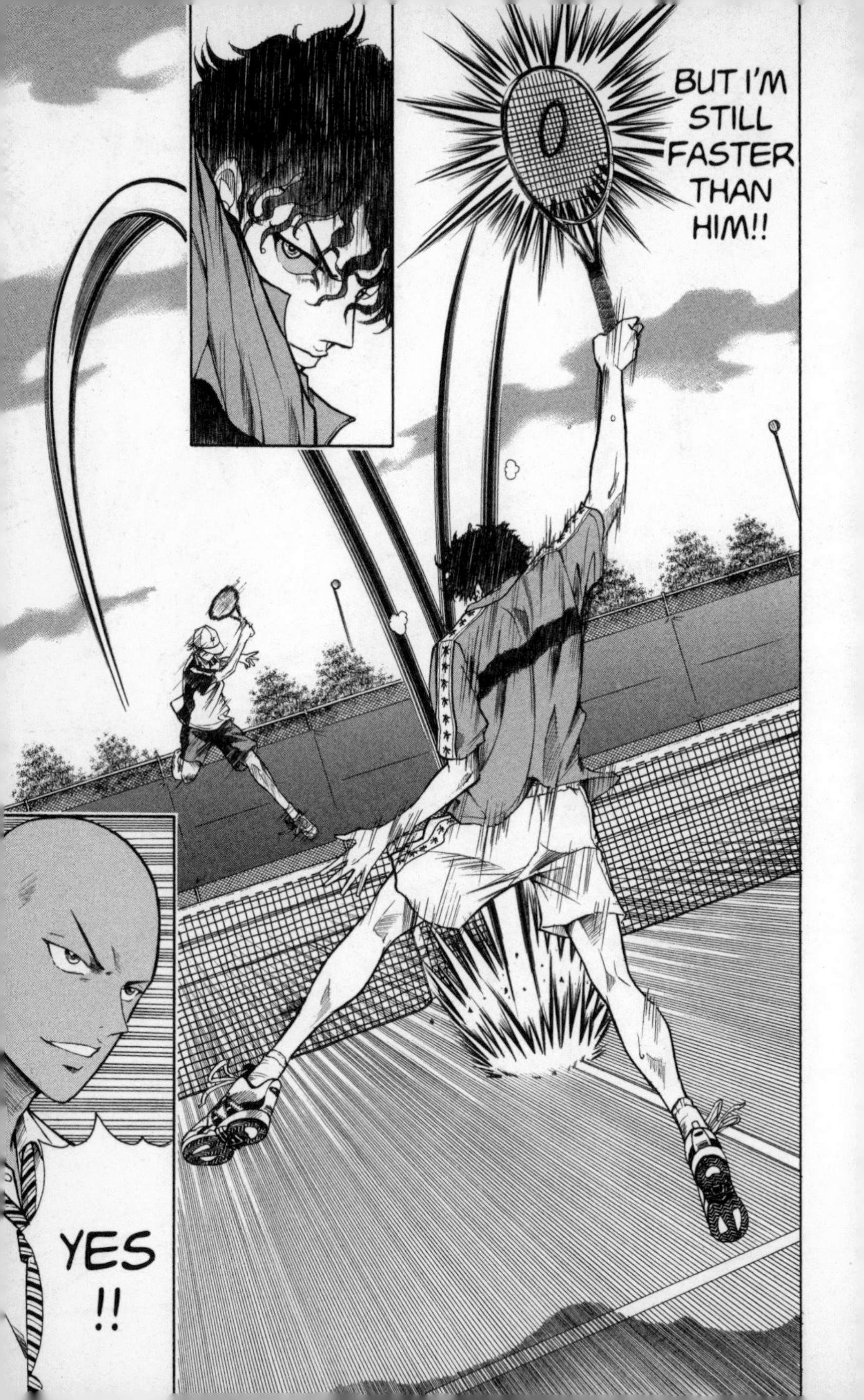
BUT I'M STILL FASTER THAN HIM!!
YES !!

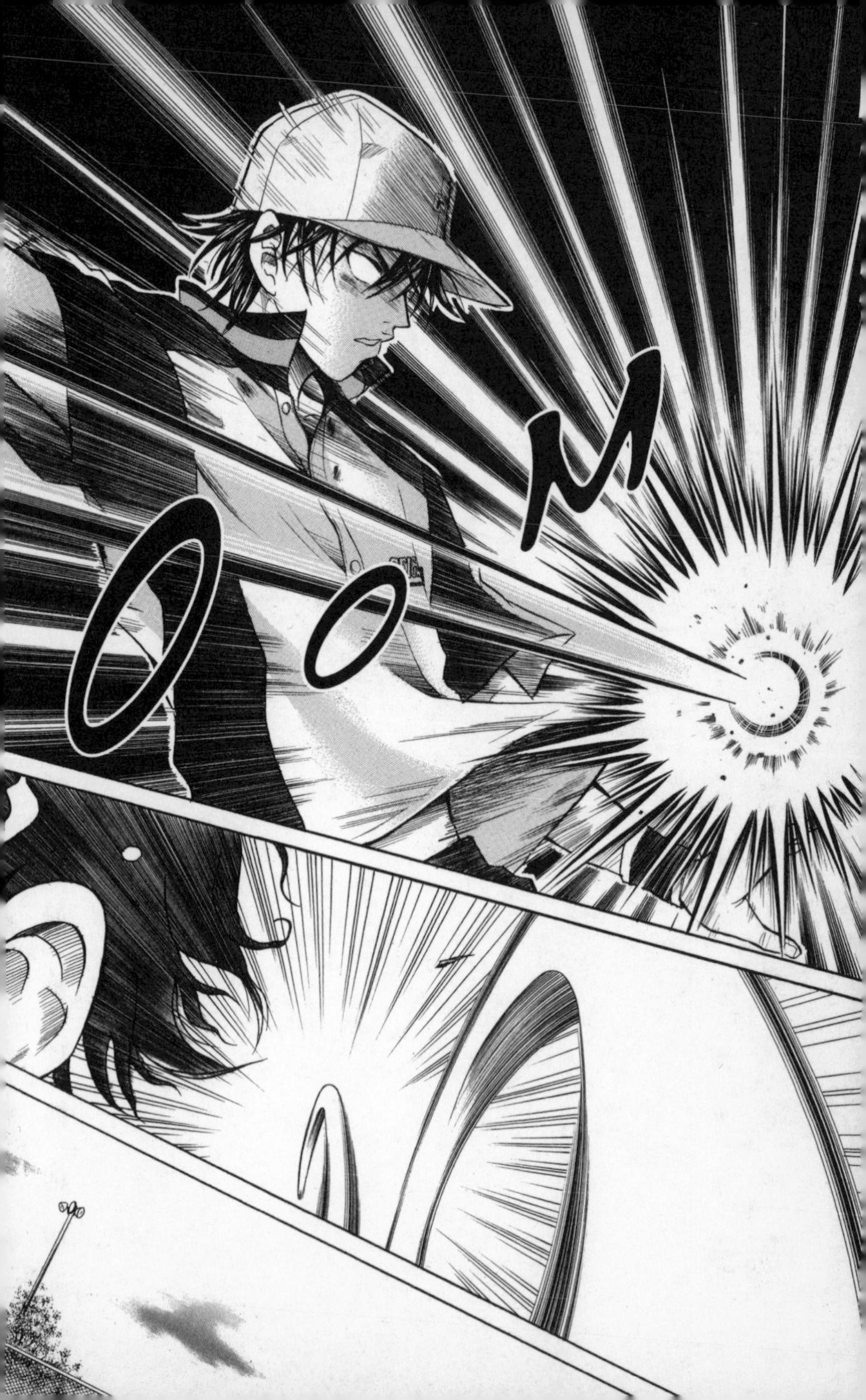
OOM

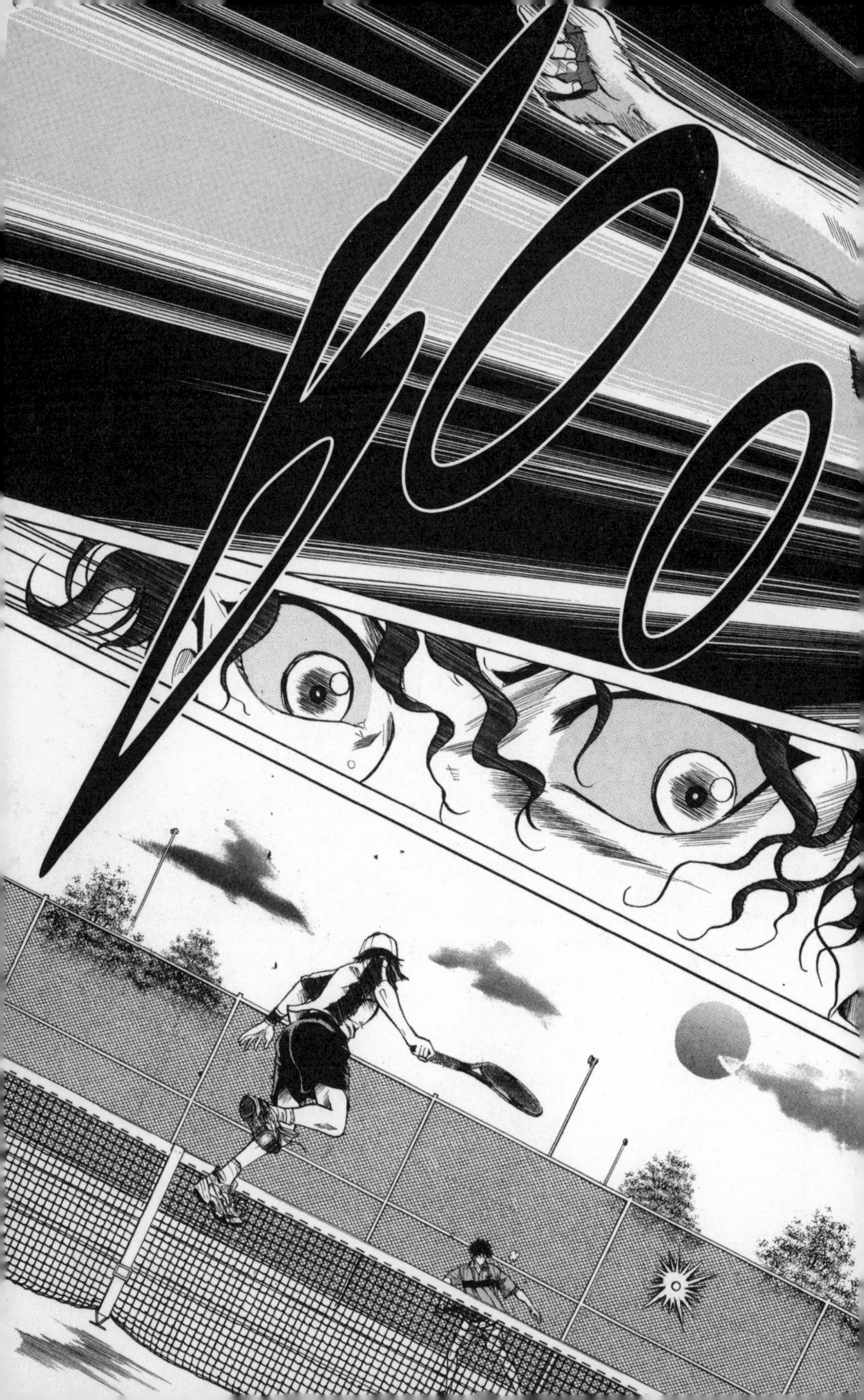

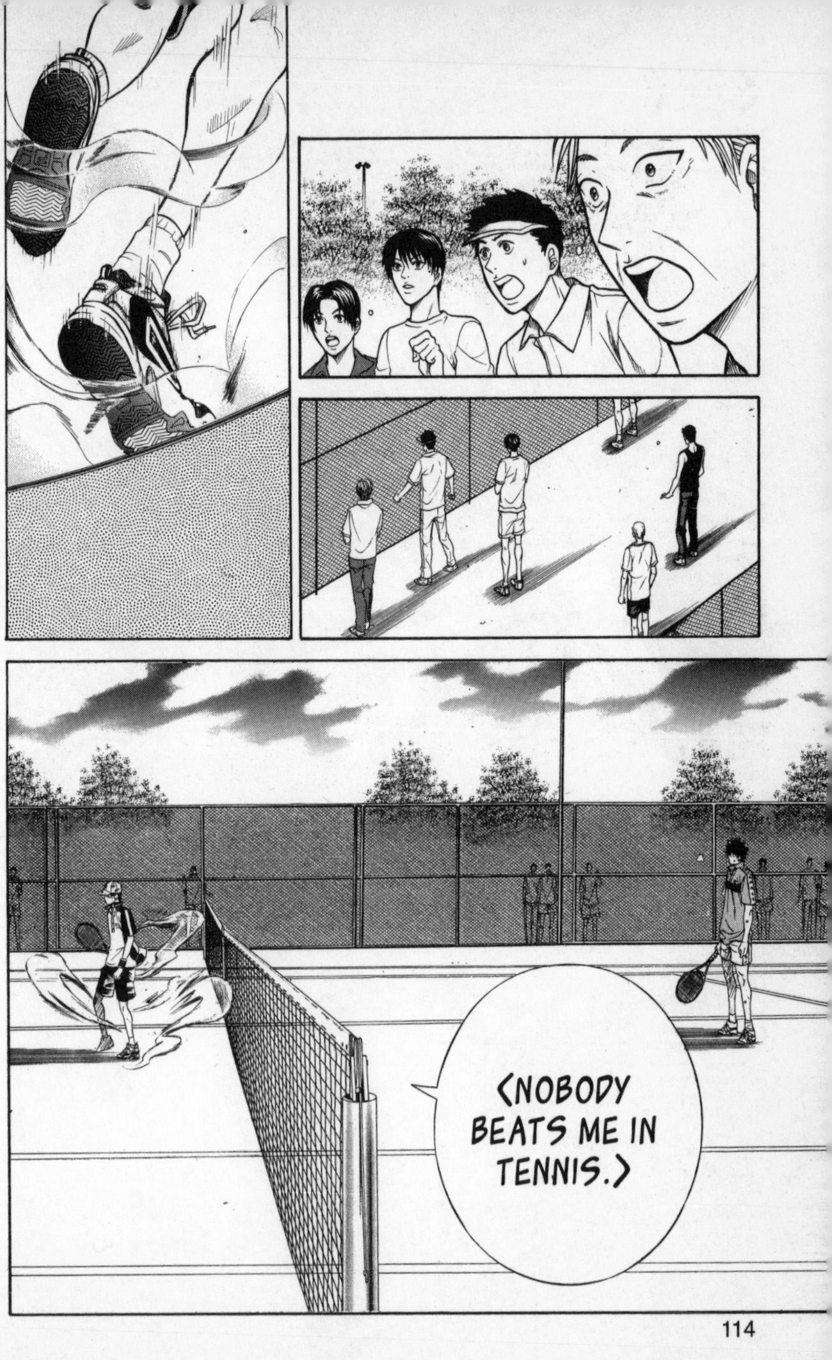
<NOBODY BEATS ME IN TENNIS.>

READ THIS WAY

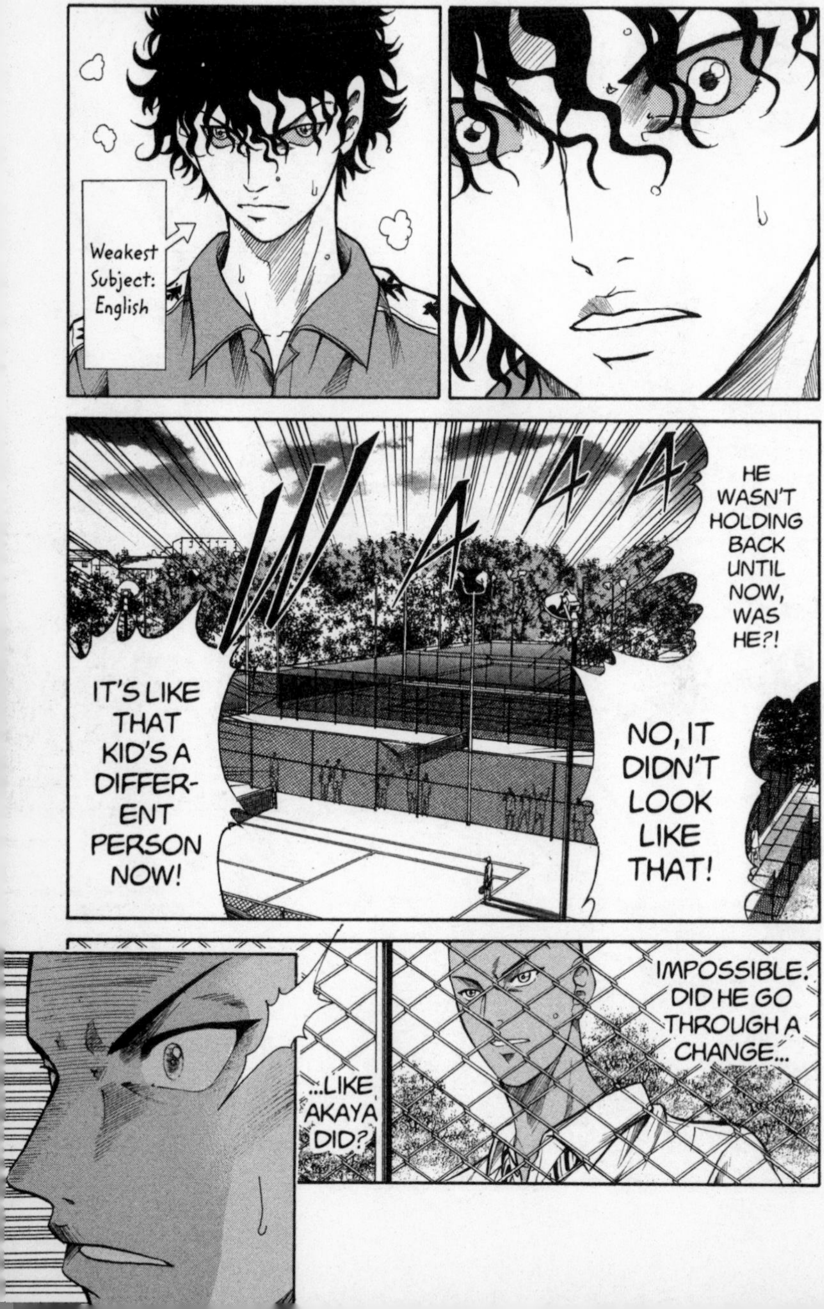
Weakest Subject: English
HE WASN'T HOLDING BACK UNTIL NOW, WAS HE?!
WAAA
NO, IT DIDN'T LOOK LIKE THAT!
IT'S LIKE THAT KID'S A DIFFERENT PERSON NOW!
IMPOSSIBLE. DID HE GO THROUGH A CHANGE...
...LIKE AKAYA DID?

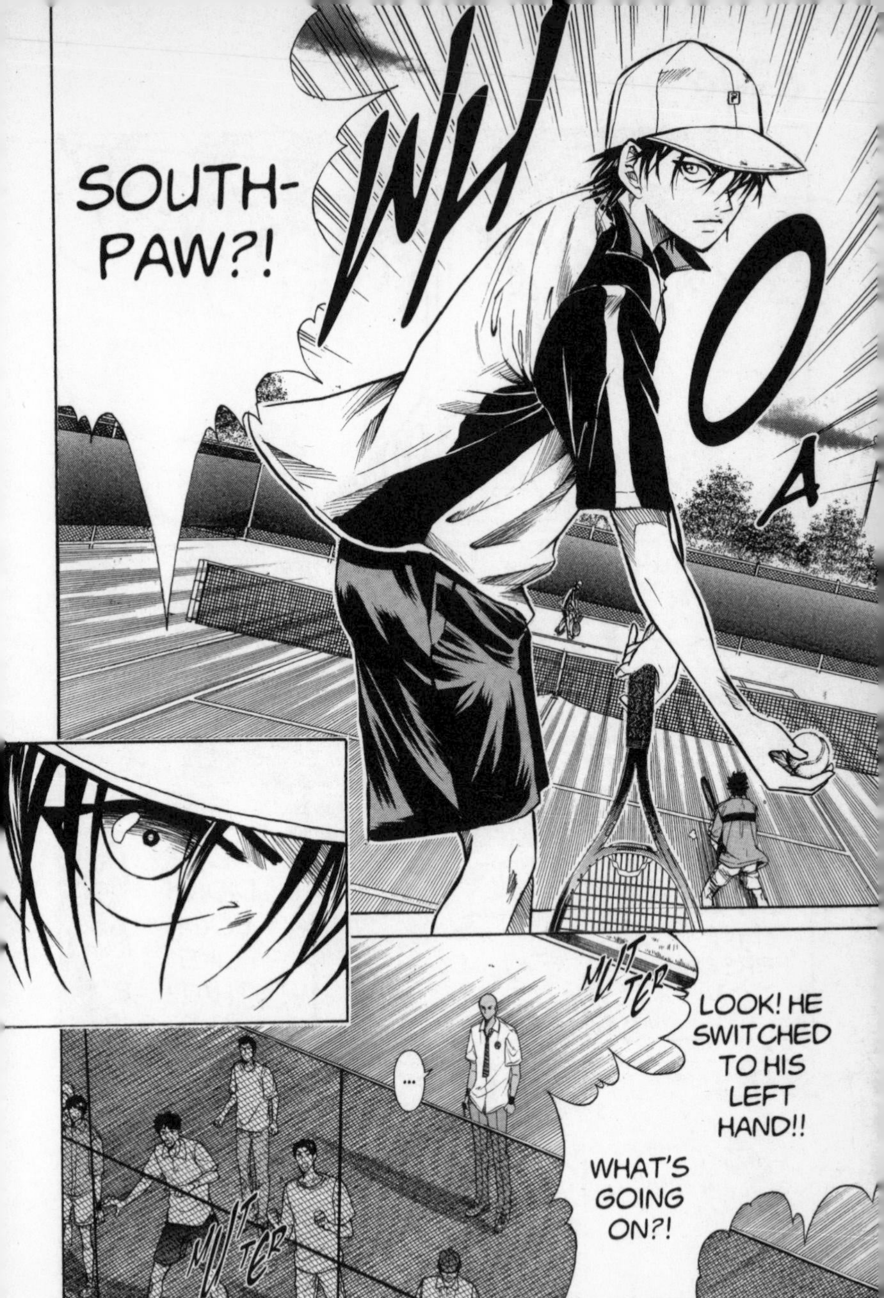
WHOA
SOUTH-PAW?!
MUTTER
LOOK! HE SWITCHED TO HIS LEFT HAND!!
WHAT'S GOING ON?!
...
MUTTER

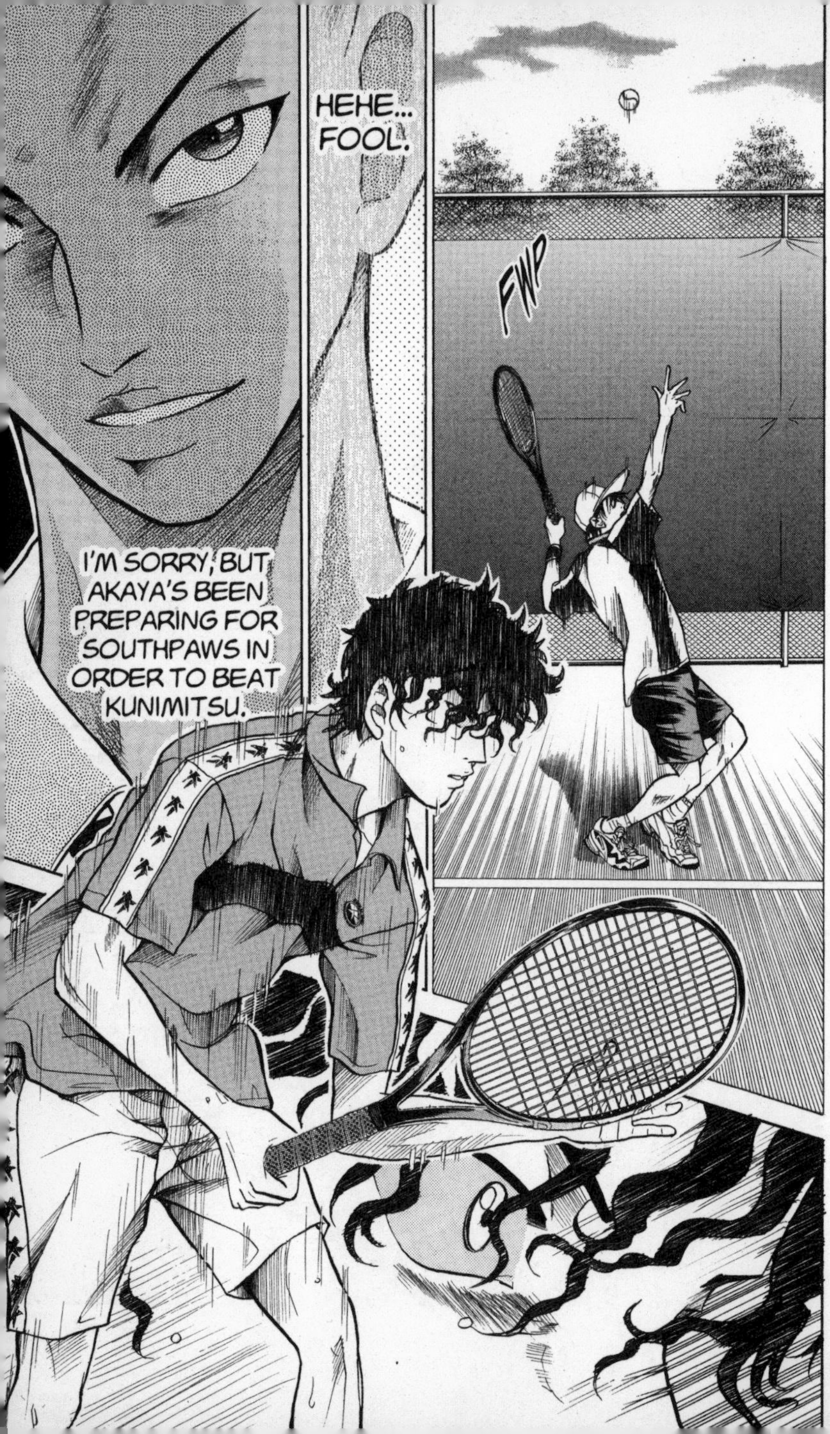
HEHE... FOOL.
FWP
I'M SORRY, BUT AKAYA'S BEEN PREPARING FOR SOUTHPAWS IN ORDER TO BEAT KUNIMITSU.

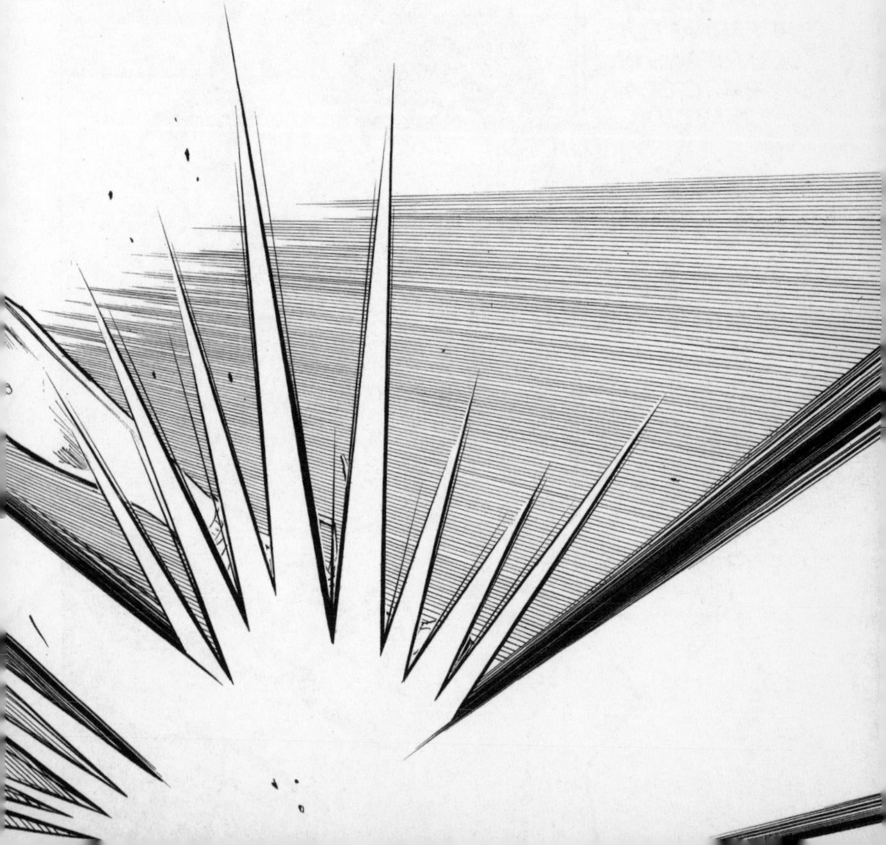

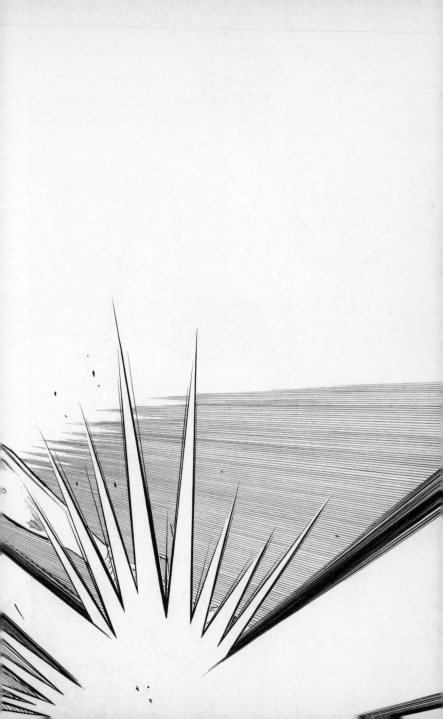

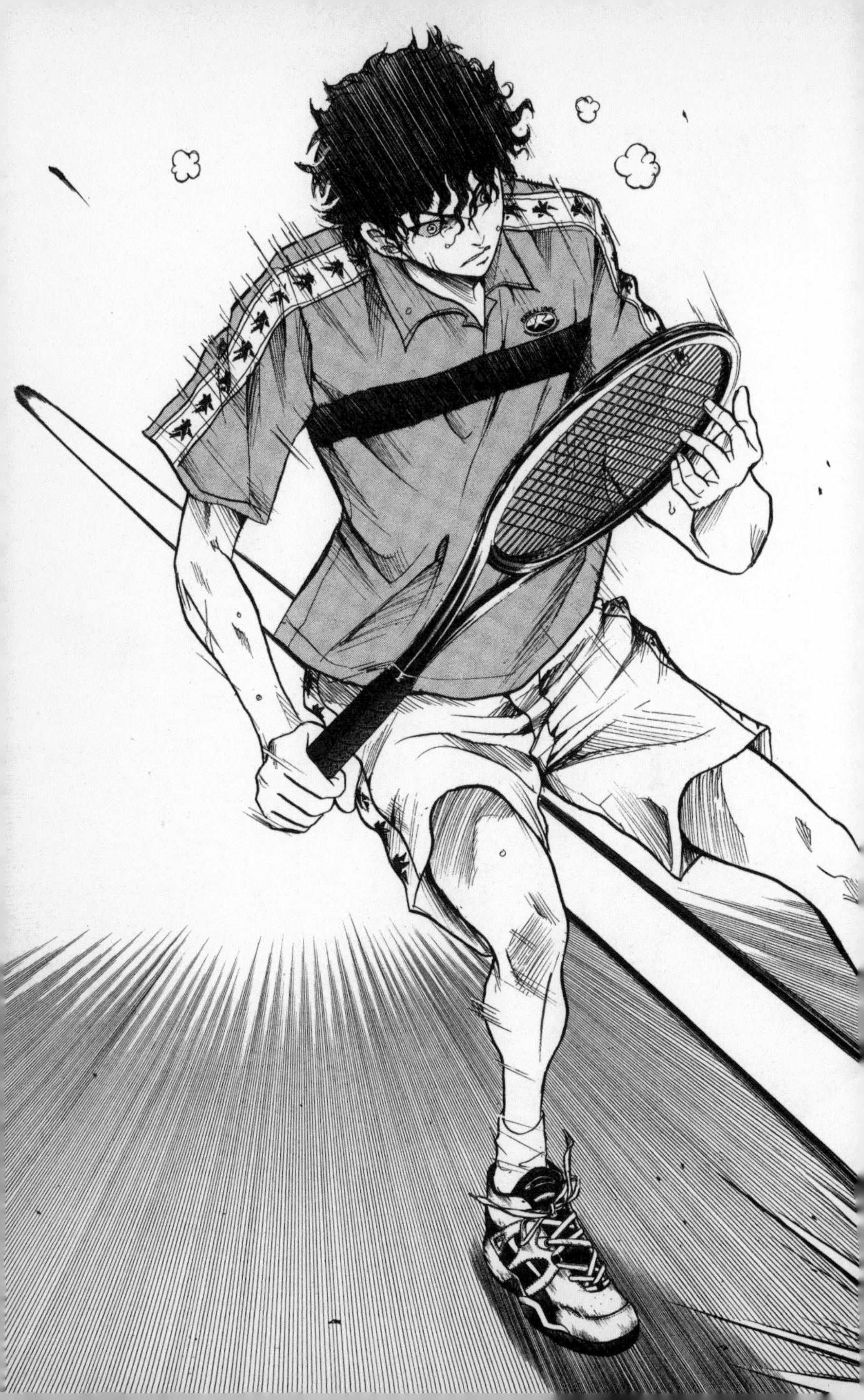

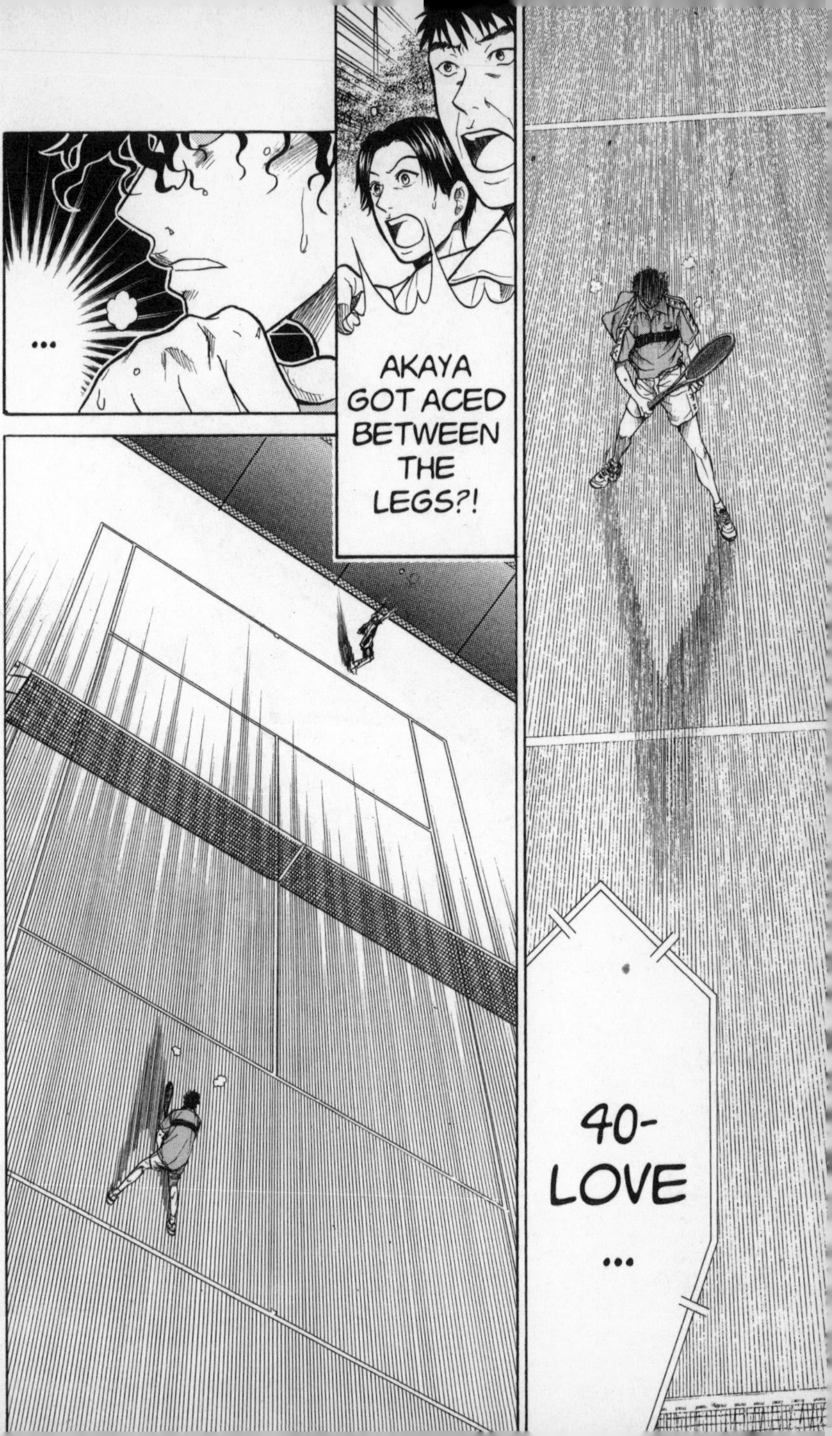
40-
LOVE
...
AKAYA GOT ACED BETWEEN THE LEGS?!
...

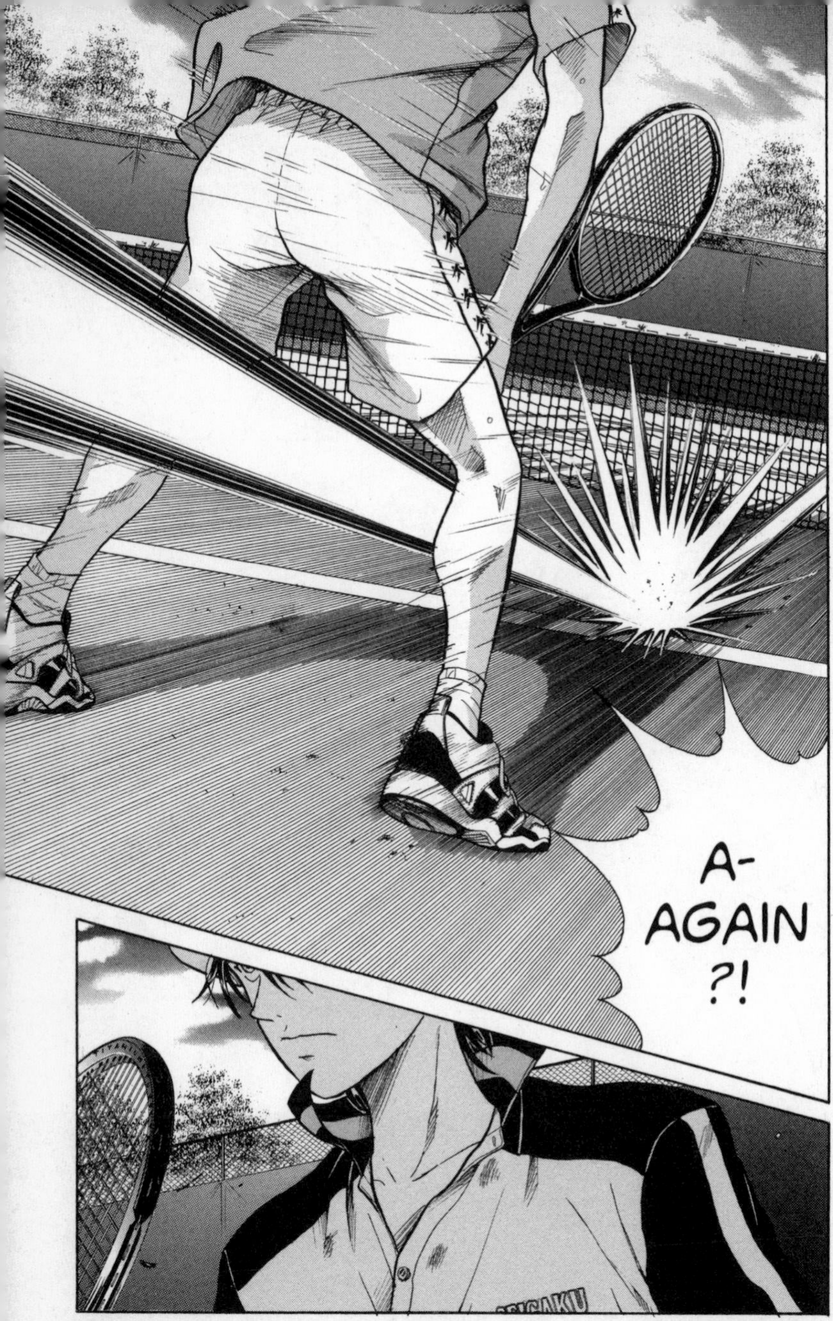
A-
AGAIN
?!

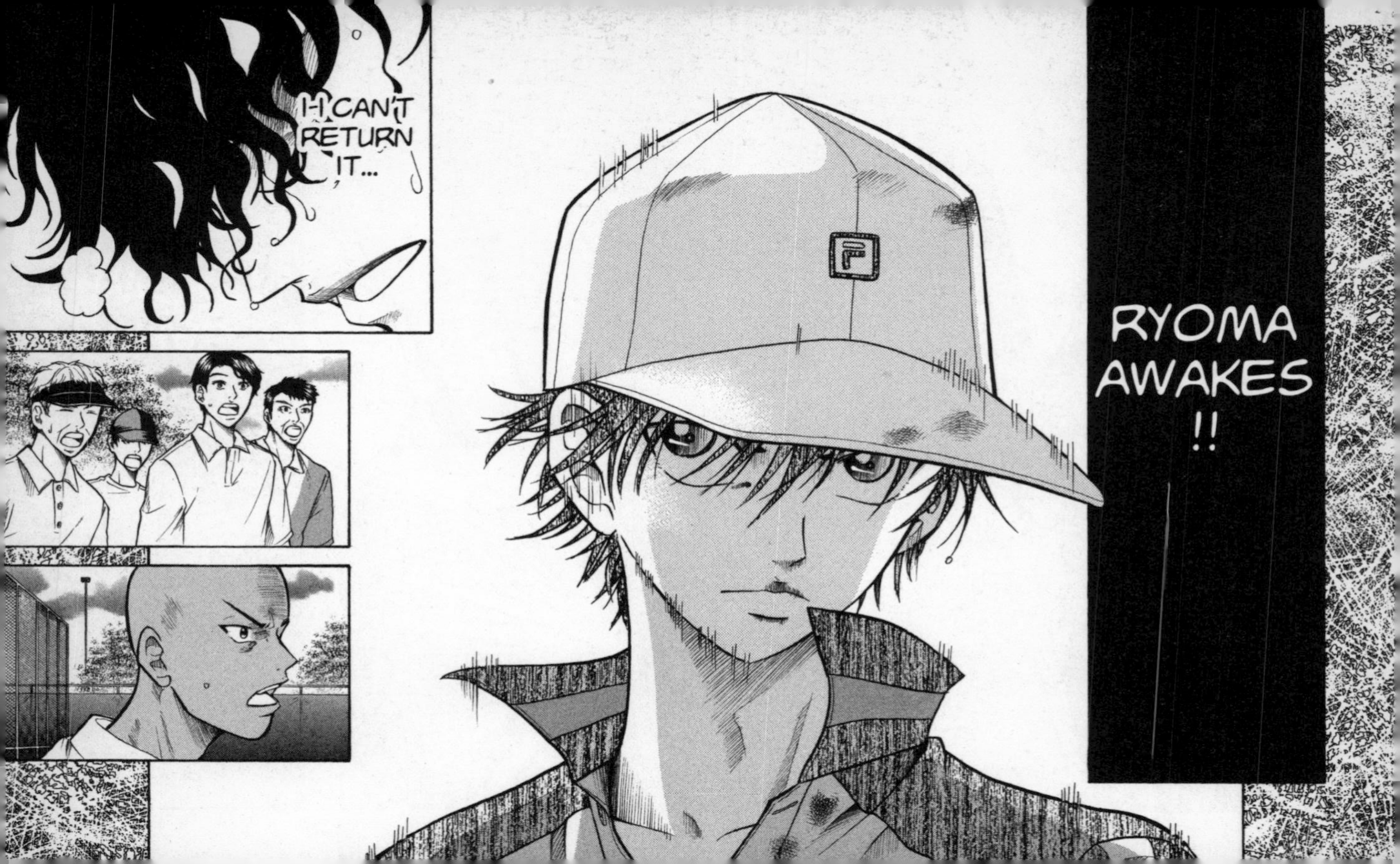
RYOMA AWAKES!!
I-I CAN'T RETURN IT...

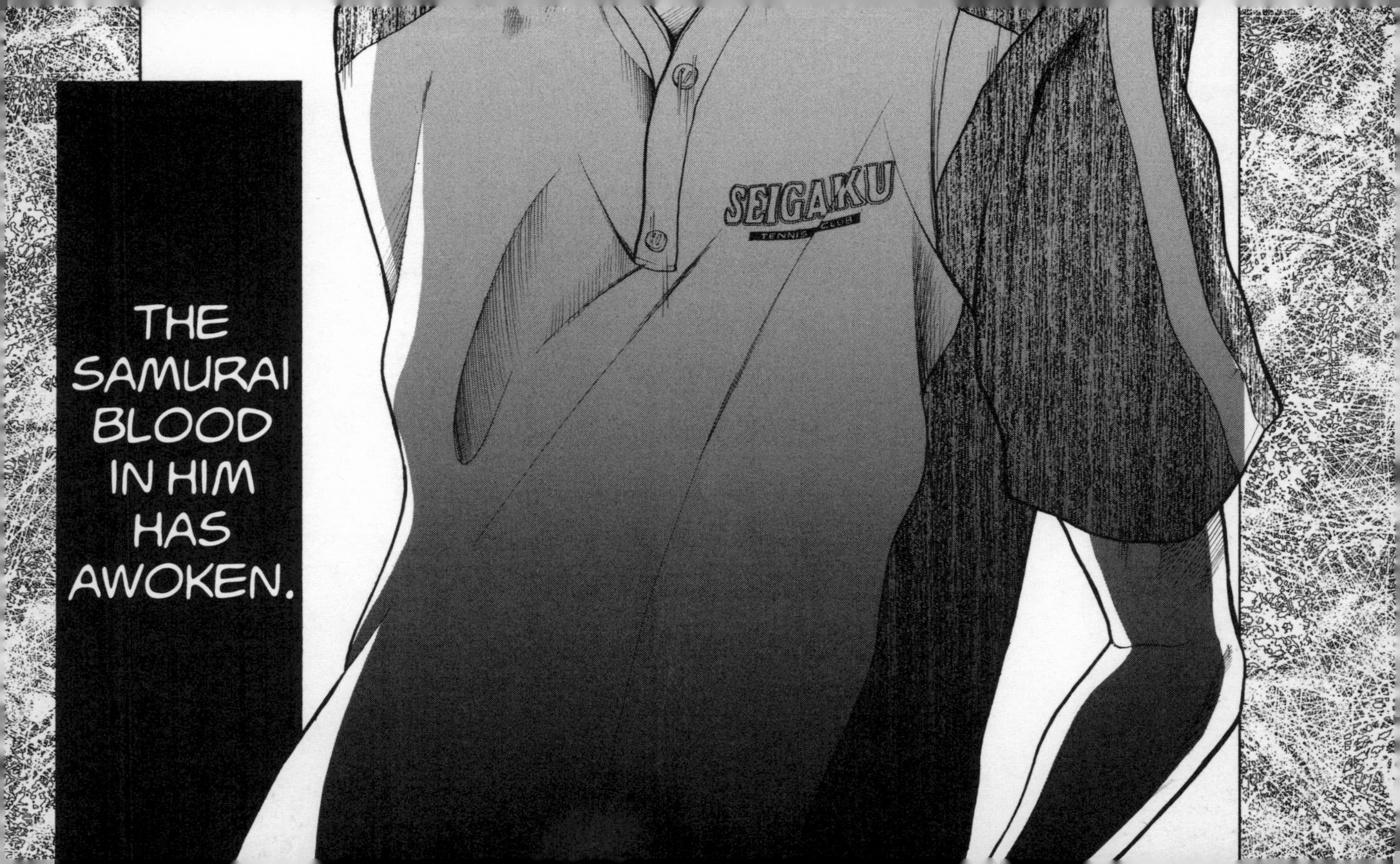
THE SAMURAI BLOOD IN HIM HAS AWOKEN.
SEIGAKU
TENNIS CLUB

テニスの王子様

THE PRINCE OF TENNIS™

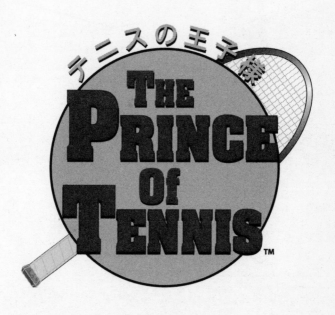

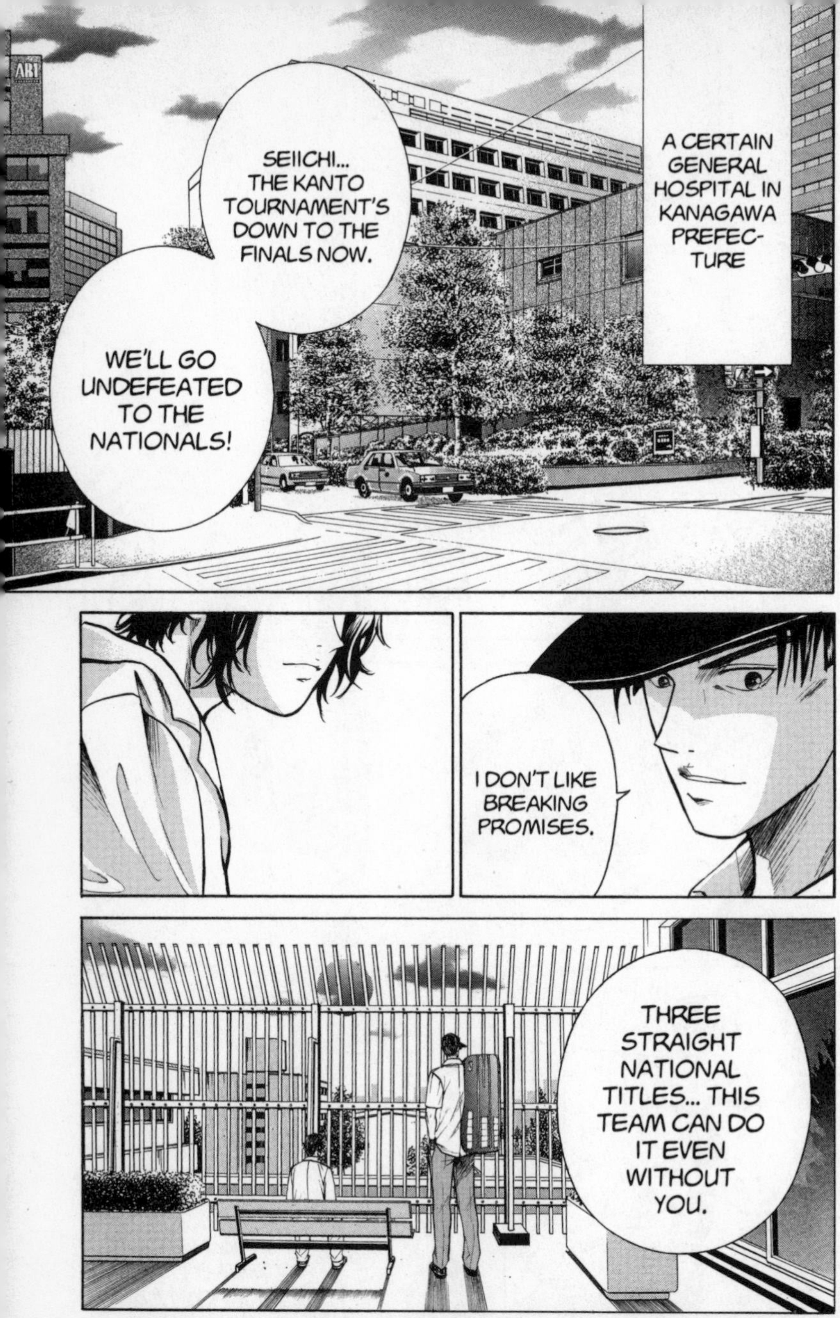
A CERTAIN GENERAL HOSPITAL IN KANAGAWA PREFEC-TURE
SEIICHI... THE KANTO TOURNAMENT'S DOWN TO THE FINALS NOW.
WE'LL GO UNDEFEATED TO THE NATIONALS!
I DON'T LIKE BREAKING PROMISES.
THREE STRAIGHT NATIONAL TITLES... THIS TEAM CAN DO IT EVEN WITHOUT YOU.

GENIUS 192: SIGNS OF AWAKENING

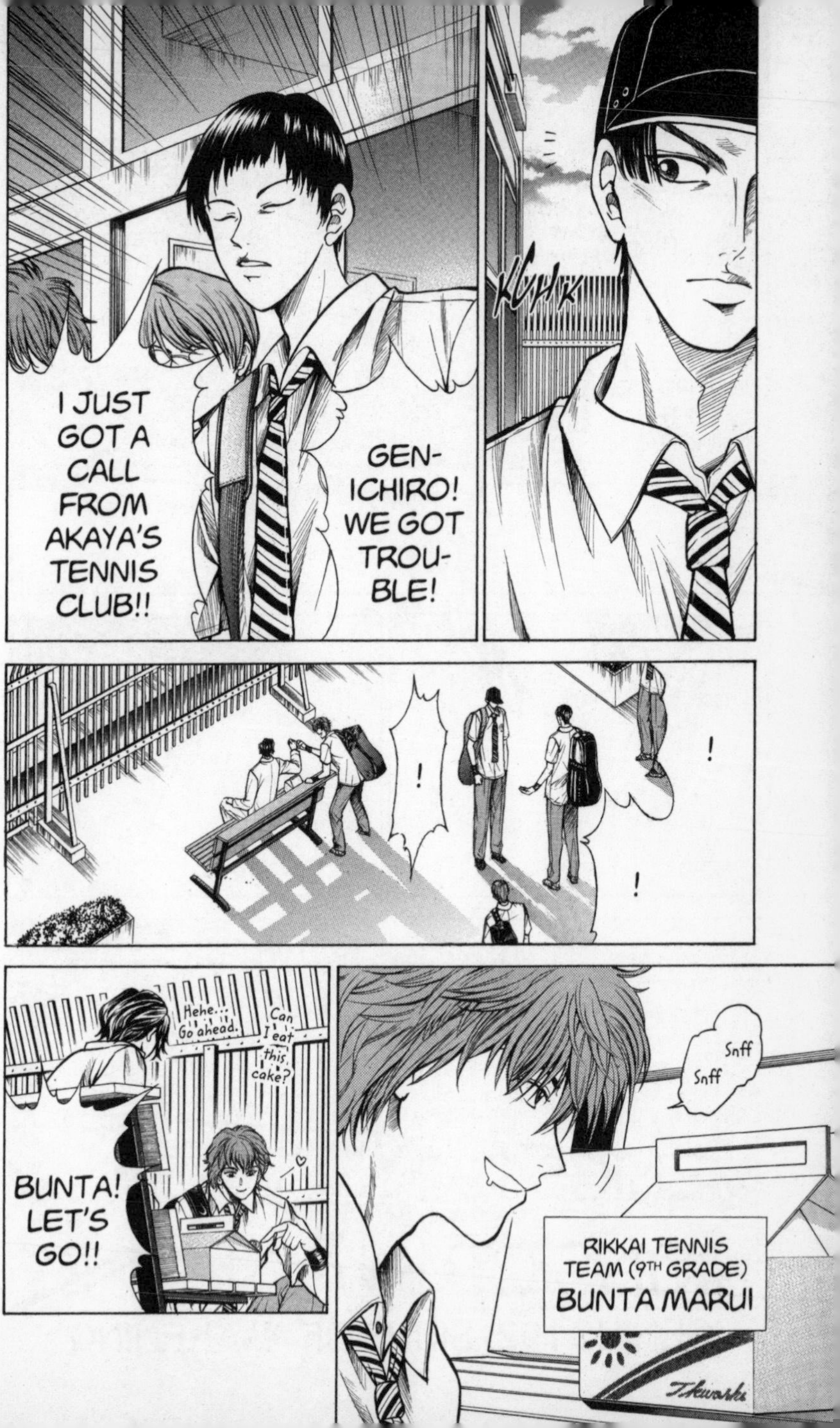
KCHK
GEN-ICHIRO! WE GOT TROUBLE!
I JUST GOT A CALL FROM AKAYA'S TENNIS CLUB!!
!
!
!
Snff
Snff
RIKKAI TENNIS TEAM (9TH GRADE) BUNTA MARUI
Can I eat this cake?
Hehe... Go ahead.
BUNTA! LET'S GO!!

...GEN- ICHIRO.

THANKS.

RIKKAI TENNIS TEAM CAPTAIN (9TH GRADE) SEIICHI YUKIMURA

GENIUS 192: SIGNS OF AWAKENING

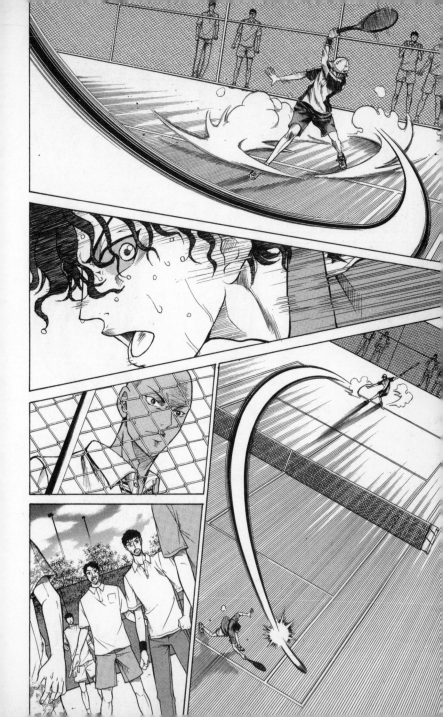

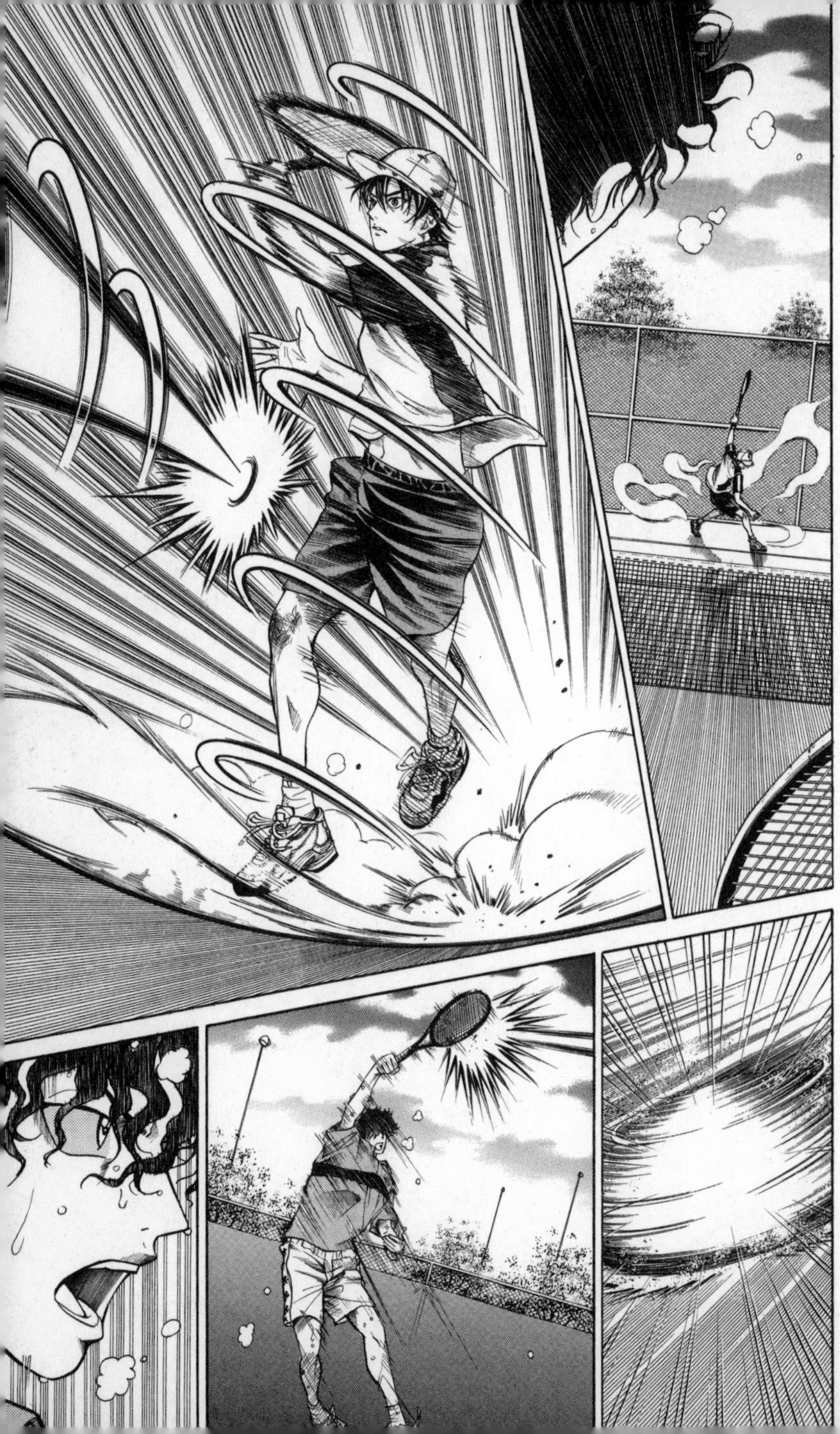

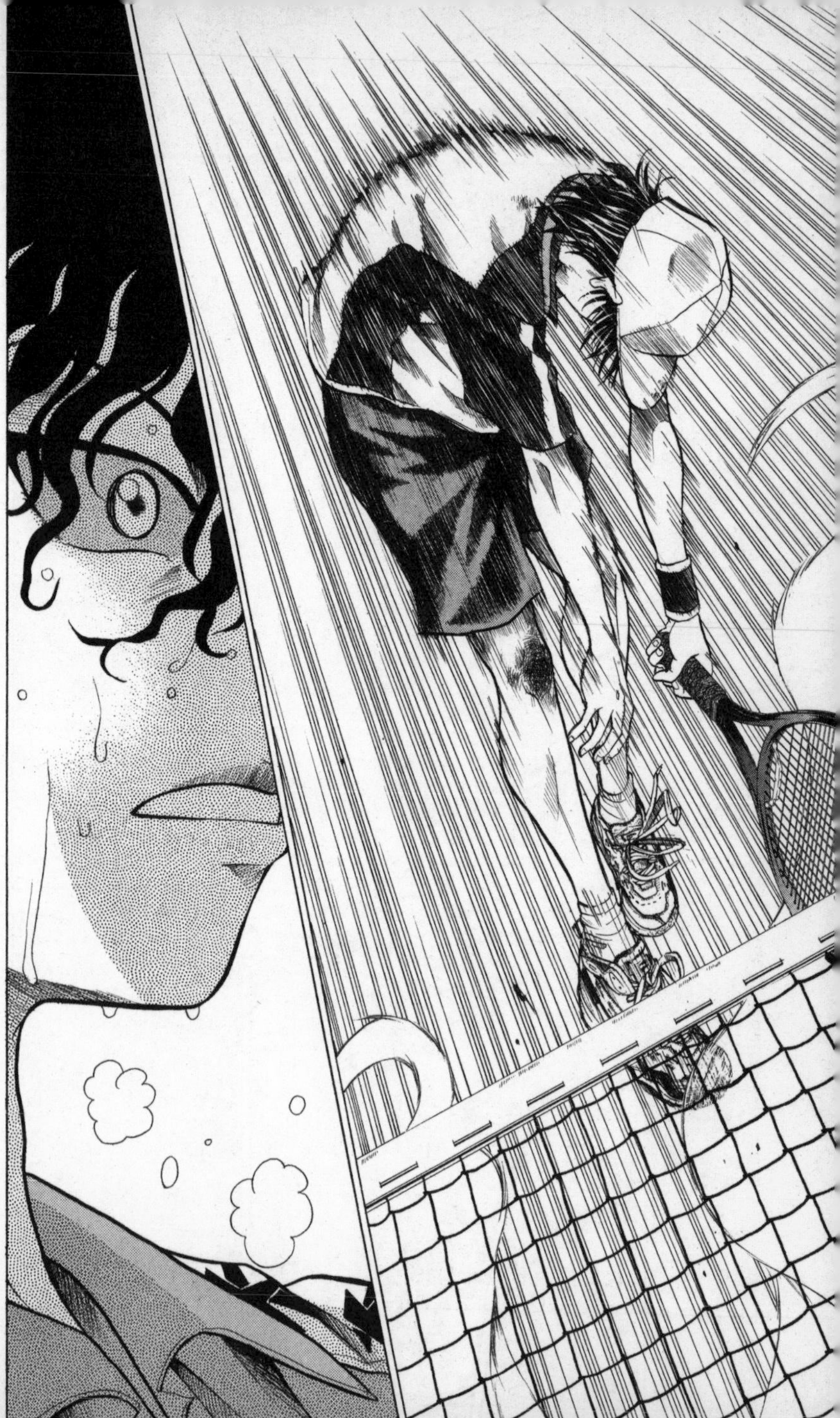

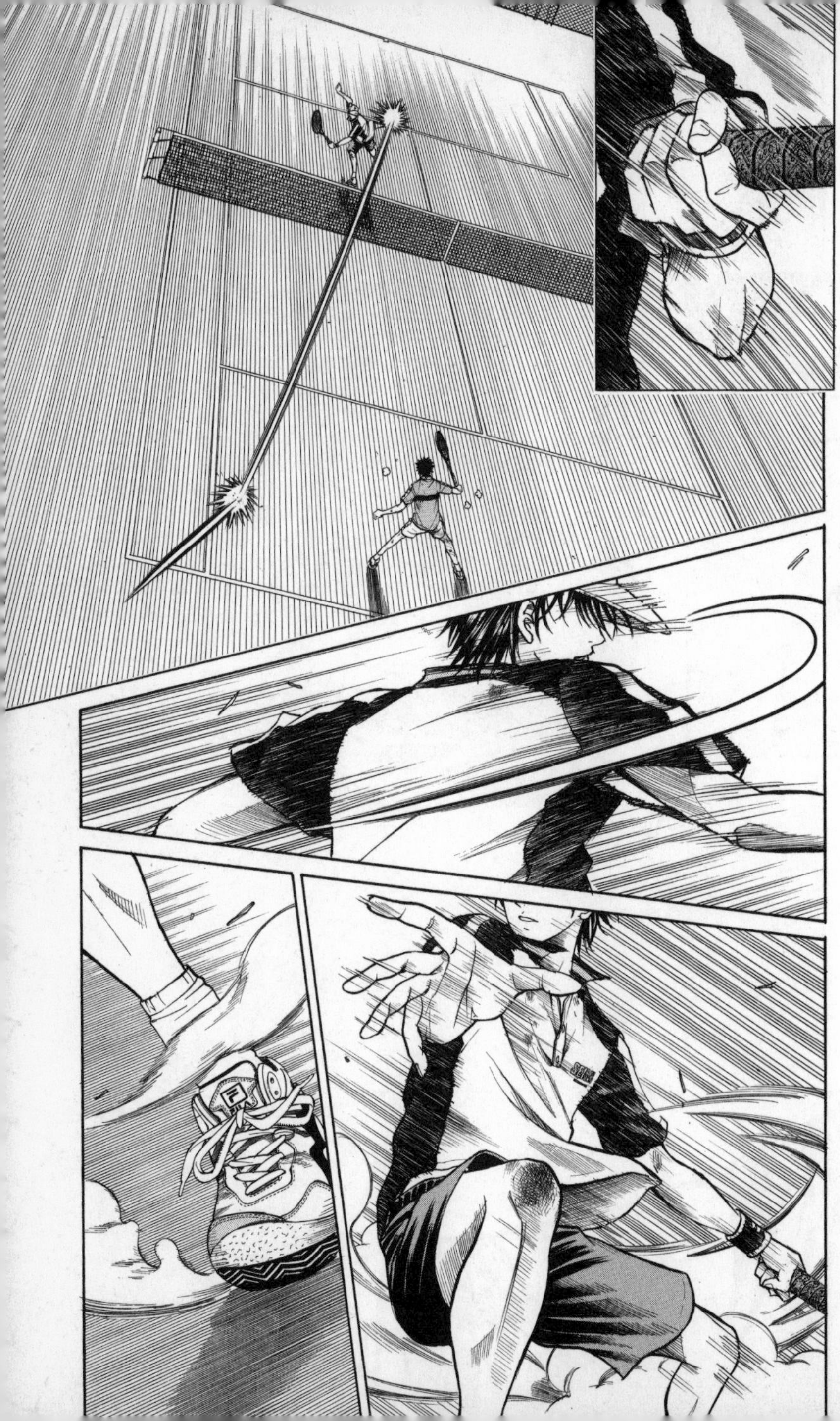

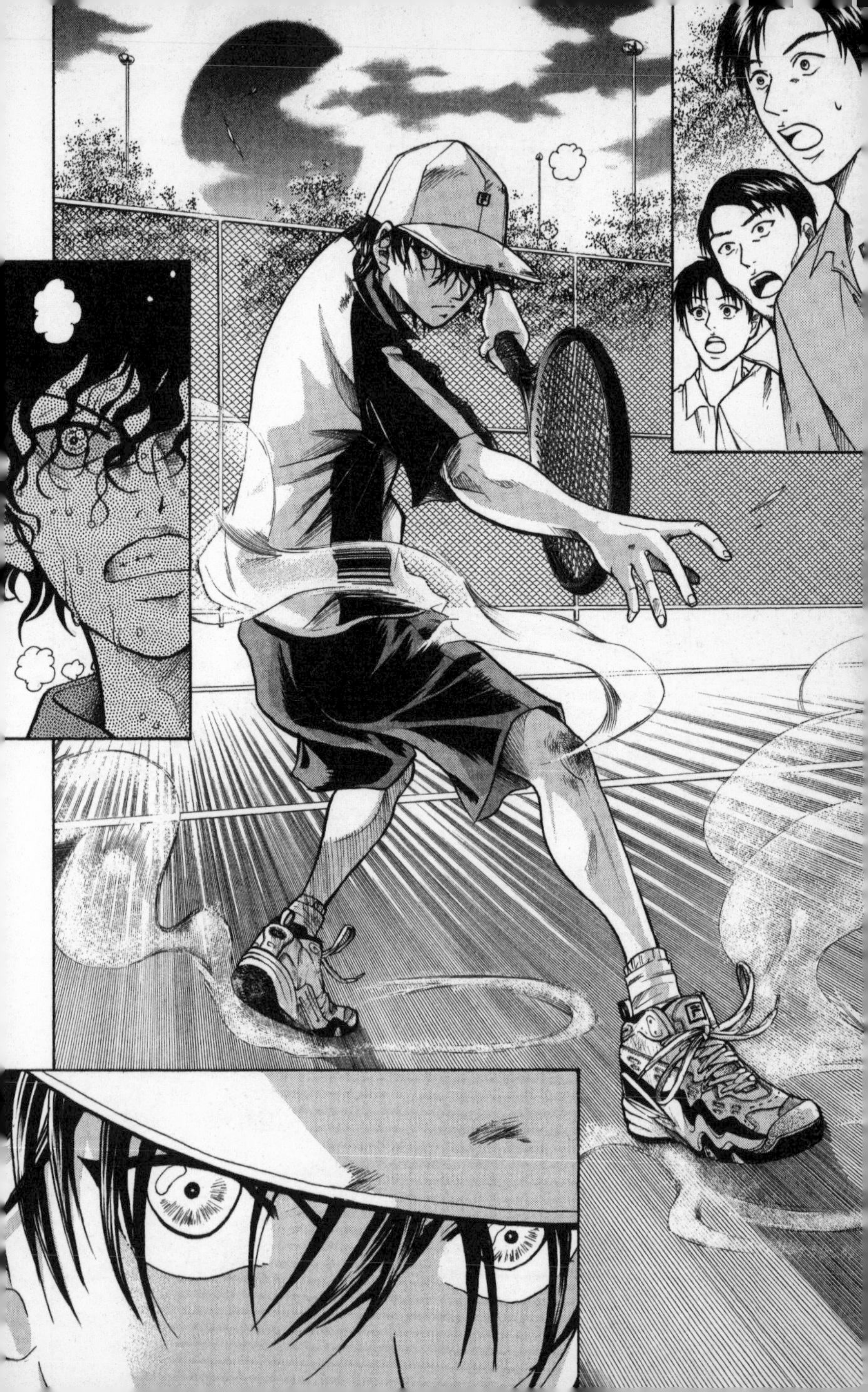

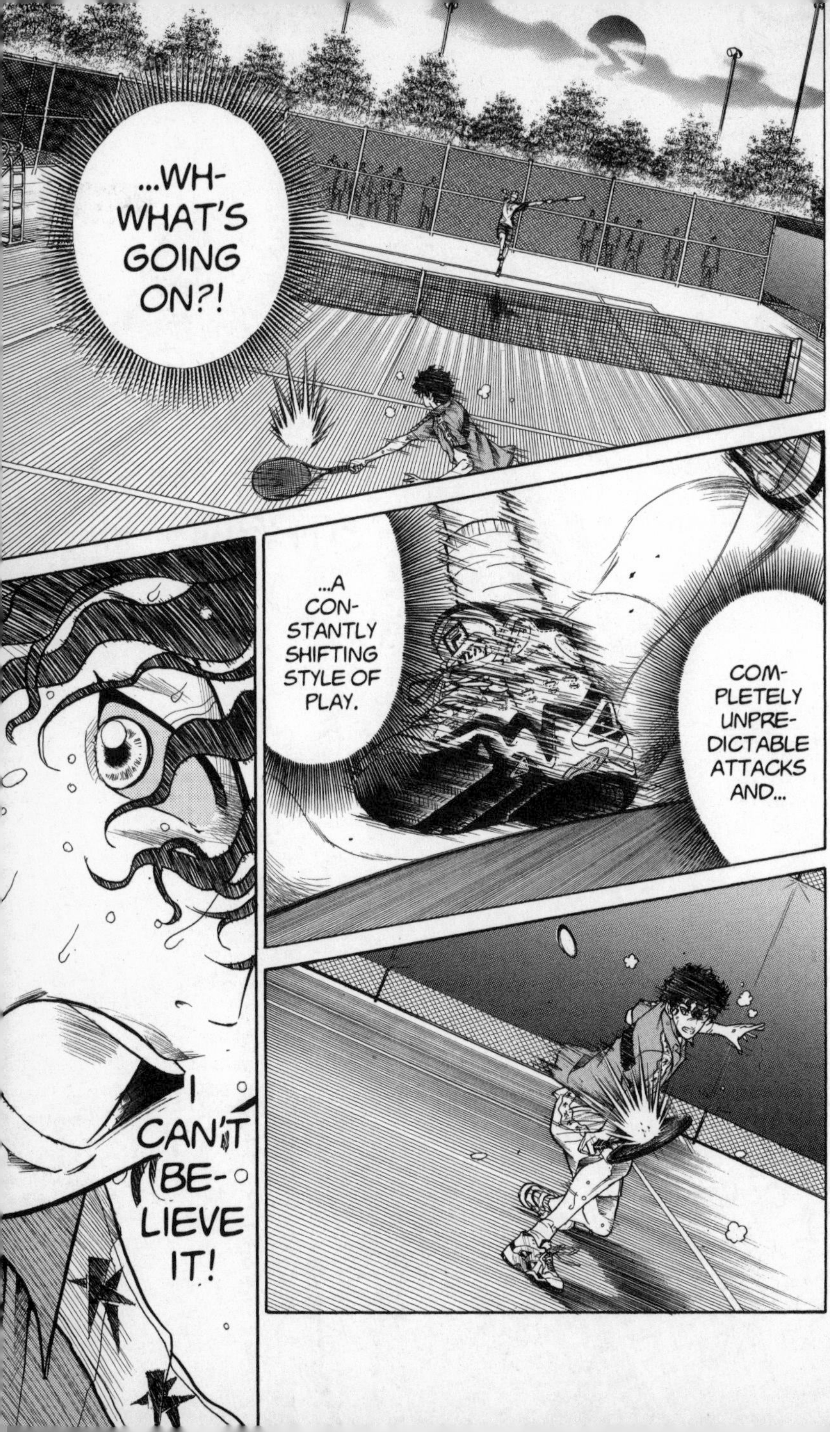
...WH-WHAT'S GOING ON?!
COMPLETELY UNPREDICTABLE ATTACKS AND...
...A CONSTANTLY SHIFTING STYLE OF PLAY.
I CAN'T BELIEVE IT!

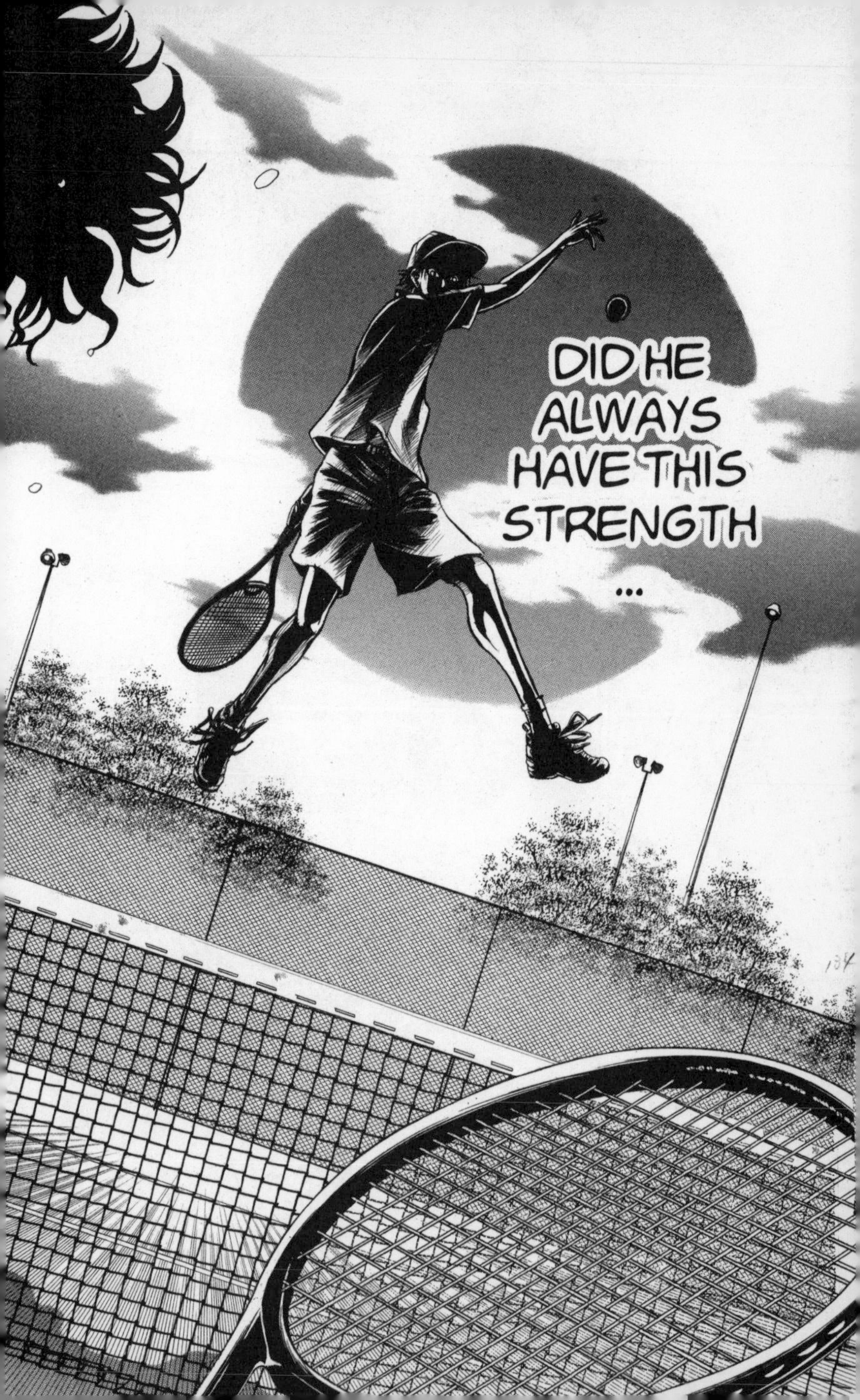
DID HE ALWAYS HAVE THIS STRENGTH ...

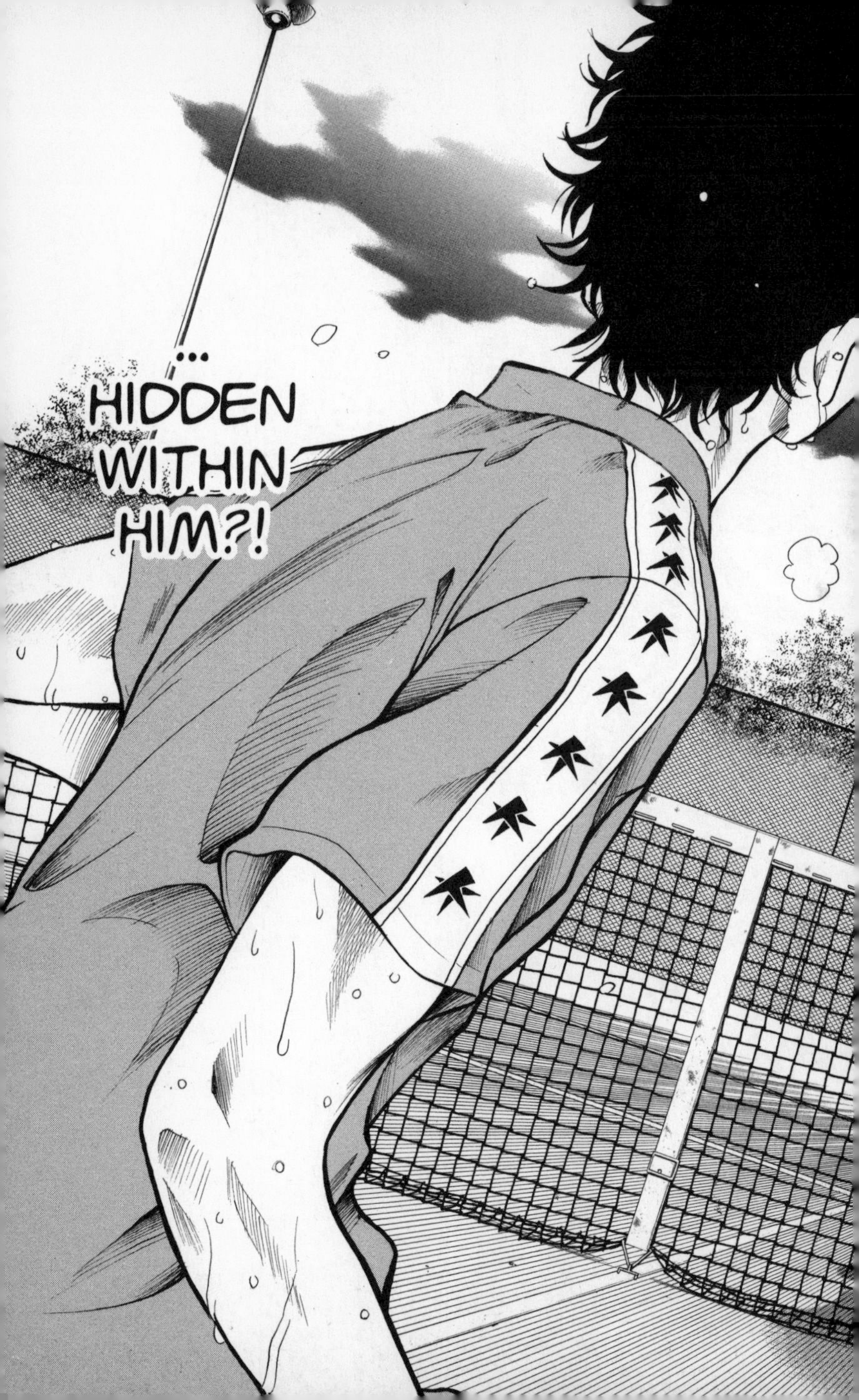
...HIDDEN WITHIN HIM?!

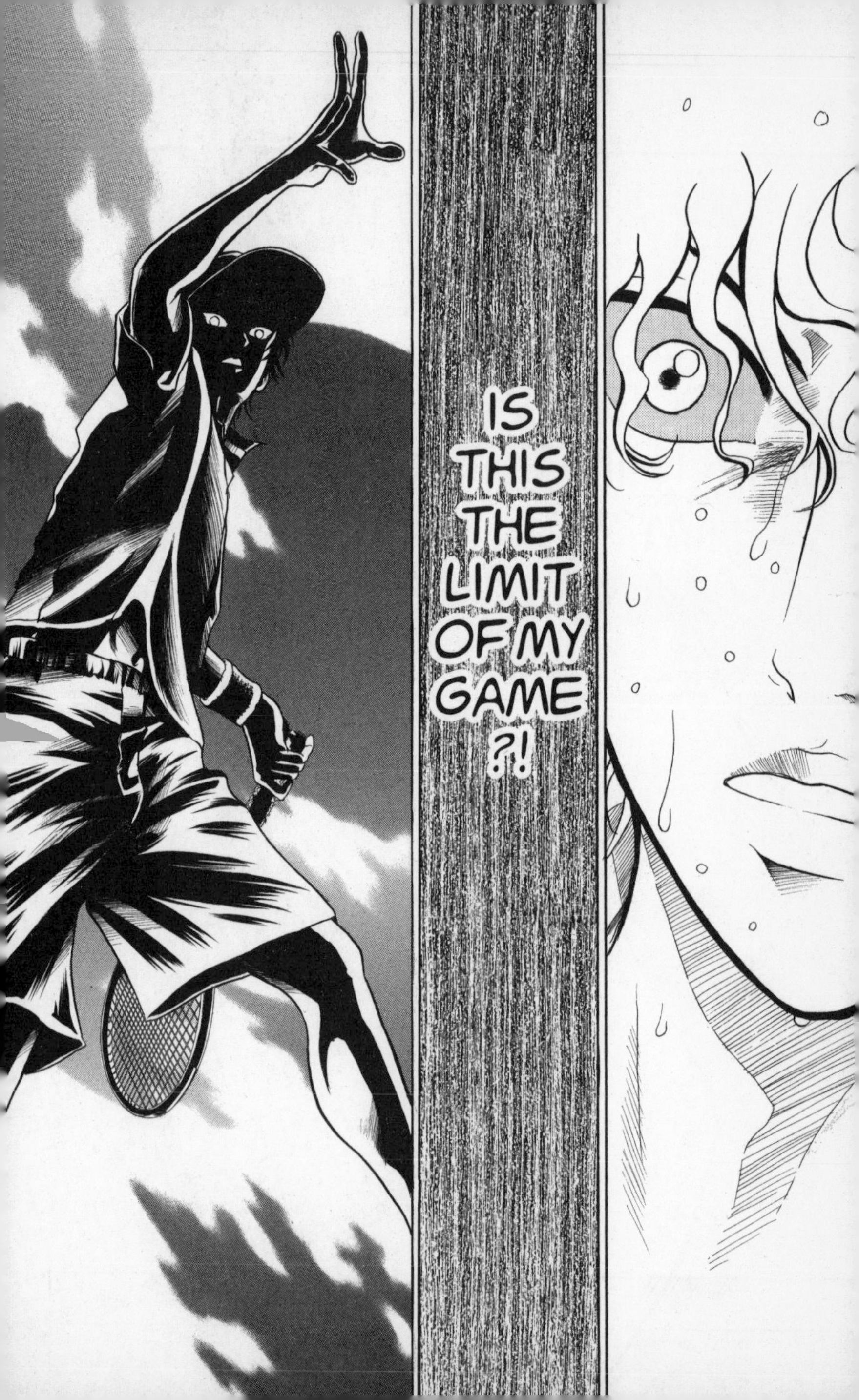
IS THIS THE LIMIT OF MY GAME ?!

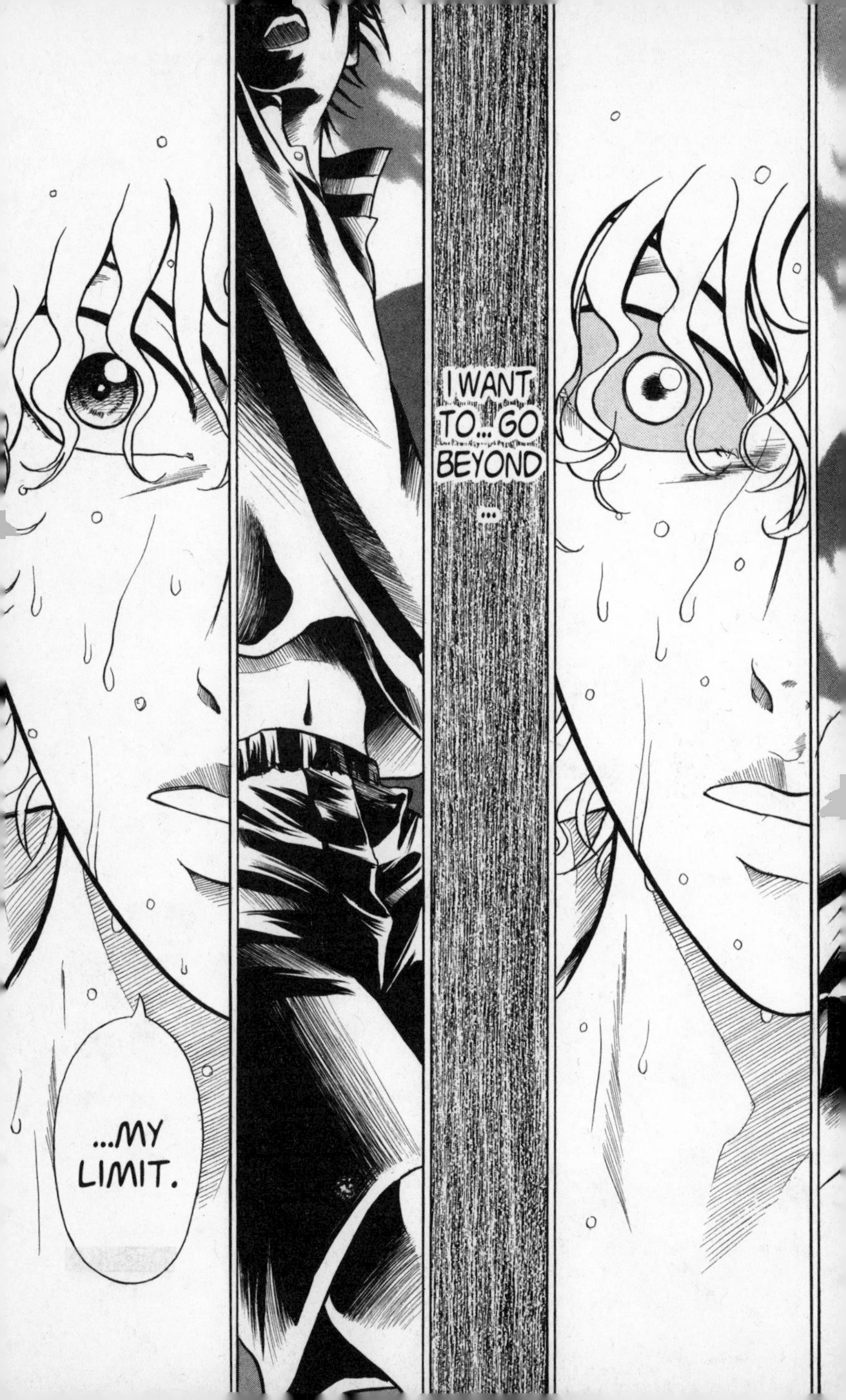
I WANT TO... GO BEYOND ...
...MY LIMIT.

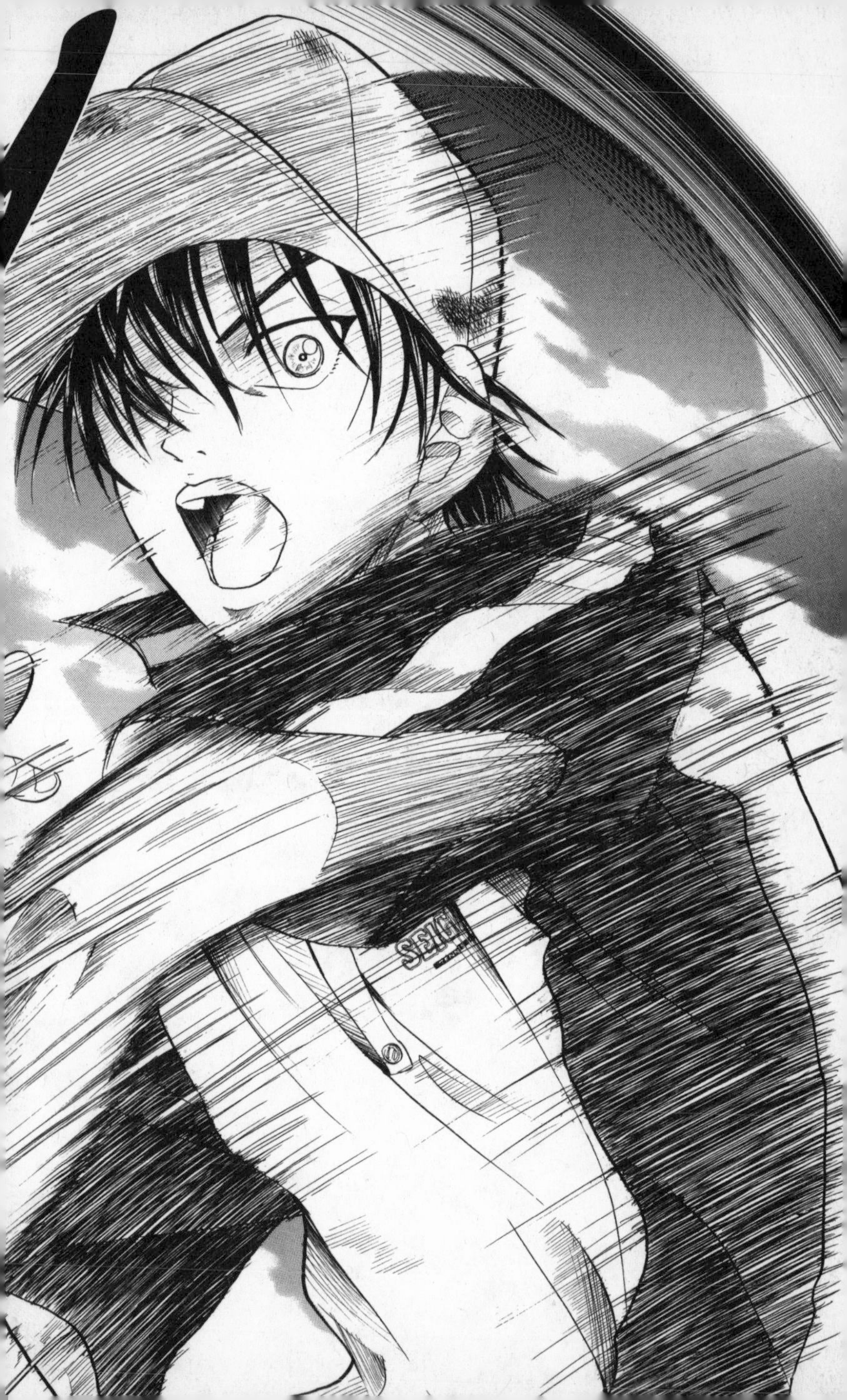

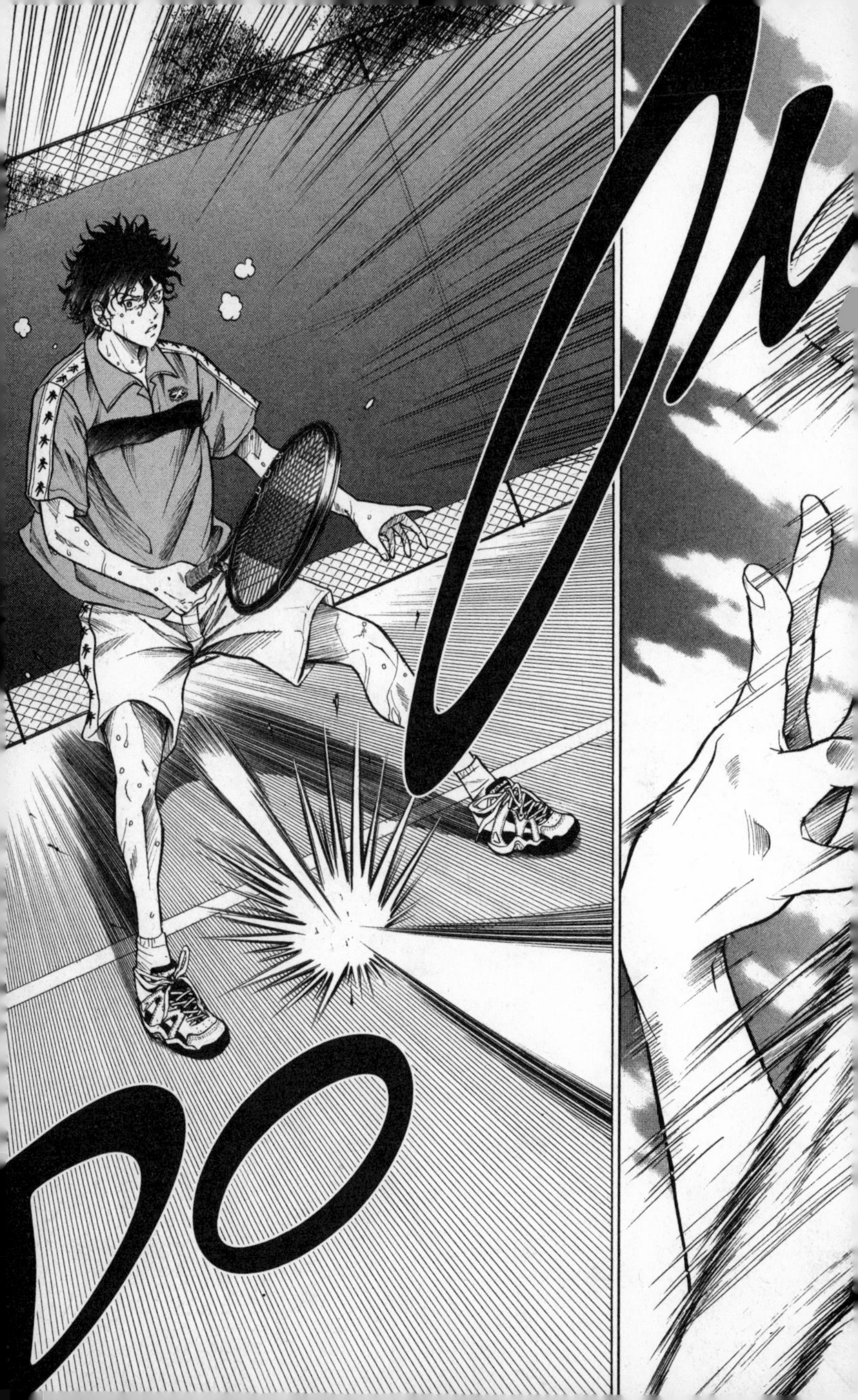

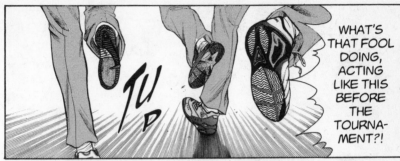

WHAT'S THAT FOOL DOING, ACTING LIKE THIS BEFORE THE TOURNAMENT?!

!

AKAYA'S EYES... ARE RED.

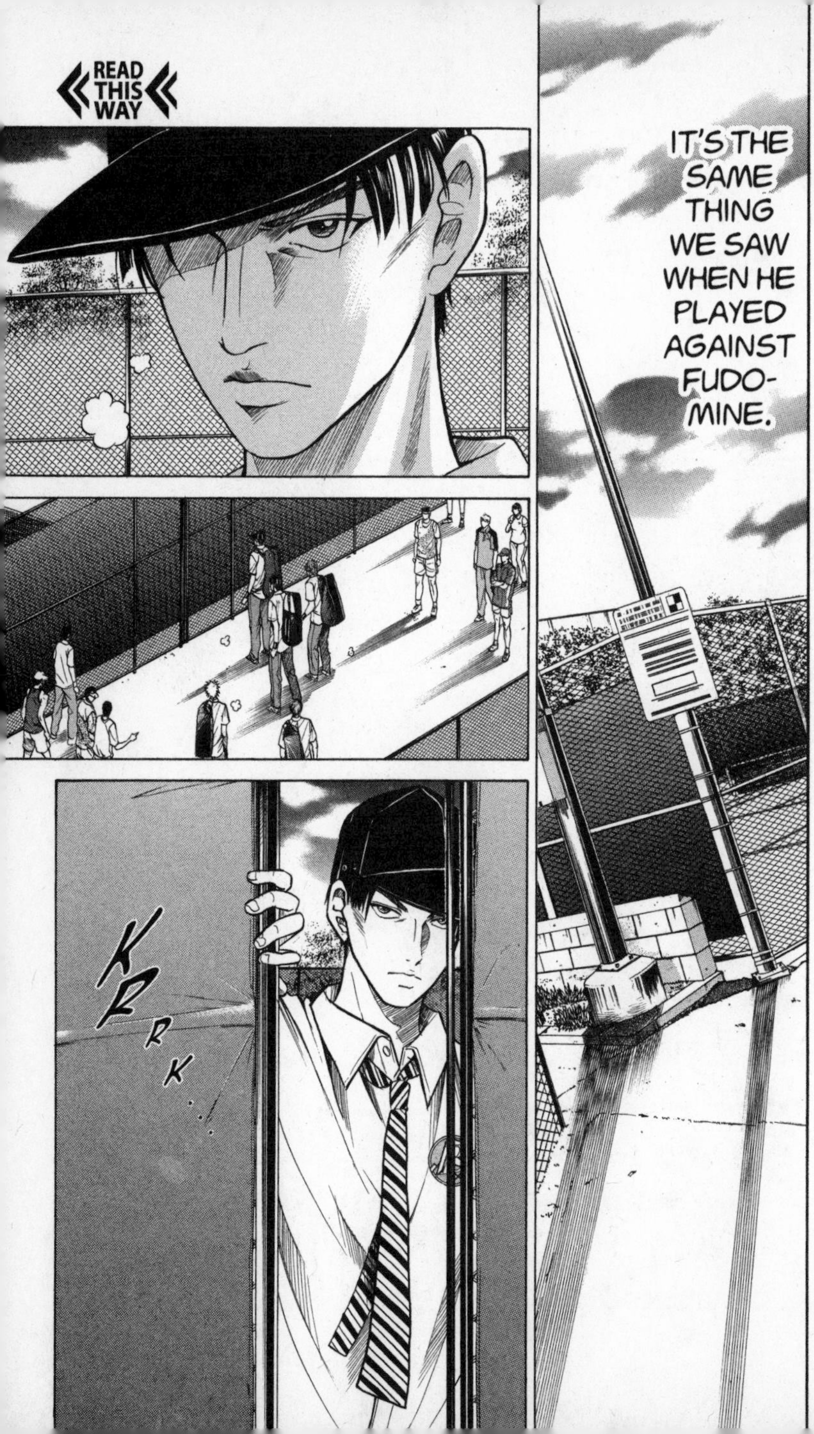
READ THIS WAY
IT'S THE SAME THING WE SAW WHEN HE PLAYED AGAINST FUDO-MINE.
KRRK..

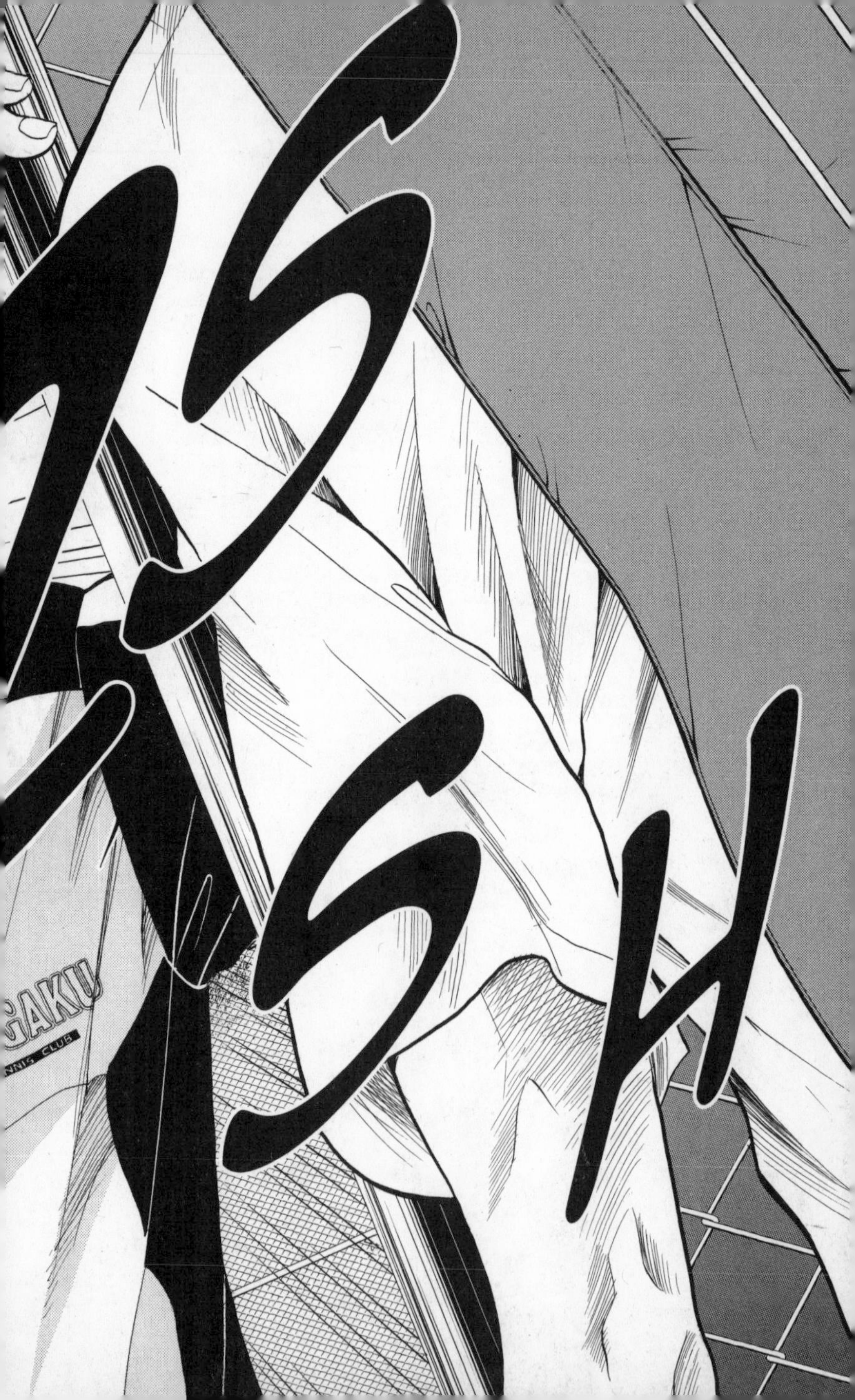
GAKU
NNIS CLUB

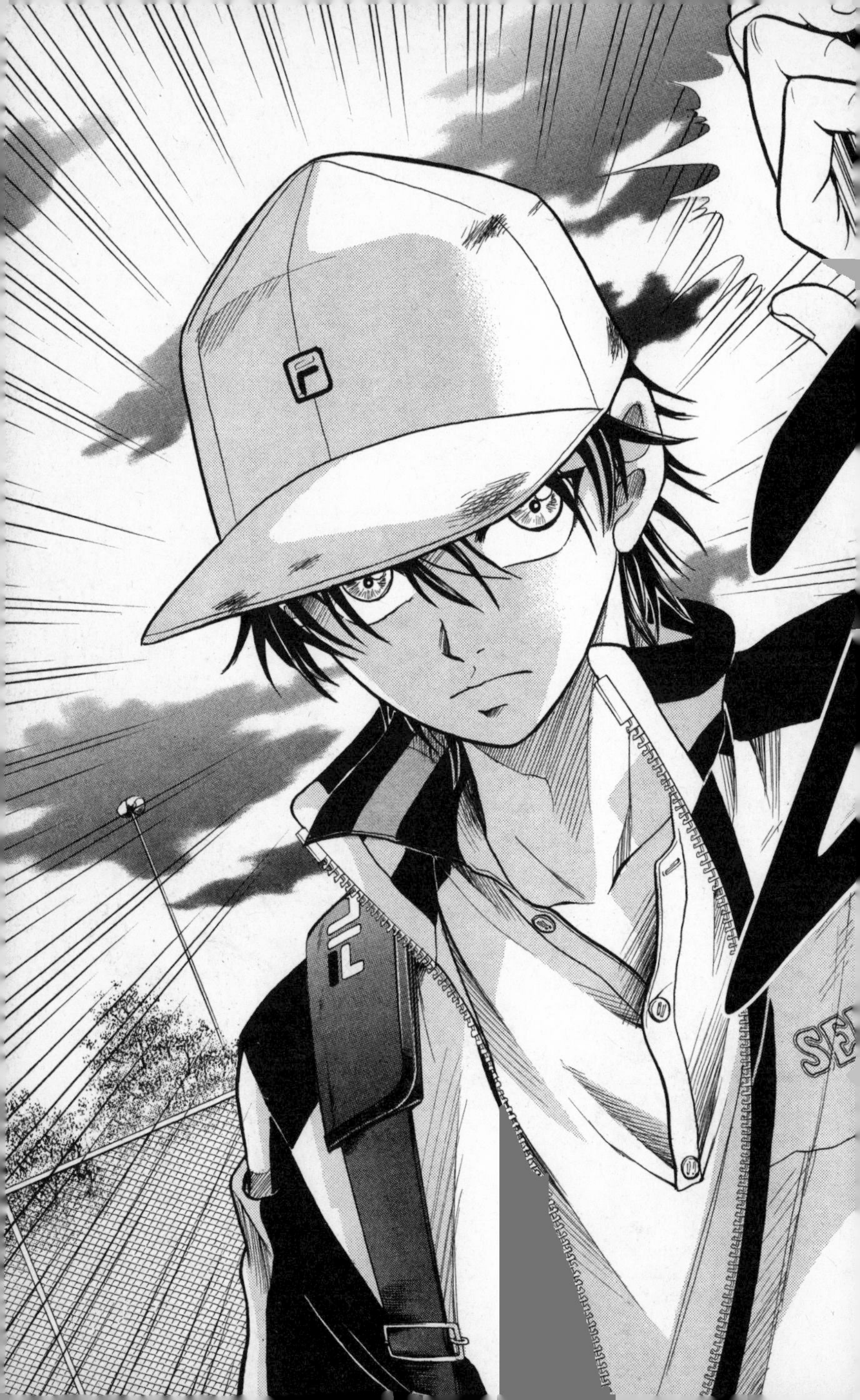

Thank you for reading *The Prince of Tennis*, volume 22.

I'm currently working while basking in the afterglow of Jump Festa*, which just ended yesterday. It was so much fun!! It's at events like that when I get to feel how much everybody loves *The Prince of Tennis* characters. This year, on the morning of the first day, I jogged around the site, and then later on I walked around in hip-hop clothing!! I was the guy dressed funny eating a hot dog and drinking tea at the Jump Café (hehehe).

This year was another huge success. They had to stop admitting people forty minutes before my segment started. Thank you so much. I'll keep working hard, so please keep up the support!! Your fan letters really are a source of energy! I read all of them!!

The end of this volume includes a short story about Ryoma's dad, Nanjiro Echizen. It was published along with "Genius 185: Versus Rikkai" in *Shonen Jump* magazine. The era may differ, but the scene where Nanjiro's looking up from the bottom of the stairway should look the same as the scene with Ryoma in the beginning of this volume. Did you catch that?

Well then, I'll see you in the next volume! Keep supporting *The Prince of Tennis* and Ryoma!!

テニスの王子様
T.KONOMI!
2003.12.22
Who is that?
He's weird.
Yo Yo—
Whatcha lookin' at, yo?

*An annual manga and anime convention in Japan.—Ed.

Send fan letters to: The Prince of Tennis Takeshi Konomi c/o VIZ Media LLC,
P.O. Box 77010, San Francisco, CA 94107

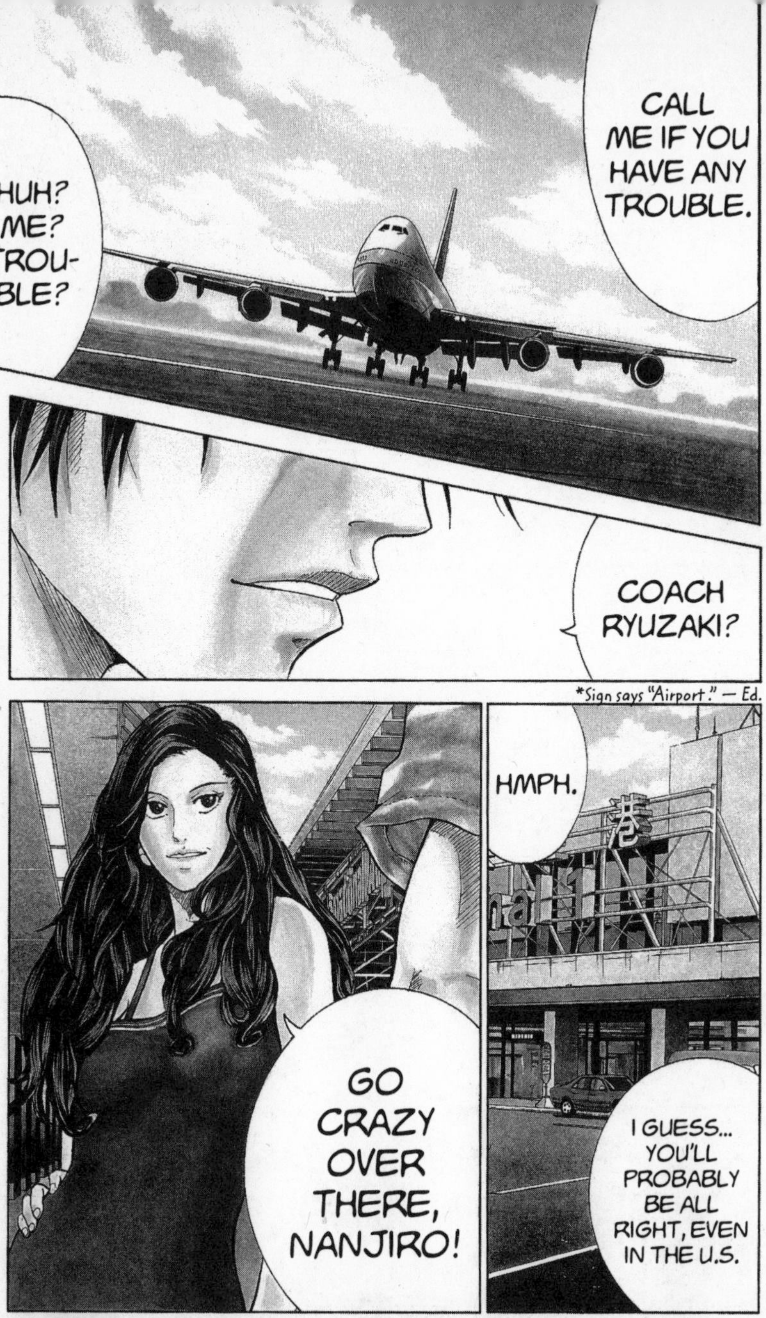
CALL ME IF YOU HAVE ANY TROUBLE.
HUH? ME? TROU-BLE?
COACH RYUZAKI?
HMPH.
港
I GUESS... YOU'LL PROBABLY BE ALL RIGHT, EVEN IN THE U.S.
GO CRAZY OVER THERE, NANJIRO!

*Sign says "Airport." — Ed.

GENIUS 0: THE SAMURAI'S STORY

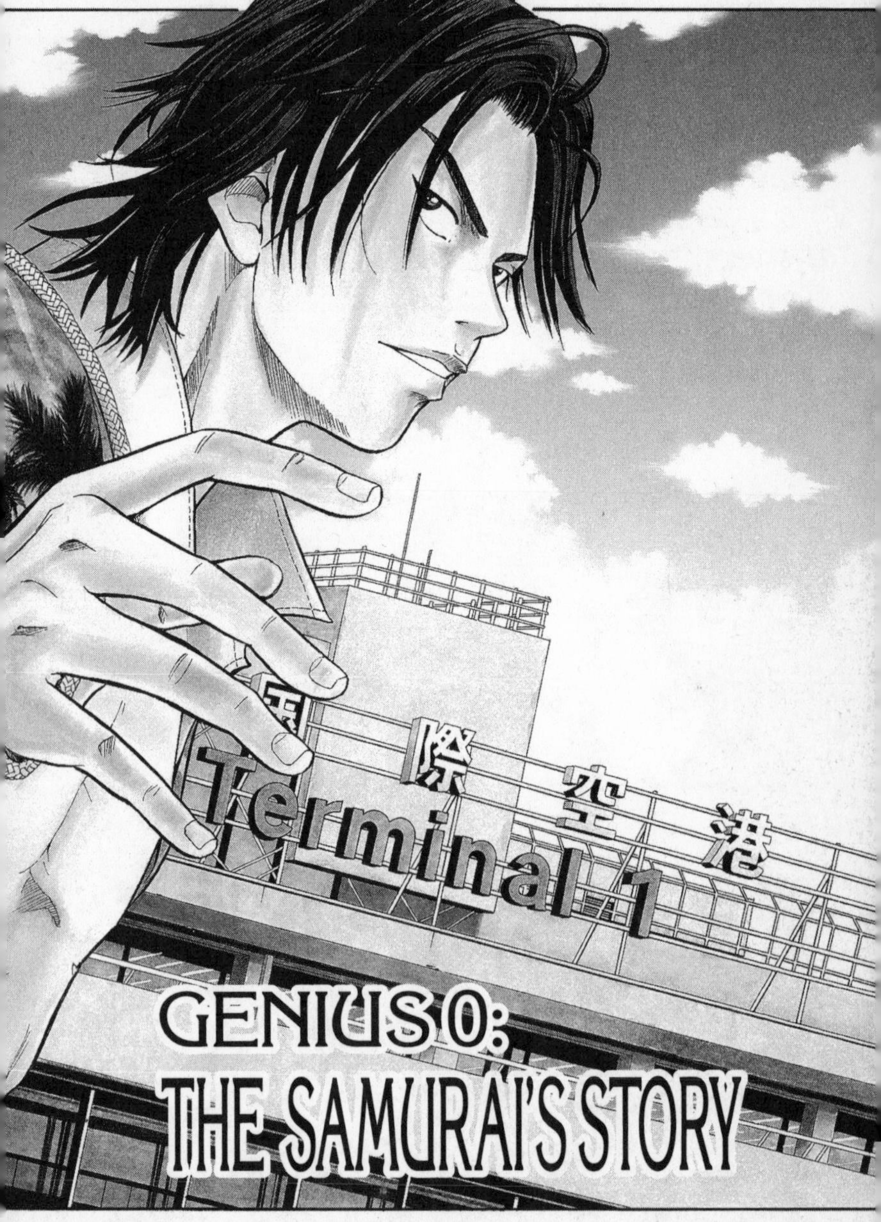
際 空 港
Terminal 1
GENIUS 0:
THE SAMURAI'S STORY

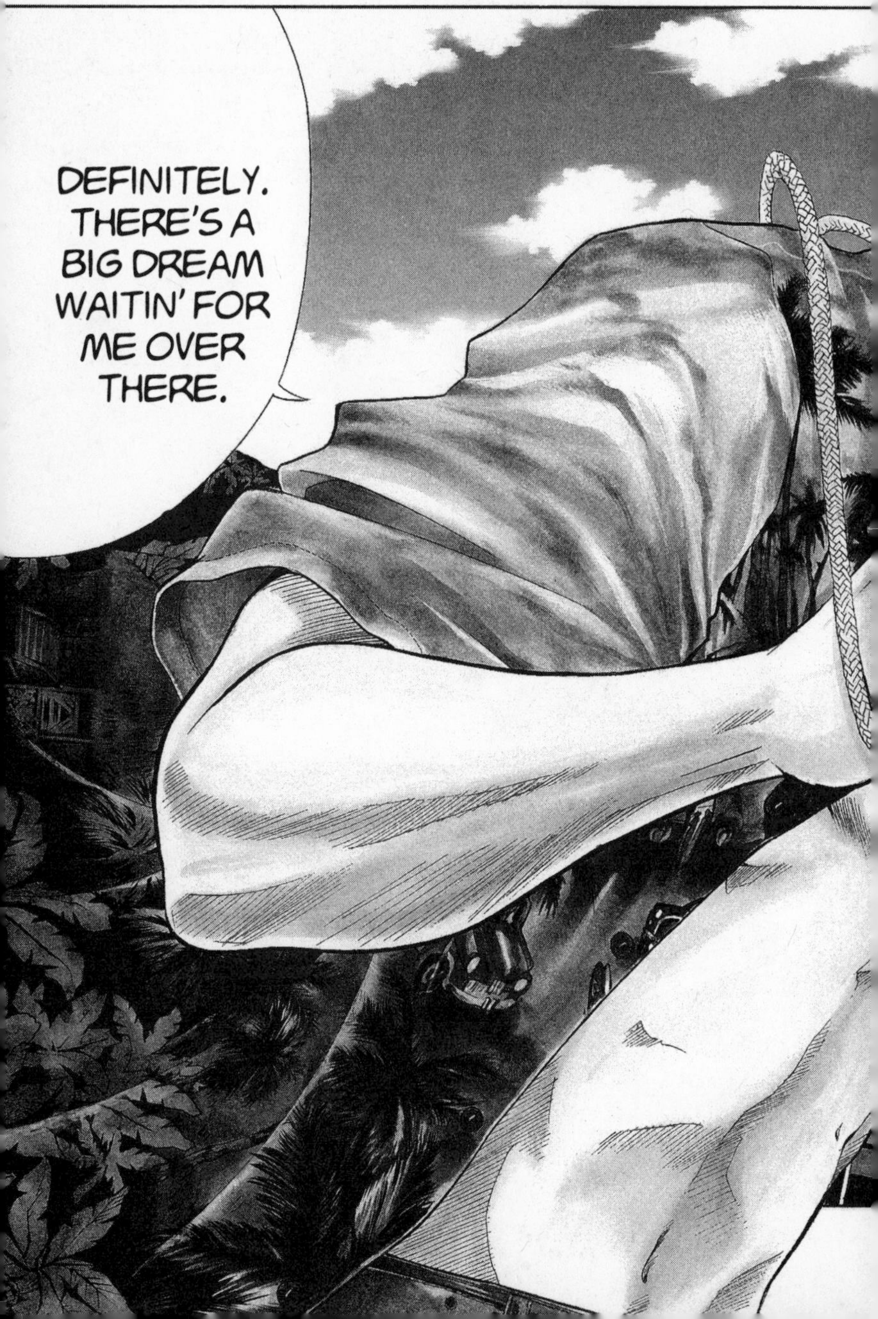
DEFINITELY. THERE'S A BIG DREAM WAITIN' FOR ME OVER THERE.

テニスの王子様

THE PRINCE OF TENNIS™

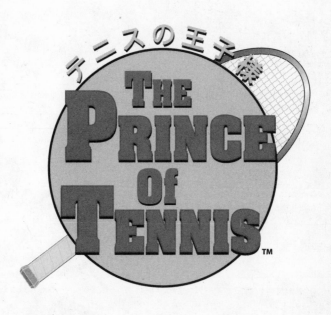

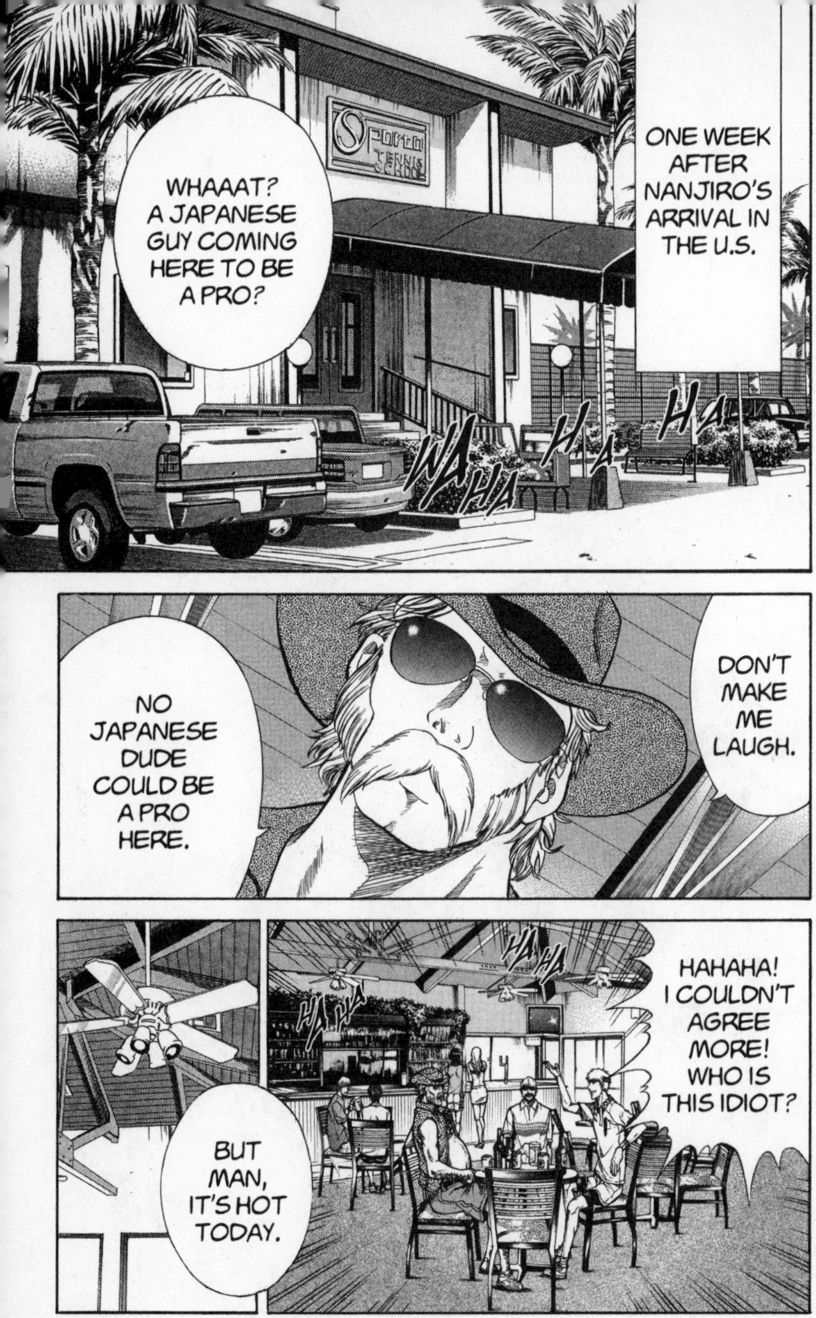
ONE WEEK AFTER NANJIRO'S ARRIVAL IN THE U.S.
WHAAAT? A JAPANESE GUY COMING HERE TO BE A PRO?
WAHAHA HA HA
DON'T MAKE ME LAUGH.
NO JAPANESE DUDE COULD BE A PRO HERE.
HAHAHA! I COULDN'T AGREE MORE! WHO IS THIS IDIOT?
HAHA
HAHA
BUT MAN, IT'S HOT TODAY.

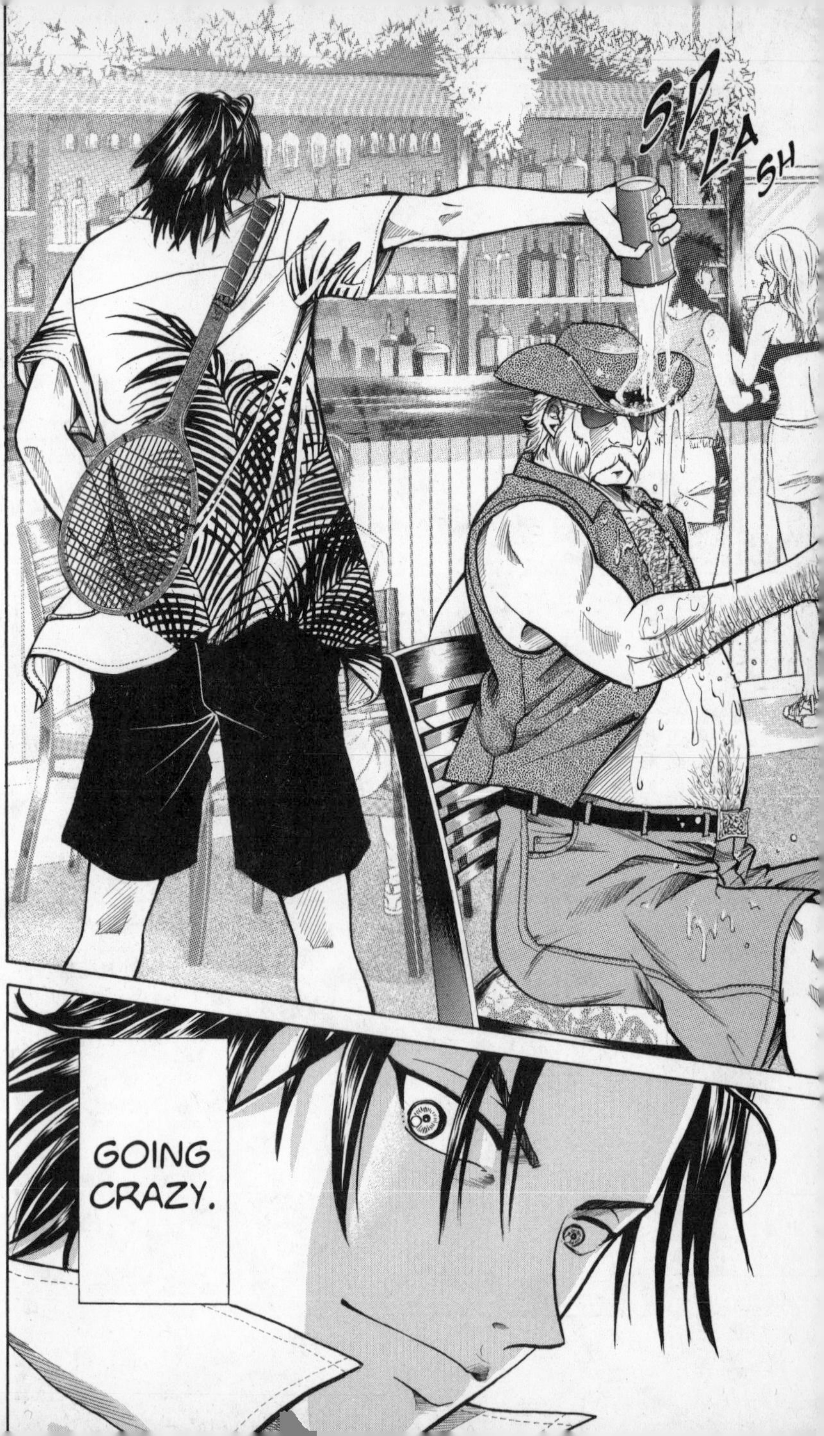
SPLASH
GOING CRAZY.

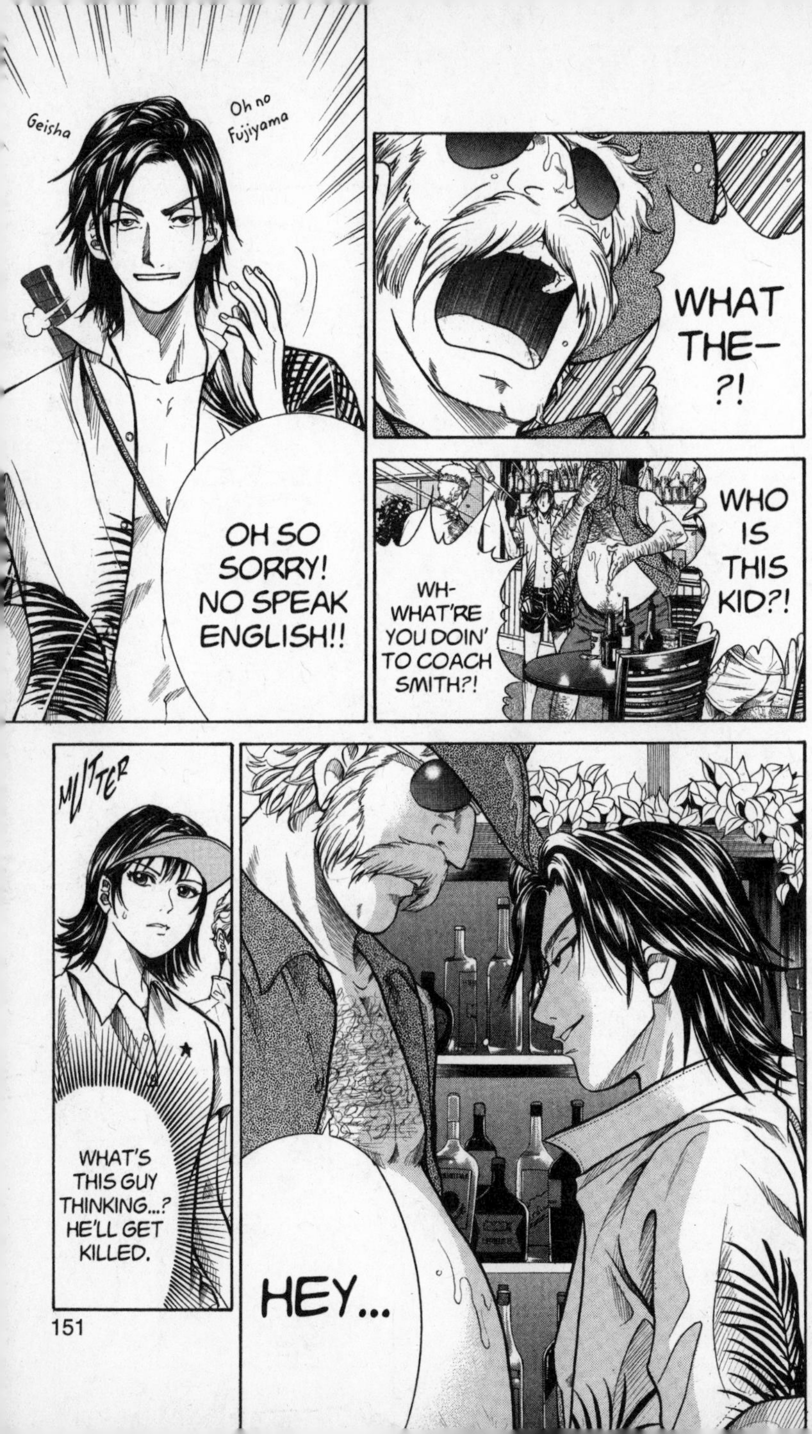
WHAT THE-?!
WHO IS THIS KID?!
WH- WHAT'RE YOU DOIN' TO COACH SMITH?!
Oh no Fujiyama
Geisha
OH SO SORRY! NO SPEAK ENGLISH!!
HEY...
MUTTER
WHAT'S THIS GUY THINKING...? HE'LL GET KILLED.

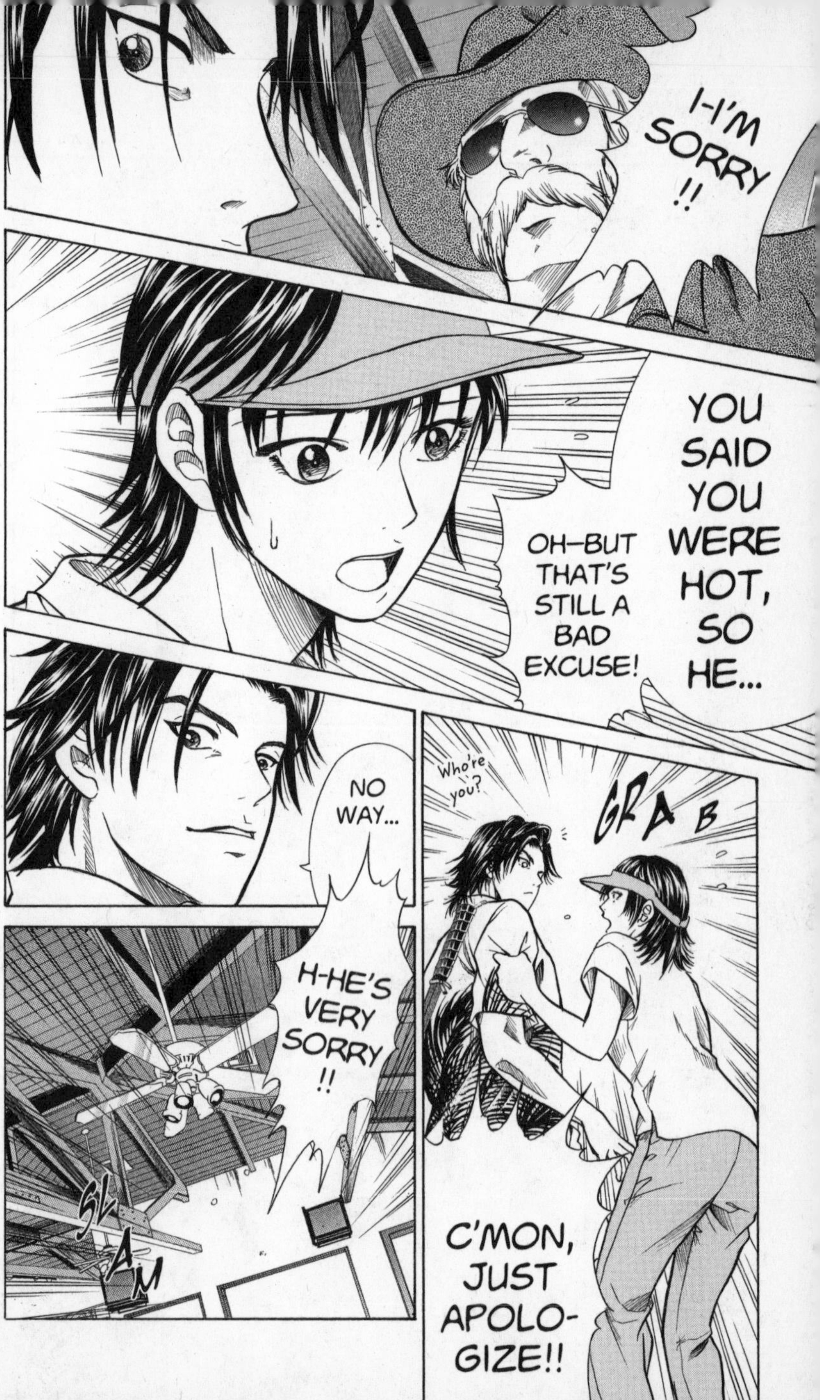
I-I'M SORRY!!
YOU SAID YOU WERE HOT, SO HE...
OH—BUT THAT'S STILL A BAD EXCUSE!
Who're you?
GRAB
C'MON, JUST APOLOGIZE!!
NO WAY...
H-HE'S VERY SORRY!!
SLAM

READ THIS WAY

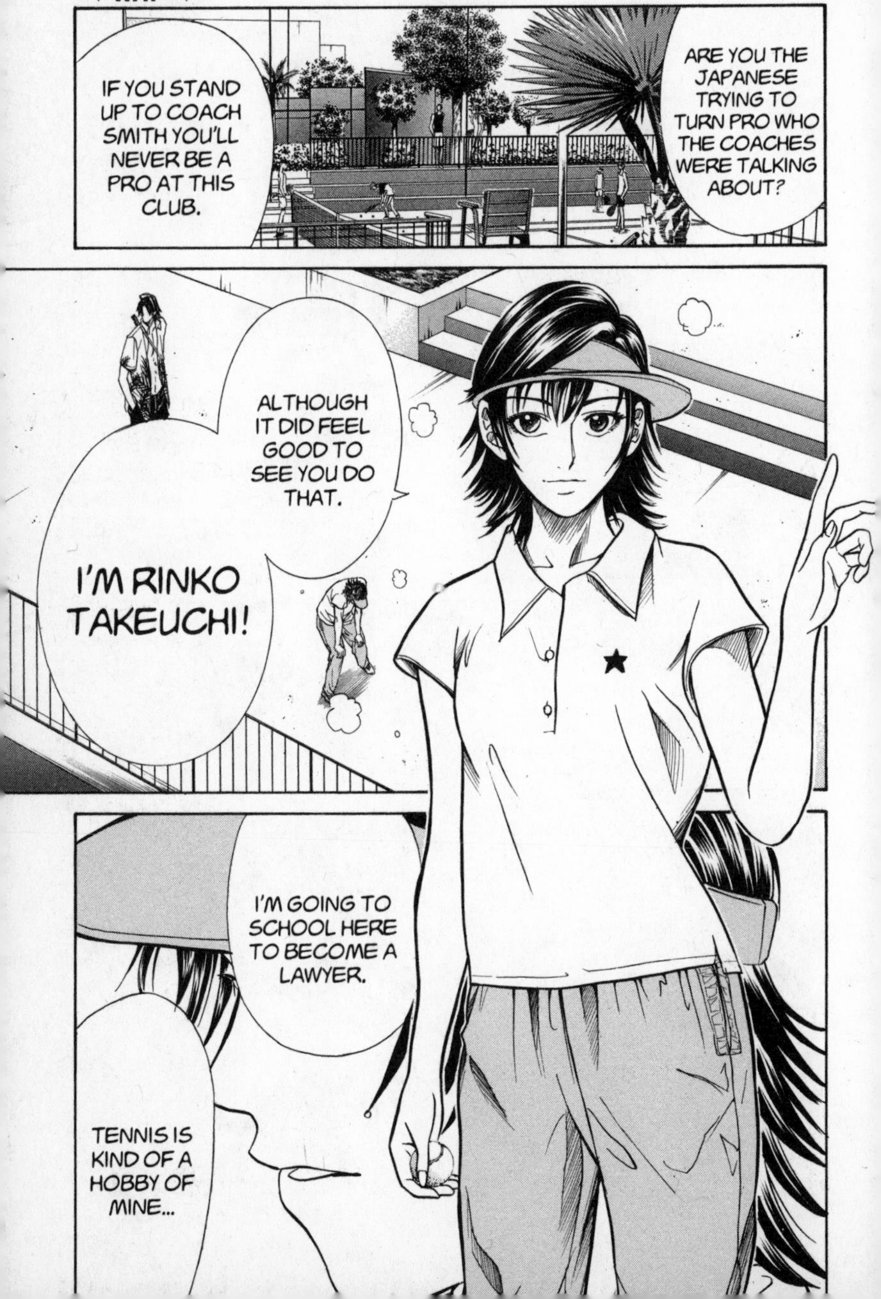
ARE YOU THE JAPANESE TRYING TO TURN PRO WHO THE COACHES WERE TALKING ABOUT?
IF YOU STAND UP TO COACH SMITH YOU'LL NEVER BE A PRO AT THIS CLUB.
ALTHOUGH IT DID FEEL GOOD TO SEE YOU DO THAT.
I'M RINKO TAKEUCHI!
I'M GOING TO SCHOOL HERE TO BECOME A LAWYER.
TENNIS IS KIND OF A HOBBY OF MINE...

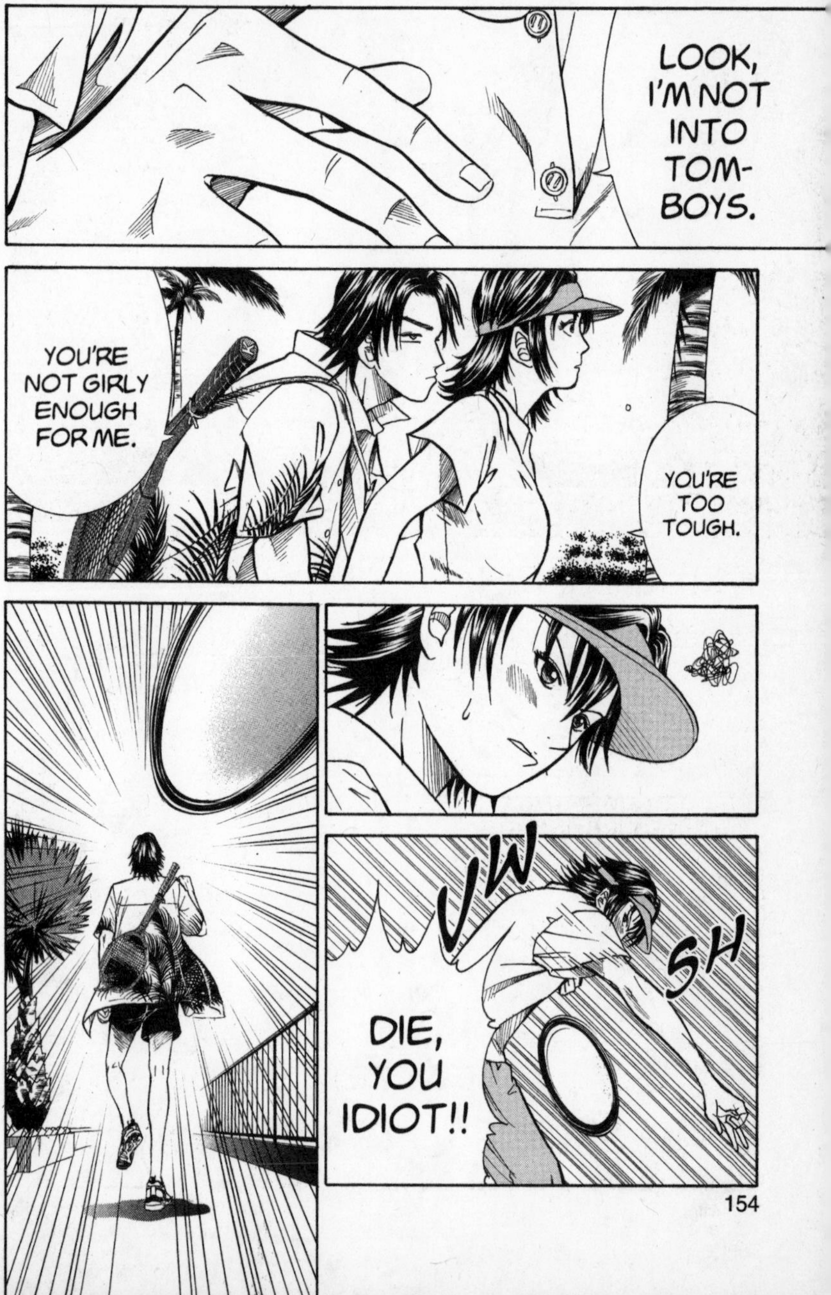
LOOK, I'M NOT INTO TOM-BOYS.
YOU'RE TOO TOUGH.
YOU'RE NOT GIRLY ENOUGH FOR ME.
VW
SH
DIE, YOU IDIOT!!

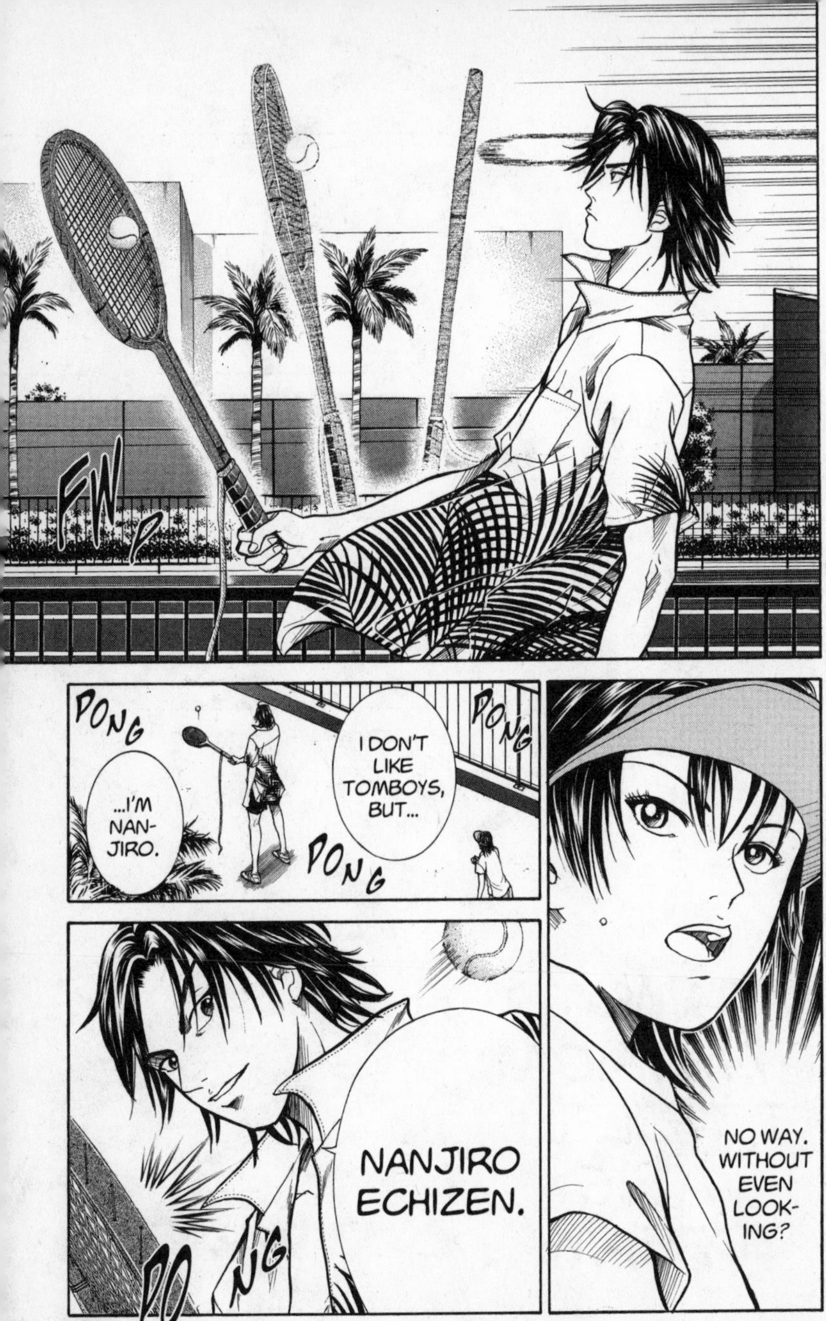
FWP
NO WAY. WITHOUT EVEN LOOKING?
PONG
I DON'T LIKE TOMBOYS, BUT...
PONG
...I'M NAN-JIRO.
PONG
NANJIRO ECHIZEN.
PONG

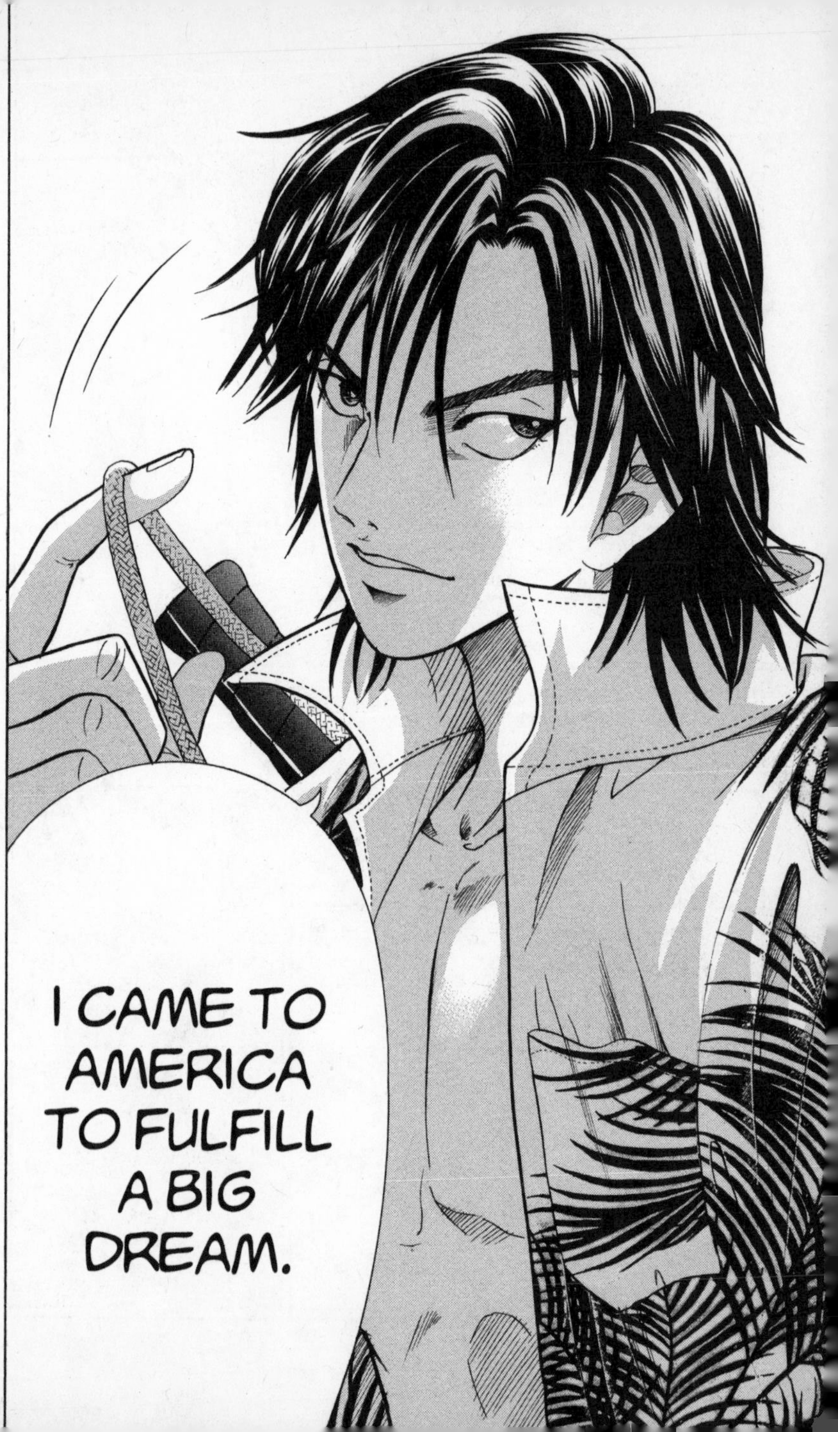
I CAME TO AMERICA TO FULFILL A BIG DREAM.

READ THIS WAY

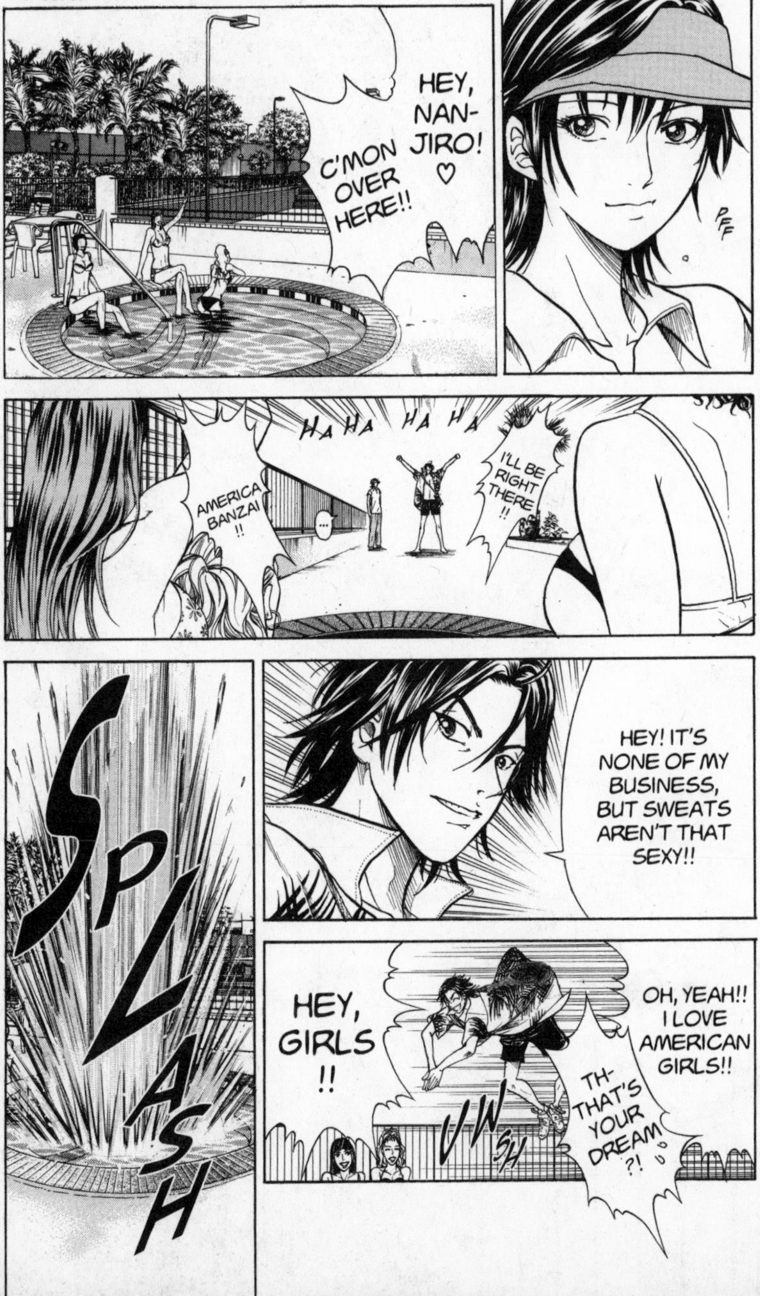
PFF
HEY, NAN-JIRO! ♡
C'MON OVER HERE!!
I'LL BE RIGHT THERE!!
HA HA HA HA
AMERICA BANZAI!!
...
HEY! IT'S NONE OF MY BUSINESS, BUT SWEATS AREN'T THAT SEXY!!
OH, YEAH!! I LOVE AMERICAN GIRLS!!
TH-THAT'S YOUR DREAM?!
VWSH
HEY, GIRLS!!
SPLASH

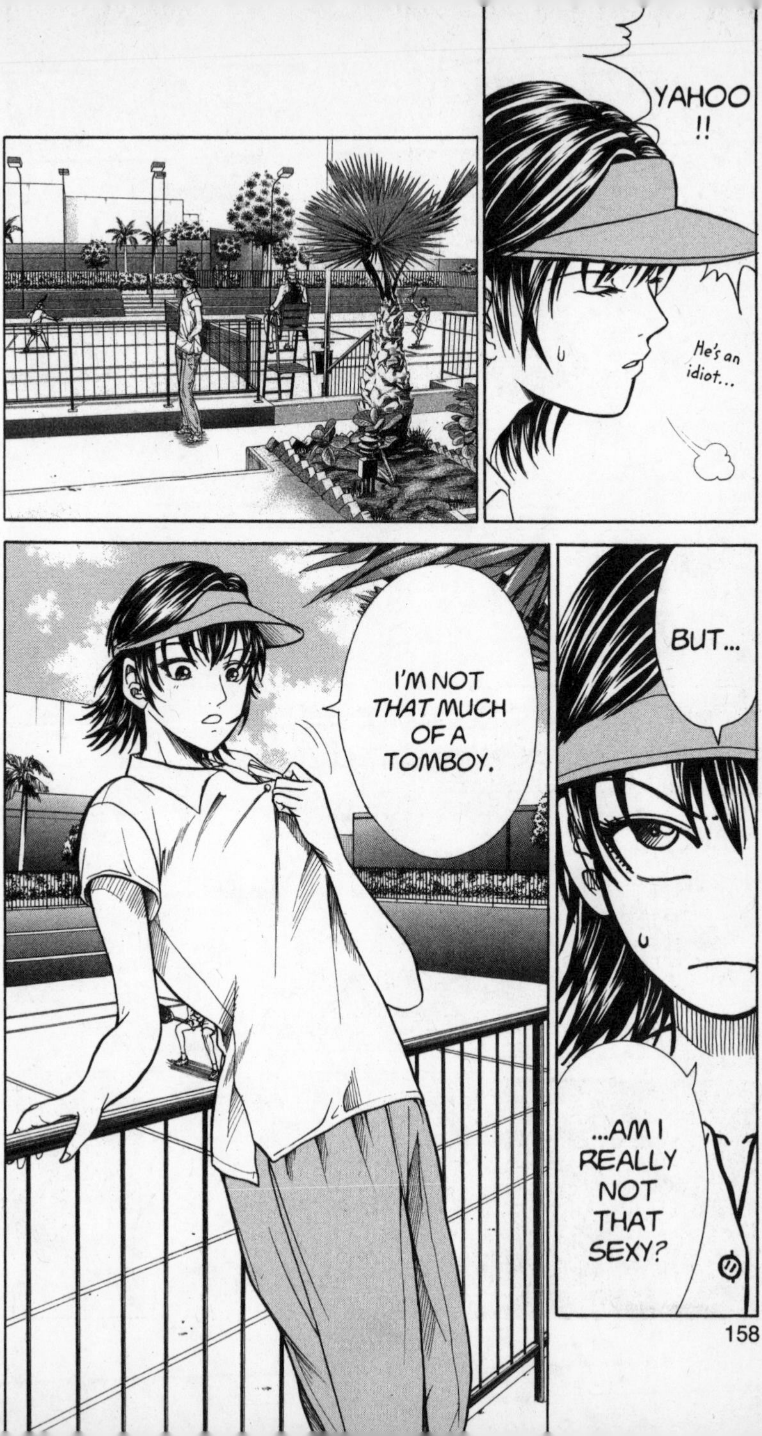
YAHOO !!
He's an idiot...
BUT...
...AM I REALLY NOT THAT SEXY?
I'M NOT *THAT* MUCH OF A TOMBOY.

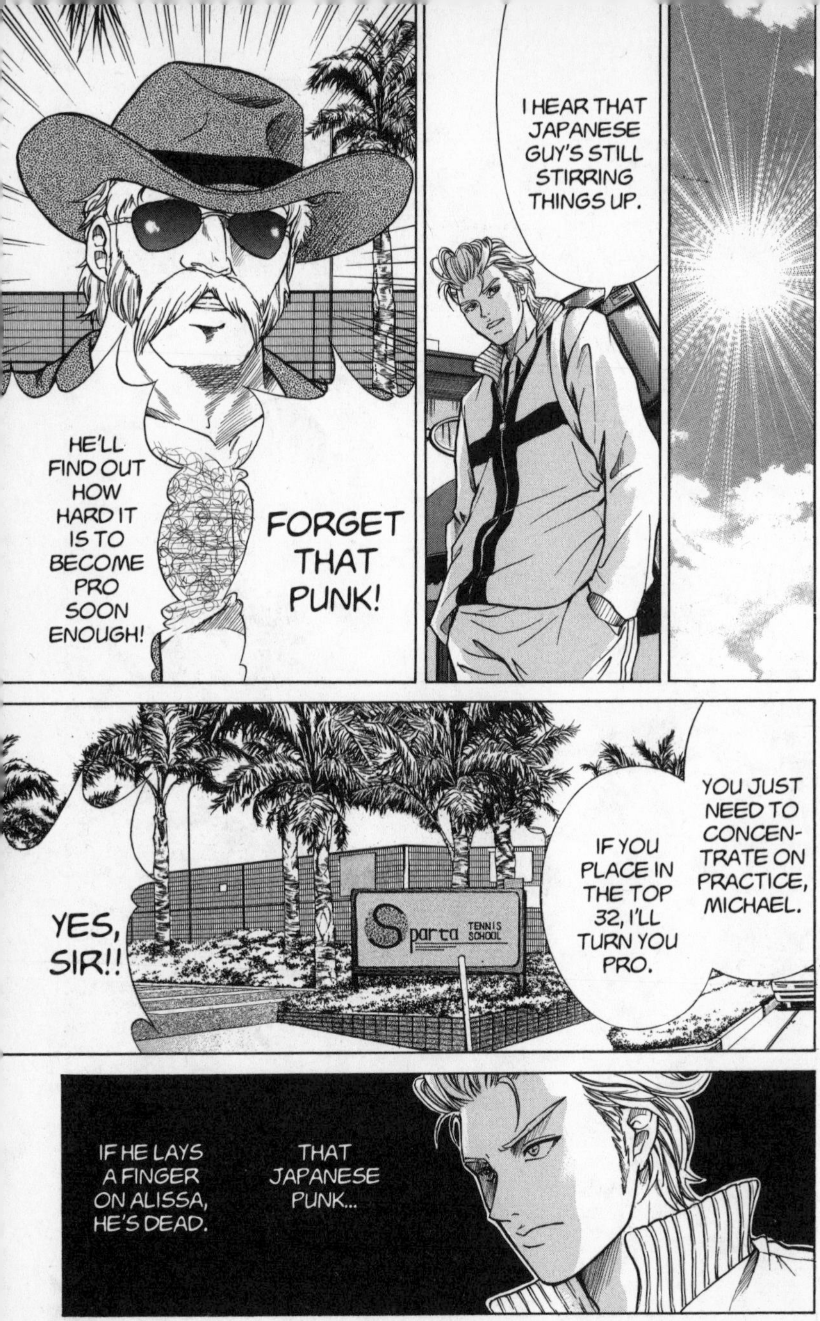
I HEAR THAT JAPANESE GUY'S STILL STIRRING THINGS UP.
FORGET THAT PUNK!
HE'LL FIND OUT HOW HARD IT IS TO BECOME PRO SOON ENOUGH!
YOU JUST NEED TO CONCEN-TRATE ON PRACTICE, MICHAEL.
IF YOU PLACE IN THE TOP 32, I'LL TURN YOU PRO.
Sparta TENNIS SCHOOL
YES, SIR!!
THAT JAPANESE PUNK...
IF HE LAYS A FINGER ON ALISSA, HE'S DEAD.

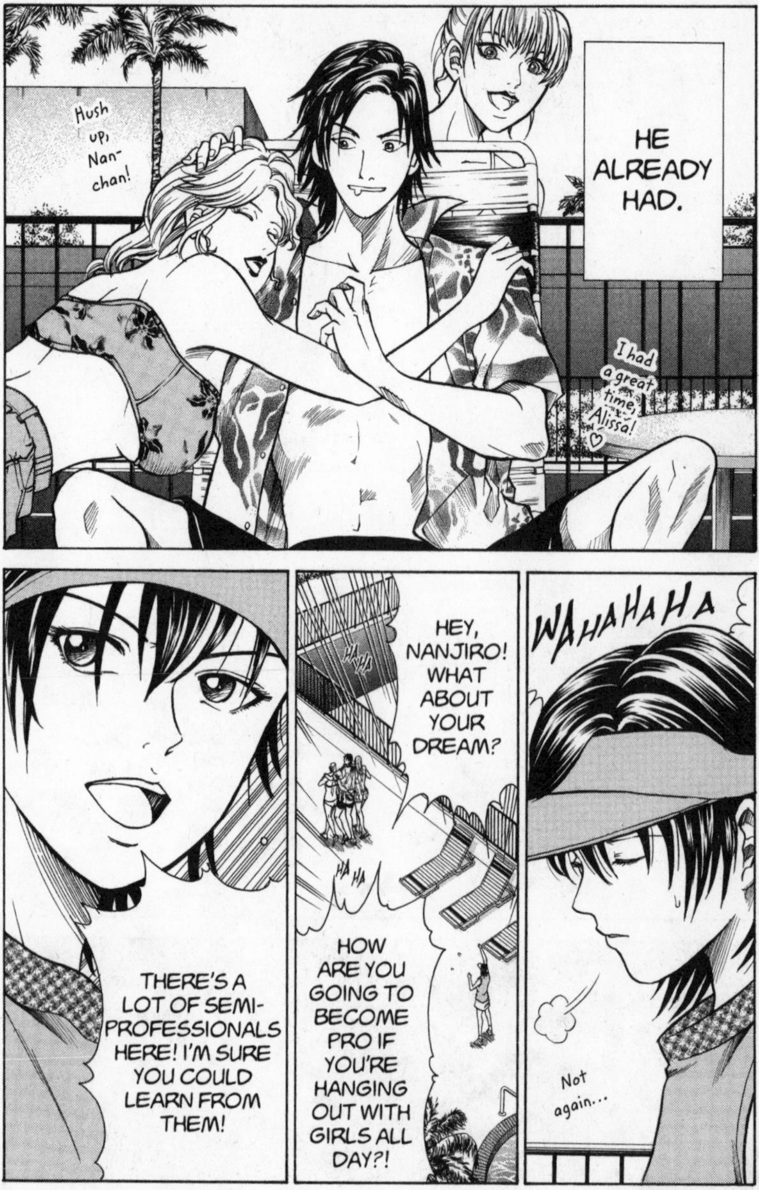
HE ALREADY HAD.
I had a great time, Alissa! ♡
Hush up, Nan-chan!
WAHAHAHA
Not again...
HA HA
HEY, NANJIRO! WHAT ABOUT YOUR DREAM?
HA HA
HOW ARE YOU GOING TO BECOME PRO IF YOU'RE HANGING OUT WITH GIRLS ALL DAY?!
THERE'S A LOT OF SEMI-PROFESSIONALS HERE! I'M SURE YOU COULD LEARN FROM THEM!

READ THIS WAY

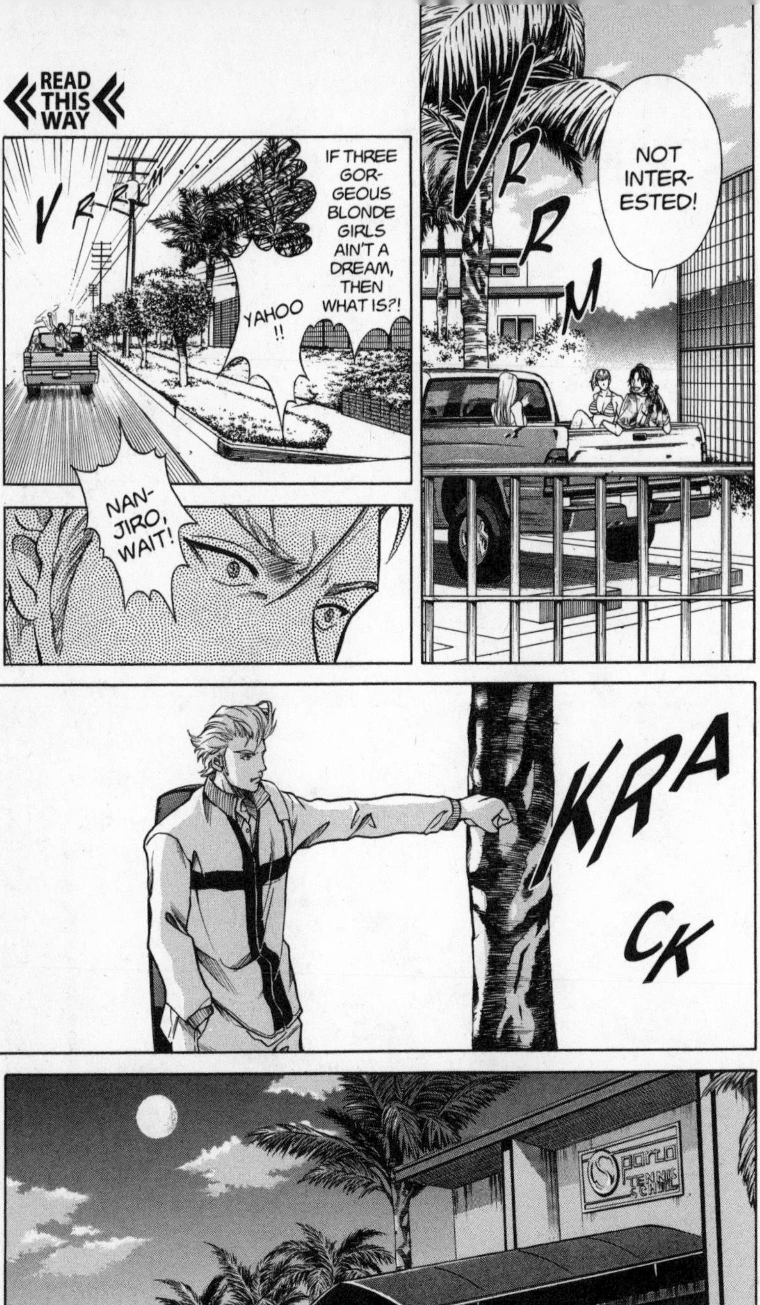

VRRM
NOT INTERESTED!
VRRRM...
IF THREE GORGEOUS BLONDE GIRLS AIN'T A DREAM, THEN WHAT IS?!
YAHOO !!
NANJIRO, WAIT!
KRACK

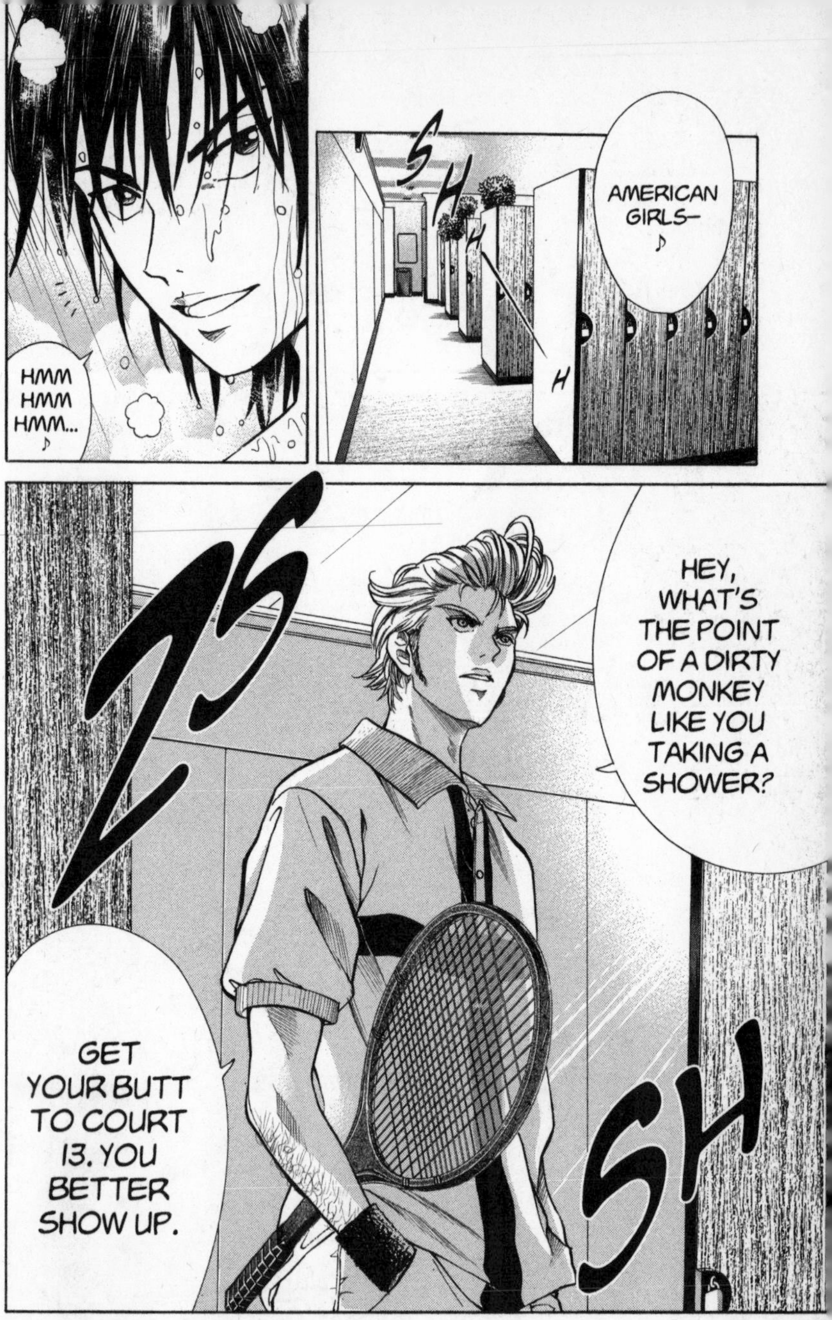
SHHH
AMERICAN GIRLS—♪
HMM HMM HMM...♪
HEY, WHAT'S THE POINT OF A DIRTY MONKEY LIKE YOU TAKING A SHOWER?
SH
GET YOUR BUTT TO COURT 13. YOU BETTER SHOW UP.

READ THIS WAY

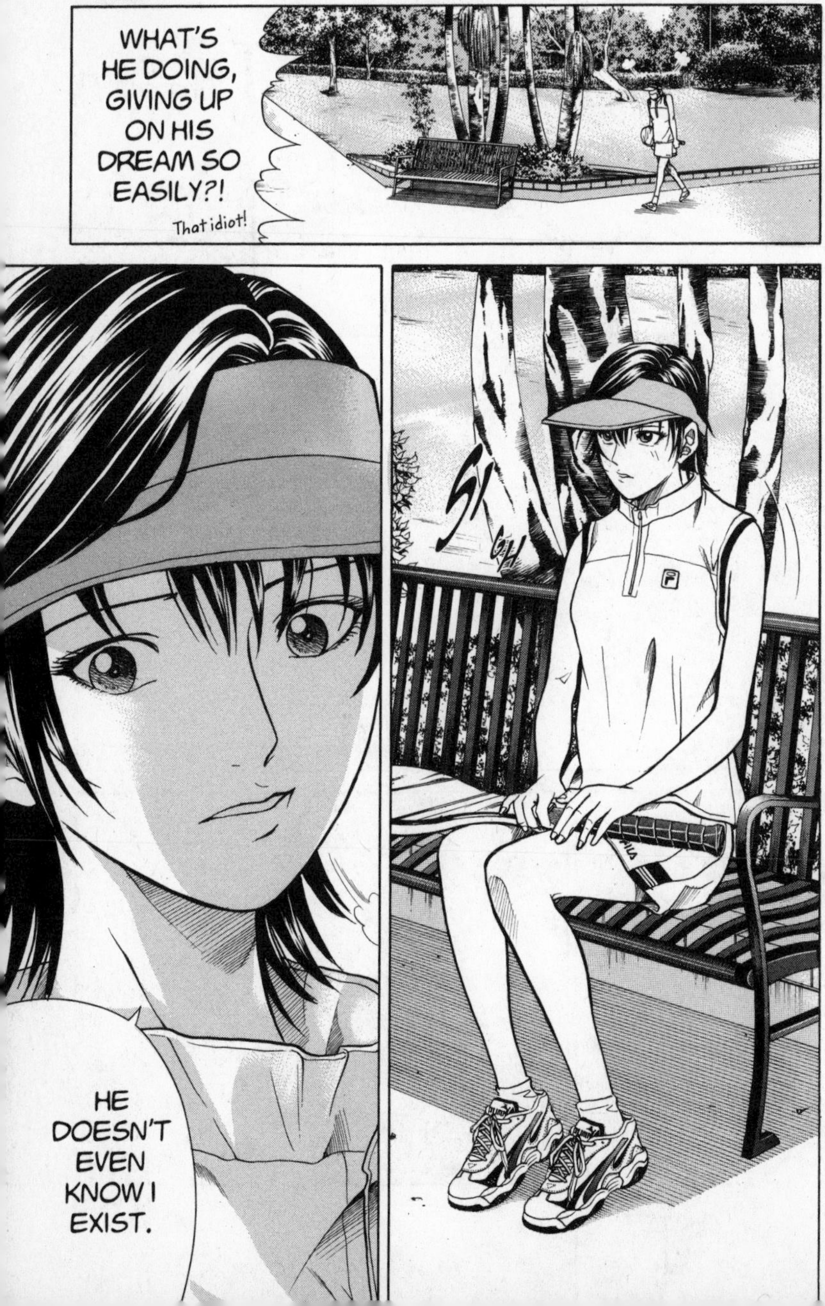
WHAT'S HE DOING, GIVING UP ON HIS DREAM SO EASILY?!
That idiot!
SIGH
HE DOESN'T EVEN KNOW I EXIST.

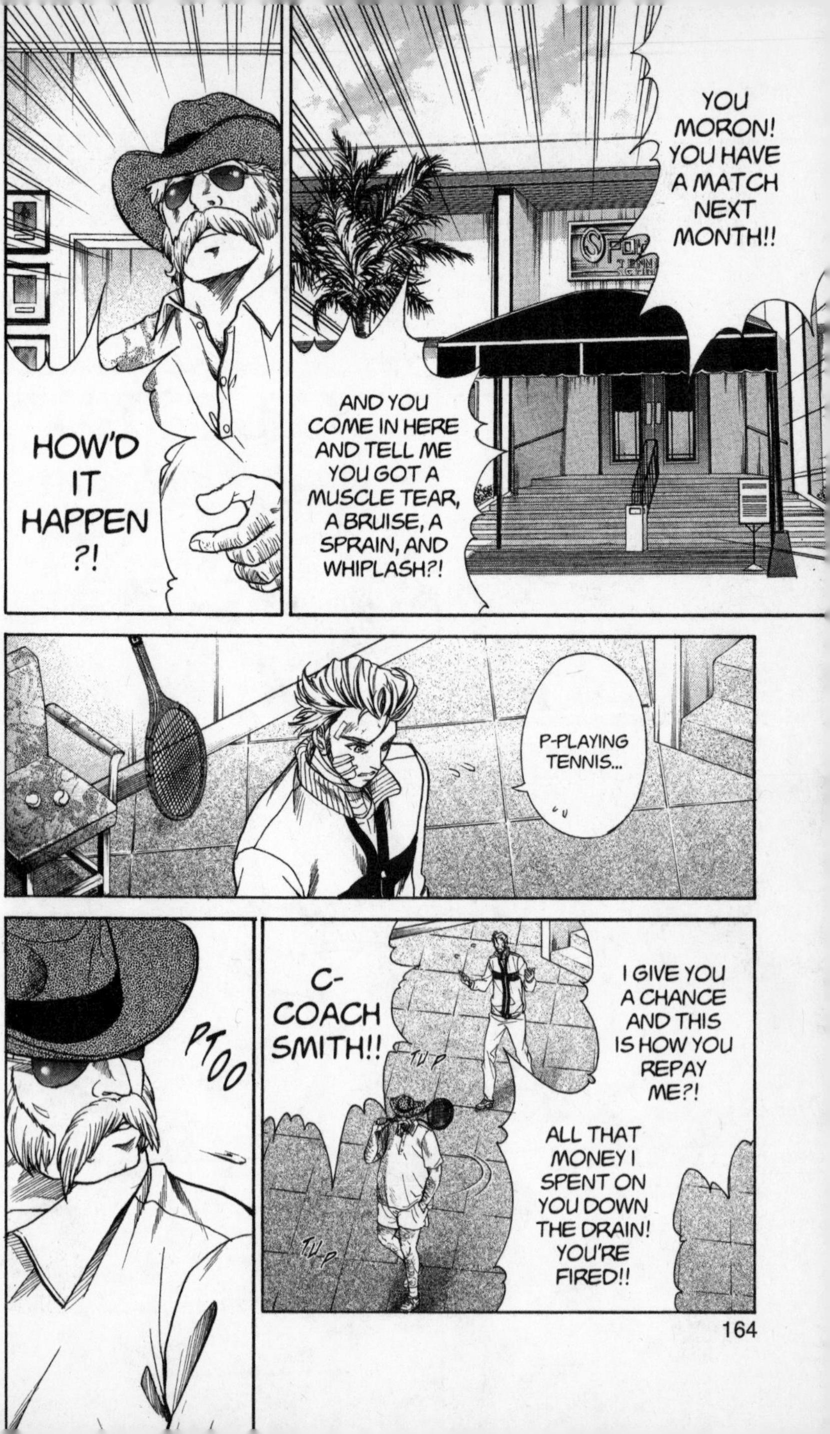
YOU MORON! YOU HAVE A MATCH NEXT MONTH!!
AND YOU COME IN HERE AND TELL ME YOU GOT A MUSCLE TEAR, A BRUISE, A SPRAIN, AND WHIPLASH?!
HOW'D IT HAPPEN?!
P-PLAYING TENNIS...
I GIVE YOU A CHANCE AND THIS IS HOW YOU REPAY ME?!
ALL THAT MONEY I SPENT ON YOU DOWN THE DRAIN! YOU'RE FIRED!!
C-COACH SMITH!!
TUP
TUP
PTOO

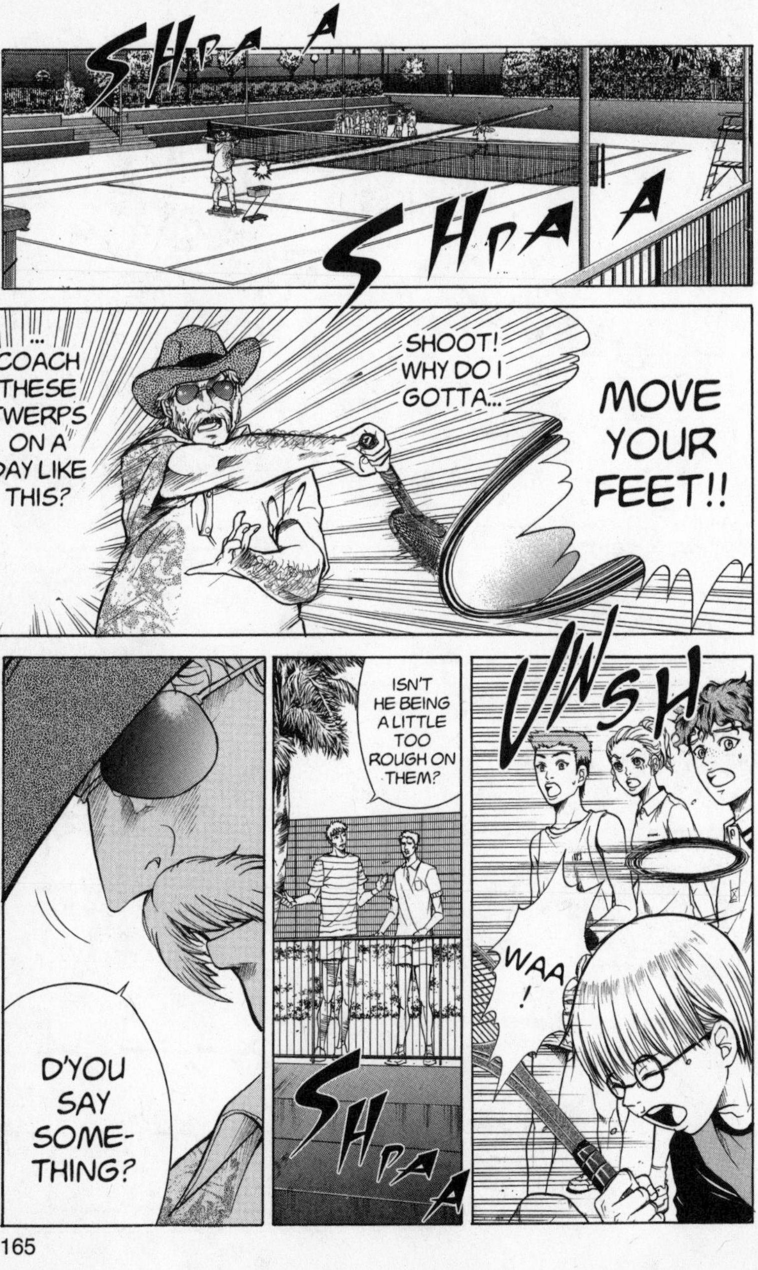
SHPAA
SHPAA
MOVE YOUR FEET!!
SHOOT! WHY DO I GOTTA...
... COACH THESE TWERPS ON A DAY LIKE THIS?
VWSH
WAA!
ISN'T HE BEING A LITTLE TOO ROUGH ON THEM?
SHPAA
D'YOU SAY SOMETHING?

N-NO, SIR...

YIKES

THAT'S RIGHT! THEY SHOULD FEEL LUCKY THEY GET TO TRAIN WITH AN EX-PRO!

HM? THAT BOY'S GLASSES...

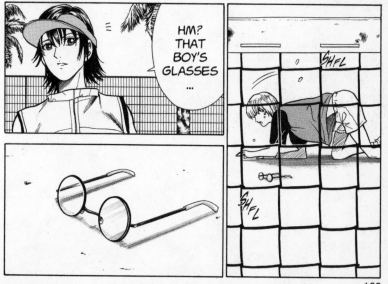

SHFL

SHFL

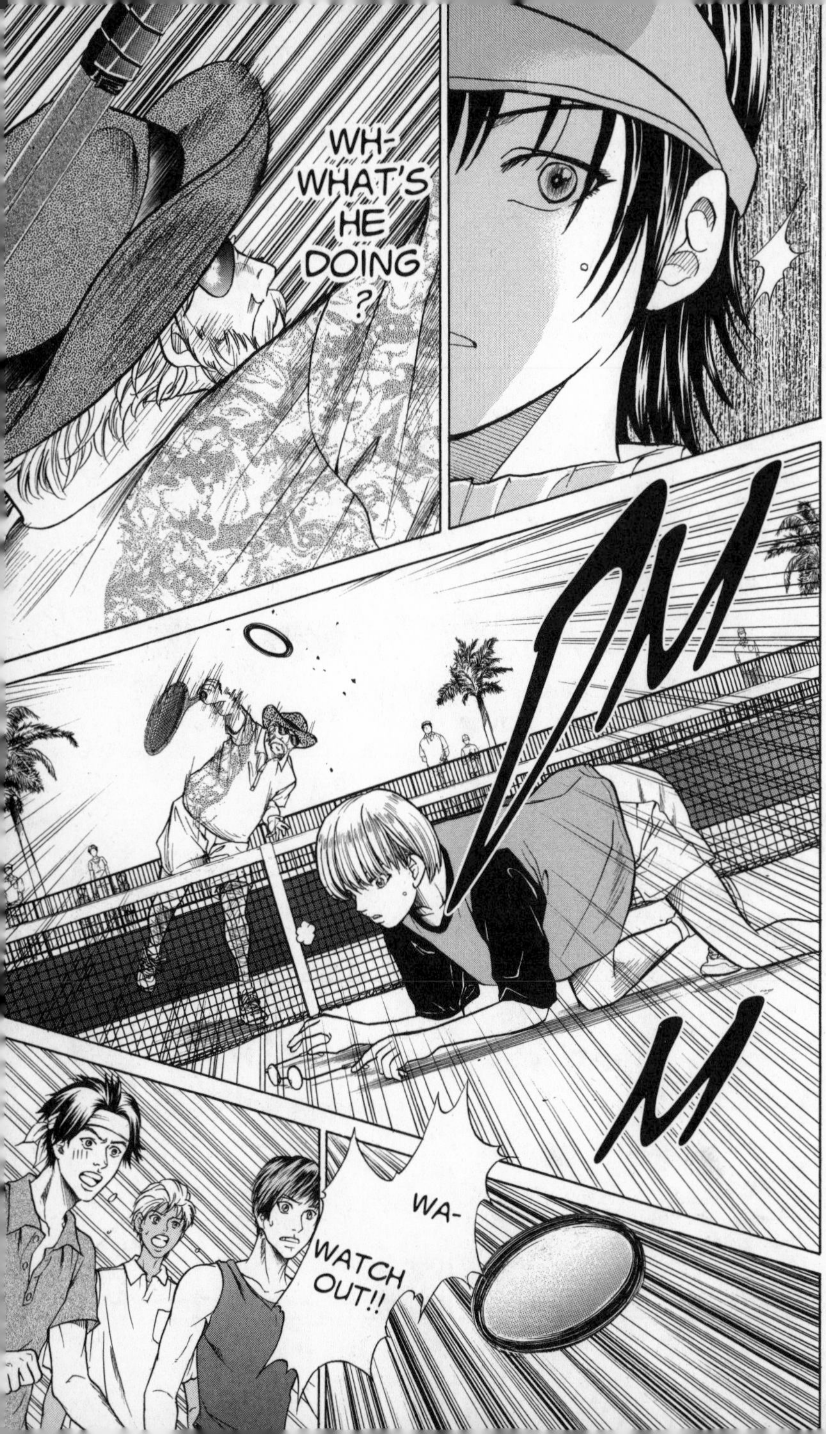
WH-
WHAT'S HE DOING?
WA-
WATCH OUT!!

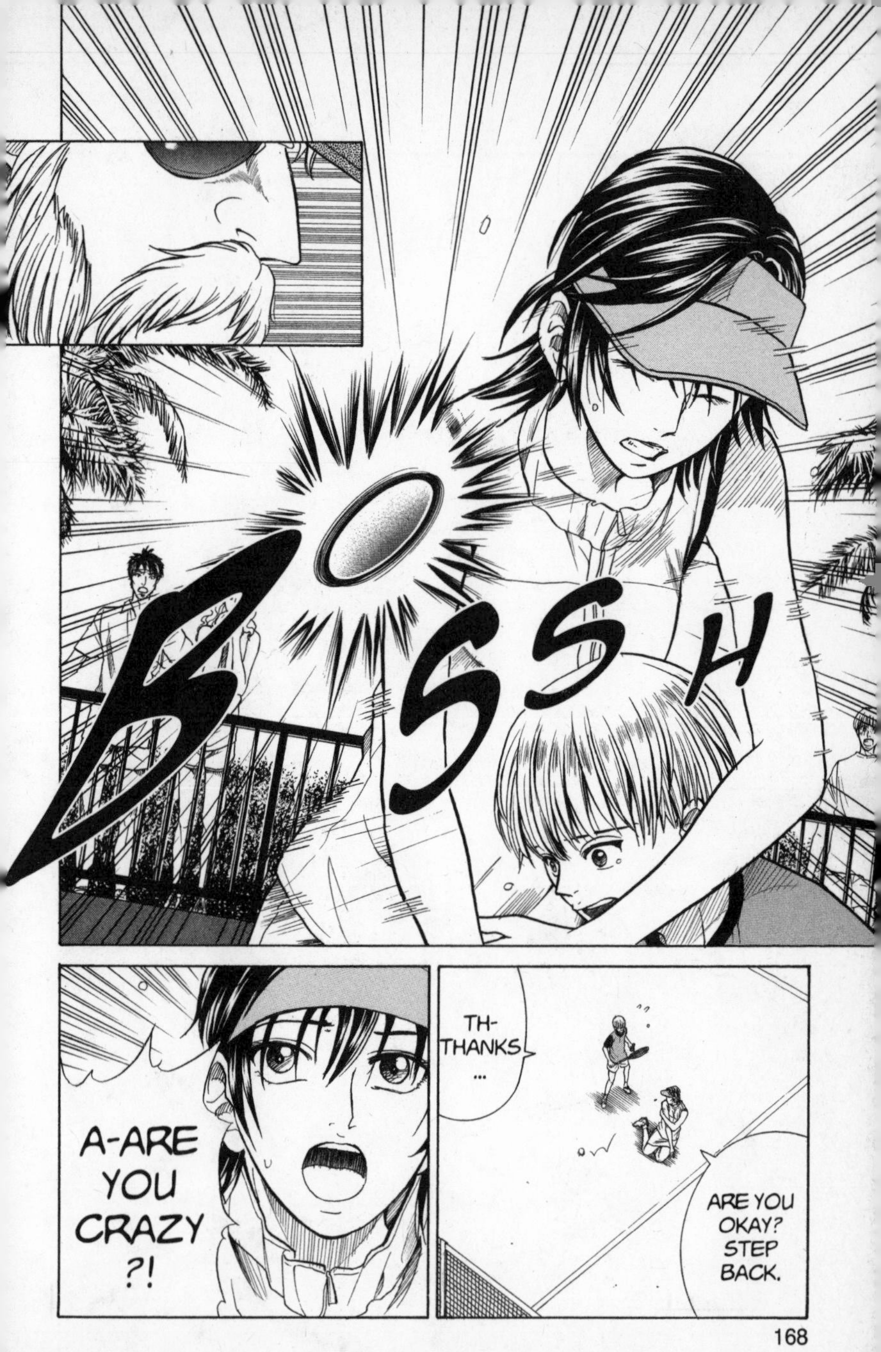
BISSH
ARE YOU OKAY? STEP BACK.
TH-THANKS...
A-ARE YOU CRAZY?!

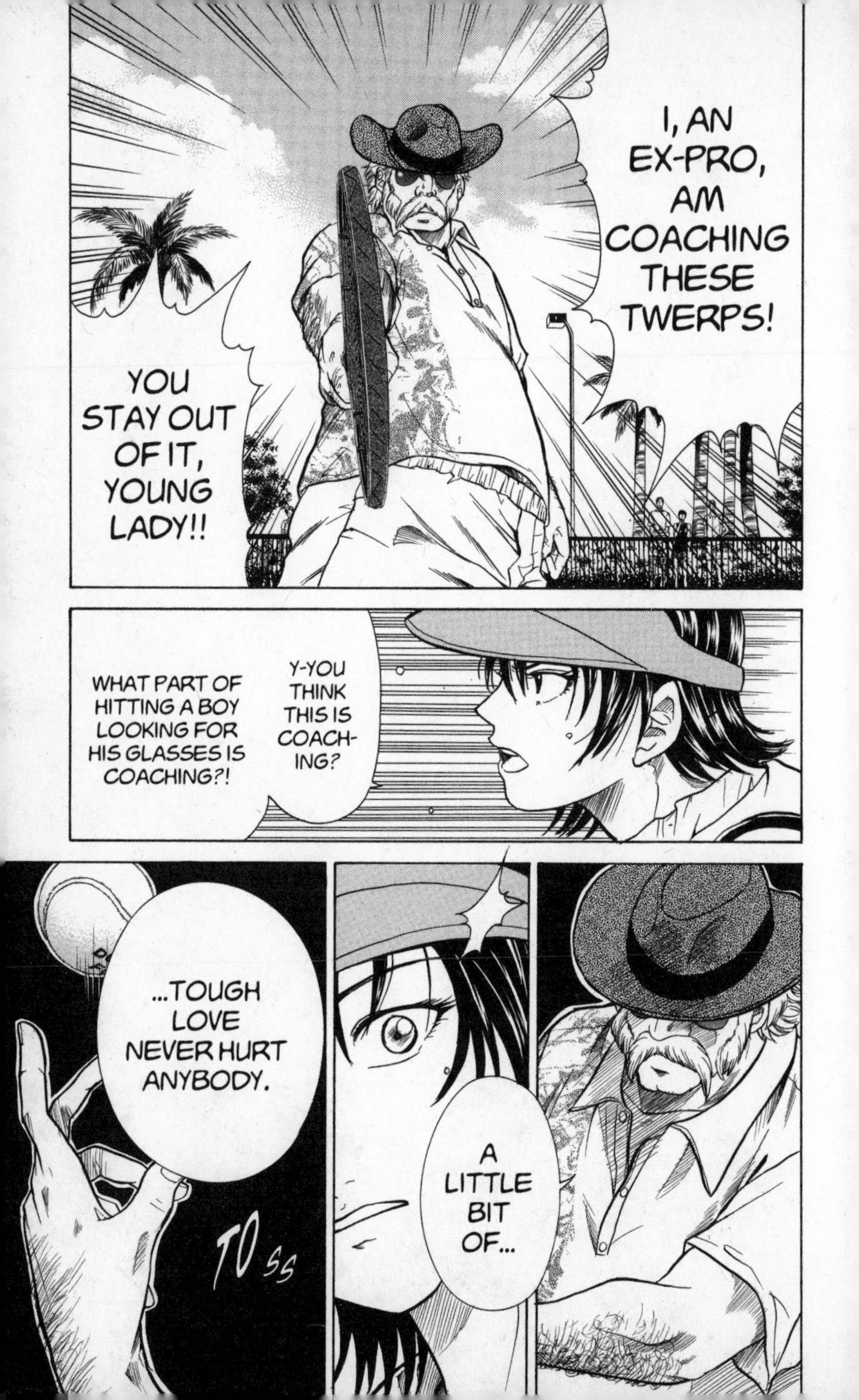
I, AN EX-PRO, AM COACHING THESE TWERPS!
YOU STAY OUT OF IT, YOUNG LADY!!
Y-YOU THINK THIS IS COACHING?
WHAT PART OF HITTING A BOY LOOKING FOR HIS GLASSES IS COACHING?!
A LITTLE BIT OF...
...TOUGH LOVE NEVER HURT ANYBODY.
TOSS

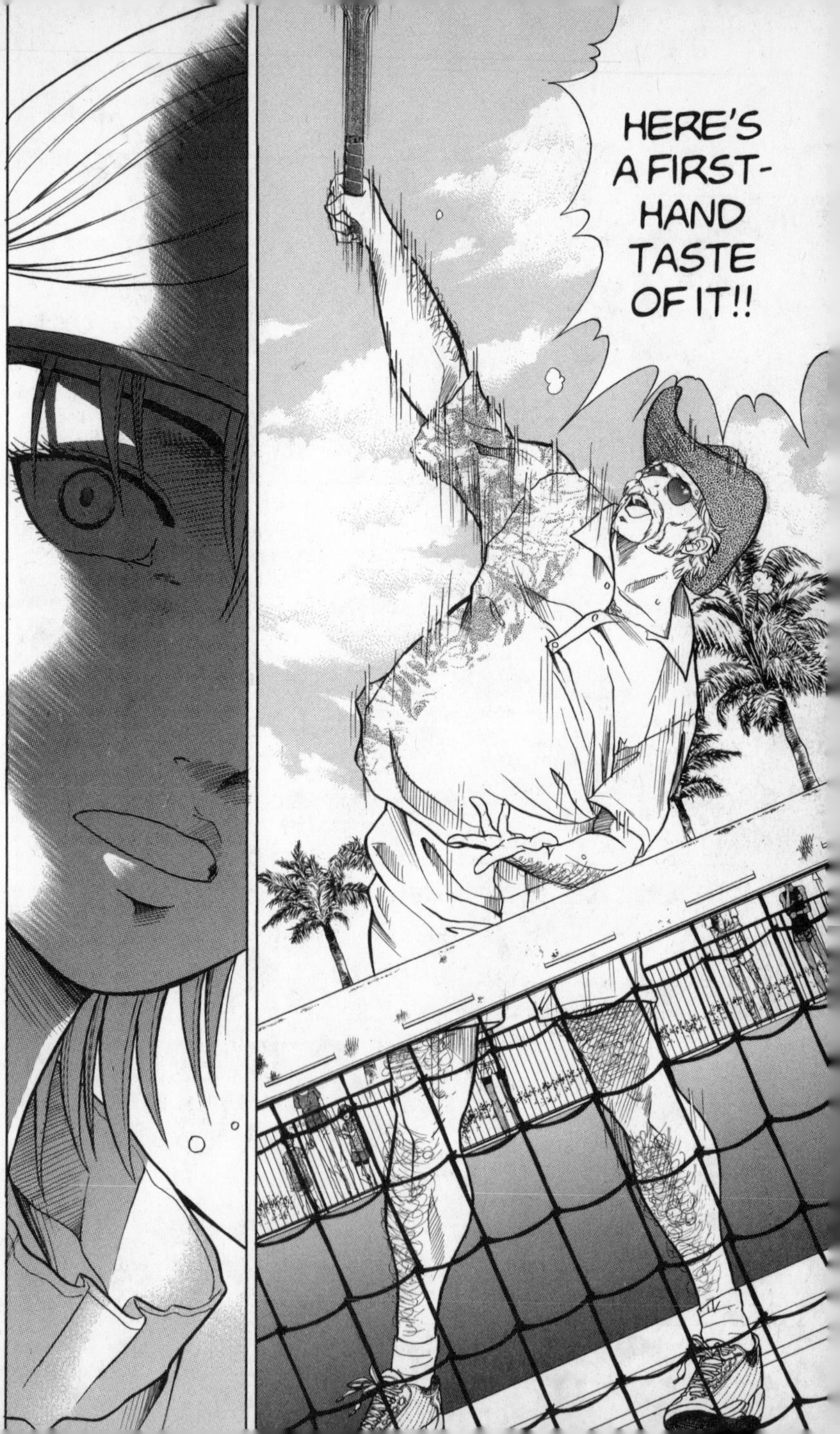
HERE'S A FIRST-HAND TASTE OF IT!!

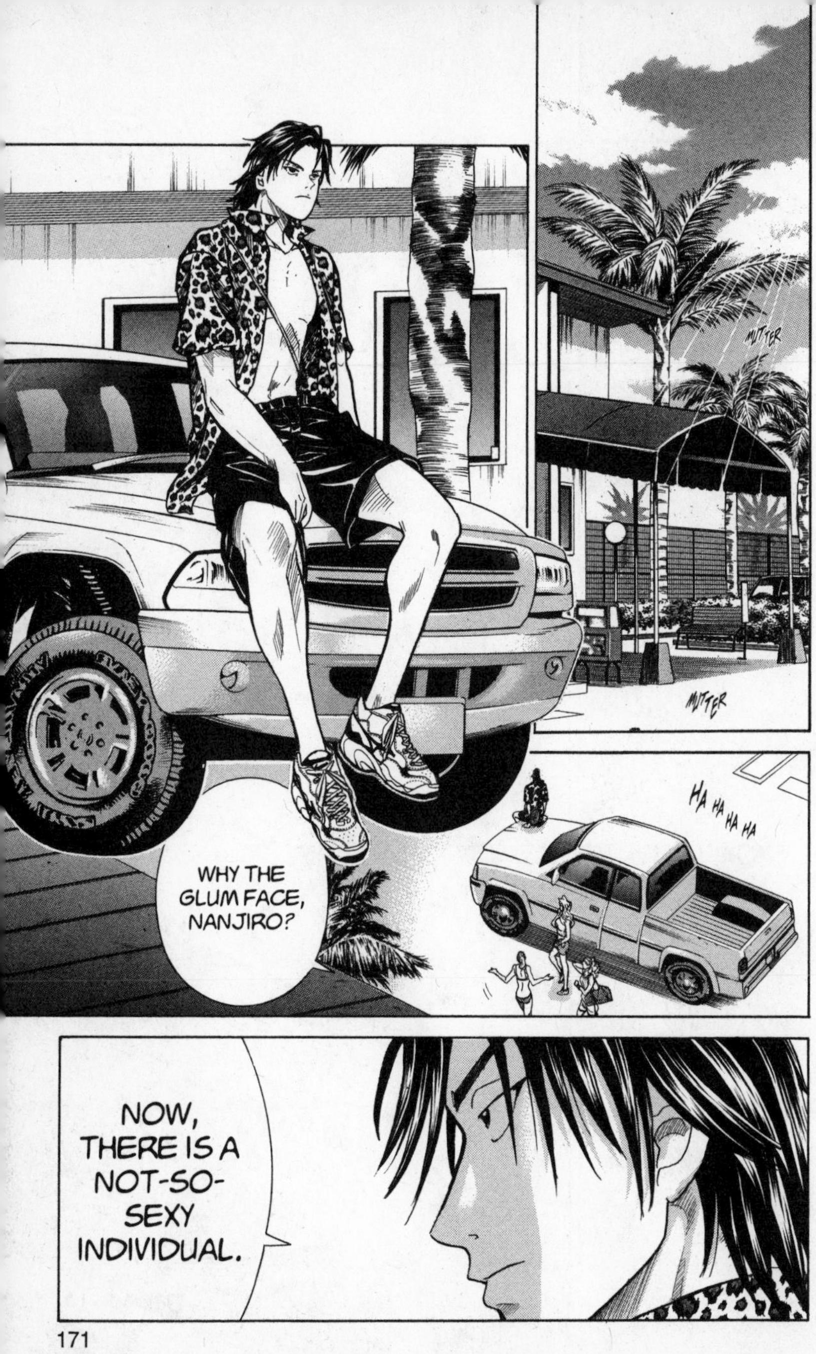
MUTTER
MUTTER
HA HA HA HA
WHY THE GLUM FACE, NANJIRO?
NOW, THERE IS A NOT-SO-SEXY INDIVIDUAL.

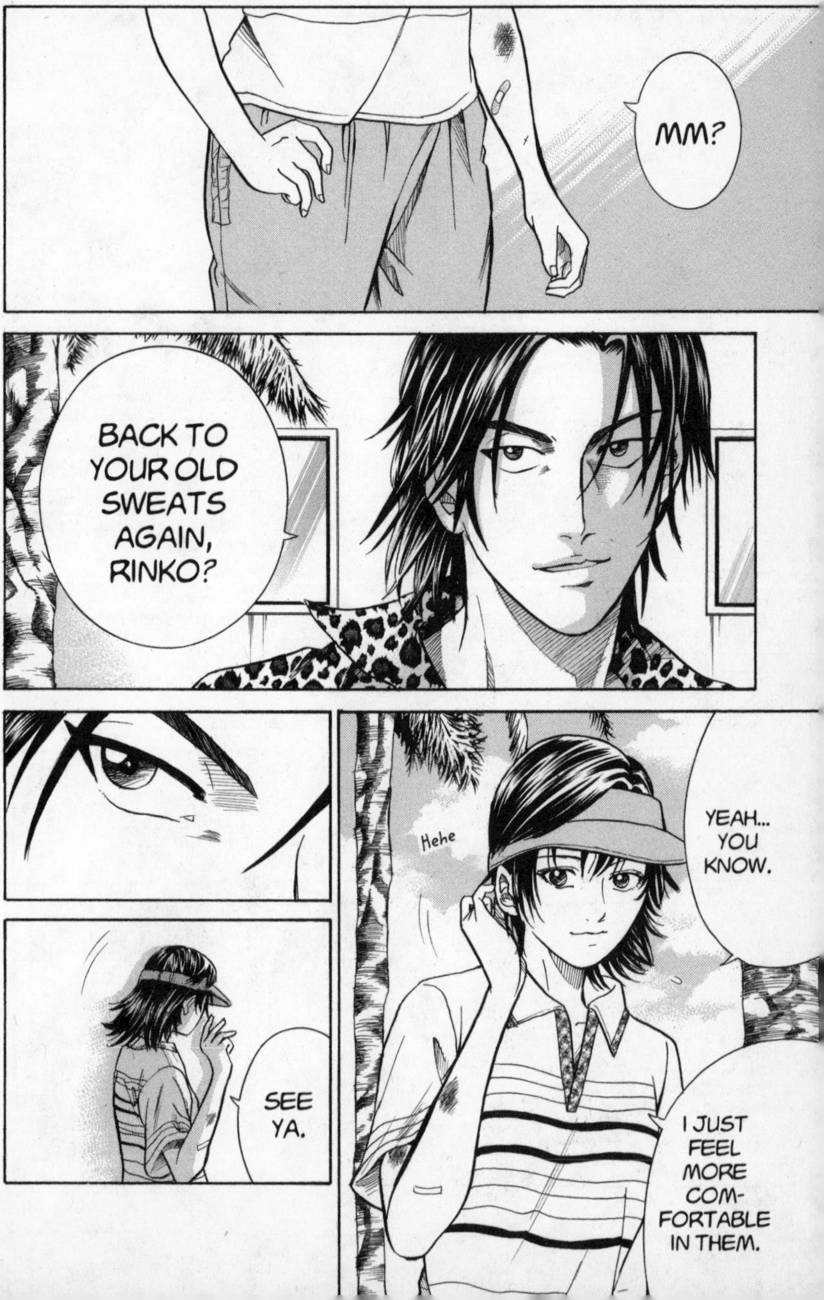
MM?
BACK TO YOUR OLD SWEATS AGAIN, RINKO?
YEAH... YOU KNOW.
Hehe
I JUST FEEL MORE COM-FORTABLE IN THEM.
SEE YA.

READ THIS WAY

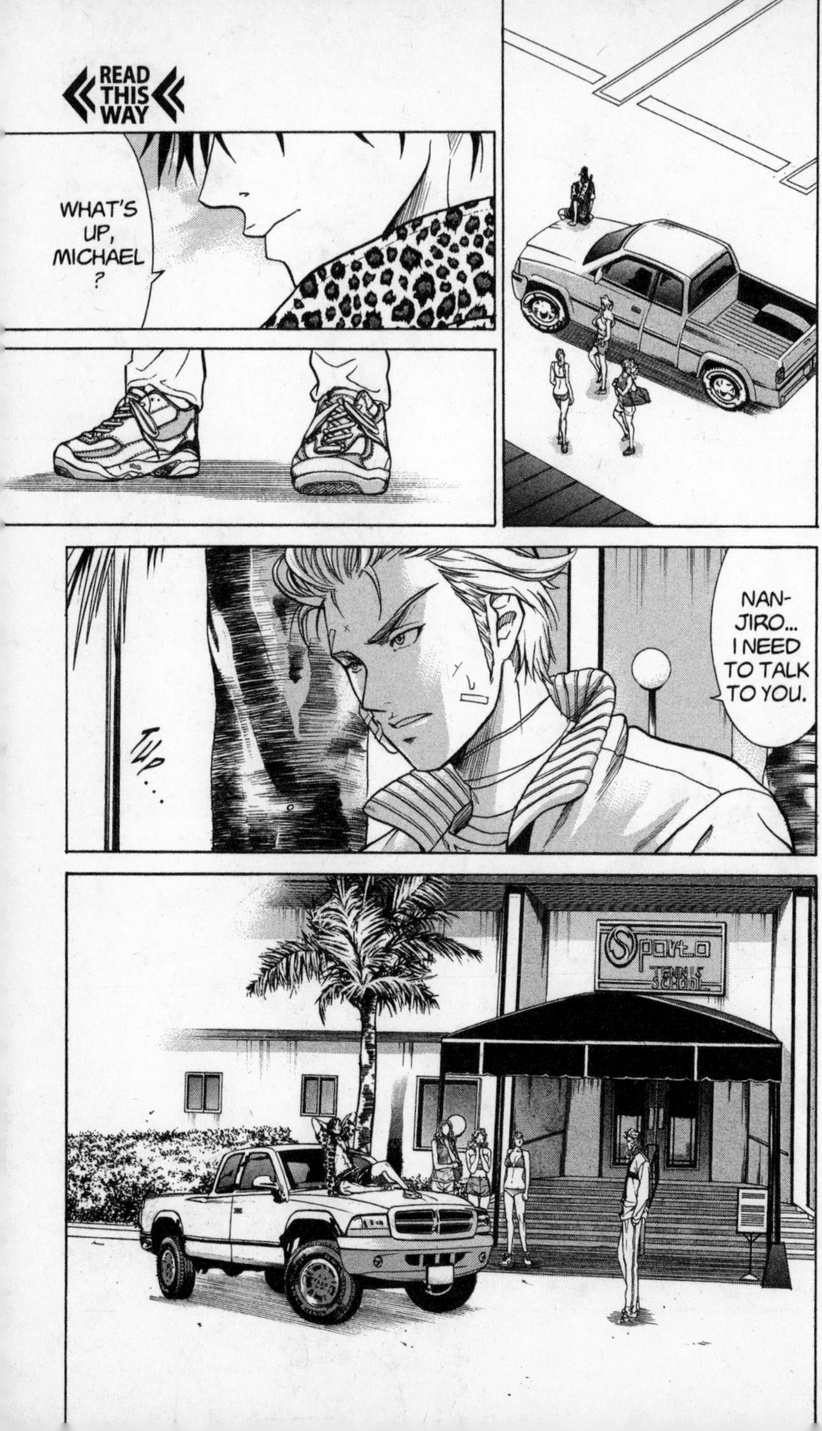
WHAT'S UP, MICHAEL?
NAN-JIRO... I NEED TO TALK TO YOU.
TUP...

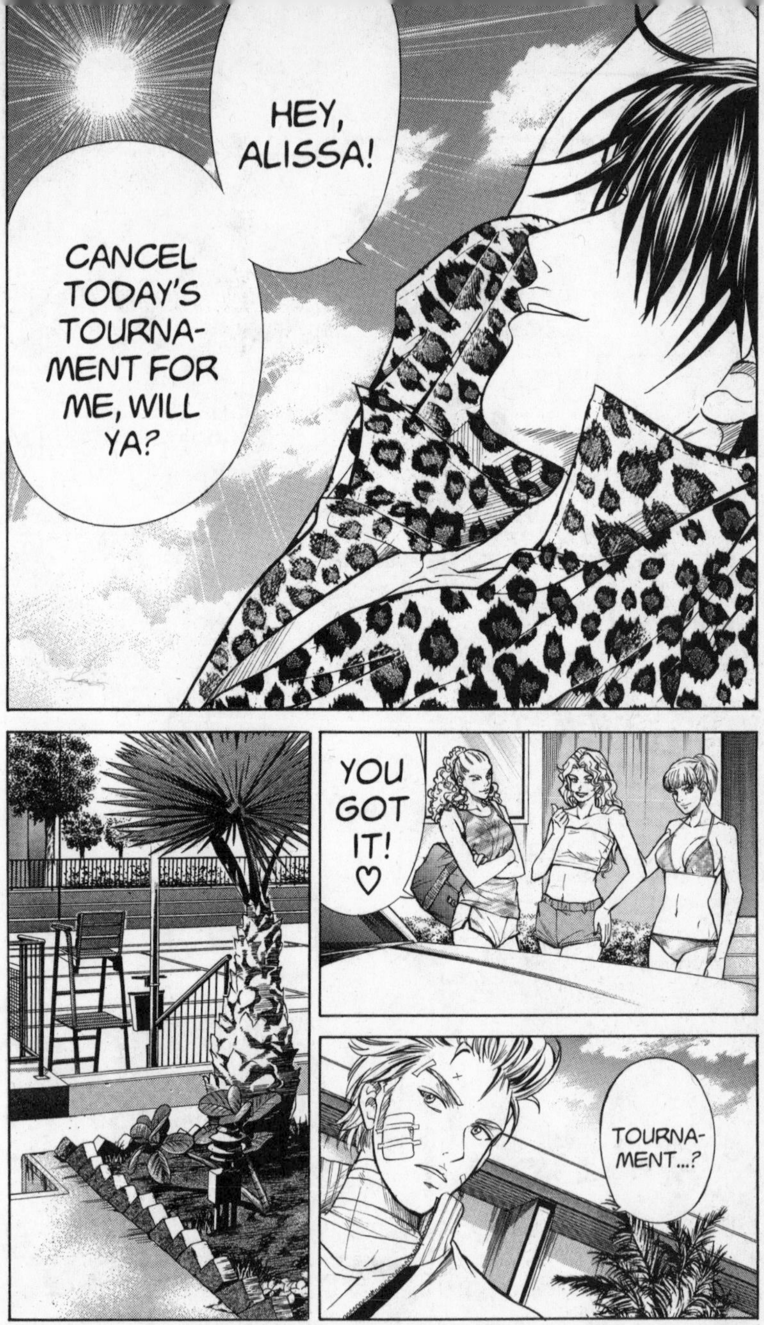
HEY, ALISSA!
CANCEL TODAY'S TOURNAMENT FOR ME, WILL YA?
YOU GOT IT! ♡
TOURNAMENT...?

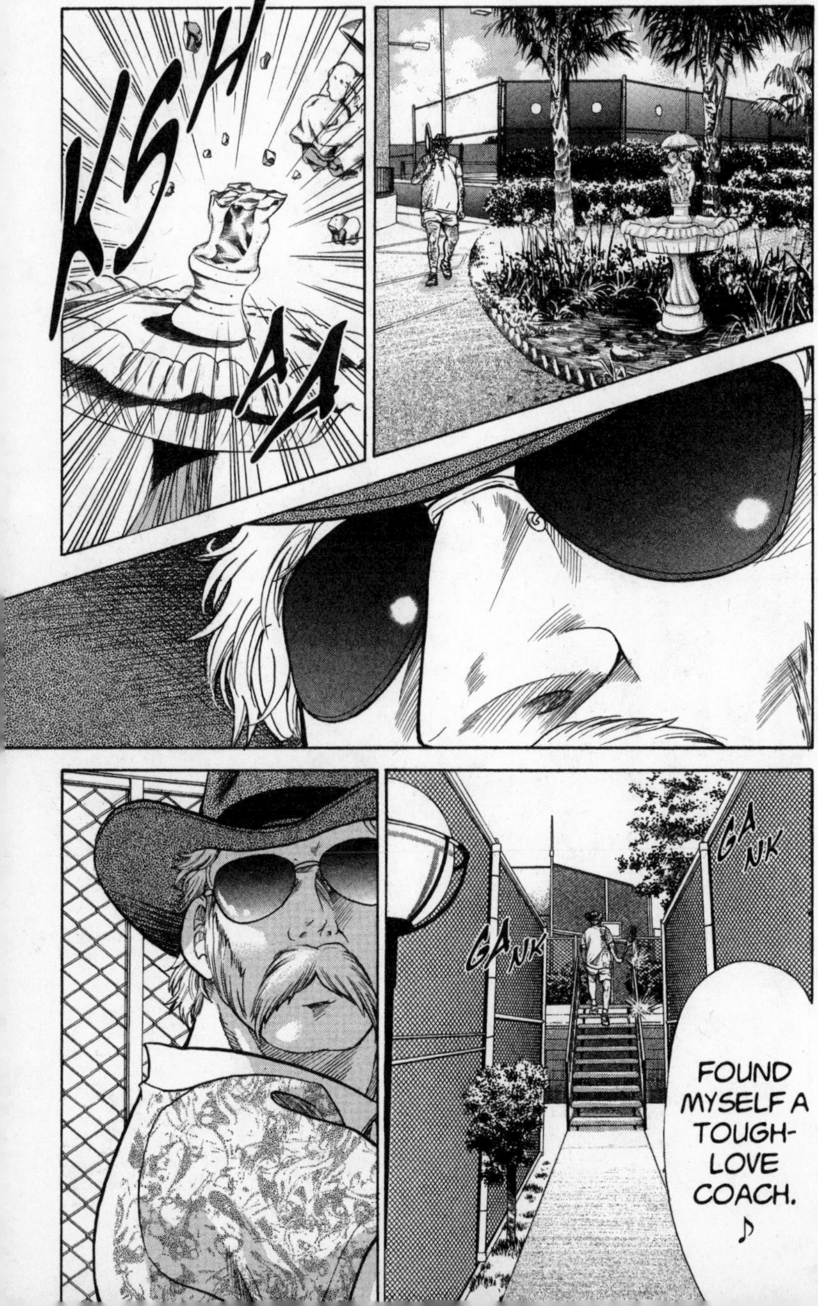
KSH
AA
GANK
GANK
FOUND MYSELF A TOUGH-LOVE COACH. ♪

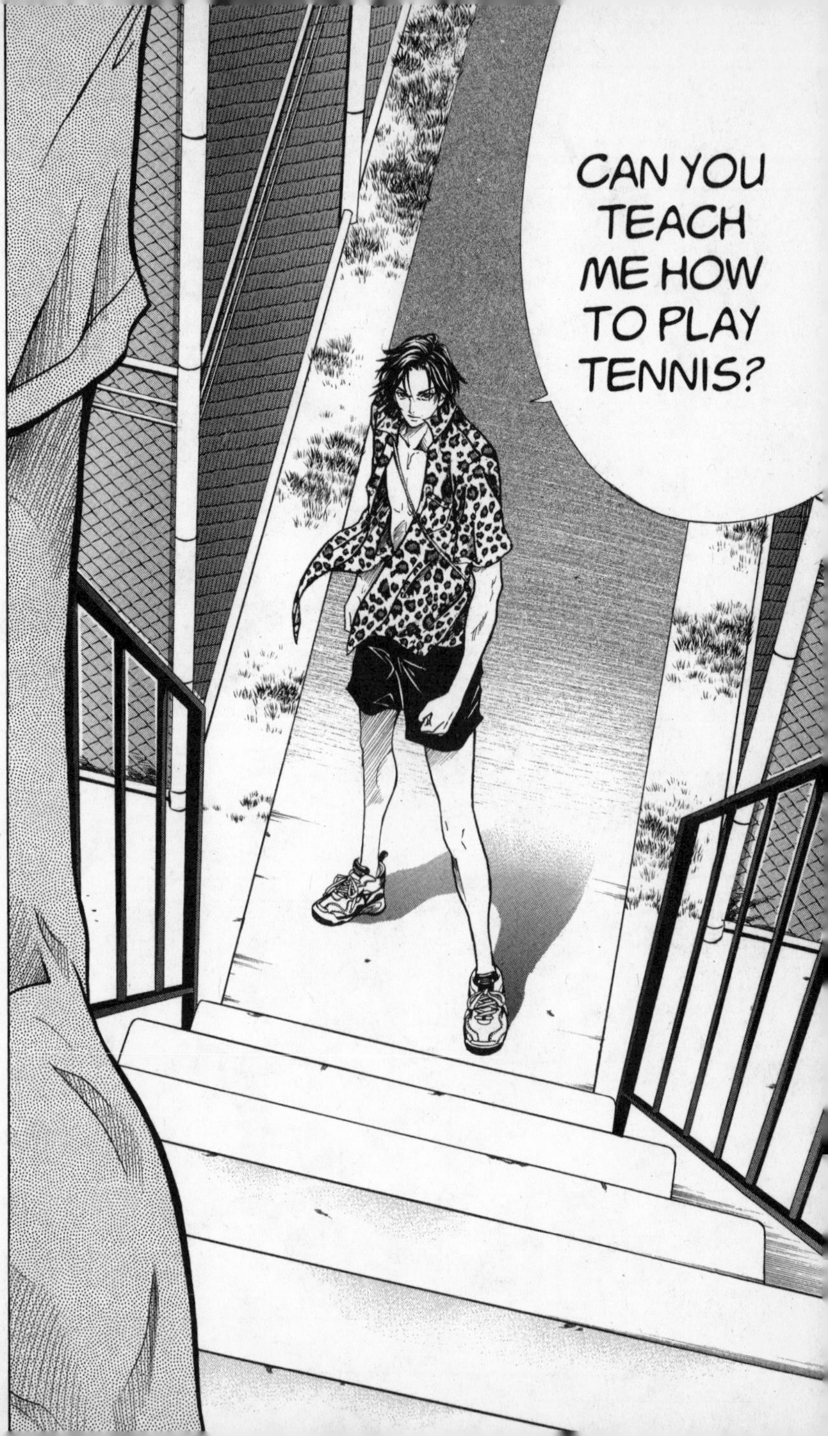
CAN YOU TEACH ME HOW TO PLAY TENNIS?

READ THIS WAY

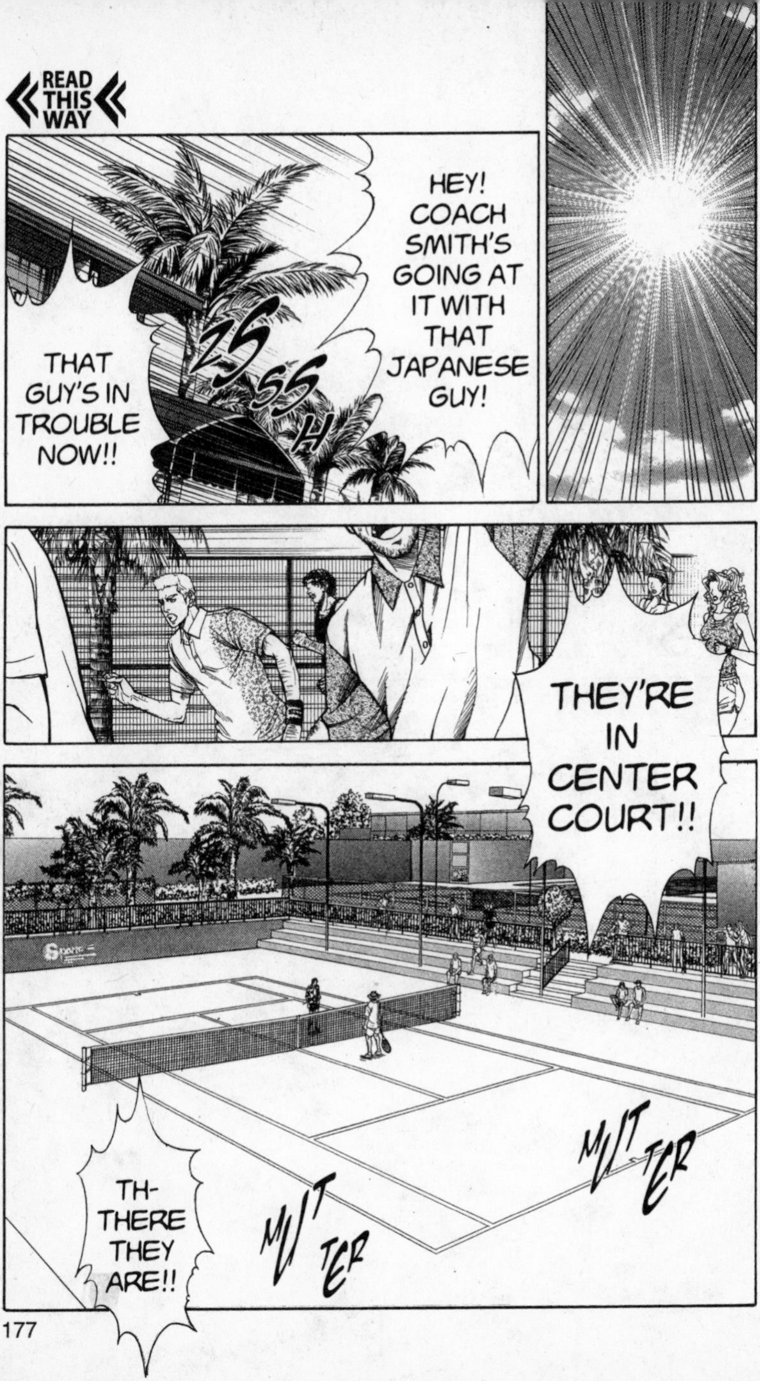

HEY! COACH SMITH'S GOING AT IT WITH THAT JAPANESE GUY!
ZSSSH
THAT GUY'S IN TROUBLE NOW!!
THEY'RE IN CENTER COURT!!
MUTTER
TH-THERE THEY ARE!!
MUTTER

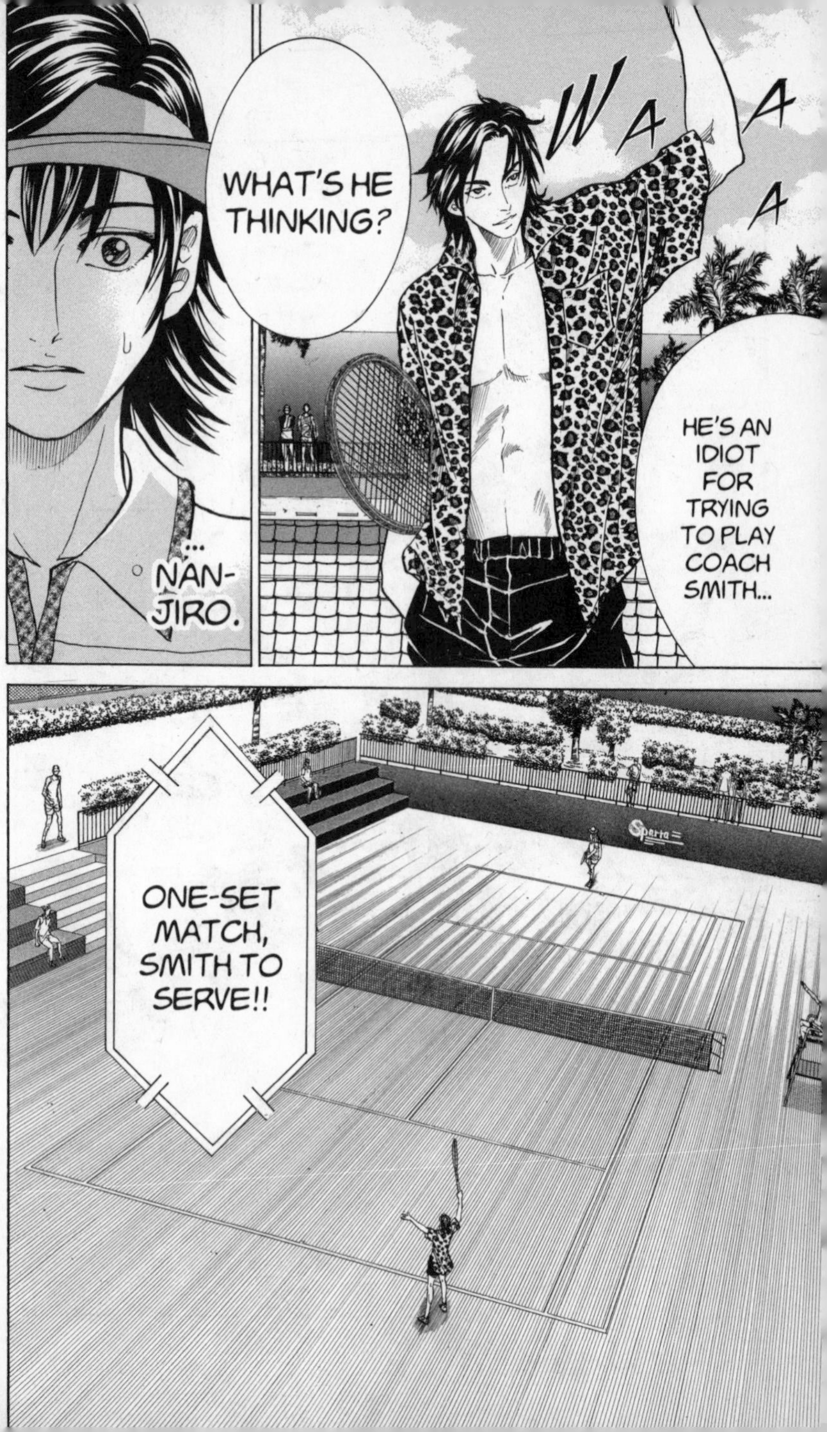
WAAA
WHAT'S HE THINKING?
HE'S AN IDIOT FOR TRYING TO PLAY COACH SMITH...
... NAN-JIRO.
ONE-SET MATCH, SMITH TO SERVE!!

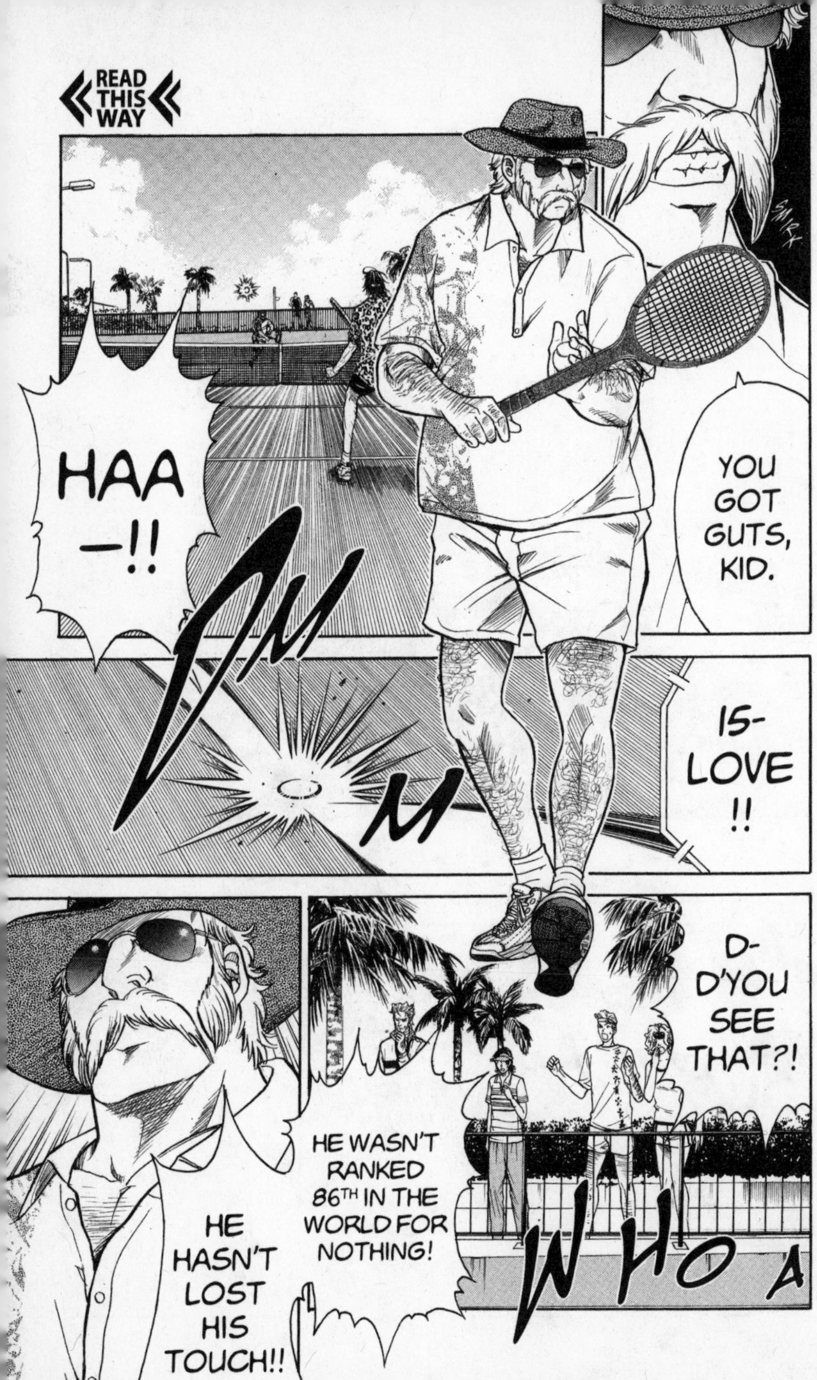
READ THIS WAY
SMRK
YOU GOT GUTS, KID.
HAA—!!
15-LOVE!!
DMM
D-D'YOU SEE THAT?!
WHOA
HE WASN'T RANKED 86TH IN THE WORLD FOR NOTHING!
HE HASN'T LOST HIS TOUCH!!

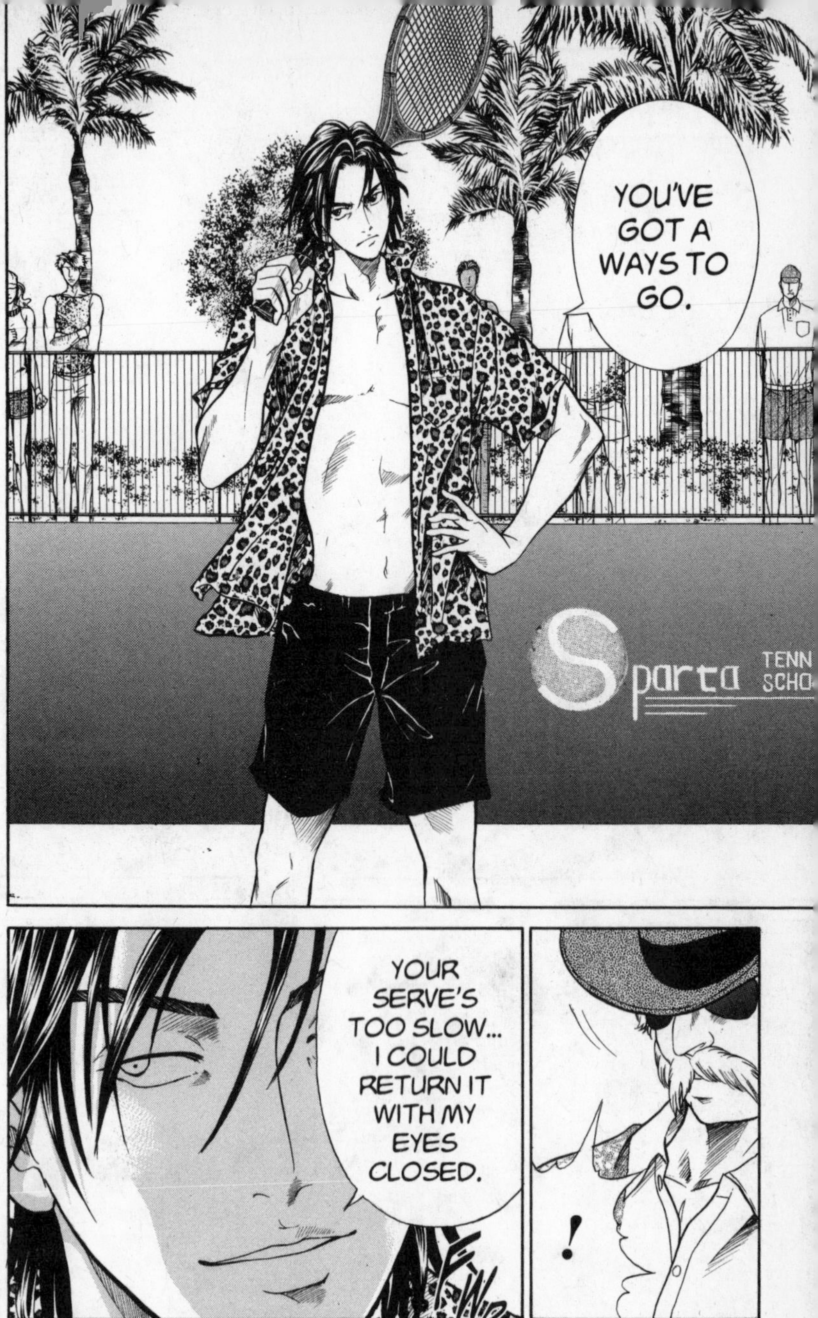
YOU'VE GOT A WAYS TO GO.
Sparta
TENN
SCHO
!
YOUR SERVE'S TOO SLOW... I COULD RETURN IT WITH MY EYES CLOSED.
FWIP

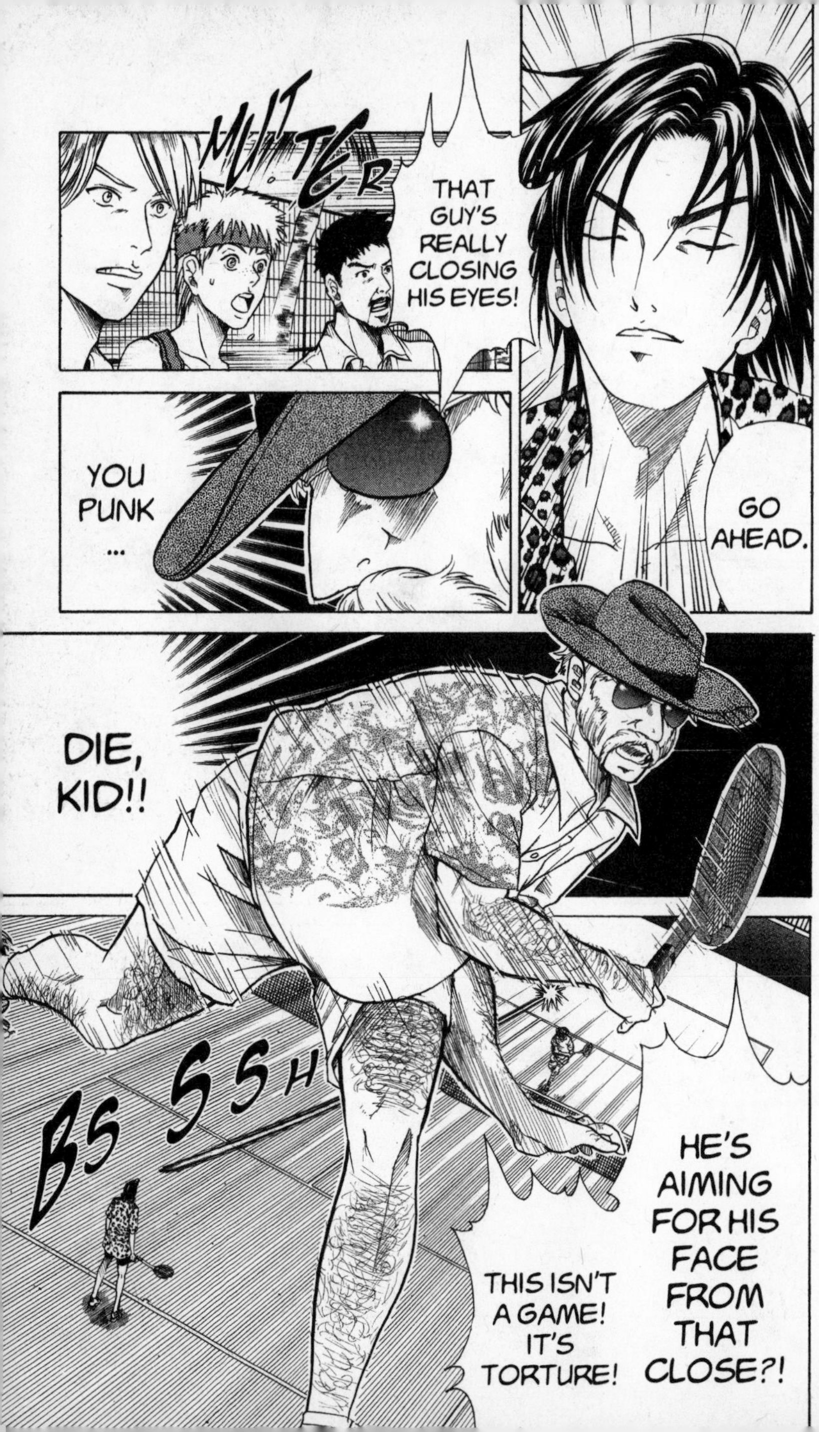
GO AHEAD.
MUTTER
THAT GUY'S REALLY CLOSING HIS EYES!
YOU PUNK ...
DIE, KID!!
BSSSH
HE'S AIMING FOR HIS FACE FROM THAT CLOSE?!
THIS ISN'T A GAME! IT'S TORTURE!

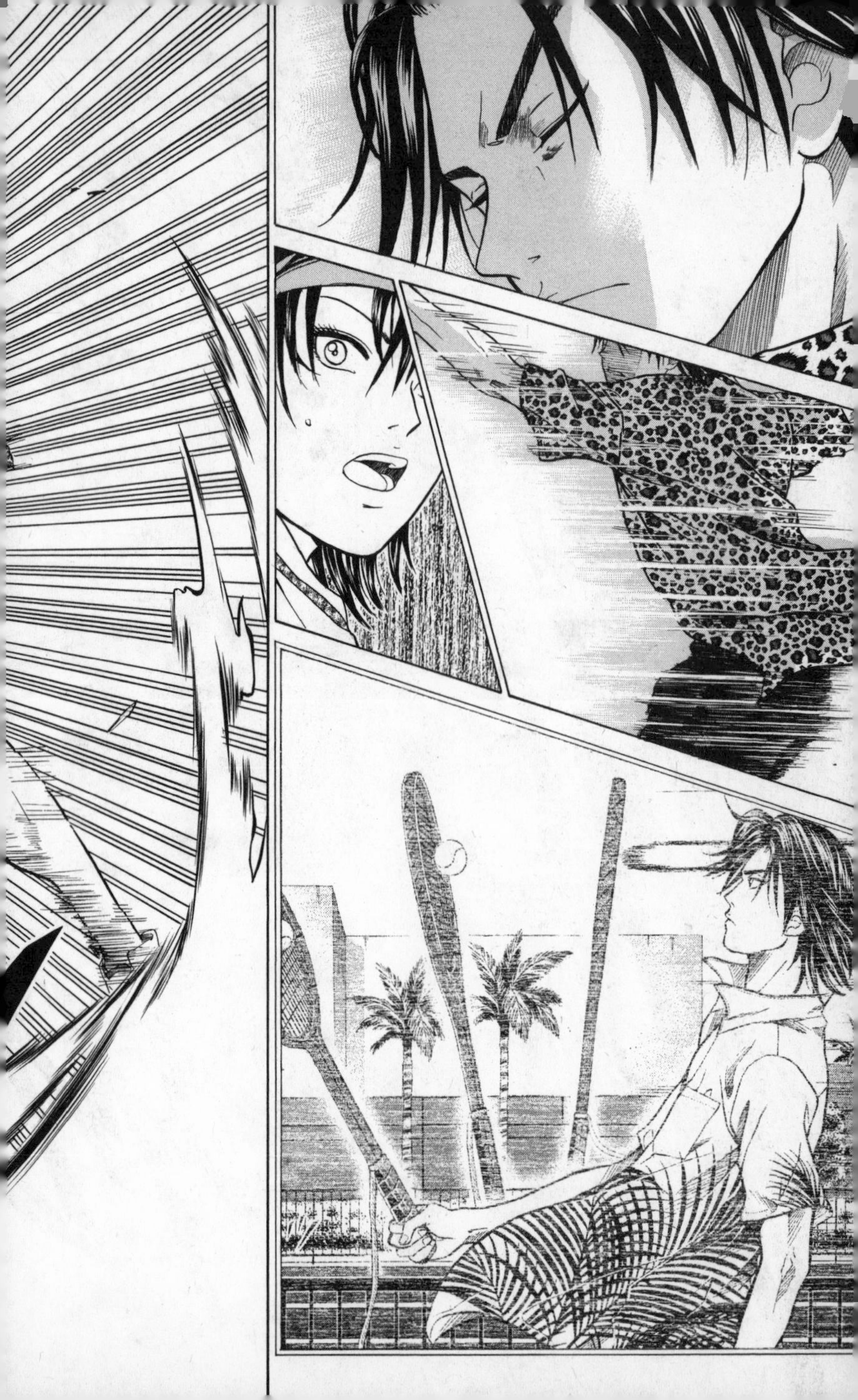

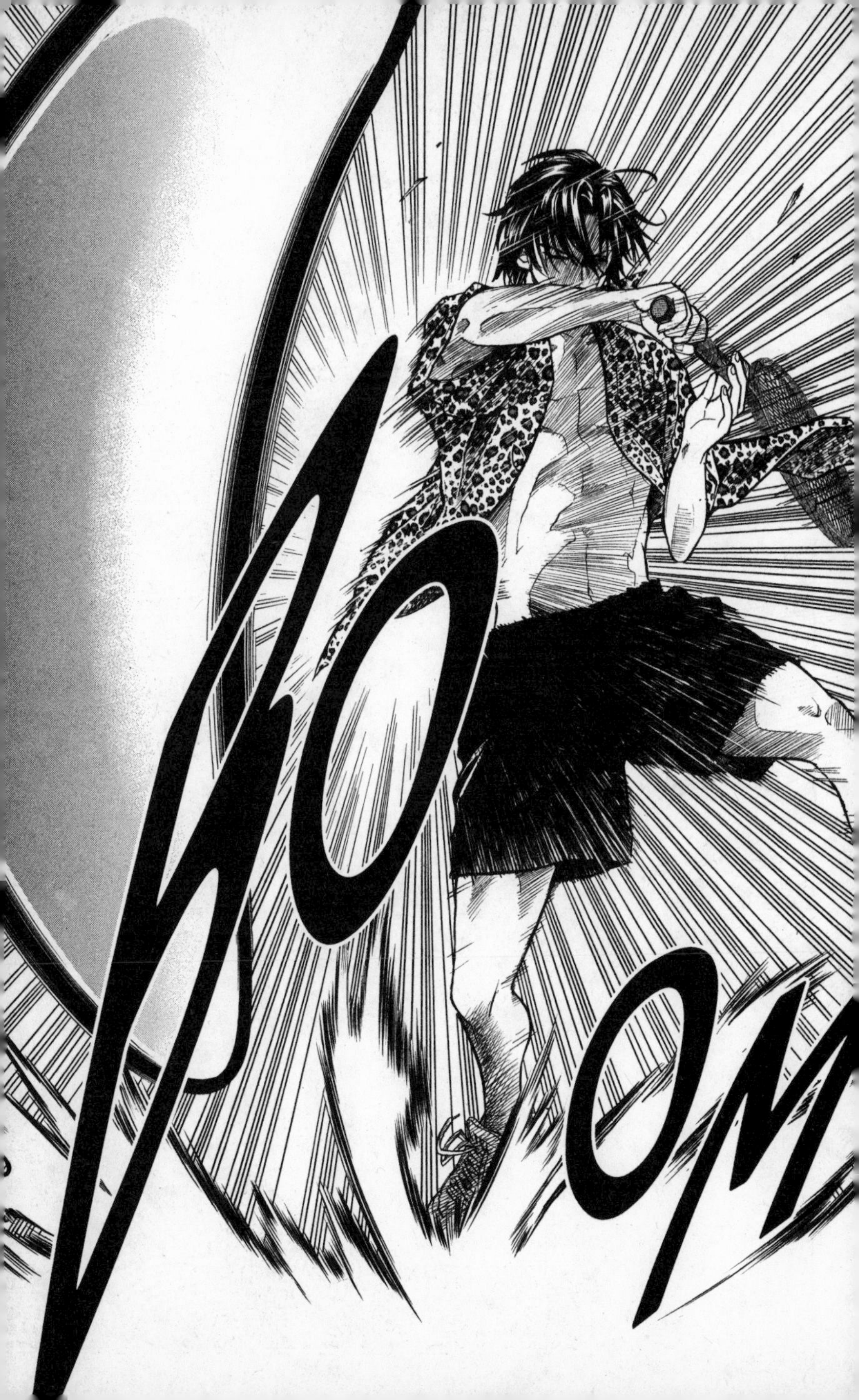

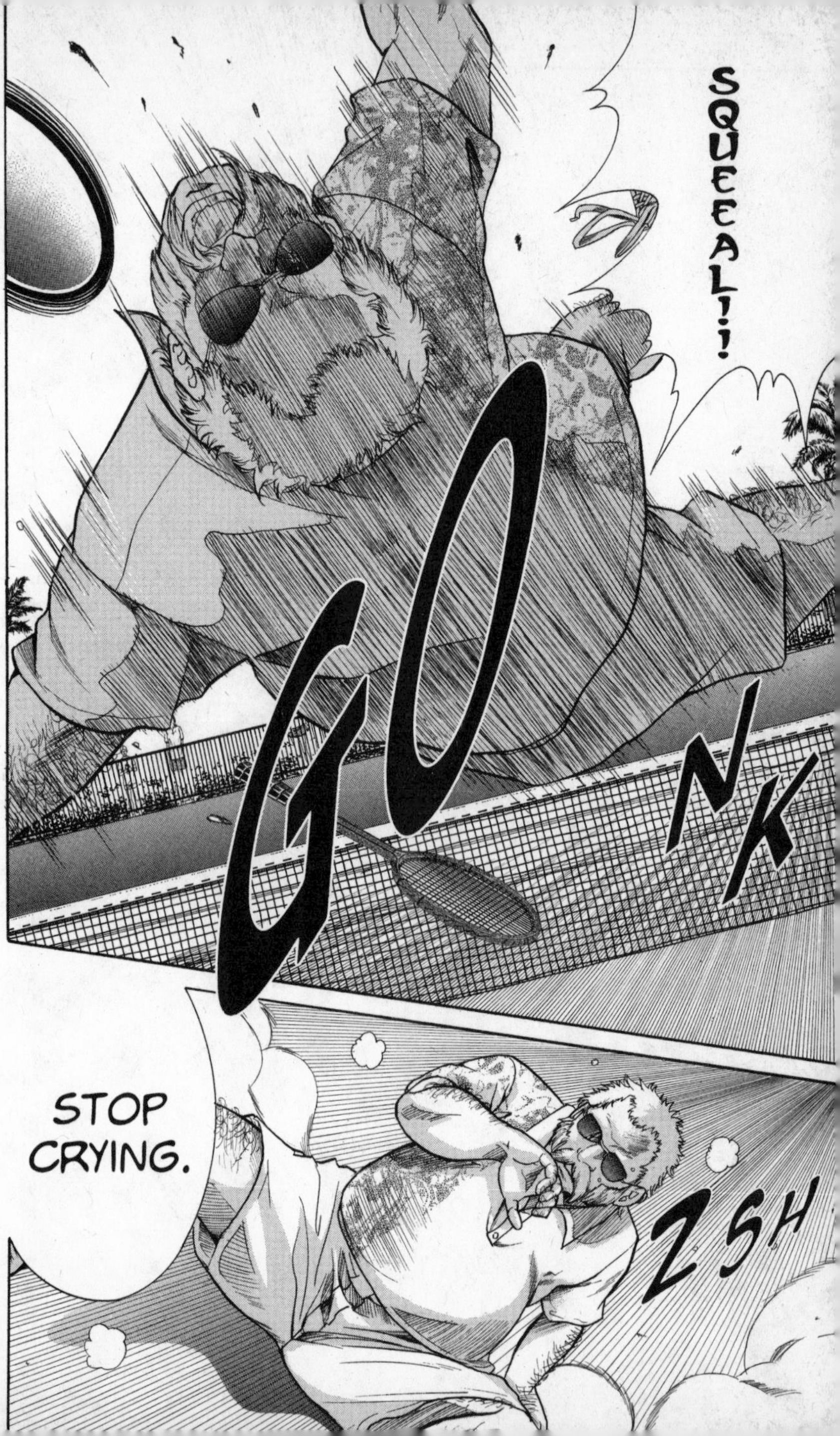
SQUEEEAL!!
GONK
ZSH
STOP CRYING.

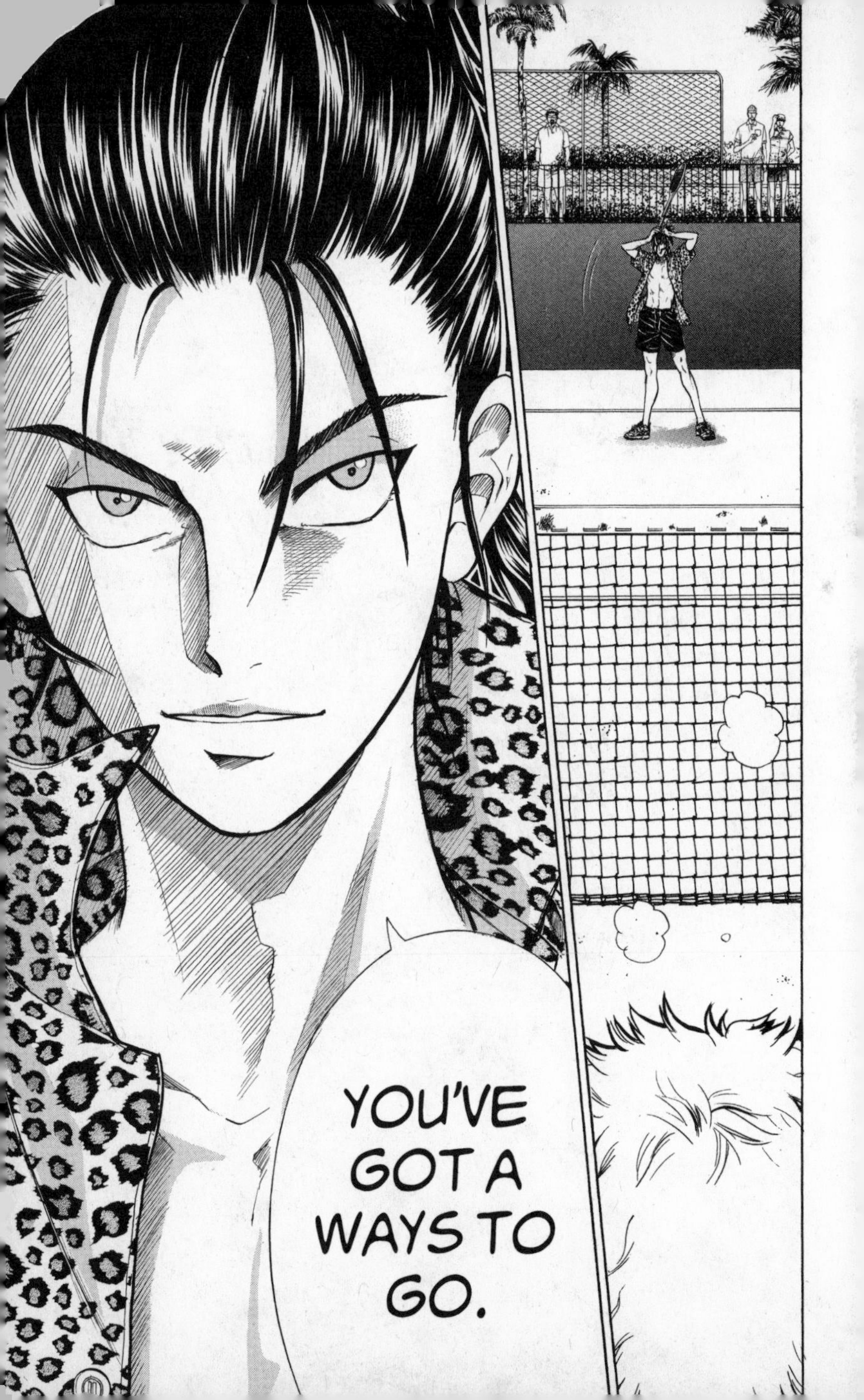
YOU'VE GOT A WAYS TO GO.

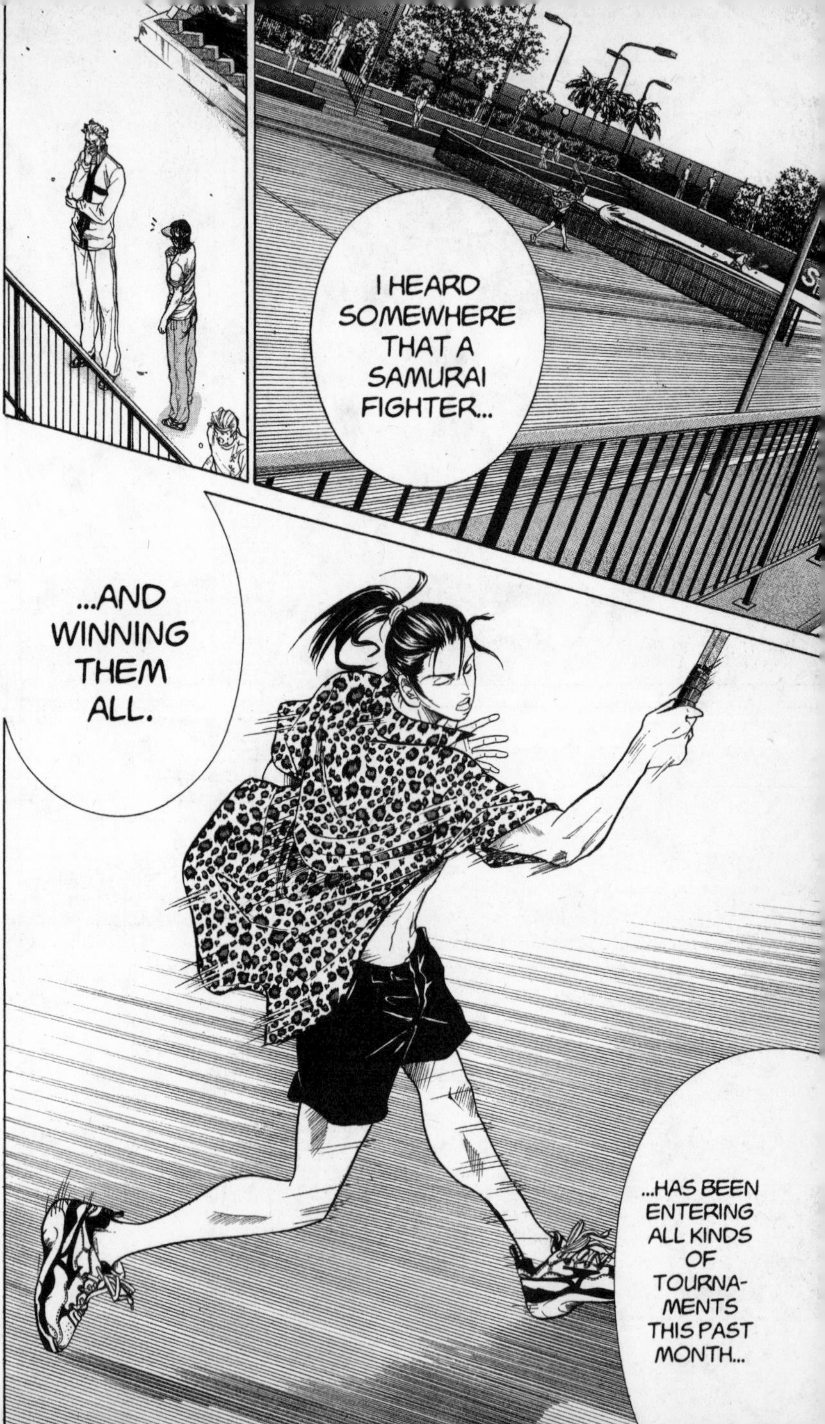
I HEARD SOMEWHERE THAT A SAMURAI FIGHTER...
...HAS BEEN ENTERING ALL KINDS OF TOURNAMENTS THIS PAST MONTH...
...AND WINNING THEM ALL.

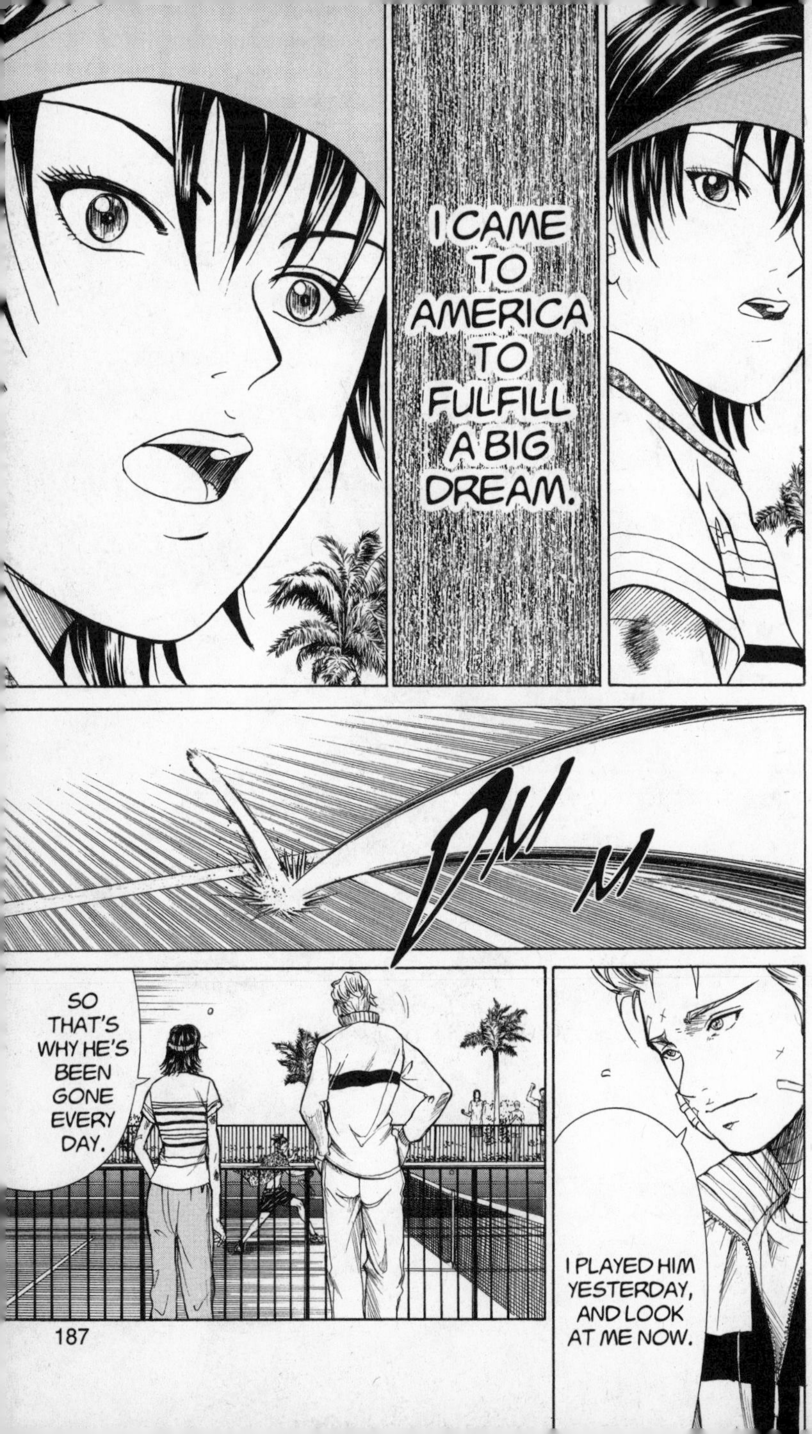
I CAME TO AMERICA TO FULFILL A BIG DREAM.
DMM
I PLAYED HIM YESTERDAY, AND LOOK AT ME NOW.
SO THAT'S WHY HE'S BEEN GONE EVERY DAY.

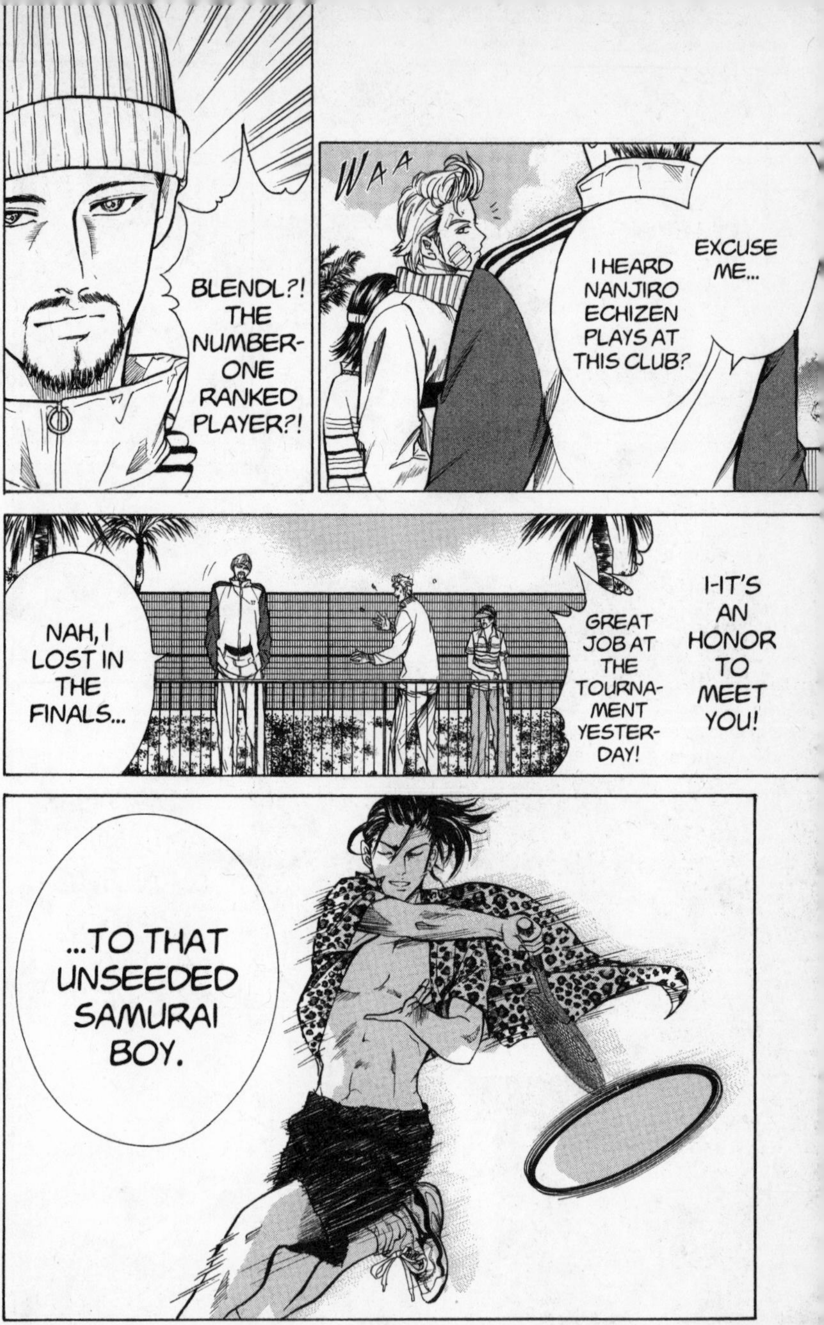
EXCUSE ME...
I HEARD NANJIRO ECHIZEN PLAYS AT THIS CLUB?
WAA
BLENDL?! THE NUMBER-ONE RANKED PLAYER?!
I-IT'S AN HONOR TO MEET YOU!
GREAT JOB AT THE TOURNAMENT YESTERDAY!
NAH, I LOST IN THE FINALS...
...TO THAT UNSEEDED SAMURAI BOY.

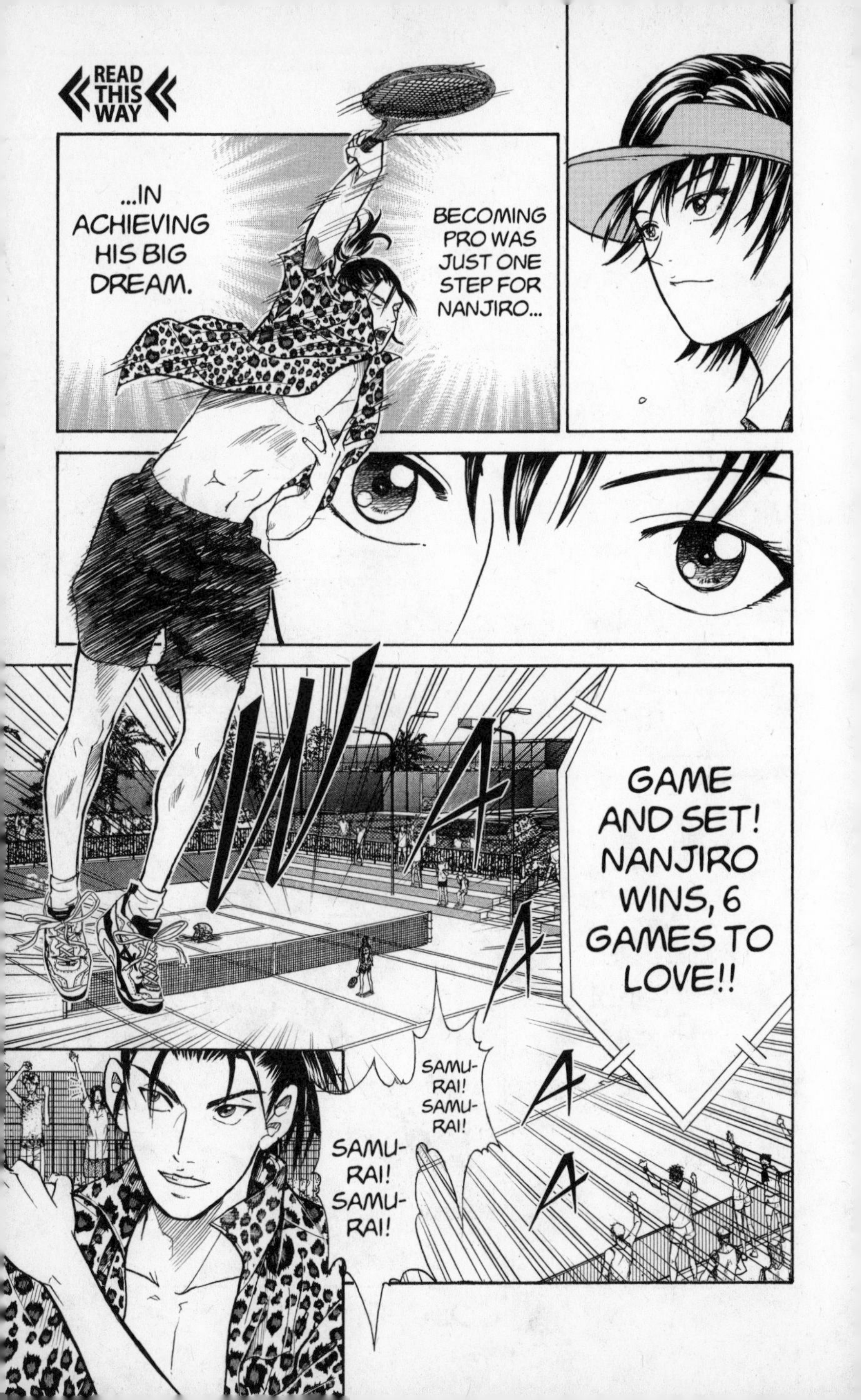
READ THIS WAY
BECOMING PRO WAS JUST ONE STEP FOR NANJIRO...
...IN ACHIEVING HIS BIG DREAM.
GAME AND SET! NANJIRO WINS, 6 GAMES TO LOVE!!
WAAAA
SAMU-RAI! SAMU-RAI!
SAMU-RAI! SAMU-RAI!

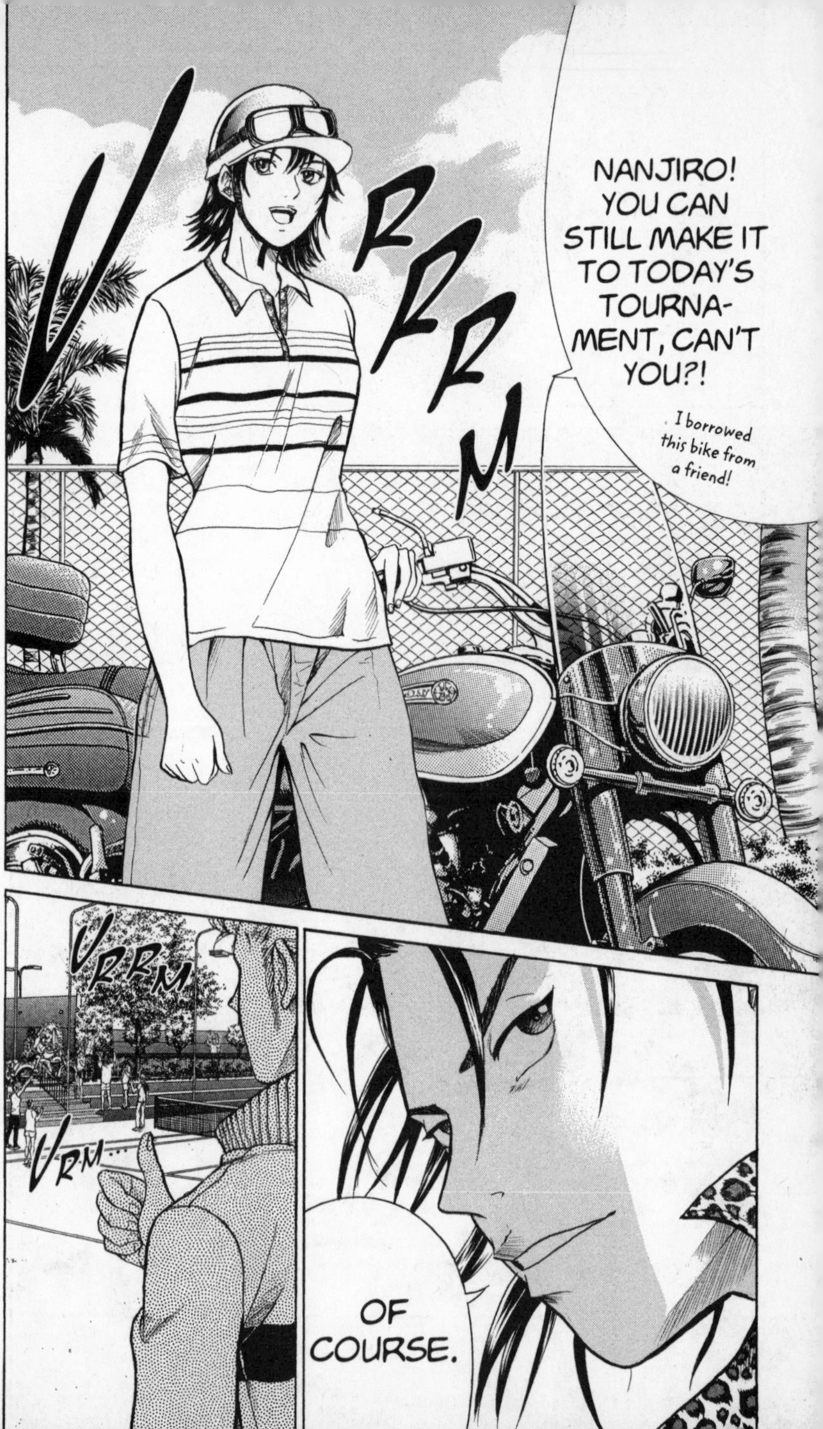
VRRRM
NANJIRO! YOU CAN STILL MAKE IT TO TODAY'S TOURNA-MENT, CAN'T YOU?!
I borrowed this bike from a friend!
OF COURSE.
VRRM
VRM...

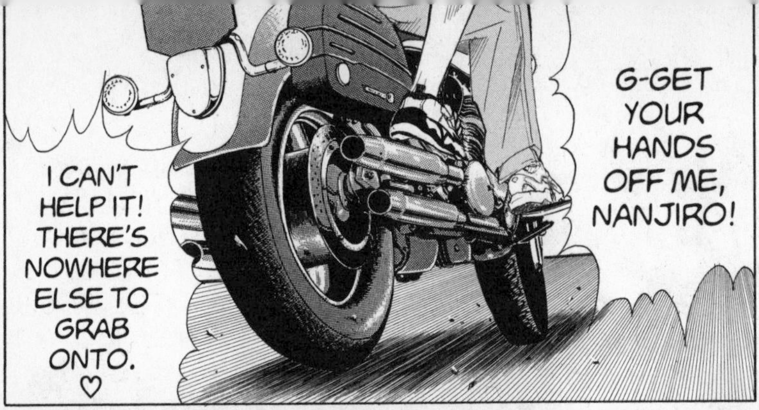
G-GET YOUR HANDS OFF ME, NANJIRO!
I CAN'T HELP IT! THERE'S NOWHERE ELSE TO GRAB ONTO. ♡

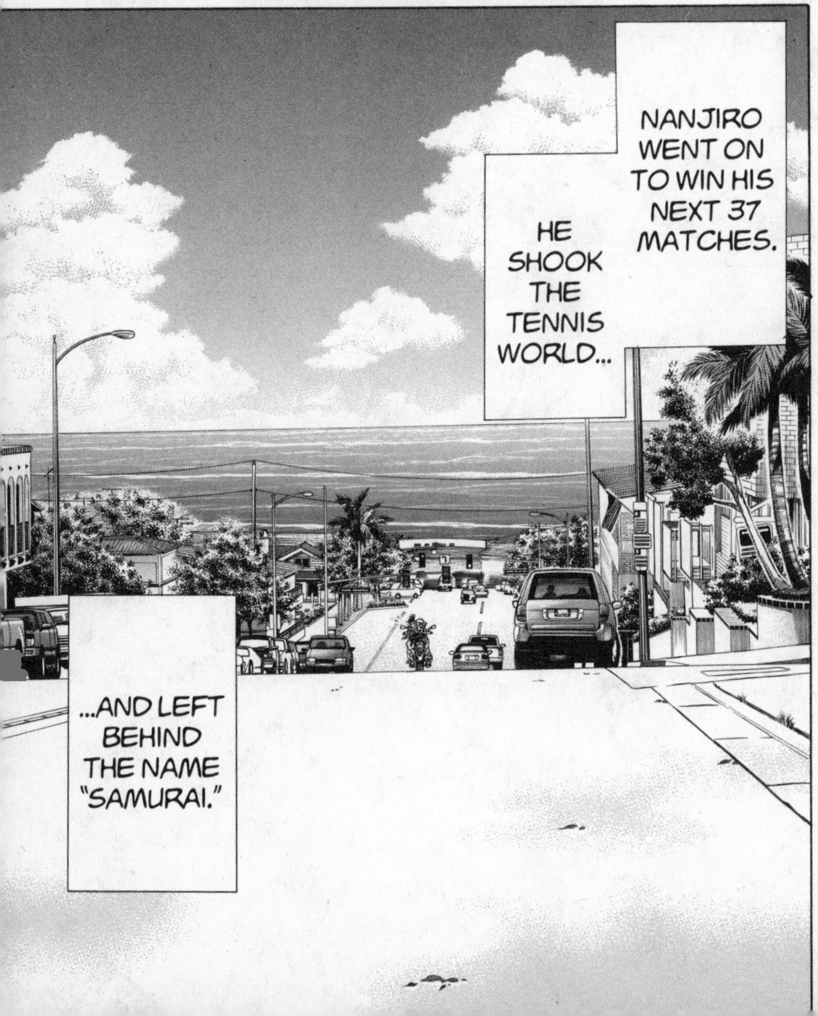
NANJIRO WENT ON TO WIN HIS NEXT 37 MATCHES.
HE SHOOK THE TENNIS WORLD...
...AND LEFT BEHIND THE NAME "SAMURAI."

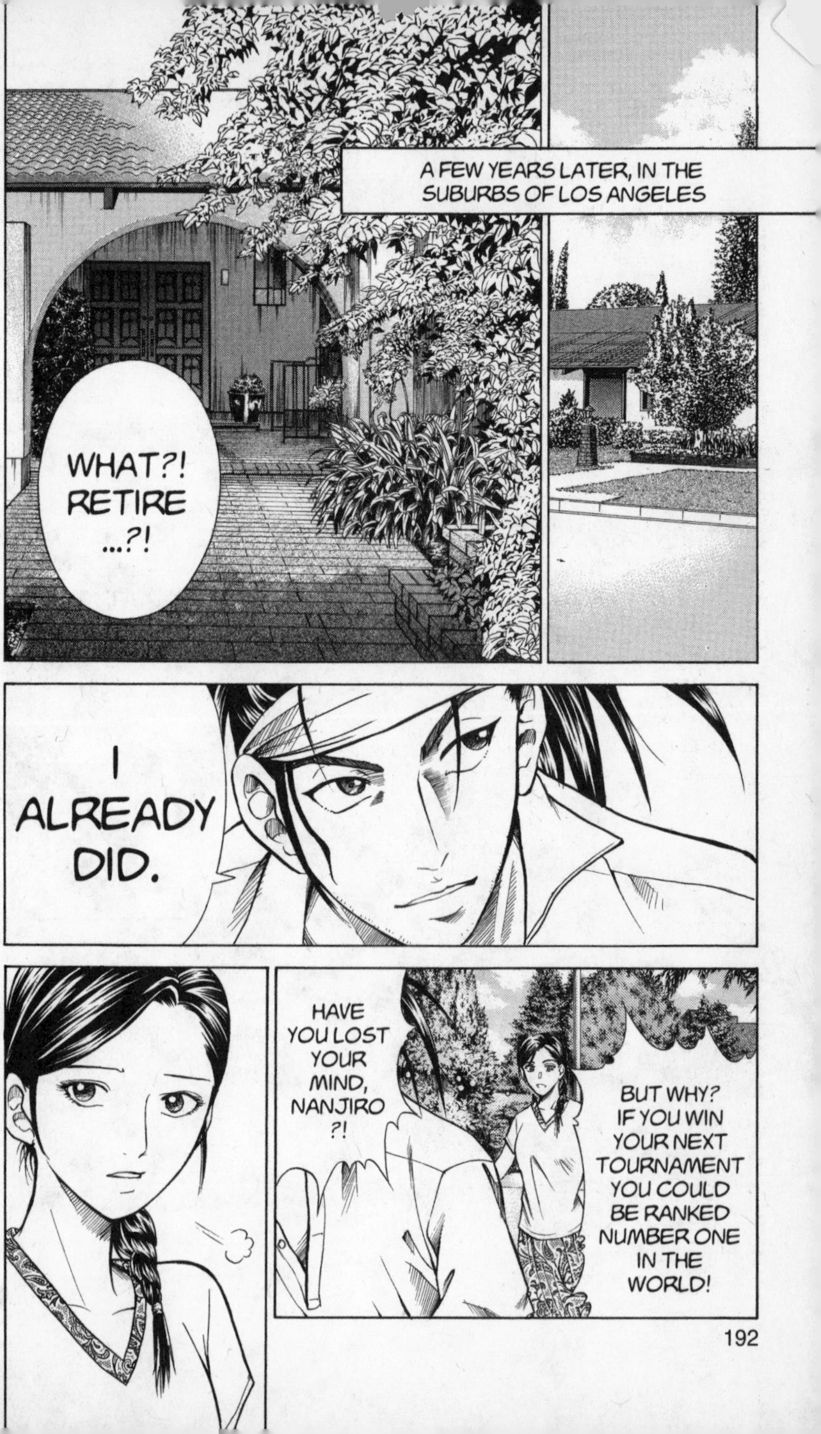
A FEW YEARS LATER, IN THE SUBURBS OF LOS ANGELES
WHAT?! RETIRE ...?!
I ALREADY DID.
BUT WHY? IF YOU WIN YOUR NEXT TOURNAMENT YOU COULD BE RANKED NUMBER ONE IN THE WORLD!
HAVE YOU LOST YOUR MIND, NANJIRO ?!

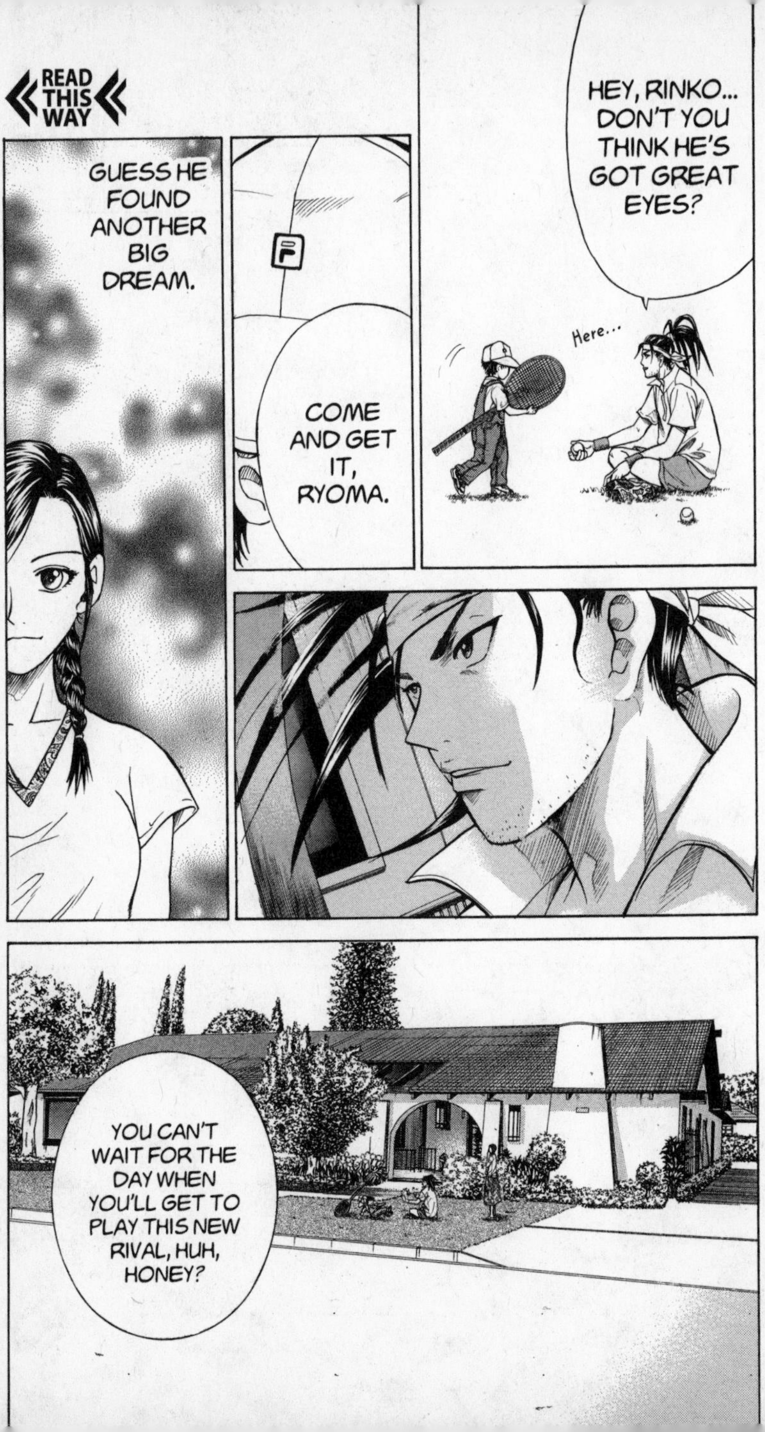
READ THIS WAY
HEY, RINKO... DON'T YOU THINK HE'S GOT GREAT EYES?
Here...
COME AND GET IT, RYOMA.
GUESS HE FOUND ANOTHER BIG DREAM.
YOU CAN'T WAIT FOR THE DAY WHEN YOU'LL GET TO PLAY THIS NEW RIVAL, HUH, HONEY?

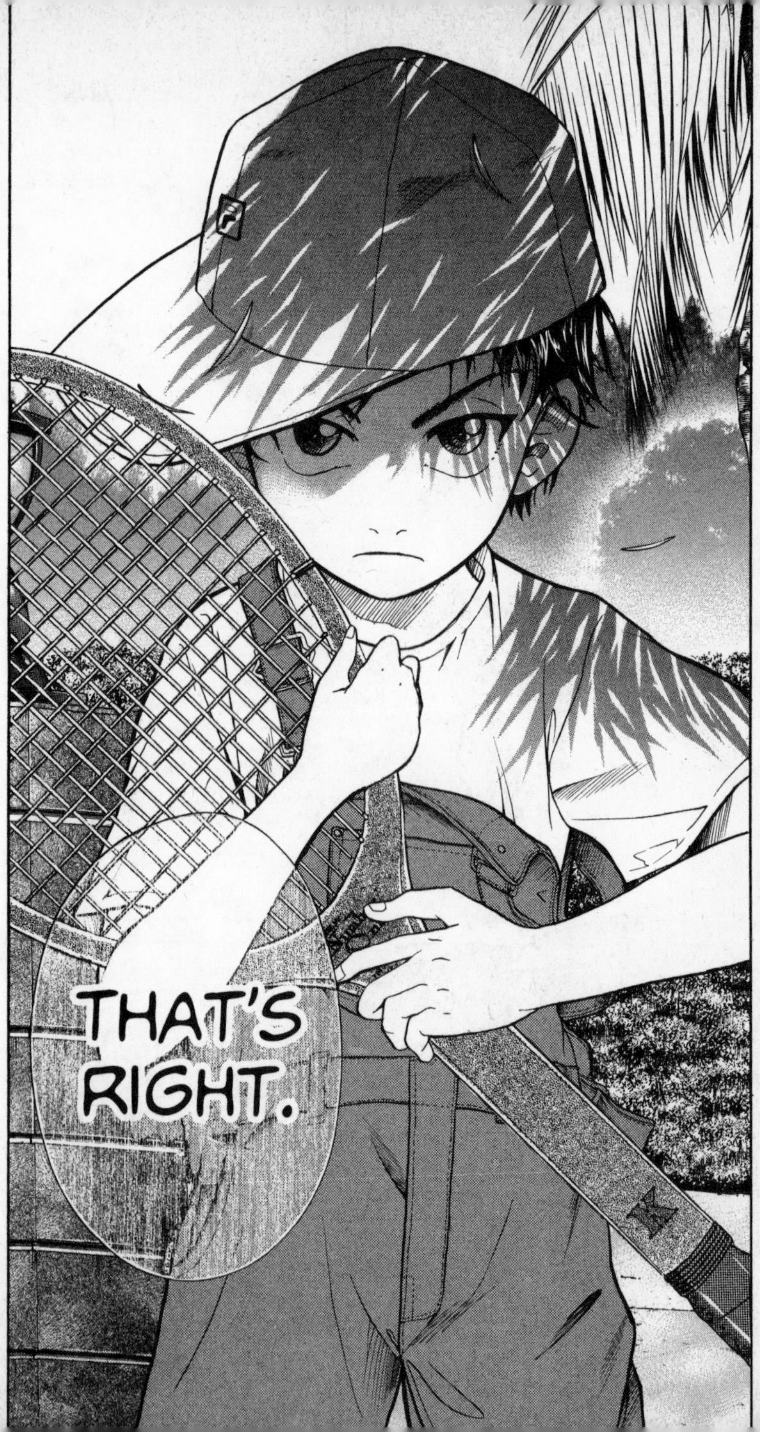
THAT'S RIGHT.

In the Next Volume...

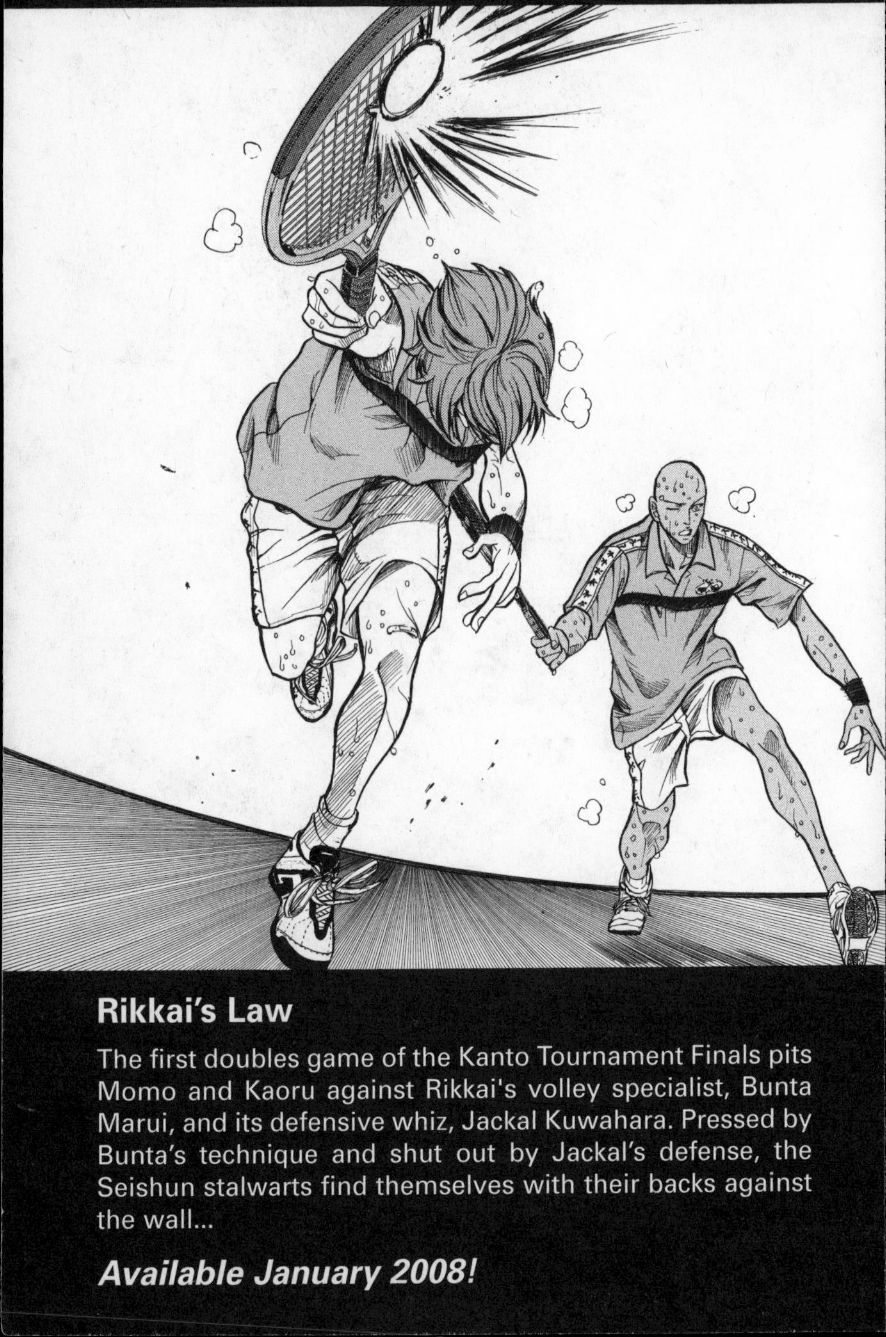

Rikkai's Law

The first doubles game of the Kanto Tournament Finals pits Momo and Kaoru against Rikkai's volley specialist, Bunta Marui, and its defensive whiz, Jackal Kuwahara. Pressed by Bunta's technique and shut out by Jackal's defense, the Seishun stalwarts find themselves with their backs against the wall...

Available January 2008!

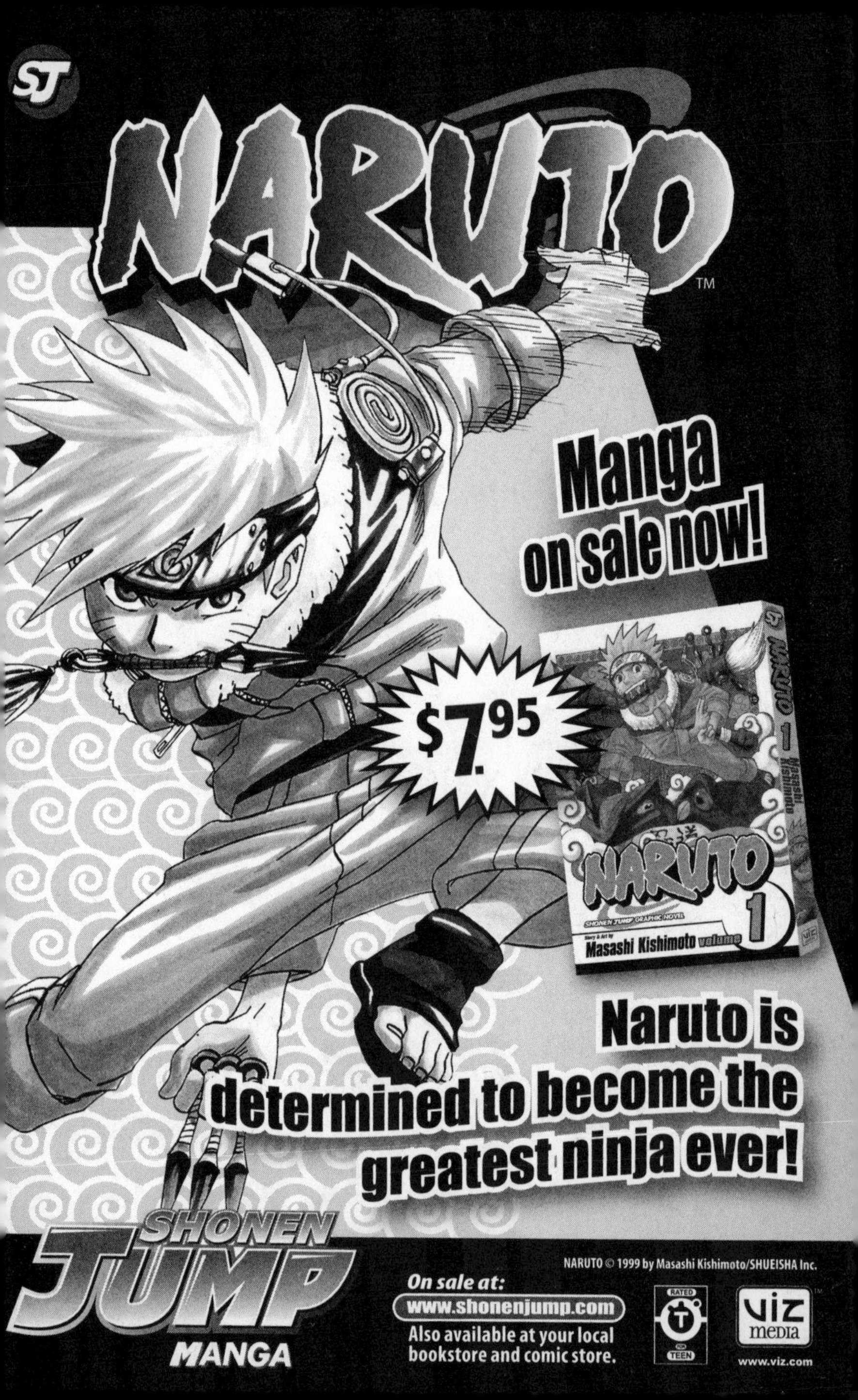

SJ
NARUTO™
Manga on sale now!
$7.95
NARUTO 1
SHONEN JUMP GRAPHIC NOVEL
Masashi Kishimoto volume 1
Naruto is determined to become the greatest ninja ever!
SHONEN JUMP MANGA
NARUTO © 1999 by Masashi Kishimoto/SHUEISHA Inc.
On sale at:
www.shonenjump.com
Also available at your local bookstore and comic store.
RATED T FOR TEEN
VIZ media
www.viz.com

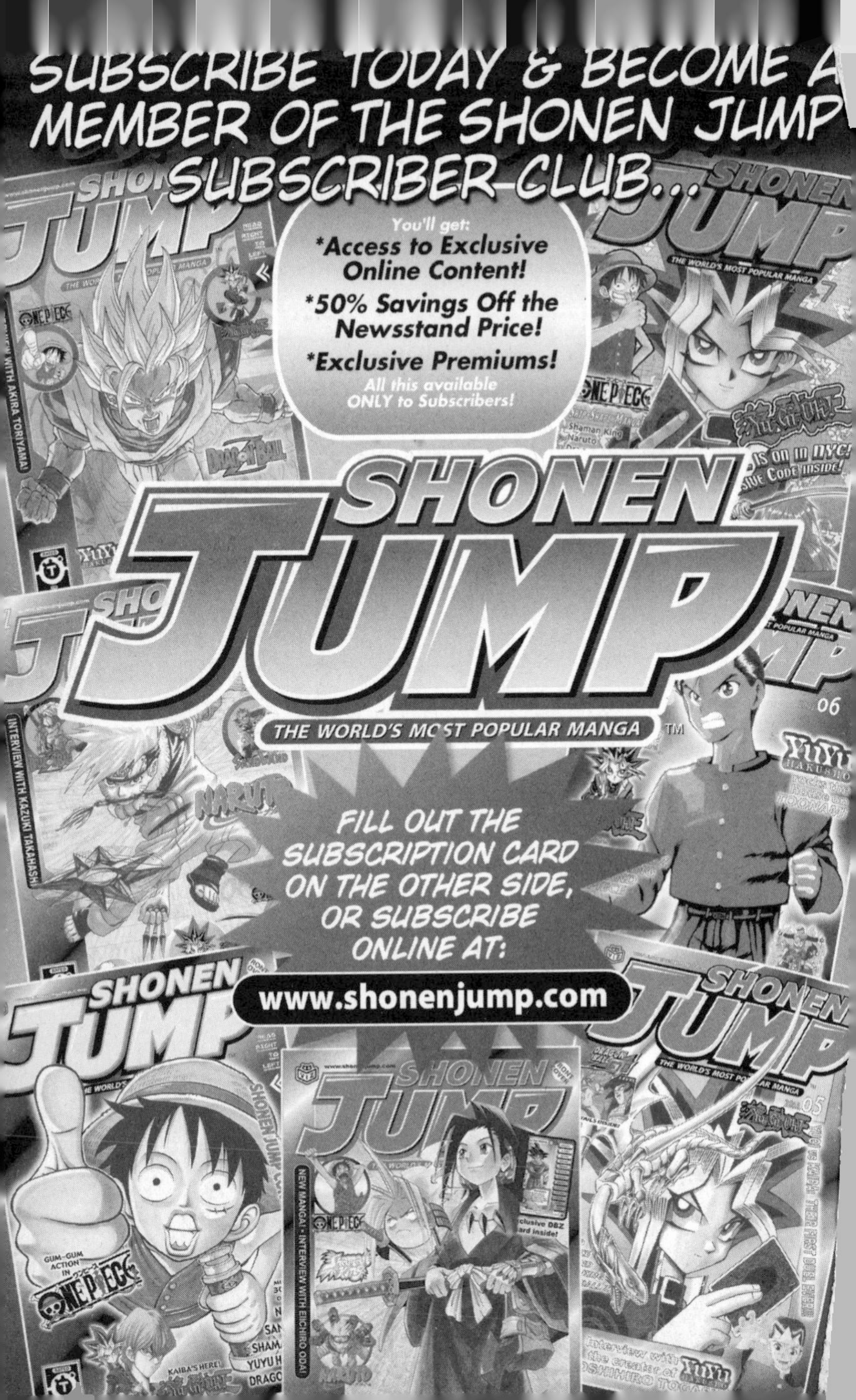
SUBSCRIBE TODAY & BECOME A MEMBER OF THE SHONEN JUMP SUBSCRIBER CLUB...
You'll get:
*Access to Exclusive Online Content!
*50% Savings Off the Newsstand Price!
*Exclusive Premiums!
All this available ONLY to Subscribers!
SHONEN JUMP
THE WORLD'S MOST POPULAR MANGA
TM
FILL OUT THE SUBSCRIPTION CARD ON THE OTHER SIDE, OR SUBSCRIBE ONLINE AT:
www.shonenjump.com

Save 50% off the newsstand price!

JUMP
THE WORLD'S MOST POPULAR MANGA

SUBSCRIBE TODAY and SAVE 50% OFF the cover price PLUS enjoy all the benefits of the SHONEN JUMP SUBSCRIBER CLUB, exclusive online content & special gifts ONLY AVAILABLE to SUBSCRIBERS!

☑ **YES!** Please enter my 1 year subscription (12 issues) to *SHONEN JUMP* at the INCREDIBLY LOW SUBSCRIPTION RATE of $29.95 and sign me up for the SHONEN JUMP Subscriber Club!

Only $29.95!

NAME

ADDRESS

CITY   STATE   ZIP

E-MAIL ADDRESS

☐ MY CHECK IS ENCLOSED   ☐ BILL ME LATER

CREDIT CARD: ☐ VISA   ☐ MASTERCARD

ACCOUNT #   EXP. DATE

SIGNATURE

CLIP AND MAIL TO ➤

SHONEN JUMP
Subscriptions Service Dept.
P.O. Box 515
Mount Morris, IL 61054-0515

Make checks payable to: **SHONEN JUMP.**
Canada add US $12. No foreign orders. Allow 6-8 weeks for delivery.

P6SJGN   YU-GI-OH! © 1996 by Kazuki Takahashi / SHUEISHA Inc.